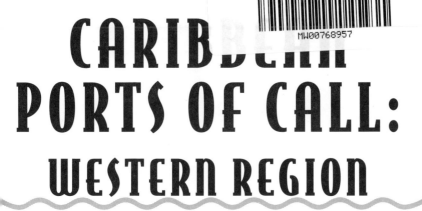

CARIBBEAN PORTS OF CALL:
WESTERN REGION

FOURTH EDITION

KAY SHOWKER

A VOYAGER BOOK

The Globe Pequot Press

OLD SAYBROOK, CONNECTICUT

Also from The Globe Pequot Press

Caribbean Ports of Call: Northern and Northeastern Regions
Caribbean Ports of Call: Eastern and Southern Regions
100 Best Resorts of the Caribbean

Copyright © 1987, 1990, 1993, 1997 by Kay Showker
All rights reserved. No part of this book may be reproduced or transmitted in any form by any means, electronic mechanical, including photocopying and recording, or by any information storage and retrieval system, except as m: be expressly permitted by the 1976 Copyright Act or by the publisher. Requests for permission should be made writing to The Globe Pequot Press, P.O. Box 833, Old Saybrook, Connecticut 06475.

Library of Congress Cataloging-in-Publication Data:

Showker, Kay.
    Caribbean ports of call: western region : a guide for today's cruise passenger / Kay Showker.
        p. cm.
    Includes bibliographical references and index.
    ISBN 1-56440-979-1
    1. Caribbean Area—Guidebooks.   2. Key West (Fla.)—Guidebooks.
    3. Ocean travel—Guidebooks. I. Title.
    F2165.S6 1996
    917.904'52—dc20   96-44974
                                                         CIP

Produced by Menasha Ridge Press
Manufactured in the United States of America
Fourth Edition/Second Printing

Contents

List of Maps

The Caribbean & The Bahamas

PORTS OF CALL

Basseterre, St. Kitts
Belize City, Belize
Bequia, the Grenadines
Bimini, the Bahamas
Bluefields, Nicaragua
Bridgetown, Barbados
Cap Haitien, Haiti
Castries, St. Lucia
Caye Caulker, Belize
Charlestown, Nevis
Charlotte Amalie, St. Thomas, U.S. Virgin Islands
Christiansted, St. Croix, U.S. Virgin Islands
Colon, Panama
Cruz Bay, St. John, U.S. Virgin Islands
Fort Bay, Saba
Fort-de-France, Martinique
Frederiksted, St. Croix, U.S. Virgin Islands
*Freeport, Grand Bahama, the Bahamas
*Guanaja, Bay Islands, Honduras
*Grand Cayman, Cayman Islands
*Great Guana Cay, Abaco, the Bahamas
Gustavia, St. Barthélemy (St. Barts)
Iles des Saintes, French West Indies
Jost Van Dyke, British Virgin Islands
*Key West, U.S.A.
*Kingston, Jamaica
Kingstown, St. Vincent
Kralendijk, Bonaire
*La Ceiba, Honduras
*Livingston, Guatemala
Marigot, St. Martin
Mayreau, the Grenadines
*Montego Bay, Jamaica
*Nassau, New Providence, Bahamas
Philipsburg, Sint Maarten

*Playa del Carmen (Cancún), Mexico
*Placencia, Belize
Plymouth, Montserrat
Pointe-à-Pitre, Guadeloupe
Ponce, Puerto Rico
*Port Antonio, Jamaica
Port-au-Prince, Haiti
Port-au-Spain, Trinidad
*Porto Progresso (Mérida), Mexico
*Puerto Barrio, Guatemala
*Puerto Cortes, Honduras
*Puerto Limón, Costa Rica
Puerto Plata, Dominican Republic
*Punta Gorda, Belize
*Ocho Rios, Jamaica
Oranjestad, St. Eustatius
Oranjested, Aruba
*Roatan, Bay Islands, Honduras
Roseau, Dominica
St. George's, Grenada
St. Johns, Antigua
Sandy Ground, Anguilla
*San Blas Islands, Panama
San Juan, Puerto Rico
*San Miguel, Cozumel, Mexico
*San Pedro, Ambergis Caye, Belize
Santo Domingo, Dominican Republic
*Santo Tomás de Castella, Guatemala
Scarborough, Tobago
Tortola, British Virgin Islands
Virgin Gorda, British Virgin Islands
Willemstad, Curaçao

*Ports covered in this volume; the balance appear in
  the companion volumes, *Caribbean Ports of Call*
  and *Eastern Caribbean Ports of Call.*

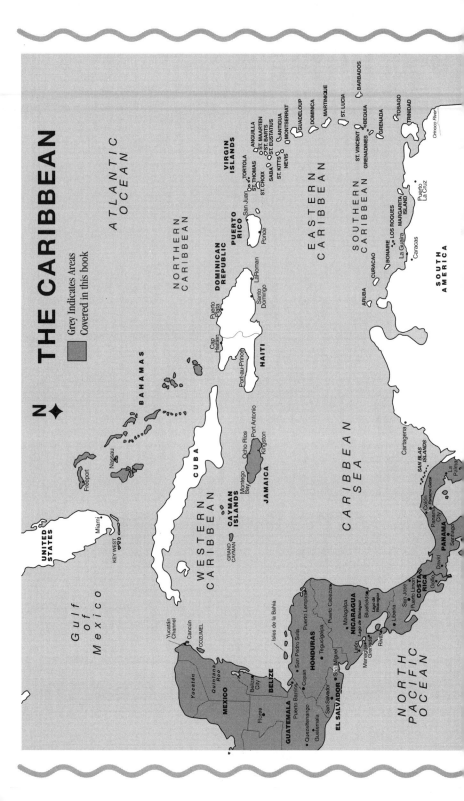

PART I

CRUISING AND THE CARIBBEAN

THE WINNING COMBINATION

very year, almost five million people take cruises and more than half of them cruise in the waters of Bahamas and the Caribbean. Superb year-round ther, proximity, prices, and the region's great vari- —of cultures, activity, scenery, sports, and attrac- s—all are reasons that make the combination of sing and the Caribbean a vacation choice that's l to beat.

estern Caribbean Ports of Call: From the amas and Key West to Central America and the ama Canal is the third in the series of Caribbean ts of Call: A Guide for Today's Cruise Passenger. n its first publication in 1988, the series has been nded to fill the gap between two kind of books: ks about cruising and books about the Caribbean. Typically, books about cruising describe the ships in great detail and are useful in selecting a cruise; however, these books give little or no attention to ports of call. Generally, once you are on board your ship heading to the Bahamas or the Caribbean, their value is marginal.

Guidebooks on the Bahamas and the Caribbean invariably assume that their readers will arrive at a destination by plane and remain several days or longer and have plenty of time to explore the attractions. They are not written for cruise passengers who spend only a few hours in port and need a special kind of guidance.

deed, neither the standard cruise guide nor the typ- Caribbean guidebook has the kind of information se passengers need to help them plan and set pri- es for their time in port. And that has been the aim ny series from the outset.

aribbean Ports of Call: A Guide for Today's Cruise senger was the first of its kind when it was first pub- ed, and although some other cruise guides and bbean books have appeared with "Ports of Call" ed to their titles, a comparison of their content would show that the books in my series are still the only ones designed specifically with the goal of helping readers plan their time in each port of call as well as serving as a reference and guide to be taken along in port.

With this new volume, Western Caribbean Ports of Call, the Caribbean Ports of Call: A Guide for Today's Cruise Passenger series has been divided into three volumes for the most practical reasons. We want each of the three books to be portable and for their inclusion of ports to reflect the pattern of Caribbean cruises.

For example, the new Western Caribbean Ports of Call is the result of the growing popularity of the Western Caribbean as an area for adding new cruise itineraries, with the number of ships offering cruises in this region more than doubling in the past decade. It also reflects a certain maturing of Caribbean cruising. As the number of cruise lines and cruise ships grows and the reservoir of past passengers expands, cruise lines need to develop new itineraries to keep up with or stay ahead of their competition to attract new passengers and stimulate repeat passengers to return.

Western Caribbean Ports of Call covers the ports on the itineraries that depart regularly from Florida to the Bahamas and Western Caribbean for lengths of two to seven days, as well as those that sail from Florida and other ports, such as Gulfport, Mississippi, and New Orleans, for the Western Caribbean and Central America or en route to the Panama Canal.

The majority of the cruises to the Bahamas are three- and four-day trips from Miami, Ft. Lauderdale, and Port Canaveral in Florida. Those to the Western Caribbean are generally five- to seven-day cruises mostly from Miami and Tampa. Some ships alternate their short Bahama cruises with Western Caribbean ones, thus enabling passengers to combine two itineraries into longer cruises.

The companion volumes are Caribbean Ports of Call and Eastern Caribbean Ports of Call. The first covers the ports of call for ships departing from Florida on one-week cruises and longer for the Northern and Eastern Caribbean; the second book covers the ships based in San Juan, Barbados, and elsewhere that cruise in the Eastern and Southern Caribbean on seven-day cruises or longer, as well as ones sailing through the Eastern and Southern Caribbean en route to the Panama Canal.

In deciding what information to include, we recognized that cruise passengers are a diverse group of travelers and their interests and needs change, sometimes from port to port. Therefore, we knew the books had to address a variety of the readers' needs. For example, you may be sports-oriented—or more interested in history, art, and culture. Someone else might want only to stroll around and shop. Some people will only venture beyond their cruise ship if they can take a tour; others would not take an organized tour if it were offered to them free. At the same time, many people who normally do not take tours will take one on their first visit to a new place to gain a quick, overall impression. Yet for others the very newness of a place causes them to want to be independent and explore on their own. Some ports lend themselves to organized touring, and others are best seen by walking on your own.

HOW TO USE THIS GUIDE

To ensure that the book has the broadest possible application and can be used by many different kinds of cruise passengers, it is organized in an easy-to-use format that enables readers to find the information they need quickly.

Part One introduces you to the delights of the Caribbean in general, to the Western Caribbean specifically, and to the delights of a cruise.

Part Two has a profile of each cruise line with cruises to the Bahamas and the Western Caribbean. It is designed to help you find the line and ship most likely to match your tastes and pocketbook. A convenient chart listing the ships, their ports of call, and range of prices appears at the end of the book.

Part Three covers the ports of call visited on Bahamas and Western Caribbean cruises. For easy reference, an alphabetical list of ports follows the Table of Contents.

PORTS OF CALL

The ports of a cruise itinerary provide a kaleidoscope of a region's history and cultures, scenery and sights, language, and music. In the Caribbean, and particularly the Western Caribbean, the destinations are very distinctive, which is one of the reasons they are the basis for such interesting itineraries. The differences are topographical and cultural, ranging from English-speaking Jamaica, Cayman Islands, and Belize to Spanish-speaking Mexico and Central America. Some

places are tropical and lush like Jamaica; others a sandy and arid like Cozumel. There are places that ha towering mountains, rain forests, vast jungles, dese and low-lying islets—sometimes all within one count like Honduras.

Port chapters start with an introduction to the cou try and a general map, Fast Facts, Budget Planning, a the Author's Favorite Attractions in addition to a p profile with information on embarkation, facilities, a local transportation. For those who prefer to tour wi a group, there are descriptions of the most frequen available shore excursions sold on board ships. F those who want to be on their own, each chapter has walking tour with a map, where appropriate, a descriptions of attractions to see if one were to ren car or hire a taxi. In any case, the objective is to he you organize and maximize your time in port to ensu you get the most out of the visit. Other sections cov shopping, sports, dining, and entertainment.

All ports, except those covered very briefly, open wi "At a Glance," a generic list of attractions with ★ ★★★★★ stars. The purpose is to give you a instant picture of the destination so you can judge ho best to use your time. The stars are not used in the sam sense as a restaurant critique; they are simply intend as an objective guide to what the destination has offer. My personal list of Favorite Attractions can also a guide.

A cruise is the best and sometimes only way to vis several Caribbean destinations in one vacation. Tha one of the main attractions of cruising. But if you dor plan you may come back thinking that the islands a all alike. Using this book will enable you to have a ba anced and varied itinerary by planning your activity each port. In other words, if you were to spend all yo time on a walking tour in Nassau or Key West, you mig want to play golf or go horseback-riding in Jamaica an try snorkeling or diving in the Cayman Islands.

Each port has a Budget Planning section. Prices a not uniform in the region. Generally, they tend to l highest in the most popular places. You might som times have the feeling there's a "soak the tourist" att tude, but do remember that a place like Nassau mu import almost all of its food and supplies. Sinc Caribbean destinations cater mainly to Americans, cos are high because American tastes often cost a great de to satisfy.

The islands depend on tourism. Local people wa you to have a good impression of their country so yo will come back and bring your friends. They are o your side. On the other hand, don't blame them fo your own gullibility or lack of planning. There are a many bad apples in New York or Miami as in Nassau o Montego Bay. This book gives you guidelines to hel you avoid the bad ones. We hope you will use these guidelines and have a pleasant and memorable cruise.

As with my other books, I invite readers to send me their comments and suggestions and tell me about their experiences—good or bad. If we can use your ideas or information we will happily reward your effort with a copy of the next edition. Please let us hear from you.

Kay Showker

THE DELIGHTS OF THE CARIBBEAN

Take a cruise to the Caribbean and you will discover a world that is foreign but familiar, close yet far. It is an exotic world of vivid color and gentle trade winds. Paradise, the Caribbean is often called, and you will see why as your ship glides gently through aquamarine and sapphire waters to reach places thick with tropical greenery down to their white sand shorelines.

The seas of the Bahamas and the Caribbean stretch across more than a million square miles from the coast of Florida to the shores of Central and South America. On the east, the islands form an arc that cradles the Caribbean Sea and separates it from the Atlantic Ocean; on the west, Mexico and Central America form the land mass that separates the Caribbean Sea from the Pacific Ocean. The Caribbean region, known as the Eighth Continent of the World, contains large and small countries, islands, and tiny islets, some no more than the peaks of long-submerged mountains; others are larger than 15 states of the United States and have the geographic variety of a continent. The Caribbean region has as many independent nations and island-states as there are countries in Europe, and they draw their heritage from the four corners of the globe.

LOCATING THE ISLANDS

On a map with the arm of the compass pointing north, the islands closest to the United States are known as the Greater Antilles; they include Cuba, Haiti, the Dominican Republic, and Puerto Rico. All but Cuba have daily air service from New York, Miami, and other major U.S. cities. Puerto Rico is a major hub for cruise ships as well as airlines.

The Bahamas and the Turks and Caicos lie southeast of Florida and north of the Greater Antilles. They are entirely in the Atlantic Ocean, but because their tropical environment is so similar to that of the Caribbean, they are thought of as part of the region. Both have daily air service from the United States but only the Bahamas is a major cruise destination.

Farther along with the compass pointing east, the area known as the Eastern Caribbean includes the Lesser Antilles, starting with the Virgin Islands on the north and curving south to Grenada. The northern group of these many small islands are called the Leewards and comprise the United States and British Virgin Islands, Anguilla, St. Maarten, St. Barts, Saba, St. Eustatius, St. Kitts, Nevis, Antigua, Barbuda, Montserrat, and Guadeloupe. The south group, called the Windwards, includes Dominica, Martinique, St. Lucia, Barbados, St. Vincent and the Grenadines, and Grenada. Most, but not all, have direct air service from the United States; the others can be reached by local airlines, and most are stops for cruise ships.

On the south side of the Caribbean are Aruba, Bonaire, Curaçao, and Trinidad and Tobago, which lie off the coast of Venezuela.

To the west are Jamaica and the Cayman Islands; Mexico's Yucatán Peninsula with the islands of Cancún and Cozumel; Belize and Honduras with long coastlines fronting the longest barrier reef in the Western Hemisphere; plus the Central American countries of Guatemala, Nicaragua, Costa Rica, and Panama, bracketing the Caribbean western shores.

Along the 2,000 miles of the Caribbean, whether to the east or the west, nature has been extravagant with its color, variety, and beauty. Verdant mountains rise from sunbleached shores. Between the towering peaks and the sea, rivers and streams cascade over rocks and hillsides and disappear into mangrove swamps and deserts. Fields of flowers, trees with brilliant scarlet and magenta blossoms, and a multitude of birds and butterflies fill the landscape. The air, refreshed by quick tropical showers, is scented with spices and fruit.

And this is only nature's act above the ground. Below the sea is a wonderland of exotic fish in a setting often called the most beautiful in the world. Rainbows of brilliantly colored fish of every size and shape dart endlessly through the crystal waters to hide in caves and grottos, mingle between the swaying purple seafans, and burrow into boulders of coral and sponge.

Yet, what makes the Caribbean region unique is not simply its beauty or geography but rather the combination of this lovely and exotic scenery and the kaleidoscope of rich and diverse cultures. Like the vibrant landscape they reflect, the people and their cultures have evolved from a wide range of traditions, music, dance, art, architecture, and religions from around the world into the greatest of the world's melting pots.

ENTER COLUMBUS

Before 1492 when Columbus sighted the New World, the lands of the Caribbean region were populated by Indian tribes, some of whom may have migrated to the region from Asia 20,000 years ago. In more recent history, we know that the Ciboneys who probably came from South America arrived in the Caribbean region about 3,000 years ago. They were followed by the peaceful Tainos (known as the Arawaks, their more frequently used linguistic name) and the fierce Caribs who had been in the region for about 600 years when Columbus arrived. It is from the latter group that the Caribbean Sea takes its name.

But in less than a century after Columbus's voyages, the native population in the islands had almost vanished because of war, disease, and enslavement. Their only survivors are a small group of the descendants of the Carib Indians on the island of Dominica and the Afro-Amerindians, known as Black Caribs in St. Vincent and as Garifunas, after their distinct language, in Belize and Honduras.

Columbus's discoveries brought waves of explorers, conquerors, settlers, merchant sailors, pirates, privateers, traders, and slavers from Europe, the Middle East, Africa, and Asia. For two centuries the West Indies, as the region came to be known, were a pawn in the battle for the New World that raged among the European nations. While they fought, they plundered the region's riches and searched for a route to the East. These were savage times that disgraced even the noblest of aims.

By the dawn of the eighteenth century, Spain, England, France, Denmark, and Holland had sliced up the region, had planted their flags on various islands, and had begun to colonize their new territories. Gradually the decimated Indian population was replaced with African slaves to work the land that yielded fortunes in sugar, rum, cotton, and tobacco. After slavery was abolished in the British colonies in the nineteenth century (three decades before its abolition in the United States), the Africans were replaced by indentured laborers from Asia. They were in turn followed by waves of immigrants from the Mediterranean to the Americas in search of a better life.

Once entrenched in the Caribbean, the European governments began to make burdensome demands on their colonies. There were many rebellions. Haiti's revolt was the only one to succeed in a complete break and led to the establishment of the first black republic in the Western Hemisphere two decades after the American Revolution.

Following abolition and the invention of the steam engine and cotton gin, the West Indies lost the base of their economy and soon became neglected outposts of European empires. With the end of the Spanish-American War, Spain gave up her holdings in the New World, and after World War II, Britain, France, and the Netherlands were forced to change their relationships with most of their colonies, granting them independence in most cases.

But the road to independence was a rough one. The 1970s, with the oil crisis, inflation, and the worldwide recession, were particularly hard on the islands, which have few resources other than their people and natural beauty. Adding to their burdens, the troubled sixties in the United States with their shock waves of black power demands and rising expectations washed ashore in the Caribbean simultaneously. But from the experience a new Caribbean has taken shape.

CARIBBEAN CULTURE

Down through the centuries, those who came to the Caribbean—conquerors and settlers, sailors and slaves, merchants and workers, and visitors and vacationers—brought with them parts of their cultures—their church steeples, temples, brogues, high tea, high mass, masks, drums, colors, songs, dances, high-rises, and hamburgers. Out of this mélange has grown a new Caribbean as colorful, rich, and diverse as the landscape in which it flowers.

Although it might be difficult to single out a Caymanian or a Cruzan by sight, there is no mistaking the lilt of a Jamaican's voice when he speaks or a Trinidadian when he sings. Haitian art is instantly recognizable. The beguine began in Martinique, the merengue in the Dominican Republic. Calypso and steel bands were born in Trinidad, reggae in Jamaica, and salsa in Puerto Rico.

Today, the region pulsates with creative energy in the arts. The best time to see the evidence is during Carnival when tradition vies with innovation as part of the show. Trinidad's Carnival is the best known and is held at the traditional pre-Lenten time, but Carnival in the Caribbean often developed from local events and is held at different times of the year. For example, Crop-Over in Barbados in July stems from the celebration of the harvest, and Antigua's Carnival in August started as a welcome to the British monarch during her visit in the 1960s.

Caribbean architecture, like its art, is a composite of world cultures. English churches and Spanish cathedrals stand alongside warm-weather adaptations of Dutch farmhouses and French manors. Victorian gingerbread mansions are pauses in the tango of brightly painted houses in the towns and villages of Haiti. Minarets and steeples pierce the sky of Trinidad; the oldest synagogue in the Western Hemisphere is a Curaçao landmark.

A New Cuisine

Caribbean cuisine, too, is a cornucopia of tastes from the four corners of the globe—a unique blend that evolved over the centuries and combines nature's bounty with the richness of the region's culinary heritage. The Spaniards not only discovered the New World, they found a continent of exotic fruits and vegetables Europeans had never seen—avocado, cassava, maize, peppers, papaya, chocolate, and potatoes, to name a few. From the natives, the Spaniards learned how to use the new ingredients and eventually adapted them for their own cooking; many became basic elements in classic Spanish and French cuisine. The Danes, Dutch, Portuguese, English, Africans, Chinese, Indians, Greeks, Turks, Indonesians, and Arabs all made their contributions.

Out of this potpourri evolved a Creole or West Indian cuisine that includes such standards as Cuban and Puerto Rican black bean soup, Jamaican pepperpot, St. Kitts goat water or mutton stew, Grenadian callaloo, and Guadeloupan accra.

Following independence, a new generation of hotels and restaurant chefs began developing a new and sophisticated Caribbean cuisine. Their creativity has been encouraged by their restaurant and hotel associations, which stage annual competitions judged by international food critics. The new cuisine has resulted in such wonderful creations as Cold Papaya Bisque, Crab and Callaloo Soup, Breadfruit Vichyssoise, Callaloo Quiche, Chicken Creole with Mango, and Avocado Ice Cream, to name a few.

The starting point in the making of Caribbean cuisine is the market—a cultural potpourri where Africa meets the Caribbean and mixes with the Orient. Mountains of mango, melon, and banana and pyramids of papaya, pineapple, and pomegranate are stacked next to the plantain, okra, dasheen, coconut, cassava, cloves, coffee, and cinnamon—alongside piles of clothes and shoes to be haggled over by the townfolk and villagers. Visitors, too, frequently join the mélange because there is no better place than a market to take in the Caribbean kaleidoscope.

A Wealth of Activity

Against the Caribbean's rich and varied geographic and cultural landscape, visitors have a cornucopia of sports and recreational facilities, entertainment, sight-seeing, and shopping possibilities.

For sports, the Caribbean has few rivals. Across its million square miles, sailing is suited for any type of boat from Sailfish to ocean yachts. Yachtsmen often call the stretch south from St. Vincent through the Grenadines the finest sailing water in the world. Snorkeling and scuba diving are excellent throughout the warm and exceptionally clear waters of the region. And while divers wander through the magnificent reefs and look for sunken treasures, nonswimmers need not miss the excitement. They can see it from the comfort of a glass-bottom boat, recreational submarines, or underwater observatories.

Golf on championship layouts created by the most famous names in golf course design is available at many ports of call. The Bahamas and Puerto Rico each offer more a dozen championship courses; Jamaica has six of them. And they have the added attraction of the Caribbean's beautiful and colorful landscape decorating the greens. Most cruise lines have golf programs or can make arrangements for their passengers to play golf at most ports of call.

You can also play tennis, squash, or polo and fish in the ocean or in mountain streams. There are horseback riding, jogging, hiking, biking, surfing, windsurfing, rafting, kayaking, waterskiing, parasailing, and more.

If you are less athletically inclined or simply want to enjoy nature and the outdoors, there are mile-long, powdery sand beaches where you can stretch out for the day with no more company than a couple of birds. You can spend the morning gathering shells, have a picnic by a secluded cove, stroll along bougainvillea-decorated lanes, or wander along mountainsides overlooking deep green valleys and sapphire seas. Throughout the region there are national parks, bird sanctuaries, mountain trails, and panoramas of magnificent scenery. Visitors can have a close-up look at a rain forest, drive into the crater of a volcano, bike over rolling meadows, hike through deep ravines, and explore some caves along the way.

Diversity of Destinations

No two Caribbean destinations are alike; each has a personality, distinctive geographic features, and special charm with which it beguiles its admirers. Some places are tiny idyllic hideaways far from the beaten path with names familiar only to mapmakers and yachtsmen. Others are big in size or seem big because of their strong character and regional influence; while still others are big on action with gambling, shopping, and sophisticated dining and nightlife. Some locales have enough sports and entertainment to keep you busy every hour of the day; others test your ability to enjoy simple pleasures.

Few Caribbean destinations fit neatly into only one category; most have features that contrast and overlap.

One of the great advantages of a cruise is the chance to visit several places at a time and sample some of this variety. This is particularly true on a Western Caribbean cruise where the kaleidoscope might change from lush, mountaineous Jamaica to low-lying Caymans, and from America's Caribbean at Key West to Mexico's Caribbean at Cozumel and Cancún, or from Mayan temples in Belize to river jungles in Guatemala.

A visit to any Caribbean destination is a visit to a foreign country—including those such as Puerto Rico and the U.S. Virgin Islands, which are under the American flag. You can have a Dutch treat in St. Maarten, order lunch in French in Martinique, and pick up some golf tips in Spanish in Costa Rica. You will be able to count francs in Guadeloupe, pesos in the Dominican Republic, lempira in Honduras, and gilders in Curaçao, and add to your kids' stamp collections from such offbeat places as Antigua, Dominica, Saba, and Grenada.

The Caribbean is a learning experience, too. The region is rich in historic monuments, old forts, plantation homes, sugar mills, churches, and synagogues that have been beautifully restored and put to contemporary use as art galleries, boutiques, cafes, restaurants, inns, and museums. They help bring the region's history to life.

THE NEW CARIBBEAN

Learning about its history is also a way to help understand the region today. It is bound to Europe by history, language, and culture, to Africa or Latin America by sentiment and emotion, and to the United States by economic and strategic necessity. So far, the region has shown it has the ability to survive on its own, but its problems have not disappeared.

The brightest prospect is tourism. Already tourist dollars pay for schools, roads, hospitals, and many other necessities. But tourism has limits. Too much can destroy the very elements that make the Caribbean so attractive.

Finally, a word about the people and pace of Paradise. Life in the Caribbean is leisurely. It is easy for Americans to become impatient with the slow pace of things, but remember, if you can, it's precisely the unhurried atmosphere you have come to enjoy. Americans often misinterpret a shyness and conservative nature toward strangers as unfriendliness. But after traveling from one end of the Caribbean to the other for more than two decades, I know from experience that the people of the Caribbean are as friendly as their music and as warm as their sunshine. They have wit, talent, dignity, and grace. They are generous and kind and will go out of their way to be helpful if you meet them with respect and greet them with a genuine smile.

I love the Caribbean. It's like magic. I recognize the elements that create the magic, although I don't quite know what makes it happen. Yet, the experience is so delightful that I am happy to let the mystery remain.

THE DELIGHTS OF CRUISING

People take cruises for various reasons. Some people are looking for fun, companionship, excitement, and romance—whether it's the romance of the sea or romance at sea. A cruise offers a change of pace and relaxation, new faces, new places, and a foreign environment. It is a different kind of holiday. Indeed, a cruise is so completely unlike other holiday experiences, it is difficult for those who have never taken one to imagine its pleasures or realize its true built-in value.

But to understand cruising today, let's step back a moment to consider the changes in the nature of steamship travel that have helped to create today's cruising. Prior to the 1960s, most ships sailed between New York and Europe; Caribbean cruising was limited to the winter season, mainly because ships were not air-conditioned then. With the advent of the jet, which all but sank transatlantic passenger steamship travel, many ships shifted to the Caribbean in search of new markets.

Once the ships had taken up their new home ports, the pressure was on the cruise lines to get passengers from big centers in the northern United States to southern warm-weather ports with a minimum of difficulty. And this led to the birth of air/sea packages—value-packed holidays hard to beat.

In other words, the steamship companies whose very existence was threatened by the jet in the early 1960s had realized by the 1970s that the airlines were their best friends. Savings in fuel and the elimination of travel to and from northern ports in inclement weather were boons. At the same time the cruise companies broadened their appeal by changing the old image of cruising from that of a pleasure only for the rich and idle to a new one that would attract people from all walks of life.

CHANGING LIFE-STYLES

In the past, people saved all their lives to make a single trip; the ultimate dream was a trip around the world by ship. Today, the stress of modern life and the pressures of work and urban living have made it desirable—even necessary—to get away often, if only for a few days. Shorter, less expensive cruises have not only enabled more people to take cruises, but to take them more often.

Speedier modes of transportation combined with greater affluence have made the short break the norm, especially for city dwellers. And nothing could be more ideal for a short, recuperative break than a cruise. No matter what your job or profession, a cruise offers a more complete break from the workaday world than almost anything you can do. The expanse of sea and open sky brings a freedom and an awareness of space that can be totally therapeutic.

Convenience and Hassle-Free Travel

A cruise ship is no farther away than the nearest airport. When cruise lines began combining air transportation with the cruise and selling them as one product—an air/sea package—they not only made the trip more economical, but also easier and more convenient for vacationers even from Salt Lake or Detroit, who had never before dreamed of taking a cruise. By assembling all the parts of a vacation in advance, cruise lines can provide a hassle-free holiday from the moment the passenger's travel begins. The air/sea combination becomes an extension of what the ship offers: namely, accommodations, meals, recreation, entertainment, sports, and transportation from port to port.

Once you have checked in at the airport in your hometown, you won't have to bother with your luggage again. It will be waiting in your cabin. You will be brought from the airport by motor coach to the ship that awaits you at your port of embarkation without having to tote bags or pay extra for the transfer or give tips.

The ease and comfort with which you can visit places that are hard to reach on your own are part of cruising's great attractions. Almost any place in the Caribbean can be reached by plane, but if you tried visiting Key West, Jamaica, and Cozumel or Nassau, St. Thomas, and Martinique in a week, you would spend most of your vacation in airports! Indeed, the more complex the travel—the more changes of hotels, trains, buses, and planes that a similar itinerary by land requires—the more attractive travel by ship can be. Your ship is not only your transportation, it is also your hotel. And that's where you gain the ultimate convenience—you pack and unpack only once. In my book, that's a real vacation!

Cruising is the ultimate escape. For a few days you can turn off your worries and live out your fantasies. There are no phones ringing and no computers blinking. Without even working at it, you relax. The pure air, the gentle movement of the ship gliding through the water, and the unhurried rhythm of shipboard life is an instant antidote to the noise, pollution, and pressures of city life.

Because people travel to escape does not mean they seek isolation. On the contrary, meeting new people is part of the fun of travel and there is no better or easier place to do this than on ship. You feel the friendly atmosphere as soon as you start up the gangplank where the smiling staff welcomes you aboard, eager to serve you and see you enjoy yourself. You meet people from all over the country and from other parts of the world in an atmosphere of camaraderie. Yet, if you really do not like to socialize, you can stand aside. Or, if you are shy about meeting people, the ship's staff has dozens of clever ways to make it easy.

ONBOARD ACTIVITIES

A cruise is what a vacation should be—fun! In fact, there are more ways to have fun on a cruise than there are hours in the day to enjoy them all. People often have the false notion they will become bored on a cruise, but there's little chance of boredom if one takes advantage of all that is available.

For active people, there are swimming, fitness classes, yoga, deck tennis, Ping-Pong, workout gyms, and exercise and dance classes. On some ships, onboard sports and fitness programs are combined with organized activity in port for snorkeling, diving, sailing, windsurfing, tennis, golf, and fishing. Or you can simply head for a beach and do these activities on your own.

With lavish meals so much a part of the cruise experience, it might seem incongruous for lines to spend millions on elaborate facilities and fitness programs to turn their floating resorts into floating health spas. But once again, it has been the cruise lines' response to changing life-styles. Most have added new light dishes to their menus and marked off parts of their dining rooms and lounges for nonsmokers.

Those who like to learn are kept busy too. Ships frequently have instructors and tournaments for bridge, language, arts and crafts, wine tasting, cooking, and computers, to name a few. These enrichment programs, as the cruise lines call them, vary from ship to ship and cruise to cruise. Some ships build a cruise around a special theme such as mystery or photography; others offer annual cruises featuring classical music or jazz festivals-at-sea. Bingo is alive and well on all ships, and so are other competitive games, along with casinos and slot machines.

Movies—new releases and old favorites—are shown daily in the ship's theater or on closed-circuit television in your cabin. The theater is also used for such special events as concerts by visiting artists, fashion shows, or Broadway-style shows. And if this array of activity is still not enough, there's the visit to the bridge, the engine room, and the kitchens.

Every evening before you go to bed, a schedule of the next day's activities is slipped under your door. You can take in all of it, pick and choose, or ignore the lot of it.

A MOVABLE FEAST

Cruising has given new meaning to "A Movable Feast." The feasting starts with morning coffee and tea for the early birds and breakfast in the dining room or on one of the parlor decks. Mid-morning bouillon, afternoon tea, and the midnight buffet are cruise traditions. These snacks are provided in addition, of course, to lunch by the pool and the regular lunch and dinner served in the dining room. There, every day at every meal, the menu has three, four, or more selections for each course and a half-dozen courses for each meal. The ships also cater to special dietary requirements and can provide salt-free, diabetic, vegetarian, or kosher meals.

Needless to say, every line believes it offers the best cuisine on the high seas, and all work hard to distinguish themselves. But dining on a cruise is a more important part of the cruise experience than simply eating a meal. In addition to sampling specialties and new dishes, you have the chance to get to know your traveling companions in a relaxed and congenial atmosphere and to enjoy the best part of shipboard service by dining room staffs who take pride in their work. The food, wine, music, dances, language, and people all give a ship its personality and ambience and make a cruise a special kind of holiday.

Nightlife is another attraction on a cruise. Cruise lines go out of their way to provide a variety of entertainment for different age groups and interests. All but the smallest ships have nightclubs and discos, and most have casinos. Most large ships offer full-scale Broadway- and Las Vegas-style shows. Best of all, they're there to enjoy only one or two decks away.

CRUISING WITH CHILDREN

A cruise is one of the best possible vacations for families with children. There is no end to a child's fascination with a ship. It is a totally new experience with an environment different from anything they have known at home. It's also an education. The crews—many of whom are away from their own children—are wonderful with young passengers. There are always babysitters around, and you are never far from the children when you want to spend time on your own.

Once strictly adult territory, some cruise ships are so well equipped for children, they could be called floating camps. Trained youth counselors, often teachers and counselors on holiday or leave from their regular jobs, plan and supervise shipboard activities geared to specific age groups. Some ships have year-round counselors; others provide them during summer and other traditional vacation periods.

On the first day at sea, the counselors meet with parents and their children to review the week's activities and answer questions about facilities. Each morning a printed schedule especially for children is slipped under their door with the program for the day. Preteens are kept busy with pool parties, arts and crafts projects, movies, masquerades, scavenger hunts, and special entertainment such as magic shows, sports tournaments on deck, "Coketails," ice-cream parties, and talent shows.

Teenagers are likely to shun structured activities, and many prefer to be on their own. But the ship helps them get acquainted with a party. There are also pizza, hamburger, and disco parties to help ensure that the shy ones don't miss out on the fun. Some ships give the teenagers exclusive use of the disco while the adults are at cocktails or dinner. Dance contests, sports tournaments, fitness classes, language lessons, and theatrical productions are some of the other activities.

Shows with magicians, puppets, dancers, and singers are big hits with kids and parents alike. And too, there is children's favorite pastime—eating. Four servings of ice cream, if they want them. A cruise might be the one time in your life you will hear your children say, "I can't eat any more."

Children often get their own tours of the bridge and even get to meet the captain. They see the radar, navigational charts, and equipment and often learn more about the ship and how it operates than many adults do. They learn about travel etiquette and different foods, experience new kinds of service, and learn how to socialize in new environments.

In port, the family can take the ship's organized tours or explore on its own. One of the great advantages of a cruise is its room for flexibility. If one member of the family does not want to go on a tour, it need not cause a family crisis. The ship is in full operation even when it is in port; one never need worry about being left alone.

FAMILY REUNIONS

Cruises are not only great for families with children but those with grandchildren too. And they are ideal for family reunions, especially for families scattered around the country who find it hard to gather in one place—and do all that cooking! A cruise gives all members of the family equal time to spend with their favorite aunts, uncles, and cousins. Thanks to a ship's wide range of activity, there's always plenty to do, regardless of the participant's age. By sailing together, family members across the country can take advantage of group rates. Your travel agent can piece the parts together for you. All you need to do is agree on the cruise and the date.

IDEAL HONEYMOON

A cruise is what a honeymoon should be—romantic, relaxing, glamorous, different, and fun. It is a fairy tale come true. And it has the ingredients for a perfect honeymoon: privacy when you want it, attention when you need it; sports, music, dancing, and entertainment to share; sight-seeing to enjoy. The atmosphere is a happy one. Honeymooners need not have a worry in the world. Everything is at their fingertips including breakfast in bed. There are no big decisions to make, no travel hassles to face.

A cruise offers them total flexibility in making plans. No matter what the wedding date, they will be able to find a cruise. And thanks to the all-inclusive nature of a cruise, a couple can know in advance the cost of the honeymoon and plan accordingly.

A travel agent can also arrange for the honeymooners' extras that most ships offer. These might include champagne on the first night, flowers in the cabin, a wedding cake, an album for honeymoon photos, and a reception by the captain. Almost all ships have tables for two and cabins with double beds, which a travel agent can request at the time the reservations are made.

Ship captains cannot perform marriages aboard ship unless they are state-licensed. Some ships have a ceremony during the cruise for reaffirmation of vows, and couples are given certificates as a remembrance. Some ships also double as a wedding chapel in their home port. The cruise line will provide a notary to conduct the wedding ceremony or you can bring your own clergyman aboard to officiate. The ceremony can be simple or lavish and can be followed by a reception. Some couples have been known to take their wedding parties with them on their cruises!

PART II

SELECTING A CRUISE

HINTS, TIPS, AND ADVICE

With so many cruises going to so many different places, selecting one can be difficult. My suggestion is to start your planning at a travel agency. [A]bout 95 percent of all cruises are purchased [thr]ough travel agents. It will not cost more than buy[ing] a cruise directly from a cruise line, and it will save [yo]u time.

[U]SING A TRAVEL AGENT

[A g]ood travel agency stocks the brochures of the lead[ing] cruise lines; these show prices and details on the [shi]p's itineraries and facilities. An experienced agent [wil]l help you understand the language of a cruise [bro]chure, read a deck plan, and make reservations. [Th]e knowledgeable agent can help you make compar[iso]ns and guide you in the selection of a ship and an [itin]erary to match your interests. Your agent can book [you]r dining room table and handle a particular request [su]ch as for an anniversary party or a special diet. Agents [als]o know about packages and discounts that can help [yo]u save money.

[I]n recent years, with the boom in cruising, there has [be]en a rapid growth in travel agencies that sell only [cru]ises. Such specialized agencies are more likely than [ge]neral agencies, which sell all the products of travel, [to] have staffs with firsthand knowledge of many ships [an]d should be able to give you a profile of the ship, its [cr]ew, and its personality. If not, you should go to [an]other agency.

[T]HE BUILT-IN VALUE OF A [C]RUISE VACATION

[Of] all the attractions of cruising, none is more impor[tan]t than value. For one price you get transportation, [ac]commodations, meals, entertainment, use of all facil[iti]es, and a host of recreational activity. The only items not included are tips, drinks, personal services such as hairdressers, port tax, and shore excursions. There are no hidden costs.

Dollar for dollar, it's hard to beat a cruise for value. To make an accurate assessment of how the cost of a cruise compares with other types of holidays, be sure to compare similar elements. A holiday at sea should be compared with a holiday at a luxury resort, because the quality of service, food, and entertainment on most cruises is available only at posh resorts.

The average brochure price of a one-week Caribbean cruise is about $200 to $250 per day including airfare and all the ingredients previously described, but with current discounts and advance purchase plans these prices can be cut in half. Shorter three- and four-day Bahamas cruises range from $130 to $150 per day and there are plenty of low promotion fares available for them, too. No luxury resorts give you transportation to and from the resort, a hotel room, four full meals plus two or three snacks each day, nightly entertainment plus a myriad of activity—all for the one price of $150 to $250. Deluxe resorts can't match such an offering even in their off-seasons.

Stretching Your Budget

Air/sea packages provide cruise passengers further measurable savings in airfare. Because cruise lines transport so many passengers to and from their departure cities on a regular basis, they can buy air transportation in volume at low group rates and offer it as "free air." Since, more often than not, the air travel is on regularly scheduled flights, cruise passengers have the utmost flexibility in making their travel plans. The packages also provide savings on baggage handling, two-way transfers from the airport to the ship, and other features.

Air/sea combinations are available in two forms: an all-in-one package combining a cruise and air transportation in one price; or a second type in which the cruise is priced separately and an air supplement is added on to the cruise price, or a credit for air transportation from one's hometown to the ship's nearest departure port is offered. The amount of the supplement or credit varies from one cruise line to another. But, usually, the supplement is slightly more the farther away from the departure port you live. Still, the total cost is far less to you than if the cruise and air transportation were purchased separately. The details are spelled out in the cruise line's brochure. Ask your travel agent to explain how the package works as it can be confusing.

Is Free Air Free?

If you are skeptical—you don't get something for nothing—every cruise company publishes pamphlets that show the rates for every cabin on its ships, regardless of how passengers elect to get to the ship. If the cruise offers "free" air transportation and quotes one price for the package without a breakdown for each component, you can still know the value by reading the section intended for those prospective passengers who live in or near the departure port of the ship.

Although air/sea packages save you money, it goes without saying that some definitely represent larger savings than others, depending on the cruise line, the cruise, and the time of year. Every line's policy is different and policies vary not only from line to line, but even from cruise to cruise on any specific ship. The introduction of new cruise lines and the addition of new cruise ships, particularly in the Caribbean, have created a buyer's market with real bargains. It pays to shop around.

SELECTING A SHIP

The ship and the cruise line's reputation are other considerations in making your selection. Not only do ships differ; so do their passengers. You are more likely to enjoy a cruise with people who are seeking a similar type of holiday and with whom you share a community of interests and activities. A good travel agent who specializes in selling cruises is aware of the differences and should be able to steer you to a ship that's right for you. But before you visit an agent or begin to cull the colorful and enticing brochures, here are some tips on the items affecting cost that can help you in making a selection.

SELECTING A CABIN

The largest single item in the cost of a cruise is the cabin, also known as a stateroom. The cost of a cabin varies greatly and is determined by its size and location. Generally, the cabins on the top deck are the largest and most expensive; the prices drop and the cabins narrow on each deck down from the top. (Elevators and stairs provide access between decks.) But the most expensive cabins are not necessarily the best. There are other factors to consider.

Almost all cruise ships cabins have private bathrooms, but the size and fittings vary and affect cost. For example, cabins with full bathtubs are more expensive than those with showers only. Greater standardization of cabins is a feature of most new cruise ships.

Outside cabins are more costly than inside ones. There is a common misconception that inside cabins are to be avoided. It dates back to the days before air-conditioning when an outside cabin above the water line was desirable because the porthole could be opened for ventilation. Today's ships are climate-controlled; an inside cabin is as comfortable as an outside one. What's more, on a Caribbean cruise particularly, you will spend very little time in your cabin; it is mainly a place to sleep and change clothes. An inside cabin often provides genuine savings and is definitely worth investigating for those on a limited budget.

For the most stable ride, the deck at water level or below has less roll (side to side motion) and the cabins in the center of the ship have the least pitch (back and forth motion). But these cabins also cost more than those in the front (fore) or the back (aft) of the ship. Fore (or the bow) has less motion and is therefore preferable to aft (or the stern) where sometimes there is vibration from the ship's engines.

A ship's deck plan shows the exact location of each cabin and is usually accompanied by diagrams of the fittings in the cruise line's brochures. It does not give the dimensions of the cabin, but one can have a reasonable estimate since beds are standard single size—about 3 x 6 feet. Some ships have double beds, but most have twin beds that can be converted to doubles on request.

A few ships have single cabins; otherwise, a passenger booking a cabin alone pays a rate that is one and a half times the price per person for two sharing a cabin. A few ships offer special single rates on certain cruises or reserve a few cabins for single occupancy at the same rate as the per person rate on a shared basis plus a small supplement. Your travel agent should be able to give you specific information about singles rates.

OTHER COST FACTORS

As might be expected, rates for the winter season in the Caribbean are higher than in the spring, summer, or fall. Cruises over Christmas, New Year's, and other major holidays are usually the year's most expensive, but often, real bargains are to be found on cruises immediately before or after a holiday season when demand drops and lines are eager to stimulate business.

The length of the cruise bears directly on its cost. Longer cruises provide more elegance and fancier dining and service. The cost also varies depending on the ship's itinerary. For example, it is more economical for a cruise line to operate a set schedule of the same ports throughout the year, such as the ships departing weekly from Florida to the Caribbean, than it is to change itineraries every few weeks.

Family Rates

If you are planning a family cruise, look for cruise lines that actively promote family travel and offer special rates for children or for third and fourth persons in a cabin. It means a bit of crowding but can yield big savings. Family rates vary from one cruise line to another. As a rule of thumb, children sharing a cabin with two paying adults get discounts of 50 percent or more of the minimum fare. Qualifying ages vary, too, with a child usually defined as 2 to 12, and sometimes up to 17 years. Some lines have teen fares, while at certain times of the year others have free or special rates for the third or fourth person sharing a cabin with two full-fare adults, regardless of age. Most lines permit infants under two years to travel free of charge.

CRUISE DISCOUNTS

In today's highly competitive market, discounts have become a way of life. Cruise lines use them to publicize a new ship or itinerary, to attract families, younger passengers, singles, and a diversity of people. Some low fares are available year-round but may be limited to a certain number of cabins on each sailing; others are seasonal or may apply to specific cruises.

You can take advantage of fare discounts in two ways. If you book early, you can usually benefit from early bird discounts, and of course, you can be sure you have the cruise you want. On the other hand, if you are in a position to be flexible, you can wait to catch the last minute "fire sales." Cruise lines do not advertise the fact, but you can sometimes negotiate the lowest price on the day of sailing. To take advantage of this situation, you need to have maximum flexibility.

And remember, when you are buying a cruise, you will have already paid for *all* your accommodations, *all* meals (three meals a day is only the beginning; most ships have seven or more food services daily), *all* entertainment, and *all* recreational facilities aboard ship, and in most cases, round-trip airfare to the ship's departure port, baggage handling, and transfers. It is this all-inclusive aspect of a cruise that makes it a good value—a particularly significant advantage for families with children and those who need to know in advance the cost of a vacation.

SHORE EXCURSIONS

Sight-seeing tours, called shore excursions by the cruise lines, are available for an additional cost at every port of call in the Caribbean. A pamphlet on the shore excursions offered by the cruise line is usually included in the literature you receive prior to sailing. If not, ask for one.

A few lines encourage travel agents to sell their shore excursions in advance; most do not. Rather, you buy them on board ship from the purser, cruise director, or tour office. Most people seem to prefer buying them on board since, frequently, their interests and plans change once the cruise is underway.

A word of caution: When I first wrote this book, in 1987, I found that there was very little difference between the cruise ships' prices for tours and those of local tour companies, if you were staying in a hotel. However, in the last few years, the situation has changed so dramatically that I must alert readers to the change. In their need to keep their cruise prices down in the face of intense competition and rampant discounting, many cruise lines have come to regard shore excursions (as well as ancillary services such as shipboard shopping, bars, and spa facilities) as profit centers; some are selling their tours at exorbitant prices.

In a preliminary survey, I found prices jacked up 30 to 50 percent; some are even double the prices you would pay on shore. To take an example, on Western Caribbean cruises, the most popular excursion, Tulum/Xel-Ha, varies from an overpriced U.S. $50 for a three-hour trip from Playa del Carmen, and reasonable $55 to $68 for five- to six-hour trips from Cozumel, to a modest $39 for a seven-hour trip from Cancún—all for what is essentially the same trip.

To help you in your selection and to gauge fair prices, each port of call in this book has descriptions of the main shore excursions offered by the majority of cruise lines, as well as some that you must arrange on your own. The approximate price of each excursion when you buy it directly from a tour company on shore is noted, where possible, along with the current price at which it is sold aboard ship. The prices were accurate at press time but, of course, they are not guaranteed.

Since tours vary from vendor to vendor and cruise ship to cruise ship, it is difficult to generalize. Therefore, when you check prices, it is important that you compare like items and, when necessary, factor in such additional costs as transportation from the pier to the vendor's office or starting point. The information and prices provided here are intended as guidelines. Even if they change, the increase is not likely to be more than a dollar or two. If you come across shore excursion prices that appear to be out of line in comparison with those found in this book, please write to me and enclose a copy of the tours with their descriptions and prices sold on your cruise.

PORT TALKS

All ships offer what is known as a port talk—a brief description of the country or island and port where the ship will dock as well as shopping tips. The quality of these talks varies enormously, not only with the cruise line but also with the ship, and can depend on such wide ranging considerations as the knowledge and skill of the cruise director to the policy of the cruise line as to the true purpose of the information.

You should be aware that most cruise lines in the Caribbean have turned these port talks into sales pitches for certain products and stores with which they have exclusive promotional agreements and in which the cruise lines take commissions or are paid directly by the stores. You will receive a map of the port with "recommended" shops. What that really means is that the shop has paid the cruise line for being promoted in port talks and advertising in the ship's magazine that might appear in your cabin. Also, sometimes cruise directors receive commissions from local stores, even though they deny it. Hence, their vested interest could color their presentation and recommendations.

There are three ways to avoid being misled. If a cruise line, a cruise director, a guide, or anyone else recommends one store to the exclusion of all others, that should alert you to shop around before buying. The recommended store may actually be the best place to buy—but it may not. Second, if you are planning to make sizeable purchases of jewelry, cameras, or china, etc., check prices at home before you leave and bring a list of prices with you. Be sure, however, you are comparing like products. Finally, check the prices in shipboard shops, which are usually very competitive with those at ports of call.

Happily, because you have this book you do not need to rely on port talks for information, but if you do attend your ship's port talks and find that they have been more sales pitch than enlightenment, please write and tell me about your experience.

WHAT YOU SHOULD KNOW BEFORE YOU GO

Luggage and Wardrobe: There are no limits on the amount of luggage you can bring on board ship, but most staterooms do not have much closet and storage space. More importantly, since you are likely to be flying to your departure port you need to be guided by airline regulations regarding excess baggage. Life on a cruise, especially a Caribbean one, is casual. It is needless to be burdened with a lot of baggage; you will spend your days in sports clothes—slacks, shorts, T-shirts, bathing suits. Men usually are asked to wear a jacket at dinner.

The first and last nights of your cruise and the nights your ship is in port almost always call for casual dress. At least one night will be the captain's gala party where tuxedos for men and long dresses for women are requested but not mandatory. Another night might be a masquerade party; it's entirely up to you whether or not to participate.

A gentleman who does not have a tuxedo should bring a basic dark suit and white shirt. Add a selection of slacks and sport shirts, one or two sports jackets, and two pairs of bathing trunks. Women will find nylon and similar synthetics are good to use on a cruise because they are easy to handle, but these fabrics can be hot under the tropical sun. It largely depends on your tolerance for synthetic fabrics in hot weather. Personally, I find cottons and cotton blends to be the most comfortable. You will need two cocktail dresses for evening wear. A long dress for the captain's party is appropriate but not compulsory. Add a sweater or stole for cool evening breezes and the ship's air-conditioning in the dining room and lounges. Take cosmetics and sun lotion, but don't worry if you forget something. It will most likely be available in shipboard or portside shops.

You will need rubber-soled shoes for walking on deck and a comfortable pair of walking shoes for sight-seeing. Sunglasses and a hat or sun visor for protection against the strong Caribbean sun are essential. A tote bag comes in handy for carrying odds and ends; include several plastic bags for wet towels and bathing suits upon returning from a visit to a beach. You might also want to keep camera equipment in plastic bags as protection against the salt air and water and sand. And don't forget to pack whatever sporting equipment and clothes you will need. If you plan to snorkel, scuba, or play tennis, often you can save on rental fees by bringing your own gear.

Documentation: Requirements for vaccinations, visas, and so on depend on the destinations of the ship and are detailed in the information you receive from the cruise lines. Among the Caribbean's many advantages is that normally no destination (except Cuba, which is not covered in this book) requires visas of U.S. and Canadian citizens arriving as cruise passengers.

Meal Times: All but the most luxurious Caribbean cruise ships have two sittings for the main meals. Early sitting breakfast is from 7 to 8 A.M.; lunch is from 12 to 1 P.M.; and dinner is from 6:15 to 7:30 P.M. On the late sitting, breakfast is from 8 to 9 A.M.; lunch is from 1:30 to 2:30 P.M.; and dinner is from 8:15 to 9:30 P.M. If you are an early riser, you will probably be happy with the early sitting. If you are likely to close the disco every night, you might prefer the late one. Of course, you will not be confined to these meals as there are usually a buffet breakfast, lunch on deck, a midnight buffet, and afternoon tea.

Requesting a Table: Your travel agent can request your table in advance, if you want a table for two or for your family, as well as your preference for early or late seating. Some cruise lines will confirm your reservation in advance; others require you to sign up for your dining table with the maître d'hôtel soon after boarding your ship. In this day of computers, it's hard to understand why any cruise line would want to put a passenger through this unnecessary inconvenience, but some do.

Electrical Appliances: Cabins on almost all new ships have outlets for electric razors and have hairdryers or are wired for them, but older ships are not. Instead, rooms with special outlets are provided. Few ships allow you to use electric irons in your cabin because of the potential fire hazard. Electric current is normally 115–120 volts—but not always—and plugs are the two-prong, American-type ones. Check with your cruise line for specific information.

Laundry and Dry Cleaning: All ships have either laundry service for your personal clothing (for which there is an extra charge) or coin-operated laundry rooms. Only a very few have dry cleaning facilities. In the Caribbean, this is not an important consideration since the clothes required are cotton or cotton blends and should be easy to wash.

Hairdressing: Almost all Caribbean cruise ships have hairdressers for both men and women. Prices are comparable to those at deluxe resorts.

Religious Services: All ships hold interdenominational services; many also have a daily Catholic mass. Services will be conducted by the captain or a clergyman. At ports of call you will be welcome to attend local services.

Medical Needs: All cruise ships are required by law to have at least one doctor, nurse, and infirmary or mini-hospital. Doctor visits and medicine are extra costs.

Seasickness: First-time cruise passengers probably worry more about becoming seasick than about any other aspect of cruising. Certainly they worry more than they should, particularly on a Caribbean cruise where

the sea is calm almost year-round. Ships today have stabilizers, which steady them in all but the roughest seas. But if you are still worried, there are several types of nonprescription medicines such as Dramamine and Bonine that help to guard against motion sickness. Buy some to bring along—you may not need it but having it with you might be comforting. Also, the ship's doctor can provide you with Dramamine and other medication that will be immediately effective, should you need it.

Sea Bands are a fairly new product for seasickness prevention. They are a pair of elasticized wristbands, each with a small plastic disk that, based on the principle of acupuncture, applies pressure on the inside wrist. I use Sea Bands and have given them to friends to use and can attest to their effectiveness. They are particularly useful for people who have difficulty taking medication. Sea Bands are found in drug, toiletry, and health care stores and can be ordered from Travel Accessories, P.O. Box 391162, Solon, Ohio 44139. Tel. 216–248–8432. They even make sequined covers in a dozen colors to wear over the bands for evening.

There are two important things to remember about seasickness: Don't dwell on your fear. Even the best sailors and frequent cruisers need a day to get their "sea legs." If you should happen to get a queasy feeling, take some medicine immediately. The worst mistake you can make is to play the hero, thinking it will go away. When you deal with the symptoms immediately, relief is fast, and you are seldom likely to be sick. If you wait, the queasy feeling will linger and you run a much greater risk of being sick.

Caution against the Caribbean Sun: You should be extra careful about the sun in the tropics. It is much stronger than the sun to which most people are accustomed. Do not stay in the direct sun for long stretches at a time, and use a sunscreen at all times. Nothing can spoil a vacation faster than a sunburn.

Shipboard Shops: There's always a shop for essentials you might have forgotten or that can't wait until the next port of call. Many ships—particularly the new ones—have elaborate shops competitive with stores at ports of call. It's another reason to pack lightly, since you are almost sure to buy gifts and souvenirs during the cruise.

Tipping: Tipping is a matter of a great deal of discussion but much less agreement. How much do you tip in a restaurant or a hotel? Normally, the tip should be about $3 per person per day for each of your cabin stewards and dining room waiters. On some ships, particularly those with Greek crews, the custom is to contribute to the ship's common kitty in the belief that those behind the scenes such as kitchen staffs should share in the bounty. On some ships, dining room staffs also pool their tips. Tipping guidelines are sometimes printed in literature your cruise line sends in advance, enabling you to factor the expense into your budget even before booking a cruise. The cruise director, as part of his advice-giving session at the end of the cruise, also explains the ship's policy and offers guidelines.

Telephone Calls—Ship-to-Shore and Shore-to-Ship: Most new ships have telephones in cabins with international direct dialing capability and fax facilities in their offices. Be warned, however, the service is very expensive—about $15 per minute. If someone at home or in your office needs to reach you in an emer-

gency, they can telephone your ship directly. Those calling from the continental United States would dial 011 plus 874 (the ocean area code for the Caribbean), followed by the seven-digit telephone number of your ship. Someone calling from Puerto Rico should dial 128 and ask for the long distance operator.

Instructions on making such calls, how to reach the ship, or who to notify in case of an emergency are usually included in the information sent to you by your cruise line along with your tickets and luggage tags. If not, your travel agent can obtain it. You should have this information before you leave home.

PART III

CARIBBEAN CRUISE LINES AND THEIR SHIPS

A GUIDE

*very effort has been made to ensure the accu-
racy of the information on the cruise lines and
ir ships, their ports of call, and prices, but do
ep in mind that cruise lines change their ships'
neraries often for a variety of reasons. Always
eck with the cruise line or with a travel agent
fore making plans. For specific information on
e itineraries of ships cruising to the Western
ribbean, see charts at the end of this book.*

ERICAN CANADIAN CARIBBEAN LINE,
1 Water Street, Warren, RI 02885;
1–247–0955; 800–556–7450;
x 401–245–8303

ips (Passengers): *Caribbean Prince* (83);
ande Prince (100); *Mayan Prince* (90);
agara Prince (84)

parture ports: Panama City or Balboa; Belize City;
atan; Nassau; Palm Beach/Key West

pe of cruises: 12 days of Bahamas to Turk and
icos; Belize/Barrier Reef/Guatemala; Honduras;
nama Canal/San Blas; Central America; Virgin
ands; Trinidad/Orinoco/Tobago; and
ba/Bonaire/ Curaçao.

e-style tips: Family-style dining; mature and expe-
nced passengers; light adventure; no frills. Emphasis
on natural attraction and local culture

f you are looking for tranquility, informality, and con-
sation with fellow passengers instead of floor shows
d casinos, American Canadian Caribbean Line offers
v-key cruises around the Bahamas archipelago,
lize, the southwestern Caribbean, and Central
erica during the winter and early spring.

n 1964, founder Luther Blount designed his first small
p for cruising Canada's inland waterways. By 1988,
line had expanded to the extent that it could add
ribbean to its name. In the intervening years, ACCL
nained faithful to the concept that small, intimate ships
h limited planned entertainment can be successful.

The ships' innovative bow ramps and shallow drafts give
passengers direct access to beaches, coves, and places
that are inaccessible to larger ships. The line's fourth
ship, the *Grande Prince,* will sail on Panama/Western
Caribbean cruises in the winter season.

ACCL's ships are popular with mature, well-traveled
passengers who like hearty American menus and the
informal atmosphere of family-style dining. It is an
atmosphere for instant friendships and complete relaxation. The line's large number of repeaters would seem
to indicate that passengers agree with its concept and
appreciate the "in-close" facility the ships bring to the
cruise experience.

CANAVERAL CRUISE LINE, 501 N. Wymore
Road, Winter Park, FL 32789;
409–975–5000; 800–910–SHIP

Ship (Passengers): *Dolphin IV* (562)
Departure port: Port Canaveral
Type of cruise: 2 nights to the Bahamas
Life-style tip: Casual, informal for budget-minded
first-time cruisers

The new cruise line was launched in 1996 after con-
tracting the *Dolphin IV* from Dolphin Cruises. The
smallest ship in Bahamas service has established a reputation for good food and friendly service. The cabins
are comfortable for two persons, but those with four
berths are snug for a family of four unless the kids are
small. The ship sails to Port Lucaya, west of Freeport on
Grand Bahama Island. The two-night cruises start at
$129 per person, double occupancy, plus $79 for port
charges. The cruise line also offers a package that couples three nights at select hotels in Orlando with the
cruise; prices range from $279 to $319 per person
double occupancy plus $79 port charges, depending
on the cabin category aboard ship.

CARNIVAL CRUISE LINES, 3655 N.W. 87th
Avenue, Miami, FL 33178–2428;
305–599–2600; 800–327–7373;
fax 305–599–8630

Ships (Passengers): *Carnival Destiny* (2,642);
Celebration (1,486); *Ecstasy* (2,040); *Fantasy*
(2,044); *Fascination* (2,040); *Holiday* (1,452);
Imagination (2,044); *Inspiration* (2,044);*Jubilee*

(1,486); *Sensation* (2,040); *Tropicale* (1,022)
Departure ports: Miami, Port Canaveral, Tampa, New Orleans, San Juan
Type of cruises: 3 and 4 days to Bahamas and Key West; 7 days to Western, Northern, Eastern, and Southern Caribbean, and the Panama Canal
Life-style tip: The "Fun Ships," youthful, casual, action-filled; high value for money

When Kathie Lee Gifford flashes her pretty smile across your television screen and says, "Carnival, the most popular cruise line in the world," that's not simply advertising hype. It's true—and the story of how it got to that position is the stuff of legends.

In 1972 Florida-based cruise executive Ted Arison and an innovative Boston-based travel agency bought the *Empress of Canada,* which they renamed the *Mardi Gras* to start a cruise line that would stand the stodgy old steamship business on its ear. But alas, the *Mardi Gras* ran aground on her maiden cruise. After staring at losses three years in a row, Arison took full ownership of the company, assuming its $5 million debt, buying its assets—i.e., the ship—for $1, and launched the "Fun Ships" concept that is Carnival's hallmark.

The idea was to get away from the class-conscious elitism that had long been associated with luxury liners and to fill the ship with so much action-packed fun that the ship itself would be the cruise experience. The line also aimed at lowering the average age of passengers by removing the formality associated with cruising and providing a wide selection of activity and entertainment to attract active young adults, young couples, honeymooners, and families with children at reasonable prices. In only a few months Carnival turned a profit and in the next two years added two more ships.

The line's next move was as surprising as it was bold. In 1978 when shipbuilding costs and fuel prices were skyrocketing—threatening the very future of vacations-at-sea, Carnival ordered a new ship, larger and more technologically advanced than any cruise ship in service. It changed the profile of ships and enhanced the "fun" aspects of cruises. But it was Carnival's next move that really set the trend of the eighties and beyond.

In 1982, less than ten years after its rocky start, Carnival ordered three "superliners," each carrying 1,800 passengers, with design and decor as far removed from the grand old luxury liner as could be imagined. Between 1985 and 1987, the three ships— *Holiday, Jubilee,* and *Celebration*—were put into service. The decor was so different, it was zany. The owners called it "a Disney World for adults." On the *Holiday,* the main promenade deck, called "Broadway," complete with boardwalk and a Times Square, runs double-width down only one side of the

ship and is lined with bars, nightclubs, casinos, lounges, and disco with as much glitz and glitter as the neon on Broadway. At one end of the deck there's a marquee and an enormous theater spanning two decks where Broadway musical–style and Las Vegas cabaret–type shows are staged twice nightly.

In 1990, Carnival outdid itself with the *Fantasy,* the first of eight megaliners even more dazzling than the earlier superliners. A ship for the twenty-first century, the *Fantasy,* with its flashy decor and high-energy ambience, is something of a Las Vegas, Disneyland, and Starlight Express in one. The heart of the ship is an atrium, awash in lights, towering seven decks high. Here and in the entertainment areas, 15 miles of computerized lights are programmed to change color—constantly, but imperceptibly—from white and cool blue to hot red, altering the ambience with each change. The ships have full-fledged gyms and spas and so many entertainment and recreation outlets that you need more than one cruise to find them all. By spring 1996, all eight megaliners were in service and *Carnival Destiny,* the world's largest cruise ship, arrives in December.

Now headed by Arison's son, Micky, Carnival is directed by a young, energetic, and aggressive team that seems determined to entice *everybody*—single, married, families, children, retirees, disabled (on the new ships), first-time cruisers, repeat cruisers, people from the north, south, east, and west, and from all walks of life—to take a cruise. To that end, the cruises are priced aggressively and offer early bird and special rates for third and fourth persons in the cabin.

The ships that sail to the Bahamas on three- and four-day cruises feature a full day at sea, instead of a beach party at a Bahamian island, which most other ships offer. Needless to say, ships make more money in the bars and casino when passengers remain on board. This revenue, in turn, helps Carnival keep down the price of its cruises.

Do all these ideas work? You bet they do! By 1997 Carnival will have 11 cruise ships in service, carrying over a million passengers a year. That's up from 80,000 passengers in its first year. In 1987 Carnival Cruise Lines went public, and the following year it began *Carnival Air Lines* and purchased the long-established Holland America Line, which in turn owned Windstar Cruises. Later it acquired partial ownership in the Seabourn Cruise Line, with ultra-luxurious ships. Although these lines operate under their own banners, the combination makes Carnival one of the world's largest cruise lines and gives it enormous marketing clout across the widest possible spectrum. Recently, Carnival acquired ownership in Airtour, a large European tour company, as an avenue for expanding in Europe.

The success of Carnival's western Caribbean cruises from Tampa and New Orleans led the line to replace its *Tropicale* with the larger *Celebration,* expanding capacity by nearly 50 percent. With the dual ports of embarkation, passengers may board in either Tampa or New Orleans for a seven-day Western Caribbean cruise to Grand Cayman and Cozumel, as well as New Orleans and Tampa.

CELEBRITY CRUISES, 5201 Blue Lagoon Drive, Miami, FL 33126; 305–262–6677; fax 800–437–5111

Ships (Passengers): *Century* (1,750); *Galaxy* (1,750); *Horizon* (1,354); *Meridian* (1,106); *Mercury* (1,750); *Zenith* (1,374)
Departure ports: Ft. Lauderdale, San Juan
Type of cruises: 7, 10, 11 nights to the Bahamas and Northern Caribbean; Western and Eastern Caribbean; Bermuda
Life-style tip: Modestly deluxe cruises at moderate prices

In 1989, when John Chandris, the nephew of the founder of Chandris Cruises, announced the creation of a new deluxe mid-priced cruise line, he said the goal was "to bring more luxurious cruises to experienced travelers but still at affordable prices." He was met with a great deal of skepticism; "deluxe" and "mid-priced" seemed a contradiction in terms. But three years later, he had made believers out of all his doubters.

Not only did Celebrity Cruises accomplish what it set out to do, it did it better than anyone imagined and in record-breaking time. A Celebrity cruise is not only deluxe; it offers the best value for the money of any cruise line in its price category.

Celebrity was a completely new product with a new generation of ships designed for the 1990s. It defined the ideal size of a cruise ship and the appropriate layout, cabins, decor, and ambience for its market and set new standards of service and cuisine in its price category.

Celebrity's ships are not as glitzy as some of the new megaliners but they are spacious and have a similar array of entertainment and recreation. The once-standard one-lounge-for-all has been replaced by small, separate lounges, each with its own decor, ambience, and entertainment, and a variety of bars to give passengers a range of options. They have stunning, stylish decor that has brought back some of the glamour of cruising in bygone days but with a fresh, contemporary look.

From its inception, Celebrity Cruises aimed at creating superior cuisine as one way to distinguish itself. To achieve their goal, they engaged as their food consultant Michel Roux, the award-winning master French chef who operates two Michelin three-star restaurants

and five other restaurants in England, a catering service, and other food enterprises. He spent six months developing the menus for Celebrity Cruises and working with the ships' chandlers and chefs.

Roux accomplished miracles and set a new standard for other cruise lines. The food is sophisticated but unpretentious; quality is more important than quantity, although there's no lack of quantity either. Using the best-quality products, Roux keeps the menus seasonal to the extent possible, changing them every three months. To make sure the cuisine stays at his demanding level, he sails on each ship several times during the year.

Celebrity was launched in 1990 with the brand-new *Horizon* and the *Meridian* (formerly the *Galileo*), which had undergone a $70 million reconstruction to match the deluxe level of the *Horizon.* The stylish, elegant *Horizon* is classic and very contemporary at the same time. It has mostly outside staterooms equipped with closed-circuit television that carries daily programs of events, first-run movies, and world news. The ship has a piano bar, a nightclub, a duplex show lounge with state-of-the-art sound and lighting systems, a disco, a casino, and an observation lounge. There are shops, a sports and fitness center, two swimming pools, and three Jacuzzis.

The *Zenith,* which lives up to its name in every way, followed in 1992 and is almost identical to the *Horizon.* Extensive use of wood and lovely warm decor make the *Zenith* especially inviting.

Celebrity received awards for its ships and its cuisine from the first year of operation. Now, in the suites, butler service is available. As a send-off on the last day of the cruise, all passengers may enjoy a classic high tea with white-glove service and classical music.

Also, in 1992 Celebrity teamed up with Overseas Shipholding Group, one of the world's largest bulk-shipping companies, to form a joint cruise company and launch three new megaliners known as the Century series—designed, the cruise line believes, for the twenty-first century. Among the innovations, Sony Corporation has provided the most advanced technology in entertainment and interactive services yet seen on cruise ships. The first ship, *Century,* made her debut in December 1995, followed by the *Galaxy* in November 1996 and the *Mercury* in 1997.

CLIPPER CRUISE LINE, 7711 Bonhomme Avenue, St. Louis, MO 63105; 314–727–2929; 800–325–0010; fax 314–727–6576

Ships (Passengers): *Nantucket Clipper* (102); *Yorktown Clipper* (138)
Departure ports: St. Thomas, Grenada, Curaçao, Panama City

Type of cruises: 13 days to Costa Rica and Panama; 7 days to the Virgin Islands; 11 days to the Eastern and Southern Caribbean

Life-style tip: Small ships for nature-oriented travelers

Clipper Cruise Line is a special niche: nature-oriented cruises on comfortable small ships with pleasing interior decor, sailing to the little-known corners of the Caribbean and Central America in winter and other parts of North and South America during the other seasons. The ships' shallow drafts often enable them to sail into places where larger ships cannot go. The cruise line has its own naturalists who travel on the ships and help plan the cruises and shore experiences.

In early spring and late fall, the *Yorktown Clipper* has a series combining the San Blas islands and Panama Canal en route to the Darien Jungle and the Pacific for birding and nature viewing in the parks and rain forests of Costa Rica. The ship carries Zodiacs that enable it to drop anchor frequently for passengers to enjoy a swim at secluded beaches, hike in a rain forest, or sail up a river to a remote village. Daily onboard seminars by a naturalist on the places to be visited are followed by discussions after the visit. The naturalist also acts as a guide for those who want to take nature walks, bird-watch, and learn more about the local environment.

The crew is American, mostly fresh out of college, and unfailingly polite and friendly. The itinerary is leisurely and so is the activity. Scuba diving, windsurfing, golf, or tennis can also be arranged, depending on the itinerary. Absent, but not missed by its passengers, are the casinos, pools, staged entertainment, and organized diversions of large ships. Both the ship and passenger complement are small enough that you get to know everyone aboard in the course of a week.

Clipper's ships have outside staterooms—most with large windows. Some are entered from the outside (as on river steamboats) rather than interior corridors. Cabins and lounges are nicely decorated with quality furnishings. Passengers dine at one seating on good American cuisine prepared by a staff headed by a chef from the prestigious Culinary Institute of America.

Clipper Cruise Line passengers are not bargain hunters or those looking for last-minute specials. Rather, they are mature, well-traveled, and, often, seasoned cruisers.

COMMODORE CRUISE LINE, LTD., 4000 Hollywood Boulevard, South Tower, Suite 385, Hollywood, FL 33021; 954–967–2100

Ship (Passengers): *Enchanted Isle* (736)
Departure port: New Orleans
Type of cruise: 7 days to Western Caribbean
Life-style tip: Tried and true; easy and casual, budget-priced; attracts families

Commodore Cruises, which began sailing from Florida to the Caribbean in 1966, moved to New Orleans and the Western Caribbean in the 1980s to get away from the intense competition of the new cruise lines. Best known for its theme cruises, it was bought and merged with other lines several times over the past decade. In 1995, the line was acquired by a group of Miami investors and its second ship, *Enchanted Seas*, was chartered to World Explorer Cruises to be used year-round.

The *Enchanted Isle* is a spacious ship with a warm feeling. Its large cabins make it especially popular with families, and its low prices are meant to attract budget-minded travelers. In most cases, passengers who sail on Commodore receive a free hotel night in New Orleans, either before or after their cruise. Its new itinerary includes the Bay Islands as well as Puerto Cortes in Honduras.

COSTA CRUISE LINES, World Trade Center, 80 S.W. 8th Street, Miami, FL 33130-3097; 305–358–7325

Ships (Passengers): *CostaAllegra* (810); *CostaClassica* (1300); *CostaRomantica* (1300); *CostaVictoria* (1,950)
Departure ports: Miami, San Juan
Type of cruises: 7 days to Western, Northern, Eastern, and Southern Caribbean
Life-style tip: More European atmosphere and service than similar mass-market ships

"Cruising Italian Style" has long been Costa Cruise Lines' stock in trade, with a fun and friendly atmosphere created by its Italian staff and largely Italian crew. The emphasis is on good Italian food, which means pasta, pizza, and espresso (there are other kinds of cuisine, too); European-style service, particularly in the dining room; and, not to forget the Italians' ancestry, a toga party, which is usually a hilarious affair, one night of the cruise.

The Genoa-based company of the Costa family has been in the shipping business for over 100 years and in the passenger business for over 50 years. Costa began offering one-week Caribbean cruises from Miami in 1959; it was the first to offer an air/sea program, introduced in the late 1960s.

With four new ships costing more than one billion dollars, Costa launched the 1990s with one of the newest fleets in the Caribbean. Each ship introduced interesting new features in its design, combining classic qualities with modern features and boasting unusually large cabins for their price category. Among the ships' nicest features are canvas-covered outdoor cafes and pizzerias serving pizza throughout the day without additional charge.

Serena Cay (Catalina Island) is Costa's "private" island off the southeast coast of the Dominican Republic featured on Eastern Caribbean cruises. The island is near the sprawling resort of Casa de Campo, which has, among its many facilities, two of the best golf courses in the Caribbean, a tennis village, horseback riding, and polo.

Costa's ships have fitness centers and spas (most services are extra), along with a health and fitness program to suit individual needs. Costa's shore excursions, which tend to be expensive, stress outdoor activities.

Costa lets you combine the cruises of two ships into one 14-day cruise, at a price considerably less than that of two separate cruises. Another popular feature: during a Caribbean cruise a couple can renew their wedding vows in a special shipboard ceremony.

In 1996, the line's largest ship, *CostaVictoria*, made her Caribbean debut in November, sailing weekly from Miami and alternating between the Western and Eastern Caribbean.

CRYSTAL CRUISES, 2121 Avenue of the Stars, Suite 200, Los Angeles, CA 90067; 310–785–9300, 800–446–6645; fax 310–785–3891

Ships (Passengers): *Crystal Harmony* (960); *Crystal Symphony* (960)
Departure ports: Worldwide
Type of cruises: 10-to-17-day transcanal
Life-style tips: Ultra luxury for sophisticated travelers

The launching of Crystal Cruises in 1989 was one of the most anticipated in the cruising world. The new cruise line had begun spreading the word two years before its first ship had seen the water, and its owners spared no expense to ensure that the sleek *Crystal Harmony* would live up to its advance billing. Its goal was to create luxury cruises that would return elegance and personalized service to cruising and be designed for an upscale mass market at deluxe prices.

The *Crystal Harmony* exceded expectations. Indeed, it has been so well received by passengers and by its competition that it has become the ship by which others in its class—or trying to be in its class—are measured. But for my money, the Crystal sisters are in a class all their own.

Crystal Symphony is essentially a copy of the *Crystal Harmony*, with some refinements and new features; for example, there will be no inside staterooms. The ships are magnificent, with exquisite attention to detail. The food is excellent and the service superb, with the staff at every level smiling and gracious and always willing to go the extra mile.

Built in Japan by Mitsubishi Heavy Industries, these are spacious ships for experienced travelers with sophisticated life-styles. The luxury is evident from the moment you step on either ship. The atrium lobby, the ship's focus, is accented with greenery and hand-cut glass sculptures. The piano bar features—what else?—a crystal piano.

Staterooms have sitting areas, minibars, spacious closets, and such amenities as hairdryers, plush robes, VCRs, and 24-hour hookup with CNN and ESPN; more than half have verandas. The ships' penthouses have Jacuzzis and butler service. Facilities include spa and fitness centers and full promenade decks for jogging. The indoor/outdoor swimming pools have swim-up bars and lap pools with adjacent whirlpools. The casinos are the first "Caesars Palace at Sea."

The ships' most innovative feature is the choice of two dinner restaurants—Japanese or Asian and Italian—at no extra cost. These restaurants are in addition to standard meal service in the main dining room and 24-hour room service.

In 1996, Crystal Cruises introduced low single supplement rates, ranging only 10–15 percent more than the per-person, double-occupancy rate for a cabin in Category A through E, which includes deluxe cabins with verandas. The line's new transcanal series has a new call in Puerto Quetzal, Guatemala, and a new itinerary between Acapulco and New Orleans that visits Galveston.

CUNARD, 555 Fifth Avenue, New York, NY 10017; 212–880–7500; 800–221–4770 (outside New York)

Ships (Passengers): *Cunard Countess* (752); *Cunard Dynasty* (800); *Cunard Sea Goddess I* (116); *Cunard Sea Goddess II* (116); *Queen Elizabeth 2* (1810); *Cunard Royal Viking Sun* (740); *Vistafjord* (736)
Departure ports: Ft. Lauderdale, San Juan, St. Thomas, Barbados, and Aruba
Type of cruises: 7 to 16 days for ships in Caribbean and transcanal on seasonal schedules
Life-style tip: Wide range but no mistaking the British touch, though in different ways depending on the ship; caters mostly to affluent travelers

Cruise lines spend billions annually on promotion, but according to some tests, the only ship that the man-on-the-street can recall by name, unaided, is the *QE2*. That's perhaps not surprising when one considers that she is heir to a family of transatlantic liners reaching back over a century and a half and the only ship still on regular transtlantic service, from April to December.

The *Queens* have set the standard of elegance at sea in times of peace and served their country with distinction in times of war. Today, the *Queen,* which recently had a multi-million dollar makeover, sets the tone for Cunard. To many, she is the ultimate cruise experience. The *QE2* is a city-at-sea, dwarfing most other ships. She is proud, elegant, formal, and as British as—well, yes—the queen. The *QE2* isn't seen often in the Caribbean as her winters are taken mostly with an annual cruise around the world.

The other ships are important to the Cunard mix. The spacious and graceful *Vistafjord,* which has long epitomized luxury cruising, maintains the ambience of traditional cruising. Her Caribbean schedule is seasonal. The top-rated *Royal Viking Sun,* which Cunard bought in 1994, cruises the world, as do the ultra-deluxe *Sea Goddess* twins, built expressly to offer the most exclusive, elegant cruises in the world.

Their cabins, decor, itineraries, and cuisine were all planned to meet the expectations of a select group of very affluent people, offering highly personalized service and an unregimented ambience. The dining room has open seating and there is full meal service in staterooms around the clock. The ships have a stern platform that can be lowered to the level of the sea, enabling passengers to snorkel, swim, and enjoy other water sports from the boat. One of the twins sails on one-week itineraries of the Eastern Caribbean and longer transcanal ones.

The *Cunard Countess,* with British officers and an international crew, is less traditional than the other ships and suited for the informal atmosphere of the Caribbean. She sails from San Juan on seven-day cruises with alternating itineraries to six or seven Caribbean islands.

The *Cunard Dynasty,* added in 1993, fits between the luxury of *Sea Goddess* and the economy of the *Countess* and is designed for a mid-range group of vacationers: 35 to 55 years old, with a middle-management income level and an active life-style. She is small enough to be cozy but large enough to have the amenities and facilities expected by today's cruise passengers. Praised for her innovative design and use of space, the *Dynasty* sails from Ft. Lauderdale on transcanal cruises September through April, when she heads to Alaska for the summer.

Even though Cunard is one of the oldest lines afloat, it has been very much an innovator, responding to today's changing life-styles with gusto and recognizing the impact of the electronic revolution on people's lives—including their holidays. The *QE2* was the first ship to have a full-fledged spa at sea, a computer learning center, and satellite-delivered world news.

DISNEY CRUISE LINE, 210 Celebration Place, Suite 400, Celebration, FL 34747-4600; 407–939–3727; fax 407–939–3750

Ships (Passengers): *Disney Magic* (1,760); *Disney Wonder* (1,760)
Departure port: Port Canaveral
Type of cruises: 3- and 4-day cruises combined with Disney World vacations
Life-style tip: Family-oriented but designed for all ages

Disney Cruise Line is scheduled to be launched in April 1998, with its first ship, *Disney Magic,* followed by a sister ship, *Disney Wonder,* in November. Both ships will have classic exteriors reminiscent of the great transatlantic ocean liners of the past, but inside they will be up-to-the-minute in fun and entertainment for people of all ages.

The line plans to combine a three- or four-day stay at a Walt Disney World Resort with a three- or four-day cruise aboard ship, sailing round-trip from Port Canaveral. The itinerary will include at least one Caribbean port of call and a daylong stop at Disney's own private island.

In addition to catering to families, passengers will find services, activities, and programs designed specifically for adults without children, honeymooners, and seniors. For example, the ship will offer themed restaurants as well as an adults-only alternative restaurant, swimming pool, and night club.

Disney promises that nightly entertainment will be "unlike any other in the cruise industry" and will feature top Disney-produced shows with Broadway-quality entertainers, cabaret, and an adult-oriented lecture and enrichment program.

The children's programs are expected to be the most extensive in the industry with the largest children-dedicated space and age-specific activities and a large number of counselors. The ship will have a separate pool, lounge, teen club, and game arcade for older kids.

Disney Magic will sport spacious suites and cabins with 73 percent outside and almost half with small verandas.

DOLPHIN CRUISE LINE, 901 South America Way, Miami, FL 33132; 305–358–2111; 800–222–1003

Ships (Passengers): *IslandBreeze* (1,146); *OceanBreeze* (772); *SeaBreeze* (840)
Departure port: Miami, Montego Bay, New York
Type of cruises: 3- and 4-night Bahamas and Key West; 7-day cruise to Western Caribbean, Panama, Costa Rica
Life-style tip: Friendly, comfortable for all ages, and economical

Dolphin Cruise Line made major changes in 1995, selling the *Dolphin IV,* dropping Aruba as a home port for the *OceanBreeze,* and acquiring Carnival Cruises' *Festivale,* which it renamed *IslandBreeze.* The *OceanBreeze* has taken over the former itinerary of the *Dolphin,* departing on Fridays for a three-day weekend cruise to Nassau and Blue Lagoon, an inlet where passengers enjoy a Robinson Crusoe day with calypso music, a cookout, and water sports. The four-day cruise leaves Miami every Monday and makes the same stops plus Key West.

During the winter season, *IslandBreeze* sails weekly from Montego Bay to Panama with a partial transit of the canal; during summer she sails from New York. The *SeaBreeze* continues on cruises that alternate weekly between the Western and Eastern Caribbean. The cruises can be combined into a two-week cruise at a special price.

When Dolphin Cruise Line started out in 1984, it had a hard time going up against the giants of Bahamas cruises, but affordable one-week packages, combining a three- or four-day cruise with visits to Disney World/EPCOT or Miami helped it succeed. Early bird discounts and special low rates for children and third and fourth persons in a cabin also helped.

Dolphin cruises are family-oriented. The *Seabreeze* has 32 cabins with adjoining doors, especially for families; the OceanBreeze has cabins with Pullman beds and a children's playroom. The ships have youth counselors on board seasonally to plan and supervise children's activities. Dolphin is the official cruise line of Hanna-Barbera cartoons; Fred Flintstone, Yogi Bear, and other cartoon characters are featured on the ships.

For active adults the ships have diving and snorkeling programs, as well as golf and tennis with instruction on board and play in port. Dolphin's sister line is Majesty Cruise Line, which caters to a more upscale traveler than Dolphin.

HOLLAND AMERICA LINE, 300 Elliott Avenue West, Seattle, WA 98119; 206–281–3535; 800–426–0327

Ships (Passengers): *Maasdam* (1,266); *Nieuw Amsterdam* (1,214); *Noordam* (1,214); *Rotterdam* (1,075); *Ryndam* (1,266); *Statendam* (1,266); *Veendam* (1,266); *Westerdam* (1,476)

Departure ports: Ft. Lauderdale, Tampa, New York, New Orleans

Type of cruises: 7 days to Western and Eastern Caribbean; 10 days to Southern Caribbean; 10 to 23 days to Panama Canal

Life-style tip: Classic but contemporary

Begun in 1873 as a transatlantic shipping company between Rotterdam and the Americas, Holland America Line stems from one of the oldest steamship companies in the world. Through the years and two wars her ships became an important part of maritime history, particularly significant as the westward passage of immigrants to America. The line also owns Westours, the Seattle-based tour company that pioneered tours and cruises to Alaska five decades ago; and it acquired the unusual Windstar Cruises in 1988. The following year the entire group was purchased by Carnival Cruise Lines, but all operate as separate entities.

Holland America now has one of the newest fleets in cruising, having added four magnificent, brand-new ships in three years: *Statendam, Maasdam, Ryndam,* and *Veendam.* They combine the Old World with the New in decor and ambience and boast million-dollar art and antique collections reflecting Holland's association with trade and exploration in the Americas and the Orient. Their Dutch officers and Indonesian and Filipino crews are another reminder of Holland's historical ties to Asia.

The ships have the space and elegance for the long cruises of two weeks or more for which they were designed. They feature a three-level atrium lobby with a large fountain, an elegant two-level dining room, small lounges and bars, disco, casino, a large state-of-the-art spa, a sliding-glass dome for the swimming pool, spacious cabins, and premium amenities. All suites and 120 deluxe cabins have private verandas, whirlpool baths, minibars, and VCRs. There are bathtubs in all outside cabins (485 cabins out of 633 total—an unusually high percentage).

The *Westerdam,* bought from Home Lines in 1988, was given a $60 million stretch job to increase her capacity. She combines the style and refinement of great ocean liners with state-of-the-art facilities and fits well into Holland America's fleet.

The *Nieuw Amsterdam* and *Noordam* are reflective of today's cruise ships, although they were thought revolutionary when they were inaugurated in the early 1980s. Each ship has a square stern that increased its open deck space by 20 percent over traditional design, providing additional room for recreational and entertainment facilities. There are two outdoor heated swimming pools, fully equipped gym and spa, sauna, massage, and whirlpool. Stateroom doors are opened with a coded card rather than a key; movies, nightclub entertainment, and other events can be viewed on television in the cabins. Many of these features, dazzling when they were introduced, have become standard on new ships.

Holland America's *Rotterdam,* launched in 1959, will be retired in 1997 and replaced by the *Rotterdam*

VI. The *Rotterdam* has the feel of a grand transatlantic liner with rich interiors, cozy bars, and big public rooms, one with a sweeping staircase that makes a passenger feel elegant just to descend it. When the ship is not on a long cruise in distant parts of the world, she sails from Ft. Lauderdale to the Caribbean.

Life aboard the ships of Holland America proceeds at a leisurely pace. Traditionally the line has attracted mature, experienced travelers and families. During the winter, all the fleet sails on Caribbean and Panama Canal cruises, some departing from Tampa, a port Holland America helped to develop for cruise ships, and New Orleans to the Western Caribbean and the Panama Canal; others leave from Ft. Lauderdale.

MAJESTY CRUISE LINE,
901 South America Way, Miami, FL 33132;
305–530–8900; 800–532–7788

Ship (Passengers): *Royal Majesty* (1,056)
Departure port: Miami
Type of cruises: 3, 4, and 5 days to the Bahamas, Key West, and Western Caribbean
Life-style tip: Upscale, mainstream, and modern

With five baby grand pianos on board and a christening in 1992 by Liza Minnelli (in New York—where else?!), the *Royal Majesty* is aimed at the affluent passenger in the short cruise market. Created by the owners of Dolphin Cruise Lines, which caters to budget travelers, *Majesty* was purposely made a separate entity to distinguish it from the Dolphin group.

The $220 million ship established some "firsts" with a totally smoke-free dining room, 25 percent smoke-free cabins, and "Kick-the-Habit" seminars on some cruises. It was the first cruise line to offer a four-night cruise of the Western Caribbean, combining stops in Key West with Cozumel and Playa del Carmen/Cancún. This cruise can be combined with the three-night cruise to Nassau and Royal Isle, Majesty's private Bahamian island, where passengers spend a day at the beach.

Some of *Royal Majesty*'s deluxe features include signature robes and premium amenities in all cabins, plus a built-in ironing board—an unusual feature. There are shops, a piano bar, a showroom, casino, nightclub, card room, children's playroom, and a pizza/ice-cream parlor. Sports facilities include a gym and jogging track, a swimming pool, two whirlpools, and a children's splash pool. The ship has a conference room for 105 persons and a boardroom for 16. The disco doubles as a sports bar with 16 television sets during the day; one of the lounges has a big-screen television for viewing sports and newscasts. Like its sister company, Majesty's ship features appearances by Fred Flintstone and other Hanna-Barbera cartoon characters.

NORWEGIAN CRUISE LINE,
95 Merrick Way, Coral Gables, FL 33134;
305–447–9660; 800–327–7030

Ships (Passengers): *Dreamworld* (1,246); *Leeward* (950); *Norway* (2,022); *Norwegian Crown* (1,000); *Seaward* (1,534); *Windward* (1,246)
Departure ports: Miami, Ft. Lauderdale, New York, San Juan, Los Angeles
Type of cruises: 3, 4, and 7 days to the Bahamas; Northern, Eastern, and Western Caribbean; Bermuda; Mexican Riviera
Life-style tip: Mainstream of modern cruising

Norwegian Cruise Line was started in 1966 by Knut Kloster, whose family has been in the steamship business in Scandinavia since 1906. Kloster is credited with launching modern cruising when he introduced the *Sunward* on year-round three- and four-day cruises from Miami to the Bahamas, thus creating the first mass-market packaging of cruises.

By 1971, Kloster had added three new ships and pioneered weekly cruises to Jamaica and other Caribbean destinations. He introduced a day-at-the-beach feature in the Caymans and bought a Bahamian island to add a day-on-a-private-island to the line's Bahamas cruises. The idea has since been adopted by most cruise lines sailing the Bahamas and Caribbean.

Yet, in its history loaded with "firsts," nothing caused as much excitement as the entry of the *Norway* in 1980. After buying her as the *France* for $18 million, NCL spent $100 million to transform her from the great ocean liner she had been to the trendsetting Caribbean cruise ship she became.

With space for 2,000 passengers, the *Norway* was the largest passenger ship afloat. Her size enabled NCL to create a completely new environment on board with restaurants, bars, and lounges of great diversity, shopping malls with "sidewalk" cafes, full Broadway shows and Las Vegas revues in its enormous theater, full casino, and sports and entertainment facilities that can keep an active passenger in motion almost around the clock. Such innovations are now standard on all large ships.

The *Norway* was readied for the 1990s in a two-stage $65 million renovation that added a 4,000-square-foot health and fitness center, a jogging track, luxury staterooms, and two glass-enclosed decks. But the most spectacular addition was the Roman spa, covering 6,000 square feet and equipped with eight massage rooms, four herbal-therapy baths—cruising's first—and a gym. Spa services are not included in the cruise price; packages are available.

Also for the 1990s, NCL has added a fleet of new ships, beginning in 1988 with the debut of the *Seaward,* taking he line in a new direction. Each ship carries 1,200 to 1,400 passengers, going against the trend of larger ships but giving the line flexibility. These mid-range ships are aimed at upscale passengers who want the facilities of a superliner but prefer the more intimate feeling of smaller ships. Among their innovations, *Dreamward* and her sister ship, *Windward,* have four small dining rooms instead of the traditional one or two large ones. The concept gets away from the mega-dining room, and their multitiered design enables passengers to enjoy extensive views through panoramic windows. One of the sun decks is also tiered, getting away from the long lineup of deck chairs.

The *Dreamward* was the first ship to have a sports bar and grill with multiple television screens featuring live broadcasts of ESPN and the NBA and NFL. Standard cabins have a separate sitting area; 75 percent are outside. In 1995, the line added the *Leeward* with many of the features that have now become NCL standards.

NCL, which blankets the Caribbean, is best known for its entertainment—some of the best in the business, ranging from comedy clubs and cabaret stars to Broadway shows. Although it did not originate water sports programs for passengers, the line has developed them further than most, offering instruction while the ships are at sea and in-water experience at ports of call. Year-round the ships have sports and fitness programs and theme cruises for golf, tennis, baseball, running, and others with specialists and sports celebrities. NCL also has an extensive youth and children's program.

In 1984, Kloster Cruise Ltd., NCL's parent company, bought the prestigious Royal Viking Line, and in 1990, it acquired Royal Cruise Line. The moves turned out to be bad ones, saddling the company with mountains of debt and forcing it to sell RVL in 1994 and to close RCL in 1996. RCL's popular *Crown Odyssey* has joined the NCL fleet as the *Norwegian Crown;* the *Royal Viking Queen* was bought by Seabourn Cruise Line; and its other two ships will have started a new life under new owners by 1997.

PREMIER CRUISE LINES, 400 Challenger Road, Cape Canaveral, FL 32920; 407–783–5061

Ships (Passengers): *Star/Ship Atlantic* (1,600) *Star/Ship Oceanic* (1,500)
Departure ports: Port Canaveral, Ft. Lauderdale
Type of cruises: 3 and 4 days to the Bahamas combined with visits to Walt Disney World
Life-style tip: Fun for the whole family

Premier Cruise Lines is another of cruising's success stories—this time, almost overnight. Its success was all the more phenomenal because there was no shortage of pundits who told its founders that their brainchild wouldn't work.

Critics cited the poor facilities in Port Canaveral, an insufficient local population to support year-round cruises, the great distance from Port Canaveral to Nassau, and other reasons. On the other hand, the founders saw Walt Disney World—the nation's biggest tourist attraction—and the Kennedy Space Center, whose visitors were an enormous untapped reservoir of potential cruise passengers.

Premier Cruise Lines was formed in 1983 by Bruce Nierenberg, a brilliant maverick of cruise marketing who has left his imprint on several cruise lines, and Bjornar Hermansen, a financial and administrative whiz with whom Nierenberg had worked at another line. With the backing of the Dial Corporation, they bought a ship to use on short excursions between Port Canaveral and the Bahamas. Then they packaged Premier's three- and four-night cruises with special airfares, three nights of "free" deluxe accommodations in Orlando, three days of admission to the Disney theme parks, and a free tour of Spaceport U.S.A. at the Kennedy Space Center, plus the use of a rental car with unlimited mileage for a week, and priced the packages so reasonably that potential passengers couldn't refuse.

Eager to live up to the "star" billing it designated for itself with its Star/Ship name, it painted the ships' hulls bright red with orange and yellow trim (whoever heard of such a thing!) and hired an experienced staff. Now known as the Big Red Boats, the result was comfortable ships with nice decor and cabins for families—some for up to five persons—with amenities such as bath items found in deluxe hotels.

For the kids, there is a full-time staff of youth counselors that runs the "Junior Cruise Club," which has its own recreational center with day and night activities for the under-17 set. Recently, Premier upgraded these facilities with computer learning centers with the latest PCs and CD-ROMs that are both educational and entertaining. The redesigned teen centers have new state-of-the-art video, light, and audio equipment for teen dances and karaoke.

For those who want to stay in shape, there's the SeaSport fitness program, which combines the use of a gym full of Universal gear, aerobics class, jogging track, and a variety of sports activities during the day at the beach on Salt Cay, an uninhabited island in the Bahamas. For night owls, in addition to the entertainment, there are a casino, theater with first-run movies, video arcade, lounges, cabaret, piano bar, and disco. And for honeymooners, there are champagne in the room and double beds, and, responding to passengers requests, the Big Red Boats have added cabins with queen beds.

The ships also have a new automated tour ticketing system that provides passengers immediate onshore tour confirmation without waiting in line. Premier's new Golf Academy provides instruction and swing analysis through video equipment and their own onboard pro. Golfing with the pro at one of the courses in Nassau and Port Lucaya is also available.

An interesting sidelight to this story is that Premier has converted prospective Disney visitors into future cruise passengers. It seems many people are hesitant about taking a cruise, but when they can get it packaged with a visit to Disney World, they are willing to take the chance on a family vacation, rationalizing that if the cruise bombs, they can still score with the kids at Disney. As it turns out, they—and the kids—enjoy the cruise as much as they enjoy the days at Disney.

After almost a decade as the "Official Cruise Line of Walt Disney World," which had generated a great deal of publicity, the Dial Corporation terminated the Disney agreement and the Big Red Boats brought on Looney Tunes under a licensing agreement with Warner Brothers Consumer Products. The Looney Tunes bunch—Bugs Bunny, Sylvester, Tweety, and friends—take a more prominent onboard role than did the Disney characters.

PRINCESS CRUISES, 10100 Santa Monica Boulevard, Los Angeles, CA 90067; 310–553–1770; 800–LOVE–BOAT

Ships (Passengers): *Crown Princess* (1,590); *Dawn Princess* (1,950); *Golden Princess* (830); *Island Princess* (640); *Pacific Princess* (640); *Regal Princess* (1,590); *Royal Princess* (1,200); *Sky Princess* (1,200); *Star Princess* (1,470); *Sun Princess* (1,950)
Departure ports: Ft. Lauderdale, San Juan, Acapulco, Los Angeles
Type of cruises: 7 to 10 days, combining Western, Eastern, Southern Caribbean, and Panama Canal
Life-style tip: Casually stylish and modestly affluent

Princess Cruises, a West Coast pioneer begun in 1965, is credited with helping to create the relaxed and casual atmosphere that typifies life on board today's cruises. For one thing, one of its ships, the *Pacific Princess*, is the ship used in the popular television series *The Love Boat*. It's impossible to calculate, but that show probably did more to popularize modern cruising than all other cruise publicity combined. It was certainly a factor in dispelling cruising's elitist image

and enabling people who might have never considered a cruise holiday to identify with it.

In 1988, Princess acquired the Los Angeles-based Sitmar Cruises, another innovative and well-established pioneer of West Coast cruising, creating one of the world's largest cruise companies and more than doubling Princess's capacity in one stroke.

The pride of the Princess fleet—its flagship, and one of the most stylish, elegant ships of the 1980s—is the *Royal Princess*, which was christened by the Princess of Wales. When she made her debut in 1983, the ship set new standards in passenger comfort with all outside cabins and refrigerators, televisions, and bathrooms fitted with tub as well as shower in every cabin category. The decor throughout is warm, inviting, and comfortable, and always with a touch of class. All suites, deluxe cabins, and some of those in lesser categories have private outside balconies—a first for cruising.

After a debut in Europe, the *Crown Princess* was officially christened by actress Sophia Loren in New York in 1990 during Princess Cruises' twenty-fifth anniversary. Very different in profile from other ships, the *Crown Princess* was designed by Renzo Piano, the architect of the Pompidou Center in Paris. Her sleek lines were inspired by the shape of a dolphin. The top of the head holds "The Dome," the forward observation and entertainment area, and the casino. The spacious ship has large cabins and a high percentage of them have verandas. Its twin, *Regal Princess*, was launched in 1991. The *Island Princess* and *Pacific Princess* are identical twins, more casual than their sisters.

Princess's latest venture—*Sun Princess*, dubbed a "Super Love Boat"—is the line's largest vessel. Designed by Njal Eide, the architect of the elegant *Royal Princess*, the ship is the most beautiful large ship afloat with exquisite interiors of the finest Italian workmanship. It introduced many new features, including two atrium lobbies and two main show lounges, a true theater-at-sea, and a restaurant offering 24-hour dining. About 70 percent of the outside cabins have verandas.

In recent years, Princess has had one of the strongest presences in the Caribbean in the winter season, with the seven ships. The line has a private beach, Princess Cays (on south Eleuthera in the Bahamas), where the ships call. Newly expanded and upgraded, the facility has just about every water sport a passenger could want; nature trails with guided walks; games; kiosks for local crafts; and a large dining pavilion where passengers are served lunch.

Princess caters to a modestly affluent clientele from 35 years of age plus, with a median age of 50 to 55. It is very aggressive with promotional fares and seasonal savings.

ADISSON SEVEN SEAS CRUISES, 600
orporate Drive, No. 410, Ft. Lauderdale,
33334; 305–776–6123; 800–477–7500;
00–333–3333; fax 305–772–3763

ips (Passengers): *Hanseatic* (188); *Radisson
amond* (354); *Song of Flower* (180)
parture ports: San Juan and worldwide ports sea-
nally
pe of Cruises: 3 to 14 days; transcanal, Eastern
ribbean, Europe, Asia
e-style tip: Luxury for affluent travelers

"Futuristic" and "revolutionary" were some of the
rds used to describe the semi-submersible *Radisson
amond,* one of the decade's most innovative ships,
en it made its debut in 1992. Well, it is certainly
vel. Viewed from the front, it looks more like a UFO
n a cruise ship.

Measuring 420 feet in length and 103 in width and
ing high in the water, the SSC *Radisson Diamond* is
largest twin-hull cruise ship ever constructed; it
rked the first time the design technology called
ATH (small waterplace area twin hull) was applied
a luxury ship of this nature. The design is intended to
ovide greater stability than that of a single-hull ship of
ilar size. Speedboats and water-skiers have been
own to race through the space between the hulls,
der the underbelly.

Diamond Cruises, a joint venture of Finnish,
anese, and U.S. interests, formed a partnership with
disson Hotels International to market the ship. In
95, Radisson Diamond joined with Seven Sea Cruises
form a new company, Radisson Seven Seas.

The focus of the *Diamond* is a five-story atrium with
ss-enclosed elevators and a grand staircase. The
bins, each with private balconies, are large, luxuri-
s, and very comfortable. They are fitted with mini-
rs, televisions, VCRs, and full baths with tubs.
rhaps because of its spaciousness and design, the
p has more the look and feel of a hotel than of a
p.

The dining room and its cuisine are, without doubt,
ship's most outstanding features. The dining room,
e of the prettiest at sea, is decorated in exquisite silks
d other fine fabrics in soft blues, beige, gray, and gold
aped from the floor-to-ceiling windows and covering
handsome dining chairs. The room functions like a
taurant, with passengers dining at their convenience.
d they dine leisurely on cuisine that is truly gourmet
d some of the finest at sea. Table service is rendered
female rather than male waiters—an unusual case
cruise ships. The waitresses are exceedingly pleas-
and efficient. The bar has women attendants as well.
e ship has a no-tipping policy.

On the top deck the Grill, with a more informal
atmosphere, offers breakfast and in the evening
becomes an Italian specialty restaurant with superb cuisine. It's probably the ship's most popular feature.

The *Diamond* has a spa and fitness center with a
gym, saunas, and a jogging track; and at the stern there
is a hydraulically operated floating marina with equipment for water sports. The ship has good facilities for
meetings at sea, with three boardrooms, a large meeting room that can be subdivided into six small rooms,
and business-related services such as in-house publish-
ing and teleconference facilities, fax machines, a broad-
cast center, and secretarial services.

Sailing from its Caribbean home port of San Juan in
the winter, the *Diamond* has a series of imaginative
itineraries of 3 to 14 days, including Panama Canal itineraries. The deluxe *Song of Flower* cruises in Europe
and Asia; and *Hanseatic,* a deluxe adventure ship, sails
on unusual, ever-changing itineraries from pole to pole.

REGAL CRUISES, 4199 34th Street, Suite B103, St. Petersburg, FL 33711; 813–867–1300; 800–270–SAIL

Ship (Passengers): *Regal Empress* (902)
Departure ports: San Juan and worldwide ports
seasonally
Type of Cruises: 3 to 14 days; Western Caribbean,
transcanal
Life-style tip: Casual, informal for budget travelers

Regal Empress, built in 1953, was the *Olympia* of
Greek Line and later became the *Caribe I* of
Commodore Cruises. The handsome ship was refur-
bished in 1993, when it was taken over by the owner of
Liberty Travel to sail on short, budget-priced cruises
from Tampa to the Western Caribbean in winter and New
York to New England in summer.

The ship's interior reflects the changes made by her
various owners over the years, although some public
rooms show the ship's quality when she was built.
Particularly outstanding is the dining room, which has
fine decorative woods, etched-glass, and some of the
original murals.

The food—steak, lobster, and other similar choices
sure to be crowd pleasers—is quite good for the budget price. The main show room offers nightly entertainment, and there are other lounges, a bar and dance
floor, a casino, and a rather unusual disco created in the
former theater.

Regal Empress has an enclosed promenade deck,
typical of older ships; an outdoor swimming pool, two
whirlpools, gym, beauty salon, boutique, small playroom, and a paneled library with glass-front bookcases
and comfortable reading chairs. The ship has as many

inside cabins as outside ones in a very wide variety of configurations. Bathrooms are small with shower only. Only suites have television. Passengers get their money's worth, but make no mistake, this lady has seen better days.

Regal Empress has a new and unusual 14-day fall cruise from New York to her base at Port Manatee in Tampa Bay with a partial transit of the Panama Canal. Ports of call include Nassau, Montego Bay, San Blas Islands, Panama Canal, Puerto Limón (Costa Rica), San Andres (Colombia), and Cozumel. The cruise can also be broken into five-night segments. Prices start at $499, $899, and $1399 for the different segments.

ROYAL CARIBBEAN CRUISE LINE, 1050 Caribbean Way, Miami, FL 33132; 305–539–6573; 800–327–6700

Ships (Passengers): *Enchantment of the Seas* (1,950); *Grandeur of the Seas* (1,950); *Legend of the Seas* (1,808); *Majesty of the Seas* (2,354); *Monarch of the Seas* (2,354); *Nordic Empress* (1,606); *Rhapsody of the Seas* (2,000); *Song of America* (1,414); *Song of Norway* (1,012); *Sovereign of the Seas* (2,276); *Splendor of the Seas* (1,800); *Sun Viking* (714); *Viking Serenade* (1,514)
Departure ports: Miami, San Juan, New York
Type of cruises: 3 to 10 days to the Bahamas and Western, Eastern, and Southern Caribbean
Life-style tip: Active, wholesome ambience

Royal Caribbean Cruise Line, launched in the early 1970s, was the first line to build a fleet of ships designed specially for year-round Caribbean cruising. The ships were established as top-of-the-line so quickly that within five years RCCL needed more capacity and did so by "stretching" two of the vessels. They were literally cut in half and prefabricated mid-sections were inserted. Although the method had been used on cargo and other vessels, RCCL's work was the first for cruise ships.

For the 1980s it added superliners with unique design features, and in 1988 it got a headstart on the 1990s with the *Sovereign of the Seas,* the first of the new generation of megaliners and the largest cruise ship afloat at the time. Few ships in history have received so much attention.

The *Sovereign,* RCCL's flagship, is three football fields in length but, miraculously, she does not seem gigantic to passengers on board because of her superb design. A dramatic midship atrium spanning five decks and featuring glass-walled elevators was a "first" for cruise ships and was quickly copied in most new ships. The atrium functions similarly to the lobby of a hotel and provides a friendly focal point for the ship. The atrium also separates the forward section of the ship, which

contains all of the cabins, from the aft, where all publ rooms, dining, entertainment, sports, and recreati facilities reside—a revolutionary design borrowed fro *Song of America.* The arrangement has a double adva tage: quieter sleeping areas and shorter walking d tances from one location to another in the public are

It would be impossible for even the most active pa senger to participate in all the daily activities offered the *Sovereign.* Fitness folks have a third-mile outsi deck encircling the vessel and one of the best-equipp health clubs at sea, complete with ballet bars, sophis cated computerized exercise equipment, and a hig energy staff to put them through their paces. The spo deck has twin pools and a basketball court.

For those with something less strenuous in min there are small, sophisticated lounges for drinks, dan ing, and cabaret entertainment. Enrichment progra run the gamut from napkin folding to wine tasting. T library resembles a sedate English club, with its woo paneling and leather chairs. Two feature films run da in twin cinemas; the shopping boulevard has a sidewa cafe; the show lounge, a multitiered theater with uno structed views, runs two different Las Vegas-style revu and variety shows.

Somewhere there's music to suit every mood, fro big band, steel band, Latin, country, rock, or strollin violins to classical concerts. The Schooner is a live piano bar; Music Man has entertainers from blues country; and the disco projects holograms on the mi rored walls and music videos around the dance flo Casino Royale offers blackjack, 216 slot machines, a American roulette. The chic Champagne Bar is a qui corner where 50 people clink flutes and scoop cavia

Sovereign's twins, *Monarch of the Seas* and *Majes of the Seas,* arrived in 1991 and 1992, with only a fe changes, such as family suites for up to six peopl When RCCL merged with Admiral Cruises in 1988, acquired *Viking Serenade,* which it rebuilt, and for th first time, RCCL entered the short cruise market whi had been Admiral's strength.

The *Nordic Empress,* launched in 1990, was bu specifically for Bahamas cruises. A smaller ship th the megaliners, *Nordic Empress* has an eye-poppi nine-deck atrium, a triple-tier casino, and a bilevel di ing room with a grand staircase and floor-to-ceili windows at the stern.

Designed as they are for Caribbean cruising, the shi have acres of open sun decks and large pools. The li offers low-fat, low-calorie fare and has a ShipSha program on all ships in the fleet. It is often combin with sports in port. Golf Ahoy! enables passengers play golf at courses throughout the Caribbean. RCCL the official cruise line of the Professional Golfe Association of America.

All the ships have bright, cheerful Scandinavian ꞏcor, enhanced by Scandinavian art. The themes used ꞏroughout the fleet relate to hit musicals and operas. ꞏe officers are Norwegian, and the hotel and enter- ꞏnment staff are a mini–United Nations. The cabins ꞏe compact—in fact, they are small, but given RCCL's ꞏccess, it would seem not to matter; they are also func- ꞏnal and spotless. A top-deck lounge cantilevered ꞏm the funnel provides fabulous views from 12 stories ꞏove the sea. These lounges are RCCL's signature.

RCCL blankets the Caribbean year-round. It has ꞏuises year-round on the West Coast and Mexico, and ꞏAlaska and Europe in the summer. In 1995, the line ꞏded Asia. CocoCay, a small island in the Bahamas ꞏherited from Admiral Cruises, is used for the ships' ꞏy at the beach. Labadee, RCCL's private resort on the ꞏrth coast of Haiti, was created in 1987 and is very ꞏpular.

RCCL's enormous success results from its smooth and ꞏnsistent operation, often winning "Ship(s) of the ꞏar" and "Cruise Line of the Year" awards. Founded in ꞏ69 as a partnership of three prominent Norwegian ꞏipping companies, RCCL went public in April 1993. ꞏt content to rest on its laurels, however, RCCL is ꞏding a new group of 1,800-to-2,000-passenger ships. ꞏThe first ship, *Legend of the Seas,* built in France at ꞏe same shipyard that constructed RCCL's three mega- ꞏers, was launched in 1995, introducing the first ꞏiniature golf course at sea and a spectacular "solari- ꞏn"—an indoor/outdoor swimming, sunning, and fit- ꞏss facility. Its sister ships *Splendor of the Seas* and ꞏandeur of the Seas* arrived in April and December ꞏ96 respectively, and others are slated for 1997 and ꞏ98.

RCCL caters to a moderately upscale market and ꞏjoys a high repeat business. The atmosphere is ꞏendly and casual, and the activities are so varied that ꞏere is something for everyone at almost every hour of ꞏe day. Most of RCCL's rates include "free" air or a ꞏ1all supplement from gateways across the United ꞏtes and Canada. All RCCL ships have programs for ꞏildren and teenagers, because the line believes that ꞏ1appy kid on a cruise now will still be a customer in ꞏ20.

With the arrival of the new ships, RCCL is making sig- ꞏficant and innovative changes. In December, the ꞏrdic Empress* moves to San Juan for the winter, sail- ꞏg on 3/4-night cruises to St. Thomas, St. Maarten, ꞏd St. Croix—the first time a major cruise line has ꞏer offered short cruises to the Caribbean from San ꞏan. The *Sovereign* has taken over the *Nordic ꞏpress*'s Bahamas cruises from Miami and is the ꞏgest cruise ship to sail the route. In summer 1997, ꞏrdic Empress* moves to Port Canaveral—another

first for RCCL—to sail on 3/4-night Bahamas cruises that will be combined with Disney World packages.

ROYAL OLYMPIC CRUISES *(See* Sun Line Cruises)

SEABOURN CRUISE LINE, 55 Francisco Street, San Francisco, CA 94133; 415–391–7444; 800–929–9595; 800–527–0999 (Canada)

Ships (Passengers): *Seabourn Legend* (214); *Seabourn Pride* (214); *Seabourn Spirit* (214)
Departure ports: Ft. Lauderdale, Barbados, Aruba, San Juan, Antigua
Type of cruises: 5 to 14 days in Eastern and Southern Caribbean and Panama Canal in winter; worldwide schedules year-round
Life-style tip: The ultimate luxury cruise

When Seabourn was formed in 1987, it set out to cre- ate the world's most deluxe cruises on the most elegant, luxurious ships afloat. To guide its debut it engaged Warren Titus, whose stewardship of Royal Viking Lines helped to set top-quality standards for the entire cruise industry. Despite very high per diem rates, Seabourn quickly won enough fans to add a second ship. In 1996, following Royal Cruise Line's demise, Seabourn acquired the former *Queen Odyssey,* which it rechris- tened the *Seabourn Legend* in July 1996 in New York.

The ships and cruises were designed with a certain type of person in mind—one who normally stays in the best rooms at a luxury hotel and books a deluxe suite on a luxury liner. The staterooms are luxuriously appointed in soft, warm colors and have television with CNN, VCRs, pre-stocked bars, refrigerators, walk-in closets, and large marble bathrooms with tub and shower. Each has a roomy sitting area beside a large picture window with electrically manipulated shades and outside cleaning mechanisms.

Passengers dine on gourmet cuisine served on Royal Doulton china and have open seating. They may also dine from the restaurant menu in their suites, and there is a 24-hour room service menu with a wide selection and a choice wine list.

Seabourn's ships have sleek profiles that resemble the most modern of yachts. A water sports platform at the stern has a "cage" that can be lowered into the water for passengers to swim in the open sea without fear. The ships carry windsurfers, snorkeling and dive equipment, and two high-speed boats. The ships' itineraries take them to all parts of the world, but at least one spends some of the winter in the Caribbean. The newly acquired *Seabourn Legend* is sailing to the Western Caribbean and Panama Canal through the winter of 1997. On select- ed cruises Seabourn offers a low singles fare of 110 to

125 percent, rather than the standard 150 percent, and offers substantial discounts to repeaters, including free cruises after 140 days of sailing with Seabourn.

Seabourn is a privately held company; 75 percent is owned by its founder, Atle Brynestad, a Norwegian industrialist, and 25 percent is owned by Carnival Cruise Lines.

SILVERSEA CRUISES, 110 East Broward Blvd., Ft. Lauderdale, FL 33301; 800–321–0165

Ships (Passengers): *Silver Cloud* (306); *Silver Wind* (306)
Departure ports: Nassau, Ft. Lauderdale, Barbados
Type of cruises: Caribbean, seasonally
Life-style tip: Ultra-luxurious surroundings in a relaxing, friendly—not stuffy—atmosphere

Silversea Cruises was launched in late 1994 with the luxurious all-suite *Silver Cloud* designed by Oslo-based Petter Yran and Bjorn Storbraaten, the architects of the *Sea Goddess* and *Seabourn* ships. Her twin, *Silver Wind,* made her debut the following year.

The Silversea ships mirror Seabourn's in many ways but carry 306 passengers (100 more than Seabourn's), and 107 of the Silversea's 155 suites have verandas (Seabourn's suites do not).

Silversea's large suites, averaging 300 square feet, have a spacious sitting area, walk-in closet, fully stocked bar, hairdryer, TV with VCR, direct-dial telephone, and marble-floored bathroom with tub. Passengers are welcomed to their staterooms with fresh flowers, a bottle of champagne, a basket of fruit replenished daily, personalized stationery, and plush terry robes for use during their cruise.

There is open seating in the dining room and 24-hour room service. The ship has a tiered show lounge spanning two decks, with a nightclub at the upper level, plus a casino, a spa, and a library.

The ships sails in Asia, Africa, and Europe most of the year, but at least one is in the Caribbean for transcanal, Central, and South American itineraries in winter. The co-owners of the line are passenger and shipping veterans Francesco Lefebvre of Rome and the Vlasov Group of Monaco, who were once partners in Sitmar Cruises. Silversea sails under the Italian flag with Italian officers and a European staff.

SPECIAL EXPEDITIONS, 720 Fifth Avenue, New York, New York 10019; 212–765–7740; 800–762–0003; fax 212–265–3770

Ship (Passengers): *Polaris* (80)
Departure ports: Panama City, San José (Costa Rica)

Type of cruises: 14 days in the Panama Canal and Costa Rica in winter; worldwide schedules year-round
Life-style tip: Light adventure for curious travelers

Founded by Sven-Olaf Lindblad, son of the late adventure travel trailblazer Lars-Eric Lindblad who pioneered modern expedition cruising in 1969, Special Expedition roams the world with its ships, *Caledonian Star, Polaris Sea Bird,* and *Sea Lion,* designed to take passengers remote corners of the world in comfort and safety. Its mission, Special Expeditions believes, is to provide traveler with "a more thoughtful way to see the world avoiding crowded destinations and seeking out natural ones."

Out of the group, only the *Polaris* currently has an annual presence in the Western Caribbean with cruise of Costa Rica and Panama. The itinerary changes from year to year and sometimes combines the Panama Can with Belize or the Mayan Coast.

Caledonian Star is usually in Asia. *Sea Bird* and *Sea Lion* sail on 4- to 12-day cruises of Alaska and the West Coast, and one ship has an annual cruise to Baja California and the Sea of Cortez timed for optimum whale watching. From time to time, the company charters the *Sea Cloud* and other ships, and operate cruises for university and other groups.

SUN LINE CRUISES/ROYAL OLYMPIC LINE, 1 Rockefeller Plaza, Suite 315, New York, NY 10020; 212–397–6400; 800–872–6400

Ships (Passengers): *Stella Solaris* (620); *Odysseus* (400); *Stella Oceanis* (300)
Departure ports: Ft. Lauderdale, Miami, Galveston, and Manaus, Brazil
Type of cruises: 7 to 15 days, Western, Eastern, and Southern Caribbean combined with South America and the Amazon during winter
Life-style tip: Low-key deluxe cruises for an upscale market to off-the-beaten-track destinations

In August 1995, Sun Line merged with Piraeus-base Epirotiki Cruise Line to form a new company, Royal Olympic Cruises. The new line operates a fleet of ten cruise ships under two brands distinguished by the colors of the Greek flag: the "blue" ships of Sun Line are more traditional and upscale and include the *Stella Solaris, Stella Oceanis,* and Epirotiki's *Odysseus*. Three "white" ships of Epirotiki, the *Triton, Orpheus* and *Olympic,* offer more casual cruises. The four other ships, Epirotiki's *Argonaut, Jason, Neptune,* and Sun Line's *Stella Maris,* are managed by Royal Olympic, primarily on charter. At the present time, only one ship the fleet, *Stella Solaris,* which has recently completed total renovation, sails in the Caribbean; other member of the fleet cruise mainly in South America in winter of the Greek Isles and Eastern Mediterranean year-round

Sun Line Cruises has been a pioneer and innovator of Caribbean cruises, being the first to combine the small islands of the Eastern Caribbean with a cruise up the Orinoco River in Venezuela; to extend an Eastern Caribbean cruise to the Amazon River; and to combine the Amazon and Panama Canal in one cruise. While it was not the first cruise line to go to Rio for Carnival, it was one of the few to combine the annual event with the Eastern Caribbean.

One of Sun Line's most popular cruises is timed for the spring equinox at Chichén Itzá in the Yucatán. Frequently, as in the case of the Yucatán and Amazon voyages, Sun Line engages experts to lecture on the cruise's destinations.

Sun Line was started in the mid-1950s by a well-respected Greek family whose patriarch, the late Ch. A. Keusseoglou, had already made his mark as head of Home Lines. At Sun Line, Keusseoglou introduced some of the first ships designed specifically for cruising that eliminated class distinction on board and provided large, sunny public rooms and outdoor areas for relaxation and deck sports.

And while many cruise lines are adding bigger and bigger ships, Sun Line's ships remain small and intimate. The size of the staff in relation to the number of passengers is high. The ships and their staffs are Greek. Many of the personnel have had 20 years of uninterrupted service with Sun Line.

Sun Line specializes in long cruises, but most itineraries can be taken in one week segments. The combination of unusual itineraries, private club-like atmosphere, and members-of-the-family crew gives the ships special appeal to sophisticated and experienced travelers. Sun Line's passengers in the Caribbean winter season are affluent and tend to be age 45 and older. Often 40 percent are repeaters, an unusually strong testimonial for the line. Sun Line offers spa cuisine on its menus, and for its high percentage of single women passengers, it has a host program.

TEMPRESS VOYAGES, 1600 N.W. LeJuene Road, Suite 301, Miami, FL 33126; 305-871-2663; 800-336-8423; fax 305-871-2657

Ships (Passengers): *Temptress Explorer* (100); *Temptress Voyager* (63)
Departure ports: Belize City or Placencia, Belize
Type of cruises: 3 or 6 nights along the cays, Barrier Reef, and mainland of Belize; others in Costa Rica
Life-style tips: Informal, light adventure cruises on unusual itineraries for experienced passengers; no frills; emphasis on natural attraction and local culture

Temptress Voyages' mainstay has been adventure

cruises of Costa Rica, particularly on its Pacific Coast, but in December 1995 with the addition of a new ship, it launched brand new, very innovative cruises of Belize. The cruises combine natural history and light adventure with snorkeling, diving, kayaking, sportfishing, and waterskiing. The line also has a children's program with trained counselors in charge.

The *Temptress Voyager* offers a six-night cruise that can also be taken in three-night segments. The ship departs from Belize City on Sundays and visits Goff's Caye for swimming, snorkeling, and a beach barbecue; Manatee Lagoon (Gail's Point), which has one of the world's largest concentration of manatee; and Rendezvous Caye along the barrier reef. The ship next sails to the coast at Sittee River, Hopkins, for jungle wildlife, followed by Tabacco Caye and Placencia, where passengers on the short cruise disembark for return to Belize City and where those taking the second leg as a short cruise join the ship. The cruise continues to Monkey River for more wildlife viewing, to remote Laughingbird Caye, Wild King Caye, and on to Punta Gorda, the southernmost town in Belize near the Guatemala border. The ship returns to Belize City on Saturday. These unusual cruises are available year-round.

The new 185-foot *Temptress Explorer* sails in Costa Rica on three- and four-day itineraries that can be combined into one week. The ship was built in Seattle, Washington, specifically to meet the requirements of the Costa Rica route, allowing for easier navigation of the rivers and shallow bays while maintaining the stability of a heavier ship. All cabins are outside and have private bath and air-conditioning. The cruise line also offers cruises of the Galapagos Islands.

WINDJAMMER BAREFOOT CRUISES, Box 120, Miami Beach, FL 33119-0120; 305-672-6453; 800-327-2601

Ships (Passengers): *Amazing Grace* (96; supply ship); *Fantome* (126); *Flying Cloud* (76); *Mandalay* (72); *Polynesia* (126); *Yankee Clipper* (66)
Departure ports: Cozumel for Western Caribbean; various ports for Eastern Caribbean
Type of cruises: 6 days for Western Caribbean; 6 and 13 days for various Bahamas and Caribbean itineraries
Life-style tip: Barefoot adventure for sailors from 7 to 70 with good sea legs and happy spirits

Windjammer Barefoot Cruises, which celebrated its fiftieth anniversary in 1992, boasts the largest fleet of tall ships in the world. The history of each ship is part of the lore and pleasure of the cruise.

The *Mandalay*, the queen of the fleet, was once the luxury yacht of financier E. F. Hutton and an oceanographic research vessel of Columbia University. The *Fantome*, extensively renovated in 1992, was originally built for the Duke of Westminster and was later owned by the Guinness family of brewery fame. They sold it to Onassis to be given to Princess Grace and the Prince of Monaco as a wedding present. But, as the story goes, Onassis was not invited to the wedding, so the present was never delivered.

Most cabins on all ships are fitted with bunk beds. They are cozy, not luxurious, and have private bath facilities and steward service. The food is good, not gourmet. The atmosphere is casual—shorts and beachwear on a full-time basis—and congenial. Most of your time will be spent enjoying the sun, swimming, snorkeling, steel band music, barbecues, and picnics on the beach.

A Windjammer cruise is a totally different, barefoot, carefree experience. Fellow passengers (who return about 40 percent of the time) come from all walks of life and many countries, although most are Americans. The company does not take children under seven years of age. Most cruises are six days. Windjammer offers all-singles cruises and fitness cruises.

Windjammer's Western Caribbean cruises are brand new and offer unusual itineraries of the Yucatán departing from either Cancún or Cozumel and sailing to Isla Mujeres and along the coast to Playa del Carmen, Tulum, Akumel, and Xcaret. The cruises can be taken as three-, four-, or seven-night trips. The first part takes in the towns of the Yucatán; the second more nature oriented.

The cruises appeal most to people with a sense of adventure who want something completely different from their routine, structured lives in a relaxed and friendly atmosphere. The ships have a romance for all who love the sea.

It's not for everyone, but then, Windjammer doesn't try to be. But if there's a Captain Mitty in you, here's your chance to stand watch at the wheel or climb the masts and to have the kind of tropical holiday that dreams and travel posters are made of.

PART IV
PORTS OF CALL

(PRESENTED COUNTERCLOCKWISE
FROM THE BAHAMAS)

The Bahamas

NASSAU, NEW PROVIDENCE ISLAND, FREEPORT, GRAND BAHAMA ISLAND, THE FAMILY ISLANDS

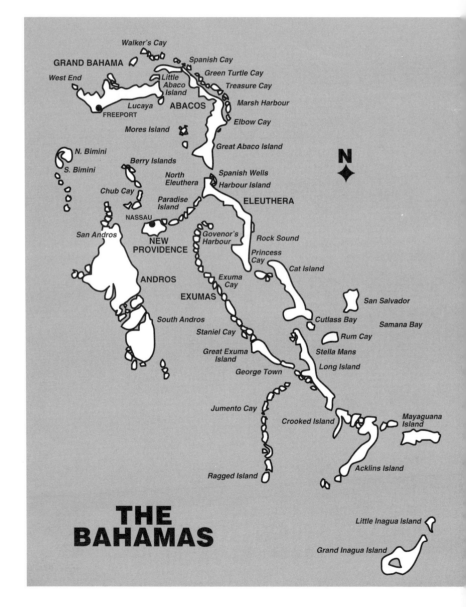

AT A GLANCE

CHAPTER CONTENTS

DISTANT NEIGHBORS

Whether your destination is Nassau, Freeport, or one of the Family Islands, your first impression of the Bahamas and the image you are likely to carry away with you is of water. Intensely beautiful with shades of aqua, turquoise, cobalt, and peacock blue, these waters have long attracted boating and fishing enthusiasts, and now they are being discovered by snorkelers, scuba divers, and cruise passengers.

The Bahamas is an archipelago of more than 700 low-lying tropical islands and islets dotting 100,000 square miles of sea. They start only 50 miles from the eastern coast of Florida and stretch for 750 miles to the northern coasts of Haiti and Cuba. They are strategically situated between the Atlantic on the north, south, and east and the Gulf of Mexico on the west; about half of the archipelago lies north of the Tropic of Cancer.

The Bahamas derives its name from the Spanish, *baja mar,* or shallows, which the early explorers used in mapping the group. Out of the hundreds of islands, islets, and cays that make up the island nation, only about three dozen are populated. Of these, three— Nassau, Paradise Island, and Freeport—get the lion's share of visitors and almost all of the cruise passengers.

The Bahamas is so close to the U.S. mainland that many people hop over for the weekend in their own boats or private planes, and ships board thousands of passengers every week for one-, two-, three-, and four-day cruises between Florida and Bahamian ports.

Yet, the Bahamas is foreign. A British colony for over two centuries and independent since 1973, the Bahamas in many ways is still more British than the Queen. This, despite the fact that throughout the history of the islands from the time Columbus made his first landfall on the Bahamian island of San Salvador and Ponce de León came in search of the Fountain of Youth, the Bahamas has been as closely linked to events in the United States as with any in Britain.

Today the British flavor combined with American familiarity, the magnificent waters and endless days of clear skies, the outstanding facilities, the variety of sports and entertainment all have made the Bahamas the most frequently visited destination in the tropics, with over three million visitors a year.

On any given day in port, you can play tennis and golf or bike and jog in the countryside. The shallow, warm waters provide a carnival of life for snorkelers and scuba divers. Protected bays and shallow waters near shore are ideal for windsurfing, waterskiing, jetskiing, and parasailing. There are an abundance of fish in the deep waters only a short distance from port and excellent opportunities for deep-sea fishing year-round.

If the sporting life is not your first requirement, a walking tour of Nassau is a stroll through history and a chance to check out the bargains in the shops and straw markets along the way. You can do it on your own or in the company of a Bahamian host that you arrange through the Tourist Office's People-to-People Program. Evening entertainment in port can range from music of a scratch band in a rustic tavern by the sea to an extravaganza with Las Vegas sizzle at a cavernous casino.

COLUMBUS AND THE AFTERMATH

The diversity of the Bahamas is the result of its variegated past. The islands' recorded history begins on the most significant date in the annals of the New World—October 12, 1492—with Christopher Columbus making his first landfall on an island the native Lucayans called Guanahani and that Columbus christened San Salvador, the Savior.

When the Spaniards who followed Columbus found no gold they abandoned all interest in the Bahamas, but not before enslaving the entire Lucayan Indian population of 20,000 and shipping them to work the mines in Cuba and Hispaniola. Ponce de León was apparently an exception. He came to the Bahamas in search of the Fountain of Youth before moving on to Florida to continue his quest. Today, four places on the island of Bimini claim to have been stops in his epic journey.

A century after the Spaniards departed from the islands, in 1648, English settlers fleeing religious conflict in Bermuda arrived on Sigatoo Island, which they named Eleuthera after the Greek word meaning "freedom." Following a dispute within the group, which was known as the Company of Eleuthran Adventurers, many of the settlers left and founded another settlement at or near Spanish Wells.

In time, the Bahamas was granted to the lords of the Carolinas, absentee landlords whose lack of interest allowed the infestation of pirates, like the infamous Edward Teach, known as Blackbeard, and Henry Morgan. The hundreds of harbors were ideal havens for smuggling and piracy; their reefs and shallows ensured—by accident or design—frequent wrecks.

Finally in 1718 the ironfisted British captain Woodes Rogers took command of the Bahamas and established order. Rogers gave the scavengers a clear choice: Give up piracy and be pardoned or be hanged. Eight who tested Rogers's will were hung in public, thus helping to bring a chapter of the Bahamas' history to a close. Ten years later, the islands were officially made a British colony with Rogers the first royal governor.

In an effort to destroy British supply lines during the American Revolution, the American Navy captured Nassau and held it for two weeks. Later the Spanish held it for a year and did not leave until they were forced out by Col. Andrew Deveaux, a Loyalist from the Carolinas and one of 8,000 who had fled to the Bahamas after the Revolution. Deveaux and the other Loyalists brought with them all their possessions including slaves, and in the Bahamas they replicated the plantation society they had left behind. The old order lasted until slavery was abolished in 1834.

Twice again events in the United States led to direct Bahamian involvement and a boom: gun-running during the Civil War and rum-running during Prohibition. After that, the American–Bahamian connection became more respectable, but no less flamboyant. During World War II, the royal governor of the Bahamas was none other than the duke of Windsor, who along with his glamorous American-born duchess set the style for what was to become the Bahamas' most important postwar enterprise, tourism.

THE NEW BAHAMAS

After the war, a weak and weary Britain welcomed foreign investments that would enable her colonies to become self-supporting. At the same time, several wealthy Americans saw the opportunity to create playgrounds in the Bahamas, which could benefit from the islands' proximity to the U.S. mainland. The most significant venture turned a spit of land facing Nassau harbor into the most complete resort in the tropics.

In the 1950s, A&P heir Huntington Hartford bought most of Hog Island, as it was known, from another millionaire and renamed it Paradise. His estate, set in landscaped gardens adorned with classic marble statues and enclosed with stones from a twelfth-century French monastery, became the centerpiece of the fashionable Ocean Club.

During the following decade, Paradise Island was acquired by Resorts International, which added hotels, casino, and extensive sporting facilities. They also made Paradise more accessible by building a multimillion-dollar bridge between the island and Nassau, and later, by adding an airline. Then, in 1989, famed television star Merv Griffin bought Resorts International and put his stamp on the island. But the greatest transformation of all came in 1994 after Sun International bought out Griffin; transformed Resort International's holdings into a new resort named Atlantis, creating an entirely new landscape of lakes, parks, and attractions; and renovated all the hotels for a total investment of $250 million.

About the same time that Hartford was creating Paradise, American financier Wallace Groves was transforming Grand Bahama Island, a little-known stretch of limestone and pine forest situated only 60 miles from the coast of Florida. Freeport, as it is better known, became the showplace of its day with hotels, casinos, a flashy international shopping bazaar, and six championship golf courses.

In the 1970s with the recession, inflation, oil crisis, and competition from newer resorts in Florida and the Caribbean, Freeport lost a great deal of its luster. But by the mid-1980s a renaissance was underway with millions of dollars being invested by the government and private developers.

Another transformation took place in the 1980s at Cable Beach, a five-mile stretch west of downtown Nassau. The multimillion-dollar Cable Beach Hotel and Casino opened in 1983, (now a Radisson hotel), followed by the thousand-room Crystal Palace Resort and Casino, the largest hotel in the tropics (now a Marriott and extensively renovated).

The Royal Bahamian Hotel, the colonial grande dame of Cable Beach which served as the fashionable resort of royalty and heads of state in its heyday as the Balmoral Beach Club when the duke of Windsor was governor, was also renovated. In 1994, it was purchased by Sandals, the Jamaican-based, all-inclusive group, and after extensive renovation and expansion reopened in 1996 as the chain's most luxurious resort. Down the road Breezes Bahamas, formerly the Ambassador Beach, is the first Bahamas member of Superclubs, also a Jamaican all-inclusive chain.

As your ship steams into Nassau Harbor, look south and you can spot Cable Beach on the ship's starboard side. The stretch of green north of the harbor on the port side of the ship is Paradise Island. Long before it became a famous playground, the island served as a natural breakwater for Nassau harbor, protecting the only safe entrance to New Providence. In the distance the arched bridge connecting Paradise Island to Nassau is the most visible evidence of the long-standing American–Bahamian connection.

 **FAST FACTS**

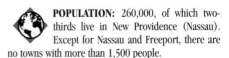 **POPULATION:** 260,000, of which two-thirds live in New Providence (Nassau). Except for Nassau and Freeport, there are no towns with more than 1,500 people.

GOVERNMENT: The Parliament, over 250 years old, has two houses. The House of Assembly has 43 members elected every five years; the Senate is an advisory group of sixteen appointed members. The Bahamas is a member of the Commonwealth and the British queen is its monarch, too.

CLIMATE: Strictly speaking, the Bahamas is not part of the Caribbean, but it enjoys a similar idyllic tropical climate. The Gulf Stream bathes the western coast with clear warm waters, and easterly tradewinds caress the shores. As a result, temperatures in the northernmost islands seldom drop below 60°F or rise above 90°F.

CLOTHING: Casual but proper. Bahamians tend to be conservative and are offended by the overly revealing dress of some tourists on the streets. Informal spring/summer sportswear for day and evening will suit most occasions, although elegant attire is not out of place in the evening, depending on your choice of dining place and activities. Generally, men neatly dressed in slacks, sports shirt, and jacket will be comfortable at any nightspot in the islands. For women, a cocktail dress or stylish pants suit is appropriate.

CURRENCY: The Bahamian dollar (B$) is freely exchanged with the U.S. dollar at par.

DEPARTURE TAX: When you leave the Bahamas by air, you pay $15 per adult and per child, age six and older. Children ages five and under are not charged.

ELECTRICITY: 120 volt, 60 cycle A.C. Standard U.S. shavers, hairdryers, and other appliances can be used.

ENTRY FORMALITIES: U.S. citizens with proof of citizenship or birth certificate do not need passports for visits of up to three weeks.

LANGUAGE: English—more British than American—and with a lilt and influences from the early settlers, African slaves and Caribbean islanders who came here to work.

POSTAL SERVICE: A letter to the United States costs 55 cents per half ounce; a postcard, 40 cents. The post office nearest the pier in Nassau is at Parliament and East Hill streets, three blocks south of Rawson Square. In Freeport, the post office nearest the pier is at Explorer's Way. Hours: 9 A.M. to 5:30 P.M.

PUBLIC HOLIDAYS: January 1, New Year's Day; Good Friday, Easter Sunday and Monday; Whit Monday (six weeks after Easter); Labor Day (first Friday in June); July 10, Independence Day; Emancipation Day (first Monday in August); October 12, Discovery Day; December 25, Christmas; December 26, Boxing Day.

TELEPHONE AREA CODE: 242. (Dial exactly as you do for a long distance call within the United States.)

TIME: Eastern Standard Time. Daylight Saving Time is adopted in the summer months as in the United States.

VACCINATION REQUIREMENT: None.

AIRLINES: Direct flights from major U.S. gateways by American Airlines/American Eagle, Bahamasair, Carnival Air, Comair, Continental, Delta, Gulfstream, Paradise Island Airlines, Taesa, Trinity Air, USAir, USAir Express, and United; and from Canada by Air Canada.

INFORMATION:

In the United States,

Bahamas Tourist Offices: 800–422–4262.
  Sports information: Bahamas Sports Line, 800–32–SPORT.
Atlanta: 2957 Clairmont Rd., No. 150; GA 30329; Tel. 404–633–1793; fax 404–633–1575.
Chicago: 8600 W. Bryn Mawr Ave., No. 820; IL 60631; Tel. 312–693–1500; fax 312–693–1114.
Dallas: 2050 Stemmons Freeway, World Trade Center, No. 116; TX 75258–1408; Tel. 214–742–1186; fax 214–741–4118.
Los Angeles: 3450 Wilshire Blvd., No. 208; CA 90010; Tel. 213–385–0033; fax 213–383–3966.
Miami: One Turnberry Place, 19495 Biscayne Blvd. No. 809; Adventura, FL 33180; Tel. 305–932–0051; fax 305–682–8758; Grand Bahamas Tourist Bureau, Tel. 800–448–3386.
New York: 150 East 52nd St., 28th Floor; NY 10022; Tel. 212–758–2777; fax 212–753–6531.
In Canada:
Toronto: 121 Bloor St. E., No. 1101;

Ontario M4W 3M5;
Tel. 800–667–3777 (Canada only);
fax 416–968–6711.

In Nassau:

The Ministry of Tourism has information booths at
Prince George Dock, Tel. 325–9155;
Ministry of Tourism Hdqs., Bay St., Tel. 322–7500.

In Freeport:

The Tourist Information Centre is located in the
Sir Charles Hayward Library, Tel. 352–8044,
and there are booths at Freeport Harbor, Tel.
352–9651, and in the International Bazaar.
Hours: 8:30 A.M. to 5 P.M., Monday–Saturday.

AN INTRODUCTION TO NASSAU

Old World charm and New World glamour come
together in Nassau and its elaborate resorts of
Cable Beach and Paradise Island. Nassau is one of the
most sophisticated and popular destinations in the
tropics.

For most people Nassau *is* the Bahamas. However,
Nassau is not an island but a town—to be sure, the main
town—on the island of New Providence, located at the
center of the Bahamas archipelago. As the seat of government, the hub of commercial activity, and the cross-
roads of the nation's air and sea lanes, Nassau has
acquired the bustle and worldliness of an international
capital. Yet it is the only place throughout the 700
islands of the Bahamas archipelago, including Freeport,
that comes even close to having this character.

For cruise passengers Nassau's combination of the
old and the new in an international city surrounded by
lovely beaches is perfect. Stretched along the north
coast of the island, the town is compact and easy to
explore on foot in a leisurely morning or afternoon. It
is situated on a low-lying island only 21 miles long and
7 miles wide that is easy to see by car, bus, or moped in
a few hours. It is also possible to combine some sight-
seeing with a sport or a shopping expedition and have
time at the beach.

Perhaps more than any other place in the Bahamas,
Nassau reflects the country's British past visually in the
colonial buildings of Old Nassau and in the trappings of
tradition that have lasted through three centuries.
Cruise passengers encounter the British legacy almost
from the moment they step off their ship. Street traffic
is directed by "bobbies" whose uniforms—white jacket,

blue trousers with a red stripe, and pith helmet—are a
tropical version of their London counterparts. Driving
is on the left as in Britain.

The graceful colonial buildings of Parliament Square
are the backdrop for a statue of Queen Victoria, and visitors on hand for the annual opening of Parliament will
see the members of the legislature dressed in striped
pants and morning coats. Were you to step into the
Supreme Court while it is in session, you would find the
judges and lawyers dressed in robes and wearing the
traditional white wigs.

NASSAU'S ORIGINS

Nassau, originally known as Sayle's Island, was settled
for the first time around 1666 by a group of
Bermudians and English, and within five years it had
over 900 settlers. By the time the Bahamas was granted
to the Six Lords Proprietors of Carolina by the British
Crown in 1670 the population had reached almost
1,000, including slaves. But the settlement developed
into a pirate stronghold, which led to Spanish raids in
1684—raids so effective, apparently, that the town was
abandoned. Some settlers returned two years later but
growth was slow until 1695, when one of the governors, Nicholas Trott, laid out a town plan for
Charlestown, as it was called. To protect the western
entrance to the harbor he built Fort Nassau, which he
named in honor of the Prince of Orange–Nassau who
later became William III of England.

Except for Trott, however, the Carolina landlords
were not interested in the Bahamas and allowed it to
become a haven for pirates and privateers. Finally, from
1718 to 1721 and again from 1729 to 1732, under the
first royal governor, Woodes Rogers, Nassau was
cleaned up, Fort Nassau restored, an assembly established, and a town plan created, which has remained,
more or less, the same to the present day. To protect the
eastern entrance to the harbor, Fort Montagu was
added in 1741.

Nassau had a burst of prosperity later in the century
when Loyalist refugees fleeing the American Revolutionary War came here to settle. Both administra-
tively and architecturally, the new arrivals made a major
impact on the island and transformed the scrappy little
port into a pretty and prosperous town with new streets
and wharfs and city ordinances for fire and health.

In 1787, the last royal governor of Virginia, John
Murray, better known to history as Lord Dunmore,
became the governor of the Bahamas. Arrogant,
incompetent, and thoroughly disliked, Dunmore left
an indelible mark on the Bahamas with his passion for
building. He cost both the Crown and the Bahamians
a great deal of money and grief. To fortify the island he

built Fort Charlotte on the west, Fort Fincastle and Fort Winton on the east, and added gun emplacements on Hog (Paradise) Island. His home, Dunmore House, served as the governor's residence until Government House was completed. On the eastern end of New Providence he built the Hermitage as his summer home. The present mansion, reconstructed in the early 1900s, is the residence of the Roman Catholic bishop of Nassau.

PORT PROFILE: NASSAU

EMBARKATION: In Nassau the piers are located on the north side of New Providence Island less than a ten-minute walk from the heart of town. Ships pull dock-side to the modern piers, known as Prince George Wharf, one block from Bay Street, the main shopping street of Nassau. An attractive pedestrian walk from the piers to the square was added as part of the port expansion in 1991. Taxis and motorcoaches are waiting for passengers at the dock when ships arrive.

Passengers are allowed to come and go freely between their ship and town. No special identification or security measures are necessary other than those required by your ship for reboarding—usually a boarding card, cabin key, or some other form of identification distributed by your ship. After leaving the pier, en route to Rawson Square, you will pass the Welcome Center of the Bahamas Ministry of Tourism where you can pick up maps, brochures, and other information.

LOCAL TRANSPORTATION: Taxis are readily available and are metered. Rates are supposed to be fixed at $2 flag-fall and 20 cents each one-fifth mile for one or two passengers; $2 for each additional passenger. Unfortunately, some Nassau taxi drivers pretend their meters do not work in order to overcharge tourists.

If you plan to engage a taxi for sight-seeing, negotiate the price in advance. Be aware that there are free-lancers who are not legal taxis and who will charge whatever they think they can get. Look for a taxi with a "Bahama Host" sticker on his windshield. They are reliable and the best informed.

In Nassau, city buses or jitneys (75-cent fare) run frequently throughout the day and early evening from two downtown departure points only three blocks from the pier. At Bay and Frederick streets next to the Straw Market is the station for buses to the north and eastern parts of the island; those to Cable Beach and residential areas on the western side of the island leave from Bay Street and Navy Lion Road, next to the British Colonial

Hotel. For Paradise Island, you'll need to take a taxi or ferry. The Paradise Island Bridge Toll is $2 per motorized vehicle. Taxis from Prince George Wharf to Paradise Island are likely to charge $6 plus toll, for a one-way trip.

Surreys, the horse-drawn carriages, which can be hired at Rawson Square, are strictly for tourists and cost $5 per person. If you are more than two or if you want to keep the surrey for a longer period than the usual half-hour tour, be sure to negotiate the price in advance.

FERRY SERVICES: Ferries for Paradise Island depart from Prince George Wharf every 20 minutes from early morning until 5:30 P.M. and cost $2.

CAR RENTALS: Car rentals from major U.S. companies are available at major hotels and various locations throughout Nassau. Those with offices nearest the pier are Avis (Tel. 326–6380) and Dollar Rent-a-Car (Tel. 325–3716) at the British Colonial Hotel. Expect to pay $50 and up for a subcompact with unlimited mileage. If you rent a car with a credit card, you must be 21 years or older; without the card, 25 years or older. Americans may use U.S. driver's licenses for up to three months. REMEMBER, Bahamians drive on the **LEFT.** The speed limit is generally 30 m.p.h. but not many drivers observe it, least of all the bus drivers.

MOPEDS/BICYCLES: Rental agencies for motor scooters and bicycles are located by the pier and on Marlboro Road near the British Colonial Hotel. A valid driver's license and a helmet supplied by the rental agency are compulsory for using a motorbike. From Motorscooter Rentals (Tel. 326–8329) at the pier, the price is $26 for half a day, plus $4 insurance, and includes helmet and full tank of gas. You must leave a $10 deposit as well. To repeat, *DRIVING IS ON THE LEFT.*

EMERGENCY NUMBERS: Police: Nassau, Tel. 911 and Tel. 322–4444. Medical Services: Nassau, Princess Margaret Hospital, Tel. 322–2861. Ambulance: Nassau, Tel. 322–2221.

BUDGET PLANNING

Nassau is not a cheap port. Taxis, car rentals, admission fees to privately operated sight-seeing and other attractions, deluxe restaurants, and drinks are usually 20 percent higher than comparable facilities in the United States and other Caribbean ports of call. These costs, however, can be avoided or offset. Here are some ways, particularly for visitors on limited budgets.

- *Walk—Nassau is a compact town that's easy and pleasurable to cover on foot.*
- *Use public transportation, which is good and low cost.*
- *Enjoy the abundant, beautiful, free, easy-to-reach beaches.*
- *Dine in restaurants serving local specialties. They are reasonably priced and clean.*

Drugs, Crime, and Today's Realities

The Bahamas, like other places, is not immune to today's social ills. Although you might be approached to buy drugs, the possession, sale, or purchase of drugs is prohibited. Penalties for breaking the law apply to tourists as much as to Bahamians; they are severe and the jails unpleasant.

Theft and crime, particularly in Nassau and Freeport, are on the rise. As a tourist, you are an easy target. Rented cars and motorscooters, for example, have special plates that make them easy to identify. However, you can reduce your vulnerability with prudence.

Do not park in secluded or isolated areas, particularly on the south coast of Nassau. Never leave valuables in your car or on the beach, including hotel beaches. Do not walk alone in remote or lightly trafficked areas, and most of all, do not engage someone as a guide who approaches you on the street or beach. All guides and taxi drivers in the Bahamas are licensed; if you have any doubt about a person's credentials, you need only step into the nearest tourist office or police station.

Author's Favorite Attractions

Walking Tour of Old Nassau
Snorkeling/scuba
A Day at Atlantis Resort
Golf
People-to-People Program
French Cloisters and Versailles Gardens/Ocean Club

Nassau Shore Excursions

Since Nassau is easy to manage on your own and has a wide selection of activities to enjoy, shore excursions offered by cruise lines tends to be limited. The attractions and sports on these tours are described elsewhere in this chapter.

Combination Tour: 3–4 hours, $25–$36. A drive through Old Nassau and around the island is combined with a visit to the Ardastra Gardens. Some visit Paradise Island, including Versailles Gardens, or Coral World. Suggested for those on their first visit who cannot make the walking tour and whose interest in sports is marginal. A shorter two-hour city tour is hardly worthwhile since most of it can be covered in a walking tour on one's own. Coral World's tour with transportation by ferry to and from the port costs US $22. *Atlantis Submarine: $74 adults; $37 child.* See description later in chapter.

Seaworld Explorer: $29 adult; $19 child. Semi-submarine drops about five feet below surface of the water for you to view the gardens. Tour begins and returns from the port and goes on a 15-minute ride to the underwater marine park, known as the Sea Gardens, at Athol Island.

Half-day Sail & Snorkel Excursion: 3 hours, $30–34 adult; $15–17 child. Several large catamarans and "pirate" sailing ships offer full party cruises to nearby beaches for swimming, snorkeling, rum punch, and/or lunch, $50. Half-day Scuba Dive, $35–55.

Golf: Most cruise lines offer packages, or you can make your own arrangements. Majestic Tours (242–322–2606), one of the major local companies, has golf packages for $90–110, depending on the course. See the Sports section later in this chapter.

Night Club Tour: $20; $35 with dinner. The tour includes admission to a nightclub with Bahamian and West Indian music and show, drink, tips, and transfers. It is suggested for those who are more interested in local entertainment than casinos but are reluctant to go out on their own.

Casino/Show: $35, cocktail show; $55, dinner show, including transportation to/from hotel at *Crystal Palace* or *Atlantis.* Las Vegas-style musical revue with long-legged showgirls baring lots of "t & a" and visit to the casino. Either can be done on your own, but you will not be saving money, as the round-trip fare by taxi costs $12 or more.

People-to-People

The Bahamas Ministry of Tourism gives you the opportunity to meet Bahamians as you would a friend through its People-to-People program, which brings tourists together with Bahamians who have volunteered to host visitors.

People to People volunteers, 500 in Nassau and 200 in Freeport, come from a cross section of the community. They might belong to the same service club, such as Rotary or Kiwanis, as you do or practice your profession or trade or share your hobby. Many have traveled themselves and know what it is like to be on one's own in a strange place. They know, too, how much more meaningful a visit can be when it is enriched with a personal experience.

These nice folks are *volunteers*. Although the program is operated by The Bahamas Ministry of Tourism, the volunteers are neither employed nor subsidized by the government. They offer their time and friendship without compensation and neither ask nor expect anything in return. They are involved because they enjoy meeting people from other countries and they want visitors to know their country in a natural, noncommercial atmosphere.

The form that the welcome takes depends on your Bahamian host. Because they, too, work for a living, they generally entertain in the evenings or on weekends. They might take you sight-seeing or to their favorite beach for a picnic or to a Sunday service at their church. Or, your host might invite you to share an afternoon or evening of conversation with light refreshments, join a family gathering or take a meal at their home. If so, you will most likely have a chance to sample food and drink you will not normally find on restaurant menus. You will be enjoying facets of Bahamian life that most visitors never see.

To participate in the People-to-People program, contact an office of the Bahamas Ministry of Tourism for a request form to be submitted about two to three weeks in advance of your visit, or write to the Ministry of Tourism, P.O. Box N-3701, Nassau, Bahamas; or P.O. Box F-251, Freeport, Bahamas. You will be contacted by a Ministry of Tourism People-to-People coordinator about the arrangements that have been made especially for you.

Cruise directors often have the forms. However, it's better to make your request in advance to give the People-to-People coordinator time to match you with your Bahamian host, especially if you have a particular interest in a social, fraternal, or religious organization, or a hobby, vocation, or profession that you would like to share.

Garden parties, sponsored jointly with the Bahamas Ministry of Tourism, are another part of the People-to-People program. In Nassau, the parties are held on the fourth Friday of the month at historic Government House and hosted by the wife of the governor general. In Freeport, the Garden of the Groves is the venue.

NASSAU ON YOUR OWN

Unless you have already been to Nassau several times, you will probably find a walking tour of Old Nassau or a boat excursion as interesting a way to enjoy your day in port as any alternative. Neither require transportation from the pier, but visiting the attractions east and west of town and on Paradise Island does. Public buses are available but they do not take you directly to the sites; from the main road, you will have a short walk. If you engage a taxi to a specific location, be sure to arrange your return transportation and set the price in advance.

A WALKING TOUR OF OLD NASSAU

The entire walk, following the sequence as numbered (see map) takes three to four hours depending on your pace. At several points along the way, you can stop for a refreshment or break off entirely and return to your ship or to Bay Street for shopping.

A walking tour of Old Nassau in the heart of town is a stroll through Bahamian history, particularly its British past. The town plan, laid out in grid fashion in 1788, is virtually intact and comprises four long, parallel east-west streets crossed by ten small north-south streets running from the harbor and Bay Street on the north to a hillside (East Hill and West Hill streets) on the south. Although modern encroachments are everywhere, many streets have retained enough of their eighteenth- and nineteenth-century buildings, gardens, and broad steps to give visitors a real sense of Nassau in bygone days.

PRINCE GEORGE WHARF (1) From Prince George Wharf where the cruise ships dock it is only a few steps to Rawson Square, the Tourist Information Office **(2)**, and Parliament Square, the heart of downtown. En route you will pass a statue dedicated to the Women of the Bahamas, by Randolph Johnston of Abaco.

The docks have been upgraded with a "Welcome Plaza," a taxi dispatch station, and shelter for the horse-drawn surreys. One building contains a "Welcome Centre," as well as information, communication, and banking services, a Bahamian product gift shop and the Junkanoo Expo **(12)** (described later in the chapter). Either now or at the end of your walk, a detour to the museum is very worthwhile.

The waterfront between Woodes Rogers Walk and the western end of Prince George Wharf is being trans-

WALKING TOUR OF OLD NASSAU

N

NASSAU HARBOR

Prince George Wharf **1**

Paradise Ferry

Customs **12**

British Colonial Hotel →

WOODES ROGERS WALK **4**

2

3

Union Dock

WEST BAY ST.

NAVY LION RD.

BAY ST.

BAY ST.

MARLBOROUGH ST.

KING ST.

American Embassy

NASSAU CT.

CUMBERLAND ST.

GEORGE ST.

MARKET ST.

FREDERICK ST.

CHARLOTTE ST.

PARLIAMENT ST.

BANK LN.

EAST ST.

see inset

14

VICTORIA AVE.

COLEBROOK LN.

DORCHESTER ST.

WEST ST.

QUEEN

28

31

29 **30** **34**

32 **33**

DUKE ST.

PRINCE ST.

24 **21**

11

13

SHIRLEY ST.

15

SHIRLEY ST.

BURNSIDE LN.

26

WEST HILL ST.

25

23
Govt. House

EAST HILL ST.

20

19

EAST ST.

Bishop's Residence

ELIZABETH AVE.

35

BLUE HILL RD.

DELANCY ST.

27

PETTICOAT LN.

Bethel Baptist

MARKET ST.

SCHOOL LN.

Post Office

SANDS RD.

16

Hospital

Hotel

DILLET ST.

Police

18

Bennet's Hill

17

Water Tower

St. John Baptist

Inset:
BAY ST.
Tourist Office
PARLIAMENT ST.
BANK LN.
5
6 **8**
7
9
10
Gardens of Remembrance

MAP LEGEND FOR WALKING TOUR OF OLD NASSAU

Note: Numbers in the walking tour correspond to the numbers on the accompanying map. An "x" after the number means the house or building is not open to the public; "s" means it can be visited by special arrangement.

1. Prince George Wharf
2. Tourist Information Office
3. Rawson Square
4. Woodes Rogers Walk
5. Parliament Square
6. House of Assembly
7. Senate Building
8. Colonial Secretary's Office and Treasury
9. Supreme Court
10. Central Police Station
11. Public Library
12. Junkanoo Expo
13. Curry House and Zion Church
14x. Cascadilla
15. Bahamas Historical Society
16. Queen's Staircase
17. Fort Fincastle and Water Tower
18. Police Headquarters
19. Ministry of Foreign Affairs

20x. Jacaranda House
21. St. Andrew's Presbyterian Church
22. Gregory's Arch
23s. Government House
24. Christopher Columbus Statue
25. Graycliff House
26. St. Francis Xavier Cathedral/The Priory (Dunmore House)
27. Buena Vista
28. The Deanery
29. Cable Beach/West End Bus Stand
30. Vendue House/Pompey Museum
31. Christ Church Cathedral
32. Balcony House
33. Central Bank/Trinity Place
34. Straw Market/Tourism Ministry; North and East End Bus Stand
35. National Museum

formed into "Festival Place," an urban water park—a themed entertainment attraction with a 315-foot observation tower, an interactive theater, and food and beverage and exhibition spaces—to be completed in 1997.

RAWSON SQUARE (3) In 1985, as part of the beautification project for the visit of Queen Elizabeth II and the meeting of the Commonwealth nations, Old Nassau's stately buildings and monuments in the heart of downtown were spruced up, and a garden and mosaic walkways were laid to connect Rawson Square and Parliament Square on the south side of Bay Street. The square is named for Sir William Rawson, governor of the Bahamas from 1864 to 1869; and it has a small statue of Sir Milo Butler, the first governor-general of the Bahamas after independence in 1973. The Churchill Building on the east side of the square was formerly the prime minister's office. On the west side, you can engage a horse-drawn surrey for a tour or stop to have your hair braided for $2 per braid at the open-air pavilion.

WOODES ROGERS WALK (4) The waterfront walkway west of Rawson Square, known as Woodes Rogers Walk, was named for the first British governor of the Bahamas. The tiny lanes with shops leads to the town's famous Straw Market (34), a lively bazaar of Bahamian crafts. You can also reach the Straw Market by walking along Bay Street, the town's oldest street and main thoroughfare. It is lined with department stores and boutiques selling anything from $2 T-shirts to French perfumes and English china at about 20 percent less than stateside prices.

If you were to continue west on Bay Street beyond the British Colonial Hotel, you would be on West Bay Street, the road leading to Ardastra Gardens and Cable Beach. East on Bay Street about two miles is the bridge to Paradise Island. Potters Cay has a native market where Bahamians buy fresh fish and provisions.

PARLIAMENT SQUARE (5) The traditional center of Bahamian government activity, Parliament Square is graced by a marble statue of a youthful Queen Victoria seated upon a throne and holding a sword and scepter. Framing the statue is the lovely Georgian architecture of the House of Assembly (6) on the west, the Senate Building (7) on the south, and the old Colonial Secretary's Office and Treasury (8) on the east. The buildings were constructed from 1805 to 1813 and are based on Tryon's Palace of New Bern, the old capital of North Carolina, praised as the most beautiful building of its time. South of these buildings facing the Garden of Remembrance, with a cenotaph commemorating the dead of the two world wars, is the Supreme Court (9). The garden with stately royal palms and tropical flowers is one of the prettiest spots

in the downtown area. On the east side of the square on Bank Lane is the Central Police Station and International Trust Building (10).

PUBLIC LIBRARY (11) The octagonal structure, built in about 1798 as a prison, was made into a library and museum in 1879. The structure, contemporary with buildings in Williamsburg, is thought to have been modeled after the Old Powder Magazine there. The first and second floors had prison cells on each of its eight sides; a central open area provided fresh air. These alcoves now hold library stacks. A domed gallery on the third floor was originally unroofed; it once held a bell that was rung to summon members of the House of Assembly to meetings. The upper floor has a collection of books and artifacts on the Bahamas, including old maps dating from 1750 and prints from 1891. Hours: Mon.–Fri., 10 A.M. to 9 P.M.; Sat., 9 A.M. to 5 P.M.

Magistrate's Court No. 3 on Parliament Street was originally built in 1894 as a chapel for the Salem Union Baptist congregation on a site known as the "Livery Stable Grounds." It is still owned by the church. South of the library, the old Royal Victorian Gardens was the site of the once grand Victorian Hotel, the center of social activity when it opened in 1861 during the American Civil War. Among its first guests were those fleeing the war; others were blockade-runners, officers of the Confederacy, spies of the Northern States, and "ladies of high quality" who were invited to the nightly parties.

In 1876 the hotel was leased to the brother of Grover Cleveland, U.S. president from 1885 to 1889; and according to a plaque in the gardens, the hotel was purchased in 1898 by Henry M. Flagler. The American railroad czar connected Florida with the rest of the nation and drew up plans for a rail/ferry service to connect the Bahamas to the U.S. mainland. In its heyday, the hotel had a long list of distinguished guests that included Winston Churchill, Prince Albert, and an array of European royalty and celebrities. The hotel changed hands many times before it closed in 1971 and was later destroyed by fire.

Curry House (13), located on Shirley Street immediately west of Zion Church, is a three-story building which opened in 1890 as a private hotel. Later it became an annex of the Royal Victoria Hotel, and in 1972 it was acquired by the government and is used by the Ministry of Finance.

[From here, you have a choice of walking east to Bennet's Hill and the Water Tower or west to Government House. If you plan to cover this entire walking tour on foot, you might do well to take the uphill climb to the Water Tower first. To reach the

Water Tower, walk east on Shirley Street and turn south on Elizabeth Avenue. It leads directly to the Queen's Staircase and hence, the Water Tower.]

CASCADILLA (14x) is one of the Nassau houses thought to have been built by ship carpenters—the island's only craftsmen for many decades. (Certain Bahamian architectural features later transplanted in Key West by Bahamians derive from this origin.) The oldest part of the house dates from 1840, when it marked the eastern boundary of town. The ruins of kitchens and other buildings indicate that it was once part of a plantation house. The property has had many owners over the years and now belongs to a real estate broker.

BAHAMAS HISTORICAL SOCIETY MUSEUM (15) Founded in 1959, the Society is a nonprofit cultural and educational organization dedicated to stimulating interest in Bahamian history and collecting and preserving material related to it. Hours: Tues. and Wed., 10 A.M. to 4 P.M.; Fri., 10 A.M. to 1 P.M.; and Sat., 10 A.M. to noon. Admission free, but contributions welcome. For information: Bahamas Historical Society, Box SS–6833, Nassau (tel. 322–4231).

QUEEN'S STAIRCASE (16) At the head of Elizabeth Avenue is a passageway of 66 steps carved out of limestone, draped with thick tropical foliage, and cooled by a waterfall. Local lore says the steps represent each year of Queen Victoria's reign. Actually, the steps were carved by slaves a century earlier and form a passageway to Fort Fincastle, thus enabling troops to reach the fort from town without being exposed to fire from enemy ships.

FORT FINCASTLE (17) Situated on Bennet's Hill overlooking the town, Paradise Island, and the eastern approaches to New Providence, Fort Fincastle was built in 1793 and takes its name from Lord Dunmore's title as the Viscount Fincastle. The fort was constructed in the shape of a ship's bow and has served as a lighthouse and signal station. Hours: Mon.–Fri., 9:30 A.M. to 4 P.M.; Sat., 2 to 5 P.M.

WATER TOWER Next to the fort, the 126-foot Water Tower built in 1928 is the highest point on the island, 216 feet above sea level. An elevator (or a circular stairway of 202 steps) goes to an observation deck at the top for a lovely panoramic view of the city, harbor, and Fort Fincastle below. The tower is open from 9 A.M. to 5 P.M. daily; the elevator ride costs 50 cents. (You may be hustled for tips by the elevator operator and self-appointed guides on the tower's observation deck; you should simply ignore them.)

From the tower, you can continue your walking tour by returning to East Street via Sands Alley or Prison Lane and walking north to East Hill Street. The Police Headquarters **(18)** was built in 1900. The green and

white building on the north side of the complex is a typical example of Bahamian wooden architecture and is reminiscent of houses built in Key West by Bahamian transplants.

When the Loyalists came to Nassau after the American Revolution they brought with them ideas about colonial architecture, particularly of the South. Although it evolved into a decidedly Bahamian version with different types of building materials, the influence is evident. Typical building materials included limestone with pink-washed walls and peaked roofs; wood was used in colonnades, fretwork balconies, and jalousies or louvered shutters that shielded the verandas from the hot sun and allowed the air to circulate. In the late nineteenth and early twentieth centuries economic hardship forced many Bahamians to leave the islands. Some became the early settlers of Key West, bringing their building habits with them.

From East Street turn west on East Hill Street. You will pass the modern Post Office building and the former East Hill Club, which houses the Ministry of Foreign Affairs **(19)**. The club was built around 1850 by the socially prominent Matthews family, who were lawyers and government officials. The Georgian colonial-style house was first renovated when it was owned by Lord Beaverbrook.

Jacaranda House **(20x)** on the corner of East Hill and Parliament streets was built about 1840 by Chief Justice Sir George Anderson, of Georgia stone previously used as ship's ballast. During World War II, the house was owned by Capt. Vyvian Drury, aide-de-camp to the duke of Windsor. It was bought in 1949 by the widow of Sir Harry Oakes and later passed to her daughter. The house is furnished with lovely antiques and has exterior features typical of classical Bahamian architecture, such as interlocking corners of large projecting stones used for strength (known as chamfered quoins).

ST. ANDREW'S PRESBYTERIAN CHURCH (21) The pretty, white church at the corner of Duke and Market streets was begun in 1810 and expanded many times over the next five decades. It was completely renovated early in this century.

GREGORY'S ARCH (22) Spanning Market Street is a picturesque entrance to Grant's Town, one of the early settlements of former slaves referred to locally as "Over the Hill," as it is literally over the ridge that divides north Nassau from the south side. The arch, named for Governor John Gregory, was built in 1852 by J. J. Burnside, the surveyor general who laid out Grant's Town. The English iron railings were added two years later. Broad stone stairways at the foot of Charlotte and Frederick streets lead from East Hill Street directly to Bay Street.

GOVERNMENT HOUSE (23s) The imposing Government House (at Blue Hill Road and Prince Street) stands on Mount Fitzwilliam, a hillside overlooking Nassau. It is the home of the governor-general, the queen's personal representative to the Commonwealth of the Bahamas. A previous structure is thought to have housed governors from Richard Fitzwilliam in 1733 to Lord Dunmore in 1787. Dunmore moved to the house he built on West Street (now a priory) and sold the former government house and its land to another Loyalist. The present house was built between 1803 and 1806 and expanded several times; the east wing dates from 1909.

The hurricane of 1929 caused a great deal of damage to the structure and, subsequently, the interior and front facade were entirely redesigned, the main entrance changed, and the car porch and main hall added. In 1940 the house was extensively redecorated, and living quarters in the west wing, known as the Windsor Wing, were added for the personal staff of the duke of Windsor who lived here for four years as the royal governor of the Bahamas.

More changes were made in 1964 and again in 1977 for the visit of Queen Elizabeth II. In addition to the queen, many members of the royal family, heads of state including President Kennedy, and other celebrities have been guests here. Monthly, the Bahamas Ministry of Tourism and the People-to-People program hold a garden party for tourists, hosted by the governor-general's wife.

CHRISTOPHER COLUMBUS STATUE (24) The entrance to Government House is marked by a bigger-than-life, 12-foot-tall statue of Christopher Columbus, made in London by an aide to American novelist and historian Washington Irving and placed here in 1830 by Governor Sir James Carmichael Smyth. It commemorates Columbus's arrival in the New World on the Bahamian island of San Salvador. The ceremonial Changing of the Guard with the famous Royal Bahamas Police Force Band takes place on alternate Saturdays at 10 A.M. sharp. (For information, phone 322–3622.)

[From the statue, you can walk down George Street in front of the Columbus statue to Vendue House (30) and the Straw Market on Bay Street, or continue your walking tour to see some of Nassau's oldest and loveliest houses.]

GRAYCLIFF HOUSE (25) This Georgian mansion set in a lovely tropical garden dates from about 1726. Now a hotel and restaurant, it was originally built by a notorious pirate, Capt. John H. Graysmith, as his home. The building may have been used as a garrison for the British West Indies Regiment, judging from the thick walls and other structural elements in the cellars,

which are now used by the hotel for its wine collection. The house is known to have been a hotel as early as 1844, but it became a private residence again in 1937 when it belonged to a Canadian couple who added a swimming pool and made alterations. In 1966, the estate was bought by Lord Dudley, earl of Staffordshire, as his winter home. The present owners acquired it in 1974. Despite the publicity you may have read, Graycliff's restaurant is highly overrated, pretentious, and grossly overpriced.

Farther west on West Hill Street are several beautifully restored private homes and the Priory **(26)**, formerly known as Dunmore House. After serving as the governor's residence, the house became the officers' quarters and mess hall for the 22nd West Indies Regiment. It later became a military hospital and in 1893 was purchased by the Roman Catholic church and made into the Priory; the Cathedral of St. Francis Xavier is adjacent.

South of the cathedral on Delancey Street is Buena Vista **(27)**, a hotel with one of the town's leading restaurants, housed in a building dating from the mid-nineteenth century.

THE DEANERY (28) From West Street continue north and turn into Queen Street to the Deanery at No. 28 Queen Street. Built in 1710, it is thought to be the oldest house in the Bahamas. The building was acquired by the Anglican church in 1800 and is the Rectory of Christ Church Cathedral. The three-story house is built of stone with chamfered quoins; originally it had three tiers of verandas on three sides. A one-story building on the west side was the stone kitchen with an eight-foot fireplace and a domed oven; it has a small room thought to have been used as sleeping quarters for domestic slaves. Across the street is the U.S. Embassy.

In the next small lane is Nassau Court, built in 1830 as the West Chapel of the Wesleyan Methodist Church. In 1864 it was sold to the government and used as a school for almost a century, although the nature of the school changed several times. In 1960 it was turned over to the Ministry of Public Works and is now occupied by the Ministry of Economic Affairs.

On the north side of Marlborough Street is the British Colonial Hotel, a Best Western Hotel, the pink colonial building which dominates the waterfront. It is on the site of the town's first fortification, Fort Nassau, built in 1670. On its east side is the stand for buses to Cable Beach **(29)**.

VENDUE HOUSE/POMPEY MUSEUM (30) At the head of George Street facing Bay Street is the site of the former slave market, originally a colonnade structure without walls dating from about 1769. It was rebuilt in the early 1900s and occupied by the Bahamas Electricity Corporation. In 1992, as part of the

Columbus Quincentennial, it was renovated to house a museum—Pompey Museum of Slavery and Emancipation—and art gallery, funded by a grant from Bacardi Corporation.

The exhibit on the African experience in the Bahamas is named after Pompey, a slave on one of five estates in Exuma owned by Lord Rolle and a hero in Bahamian history. Meanwhile, there are changing exhibits on various aspects of the Bahamas and, on the second floor, a collection of paintings by Amos Ferguson, the Bahamas' internationally acclaimed intuitive artist. Hours: Mon.–Fri., 10 A.M. to 4:30 P.M.; Sat., 10 A.M. to 1 P.M.

CHRIST CHURCH CATHEDRAL (31) Turn east on Marlborough Street and walk to the corner of King and George streets to Christ Church Cathedral. In the original layout of the town this area was a park known as George's Square, the site of the colony's first church.

BALCONY HOUSE (32) Facing the Central Bank on Market Street is the two-story Balcony House, whose construction indicates it may have been built by ships' carpenters around 1790. The house was constructed of American soft cedar and has a second-floor balcony that hangs over the street. An unusual inside staircase is said to have come from a ship. The property, which includes three other houses and slave kitchens, was acquired by Lord Beaverbrook, who sold it in 1947. More recently, it was acquired by the Central Bank and renovated as a museum by the Department of Archives to show life of a prosperous family in the nineteenth century. Hours: 9 A.M. to 5 P.M. daily except holidays.

The Central Bank **(33)** has a collection of the Bahamas' leading artists on display in its lobby. The bank is on the corner of Trinity Place, a small street between Market and Frederick streets. One of the oldest streets in Nassau, Trinity Place is home to the Trinity Church.

STRAW MARKET (34) Both Market and Frederick streets lead to Bay Street, directly in front of the Ministry of Tourism Building, the Straw Market, and the local bus stand for buses to the North and East End. You can return to your ship by walking east on Bay Street. Or you can walk through the Straw Market to the north exit and return to the dock via Woodes Rogers Walk and the Junkanoo Expo **(12)**.

NASSAU AND ITS ENVIRONS

New Providence has many good roads, making any section of the island accessible in a few minutes' drive.

At least four highways cut the island north-south, making it easy to reach the south coast from Nassau by a direct route.

ATTRACTIONS WEST OF NASSAU

In contrast to the Old World ambience of Old Nassau are the modern resorts of Cable Beach that stretch west from town along five miles of lovely, white sand beaches on the north shore. Dubbed the Bahamian Riviera, they include the eye-popping Nassau Marriott Resort & Crystal Palace Casino, which recently completed a $30 million renovation; Radisson Cable Beach; Breezes Bahamas (formerly the Ambassador Beach Hotel), next to Nassau's oldest golf course; Nassau Beach; and Sandal's Royal Bahamian. Between Old Nassau and modern Cable Beach, in the shadow of Fort Charlotte, there are several attractions that usually can be visited in one tour.

If you visit any of the following places on your own by taxi, be sure to arrange for your return transportation. In most cases, public buses pass within walking distance.

Ardastra Gardens and Zoo: One mile west of town in the shadow of Fort Charlotte is a nature park with the world's only trained flamingo corps. The pink birds are put through their paces in a 25-minute show thrice daily. The pretty birds, which are the national bird of the Bahamas, have a mating display of strutting that lends itself to being trained to parade. The five-acre gardens also offer the chance to see in one place a wide variety of tropical plants as well as endemic birds, four species of iguana (which look like miniature dinosaurs), and other wildlife remaining in the Bahamas.

Visitors are allowed to take photographs, including ones of themselves amidst the flapping flamingos. The flamingos come from the southern island of Inagua where 50,000 birds—the world's largest breeding colony—are protected in a nature preserve administered by the Bahamas National Trust. Ardastra also has several beautiful Bahama parrots in a captive breeding program with the trust. This endangered species, one of 16 Amazon parrot species in the Caribbean, is found only in Inagua and the Abacos in a sanctuary within a large forest reserve. Hours: 9 A.M. to 5 P.M. Admission: $10 for adults; $5 for children. Shows are Mon.–Sat., 11 A.M., 2 P.M., and 4 P.M. (Tel. 323–5806.)

Nassau Botanical Gardens: Adjacent to Fort Charlotte is an 18-acre spread of tropical plants and flowers, a delightful oasis with a large variety of flora typical of the tropics. The gardens are popular for weddings. It also has a re-created Lucayan village. Hours: Daily from 9

A.M. to 4:30 P.M. Admission: $1 for adults; 50 cents for children. (Tel. 323–5975.)

Fort Charlotte: One mile west of town. Named in honor of the wife of George III, the fort was begun by Lord Dunmore in 1787 and built in three stages. The eastern part is the oldest; the middle portion was named Fort Stanley; and the western section, Fort D'Arcy. Much of it was cut out of solid rock; the walls were buttressed with cedar to "last to eternity," according to Dunmore. It still has its moat, open battlements, and dungeons, plus a good view of the harbor. The fort was restored extensively in 1992. Hours: Daily from 9 A.M. to 4:30 P.M.

Coral World: Entrance north of Chippendale Road. Located on Silver Cay and connected to the mainland by a bridge, Coral World is a marine park with an underwater observatory that enables you to walk down into the sea to observe coral reefs and fish through 24 large windows. There is also a reef tank, said to be the largest manmade reef in the world, a shark tank where you can watch sharks being fed by divers, a stingray pool with several kinds of ray, and a turtle pool with breeding populations of rare sea turtles. Visitors may "adopt" a turtle for $50, which helps defray the expenses of a turtle conservation program. Adjacent to the park are shops and walkways among tropical flora that is labeled. Coral World's free shuttle bus stops hourly from 9 A.M. to 4 P.M. at hotels on Cable Beach; its free ferry service departs from the British Colonial Hotel's dock at 10:15 A.M. and 2:45 P.M. and several times daily from Paradise Island. Hours: Daily from 9 A.M. to 6 P.M., and to 7 P.M., Apr.–Oct. Admission: $15 for adults; $10 for children ages 3 to 12. (Tel. 328–1036.)

From Cable Beach, a road hugging the coast continues west around the island to Love Beach, one of the island's loveliest beaches and the home of the new Compass Point. Created by the Island Outpost Group, the oceanfront resort is made up of 18 huts, cottages, and cabanas painted in the vibrant colors of Junkanoo, the Bahamian carnival, and decorated with whimsical Junkanoo motifs such as owls, roosters, sunbursts, and fish. The resort takes its name from the renowned recording studios across the road, where artists such as the Rolling Stones have recorded. Compass Point's seaside restaurant is very popular for its Caribbean cuisine.

Farther west is Lyford Cay, a private, 4,000-acre residential resort that one can visit only as a guest of a member. Lyford Cay, as much as any development, caused the Bahamas to be called the jet-set capital because of the many famous international personalities who own homes here.

The western end of the island has many elegant Bahamian mansions, frequently painted in the deep-pink color associated with the Bahamas or other pastels with white trim, and surrounded by tropical gardens. Among the loveliest are the home of the former prime minister, on Skyline Drive; the residence of the U.S. ambassador to the Bahamas, on Saffron Hill; and on Sandford Drive, the mansion of Canadian millionaire Sir Harry Oakes, one of the island's most famous residents and benefactors, whose murder in 1943 sent shock waves through the island and continues to be a mystery.

Large areas of the south side of the island are uninhabited and covered by miles of pine forests. From Adelaide and Carmichael roads you can circle back via Gladstone Road over Prospect Ridge to see one of the island's biggest surprises—Lake Killarney and Lake Cunningham—large bodies of water whose wooded shores are richly populated with birds.

ATTRACTIONS EAST OF NASSAU

Fort Montagu: The first fortification at the northeastern end of the island was built in 1728 to protect the eastern approach to Nassau harbor. In 1741 it was replaced by the present structure, designed by Peter Henry Bruce, an engineer previously employed by Peter the Great of Russia. The fort was seized by the Americans briefly during the Revolutionary War.

The Retreat, Bahamas National Trust: The Trust's headquarters, east of Nassau near Queen's College, is on an eleven-acre site where Arthur and Margaret Langlois, beginning in 1925, created one of the world's largest private collections of palm trees—about 175 species from around the world. The property was donated to the Trust and officially opened in 1985. The palm trees grow in a thick coppice forest with other native trees and shrubs. The gardens are maintained by volunteers from local garden clubs. Hours: Mon.–Fri., 9 A.M. to 5 P.M. Guided tours are given on Tues., Wed., and Thurs. at 11:45 A.M., or by appointment. (Tel. 393–1317.)

St. Augustine's Monastery: Near Fox Hill village. Father Jerome, the architect of several Anglican and Catholic churches in the Bahamas, designed the school and cloister of the monastery.

Wealthy colonialists originally settled in the area east of Nassau; there, dozens of fine mansions stand witness to the enormous wealth the early settlers amassed. Some sections also have small settlements of colorful West Indian–style houses built, after slavery was abolished, by former slaves granted plots of land. Four of the original settlements are Adelaide, Carmichael, Fox Hill, and Gambier.

EXCURSION BOAT TRIPS

Glass-bottom boats, catamarans, and other excursion boats depart from the pier area frequently throughout the day for guided tours of nearby reefs, Coral World, and the 40-acre Sea Gardens. Some boats stop for a swim and snorkeling in the vicinity of the north shore; other boats take bathers and sight-seers to Paradise Beach or other nearby islets. Some offer sunset and moonlight dinner cruises as well. Prices range from $40 and up.

The *Atlantis I* recreational submarine departs from West Bay near Lyford Cay to visit nearby coral reefs. These excursions are sold on almost all cruise ships for $74, adults; $37, children. You will not save money doing it on your own as the departure point is a 20-minute ride from the pier.

ATTRACTIONS ON PARADISE ISLAND

Facing Nassau's north shore is Paradise Island, connected to Nassau by a half-mile bridge and a ferry from Prince George Wharf. Initially, the island resort was put on the map by A&P heir Huntington Hartford, whose home became the centerpiece of the fashionable Ocean Club. In 1994, Sun International acquired Paradise Island, changing the name of the resort to Atlantis and making major changes.

Atlantis Resort and Casino complex includes eight hotels, 12 restaurants, a cavernous casino, an enormous dinner theater, an 18-hole championship golf course, a 12-court tennis complex, horseback riding, a marina, a full range of water sports, and an interna-tional airport with flights to several Florida cities. Atlantis' centerpiece is a 14-acre Waterscape, with the largest outdoor, open-water aquarium in the world with six exhibit lagoons, more than 40 waterfalls, five swimming pools, three underground grottos, and an underwater walkway with windows for viewing sharks and artificial coral reefs.

The resort has a new day-rate option based on availability, which is especially useful for cruise passangers. For $30 per person, day guests may use any of the water facilities, which include five swimming pools, and have access to the "hospitality cavern," which has changing rooms, showers, and towels. Since the option is extended when the resort is not fully booked and space is available, you may want to call in advance: 809–363–3000. Ask for the Lagun Pool Towel Hut. The hotel also has tours of the resort and aquarium.

Versailles Gardens and French Cloister: Landscaped gardens, adjacent to the Ocean Club on the island's northeast side, are enclosed by the stones and arches of a twelfth-century Augustinian monastery, which Huntington Hartford had shipped from France stone by stone and reconstructed here. From the hotel's swimming pool, the gardens rise in seven terraces to the cloisters, which overlook a small garden and the sea; each terrace is embellished with ancient as well as modern statues of historic figures such as Empress Josephine of France, Franklin D. Roosevelt, and Dr. Stanley Livingstone. A visit to the gardens can be combined with lunch at the Ocean Club's Terrace Cafe, one of the Bahamas' prettiest settings.

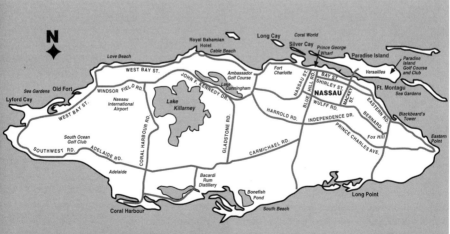

NEW PROVIDENCE

SHOPPING IN NASSAU

With the increase in the number of cruise passengers in recent years, shopping in Nassau has greatly improved in quality and selection and closely rivals St. Thomas with goods from the four corners of the globe. Now, too, the Bahamas' advertising tagline "It just keeps getting better in the Bahamas" has new meaning. After dropping the duty on most luxury goods—such as jewelry and perfumes—in January 1992, making prices on these items 25 percent or more below those in the United States, the Bahamian government recently passed an ordinance to allow stores to open on Sunday, particularly to accommodate cruise ships that are in port on that day. The Tourist Information Center in Rawson Square can provide information about duty-free shopping.

At Rawson Square, you can turn east or west on Bay Street and you will find every type of shop—dress, sportswear, shoes, men's clothing, liquor, perfume, and more. The newest shops and small shopping plazas are east of the square, while the stores on the west are generally the more established ones. The free promotional booklet *Best Buys in the Bahamas* is useful for maps and store descriptions. It usually has coupons for free gifts and discounts too.

Before the day has ended, you will certainly want to visit the Straw Market on Bay Street; it is open daily. It is one of the best of its kind in the tropics and crammed full of handcrafted baskets, hats, handbags, dolls, and other inexpensive gifts to take home to relatives and friends. You can watch the items emerge from the skilled fingers of a Bahamian craftswoman and even have them handmade-to-order with your own design and initials. Don't hesitate to bargain in the market; the ladies expect it and enjoy the exchange. And it's fun!

In addition to Bay Street, there are shopping arcades in hotels, particularly on Paradise Island and Cable Beach. Stores are open Monday through Saturday from 9 A.M. to 5 P.M. Many also open on Sundays; some close on Thursday afternoons. All stores mentioned below are on Bay Street unless indicated otherwise.

ART AND ANTIQUES: *Caripelago* (East Bay St.) is the new location of the most attractive art store in Nassau. You will find paintings, masks, and carvings along with stylishly designed T-shirts and jewelry by leading Bahamanian artists such as Maxwell Taylor, as well as promising unknowns. At the back of the store is a coffee bar will the latest flavors; it also sells spices and jams from the islands. *Marlborough Antiques* (Marlborough Street) has English antiques, old maps, gifts, and works by local artists, particularly R. Brent Malone, who is best known for his brilliant canvases of Junkanoo. Other names to look for are Manon Selby who sketches expressive, pensive faces; Reynolds, who uses humorous local settings for subjects; Eddie Minnis, who is also a singer and songwriter; and Chan Pratt.

BAHAMIAN BATIKS: Native Bahamian designs on cotton and other fabrics are printed by *Androsia* on the Bahamian island of Andros and made into sportswear sold in high-quality stores. The widest selections are available at *Mademoiselle.*

BOOKS: *The Island Shop* is something of a department store and sells everything from cameras to cashmeres, swimsuits, and sportswear; the book department on the second floor is the best in town.

CHILDREN: If you want a fun, unusual, and interesting gift for a small child, bookstores, newsstands, and pharmacies stock a series of coloring books on Bahamian flowers, birds and fish, shells, ships, and Junkanoo. For expensive items, *Linen & Lace* has lovely hand-smocked and embroidered children's clothes.

CHINA AND CRYSTAL: For the best selections of English bone china, Waterford, and other fine crystal, *Bernard's China and Gift Shop, John Bull,* and *Little Switzerland* have large selections with savings of up to 35 percent on china and crystal, representing among the best buys in duty-free goods in the Bahamas. You will be better prepared to recognize a bargain when you come with prices from home. Have the name of the pattern as well as the manufacturer for accurate comparisons.

DIVE SUPPLIES: *Bahamas Divers* outfits divers and snorkelers; *Pyfrom's* carries T-shirts, Sea Island cotton shirts, and souvenirs, as well as masks and flippers for children and adults.

JEWELRY: *Coin of the Realm* (14 Charlotte Street) has not only coins but also a large selection of precious and semiprecious stones, gold and silver jewelry, and stamps.

LEATHER: *Leather Masters* (17 Bank Lane) and the *Brass and Leather Shops* (14 Charlotte Street) carry fine Italian bags, briefcases, shoes, and other leather goods. *Fendi* and *Gucci* have their own shops in prime locations. Savings are about 20 percent, if that much, over U.S. prices.

PERFUMES: *The Perfume Shop* has several outlets on Bay Street and in the Paradise Island Shopping Centre. Their prices are as competitive as any we have found. Actually, French perfume prices are set by French perfume makers; any dealer who undercuts the price is cut off from the supply. For local products, *Bahamas Fragrance and Cosmetic Factory* (Charlotte Street) has skin creams, sunscreens, and perfumes.

SPORTSWEAR: Many shops along East Bay Street have inexpensive selections. *Cotton Ginny* has attractive, all-cotton sportswear at reasonable prices. *Everyone's Talking* (Prince George Plaza) has very original playclothes and sportswear for women. *Seventeen Shop* has a large selection of large sizes, along with a full range of standard sizes, in dresses as well as shorts, shirts, and slacks.

SWEATERS AND WOOLENS: *The Scottish Shop* has many of the best-known Scottish cashmeres and a full line of Shetlands.

WATCHES: *John Bull* (Bay Street and Paradise Island) is one of the oldest and largest stores in the Bahamas. It carries all the famous makes from novelty watches to Corum and Cartier, as well as a full line of cameras and photo equipment.

WOMEN'S FASHIONS: *Cole's of Nassau* (Parliament Street) has the largest selection of sophisticated women's fashions, but many are familiar labels that sell for less in New York. For less expensive clothes, check the shops on Bay Street east of Rawson Square.

DINING AND RESTAURANTS IN NASSAU

Restaurants and hotel dining rooms range from elegant and sophisticated as befits a world capital to simple and unpretentious as suits an unhurried tropical resort. You can enjoy a barbecue on the beach, a fish fry by the harbor, or a gourmet treat in the romantic ambience of a colonial home.

The variety of international cuisine includes French, English, Italian, American, Chinese, Indian, and Greek, but you really should try some Bahamian specialties before the day is out. The best known are johnnycakes, a corn bread; conch chowder, spicy and delicious; conch fritters or deep-fried grouper; or pigeon peas and rice, to mention a few. Prices range from $4 for lunch at a typical local restaurant to $100 for dinner at the top gourmet havens.

Always check your bill before you leave a tip. Many restaurants in the Bahamas and the Caribbean have taken up the European custom of adding a 15-percent service charge to the bill. If so, you do not need to leave a tip, unless the service has been exceptional and you want to leave something more.

Bahamian Kitchen (Trinity Place; Tel. 325–0702), one block from the Straw Market, has Bahamian specialties. Moderate.

Buena Vista (Delancy Street; Tel. 322–2811). Continental cuisine by candlelight in the elegant setting of a historic eighteenth-century house surrounded by beautiful gardens. Dinner only. Expensive.

Coco's Cafe (Marlborough Street, across from British Colonial Hotel) has good salads, sandwiches, and snacks in a cheerful setting resembling a large ice-cream parlor. Inexpensive.

Gaylords (Dowdeswell Street, off Bay Street; Tel.356–3004). Situated in a 125-year-old Bahamian house, Gaylords is the first member of the international Indian restaurant chain to open in the Bahamas and Caribbean. The menu includes Tandoori, Punjabi, Nepalese, and Mughali dishes. It has carry-out service, too. Moderate. Next door is *Gaylords Spice Shop*, which sells the ingredients for preparing Indian receipes.

Green Shutters (Parliament Street; Tel. 325–5702) is an English pub serving five kinds of draft beer and Bahamian and English specialties. Moderate.

Palm Tree Restaurant (Market and Cockburn streets; not to be confused with one of a similar name on Bay Street) is a local takeout restaurant "over the hill." It's famous among Bahamians for having the best conch fritters in town. Next door, *Mama Liddy's* offers table service. Inexpensive.

Pick-a-Dilly (18 Parliament Street; Tel. 322–2836) has an eclectic menu of Bahamian cuisine and American selections in an outdoor garden, only two blocks from the port. Most of the selections are good original recipes. There is usually music by a guitarist or small combo. Moderate.

Pisces Restaurant & Lounge (West Bay Street; Tel. 327–8827), part of Sun Fun Resorts, is one of Nassau's best restaurants for local dishes, particularly seafood. And Sun Fun's *Seaside Sports Bar* has live satellite sports on a 54-inch TV. Moderate

The Poop Deck (East Bay Street; Tel. 393–8175). For Bahamian and seafood specialties in a rustic atmosphere at lunch or dinner. The restaurant has great conch chowder, fritters, and key lime pie in a fabulous setting by the water overlooking Paradise Island Bridge. Moderate.

Sugar Reef Harbourside Bar and Grille (Bay & Deveaux Streets; Tel. 356-3065) is one of Nassau's newest restaurants overlooking the harbor. It has a casual atmosphere for enjoying salads, sandwiches, and burgers at lunch; pastas, seafood, and Bahamian and Caribbean specialties for dinner. There's a daily happy hour, 5–7:30 P.M.

Sun and . . . (Lakeview Drive; Tel. 393–1205), one of the most popular restaurants in Nassau, serves continental cuisine on the patio of a Bahamian house created by a Belgian chef and his wife. Dinner only; closed Mondays in August and September. Jacket required for men. Expensive.

Tamarind Hill Restaurant and Music Bar (Village Road; Tel. 393–1306), in an old Bahamian house painted up like a tapestry, is breezy and fun. It's a popular stop for happy hour and live guitar music on Wednesday, Friday, and Saturday. The eclectic menu has mango glaze pork, grouper in nut crust, and oven-roasted vegetarian pizza. It's at least a 15-minute drive east of the port.

Traveller's Rest (West Bay Street; Tel. 327–7633) is something of a drive from town, but it's worth it for the food and delightful country setting under huge shade trees overlooking the aqua sea. Here you can try fried grouper with peas and rice, and plantains, which are similar to fried bananas. Moderate.

And lots of places can satisfy your pizza craze— *Domino's, Paradise Island,* and *Swank's,* to name a few.

SPORTS IN NASSAU AND ENVIRONS

The Bahamas has some of the best sports facilities in the tropics, available in or near enough to Nassau or Freeport for cruise passengers to use them with relative ease. When facilities for sports such as tennis or golf are available at a hotel, contact the hotel or the sports operator in advance, particularly during the peak season when demand is likely to be high. When you want specific information on any sport, phone the Bahamas Sports Line, 1–800–32–SPORT.

BEACHES: So fine are the beaches that picking the best is difficult. For hotel beaches, the nearest to the port is the British Colonial, but if you go a little farther west, you have all of Cable Beach, dubbed the Bahamian Riviera. Most of Paradise Island is fringed by white sand.

BIKING: The island is rather flat, and roads away from the main arteries with heavy traffic are easy for biking. Bikes can be rented within walking distance of the pier, at a stand next to the British Colonial Hotel, for about $10–15 per day.

BOATING: It may seem strange for a cruise passenger to get off one vessel only to climb aboard another, but many people find it a wonderful way to spend their day in port. What better way to enjoy the magnificent waters than by chartering a boat? Almost any size or type, sail

or power, with or without crew, is available. You can explore, swim, and picnic at your own pace. *Nassau Yacht Haven* (P.O. Box SS 5693, Nassau; Tel. 393–8173) can provide information on yachts and fishing boats.

DEEP-SEA FISHING: The Bahamas is a magnet for sports fishermen. World records for marlin and other big game are made and broken year after year. Deep-sea fishing can be enjoyed almost anywhere in the Bahamas in ideal weather conditions throughout the year, and the variety of fish is endless. January to late April is the best season for white marlin and amberjack; June through August for blue marlin and kingfish. Ocean bonito, blackfin tuna, and Allison tuna are caught from May to September. Grouper can be found in reefy areas year-round; kingfish are plentiful in winter; dolphin is found in deep waters in winter and spring. And there is bluefin tuna, sailfish, wahoo, and more. Andros calls itself the bonefishing capital of the world.

Boats depart from Nassau Yacht Harbor on regular half-day fishing trips at 8:30 A.M. and 12:30 P.M. for $50 per person, with six persons per boat. The price includes bait and tackle. Contact *Chubasco Charters,* Capt. Mike Russell, 242–322–8148; fax, 242–326–4140. Charter rates, which include tackle, bait, ice, and fuel, range from about $200–300 for a half day; $400–500 for a full day for boats accommodating up to six people.

The Bahamas Sports Information Center (800–32–SPORT) has copies of *The Bahamas Fishing Guide* with pictures and descriptions of the main sportfishing targets and their seasons, plus a wealth of other information. The center can provide you with an up-to-date schedule of the fishing tournaments held during the year.

GOLF: A baker's dozen of Bahamian courses, designed by the most famous architects in the world of golf, are as beautiful to see as they are challenging to play. The Bahamas' tropical island landscape provides lovely emerald fairways bordered by flowering trees and palms. Most courses are part of resort complexes and have resident pros, pro shops, and clubhouses.

Nassau/Paradise Island has five courses. The closest to the port is the *Cable Beach Golf Course;* 800–327–6000 (7,040 yards, par 72). This championship course was the Bahamas' first when it was built in 1926. Renovated in 1990 and again in 1996, it has a clubhouse, pro shop, and restaurant. Greens fees for 18 holes are $60 per person; cart for two people, $45.

Paradise Island Golf Course; 800–321–3000 (6,776 yards, par 72). Designed by Dick Wilson and part of the Atlantis Resort and Casino complex. The championship course has what may be the world's largest sand trap—the entire left side of the fifth hole is a white sand beach. The course hosts the PGA-sanctioned Bahamas Classic in January, which attracts many top pros and is carried on ESPN. Greens fees for 18 holes: $100 including cart.

(For Freeport golf clubs, see section on Freeport. For those in the Family Islands, see Eleuthera later in this chapter.)

HORSEBACK RIDING/RACING: *Happy Trails Stables* (Coral Harbour; Tel. 362–1820), open daily except Sunday. A riding tour costs about $40 including round-trip transportation to the stables from town.

PARASAILING: *Paradise Para-sail, Ltd.* (Britannia Towers, Tel. 363–3000) will give you a bird's-eye view of Paradise, and offers waterskiing and windsurfing too. The cost is $20 for five minutes; $35 for ten minutes.

SNORKELING AND SCUBA DIVING: The spectacular underwater world of the Bahamas has something for everyone, no matter what your level of expertise. Snorkelers and novice divers can simply swim off a beach to discover fantastic coral gardens only 10 or 20 feet below the surface of the water.

More experienced divers can explore drop-offs that start at 40 feet and plunge thousands. They can swim into underwater caverns and tunnels teeming with fish and roam through waters with visibility as great as 200 feet. Masks and flippers are readily available, as are diving equipment and instruction. And those who cannot swim need not miss the fun. At *Coral World* (Tel. 328–1036), one can walk down into the sea in an underwater observatory.

Most ships that sail on three- and four-day cruises from Florida visit their "own" island, usually one of the Out Islands. The highlight of the day is snorkeling or diving directly from shore in water so incredibly clear you don't need a mask to see the colorful fish and fantastic coral. (It is, of course, more practical to wear a mask.) *Bahamas Divers* (East Bay Street; Tel. 393–5644); *Divers Haven* (Tel. 393–0869); and *Nassau Scuba Centre* (Tel. 362–1964) have daily snorkeling excursions for $20–25. They also offer dive trips (all gear provided) with one-tank dives for $35 and two-tank dives for $55 or $60. *Nassau Scuba Centre* has a learn-to-dive course for $50. The selection of dive sites often depends on level of skill of participants. Dive operators offer instruction as well.

The hottest fad is shark diving—yes, shark! *Dive Dive Dive Ltd.* (Tel. 362–1143) takes experienced divers to see bull, reef, and silky sharks, several days a week, for $75.

TENNIS/SQUASH/RACQUETBALL: In the Bahamas, where the weather is ideal for play year-round, tennis is

as popular as any water sport. There are no less than 100 courts and excellent facilities with pros and pro shops, instruction and daily clinics available at hotels and resorts in Nassau, Cable Beach, and Paradise Island. Many courts are lighted for evening play. Since most hotels do not charge guests for the use of courts, you will need to make special arrangements in advance by writing or calling the hotel to request court time.

Hotels nearest the port with the best facilities and night lights are on Cable Beach. *Nassau Beach Hotel* (Box N 7756, Nassau; Tel. 327–7711; 800–223–5672) has six Plexipave courts. The resort also offers windsurfing, sailing, snorkeling, and other water sports. The *Palace Spa* at the *Nassau Marriott Resort* (Box N 8306, Nassau; Tel. 327–6200; 800–453–5301) has 18 Har-Tru courts, 3 squash courts, and 3 racquetball courts. The sports center has a well-equipped health club, jogging area, spa treatments, and other programs.

On Paradise Island, *Ocean Club* (Box N 4777, Nassau; Tel. 363–2518; 800–321–3000) has nine Har-Tru courts. The lovely setting is the site of the annual Marlboro Open in December, which attracts top-ranked international players. *Atlantis Resort* complex (Tel. 363–3000; 800–321–3000) has 12 Laykold courts. The Bahamas International Open is held here annually in late summer. The resort has water sports on a 3-mile beach, golf, and health club.

WATERSKIING: It is easy to do in the calm Bahamian waters and available at hotels at about $20 for 3 miles or three "falls" in Nassau for up to $40, for 30 minutes.

WINDSURFING: The protection the shallows and reefs give to most parts of the Bahamian coast also makes its many bays excellent places to learn to windsurf. Try it once and you'll be hooked! Instruction is available to get you started. The cost is about $20. The annual Windsurfing Regatta is held in January.

ENTERTAINMENT

CULTURAL EVENTS AND NIGHTLIFE

Bahamians—and visitors—make something of a ritual of watching the pretty sunsets. So when the air begins to cool and the sun starts its fall, you can grab a *Bahama Mama* (that's the local rum punch) and head for the beach. You'll probably be joined by kindred spirits, a scratch band, or other local musicians for some impromptu jamming.

After the sun disappears and the stars are out, you can stay on the beach with the calypso beat or change into something a bit dressier for a round of the Bahamas' razzle-dazzle nightlife. The 1,000-seat theater of *Crystal Palace Casino* and *Atlantis Show Room* (Paradise Island) have Las Vegas–style shows nightly. Their theaters are adjacent to the casino, where you can choose blackjack, roulette, craps, baccarat, or slot machines to play, and if your luck runs out, you can laugh it off at Atlantis' *Jokers Wild Comedy Club*. The resorts also have discos, several bars, and restaurants. *The Zoo* (West Bay Street; Tel. 322-7195) is Nassau nightlife bigtime—a three-story night club with a tri-level dance floor and one of the biggest sound and light systems in the Caribbean. You can dance to soca, calypso, or reggae or hang out at one of the six theme bars or outdoor section with live entertainment. Happy hour starts at 8 P.M. and the dancing goes to 4 A.M. There is a cover charge of $20 weekdays, $40 weekends. *Rock 'n' Roll Cafe* (Cable Beach; Tel. 327–7639) in the Frilsham House, a beautiful Bahamian beachfront mansion next to the Nassau Beach Hotel, is open seven days a week from noon to 2 A.M., with music at a volume that separates generations.

For those who want something on the cultural side, the *Dundas Centre for the Performing Arts* (Mackey Street; Tel. 322–2728) offers plays, musicals, ballets, and folkloric shows.

FESTIVALS AND CELEBRATIONS

Bahamians love to celebrate. From January to December the calendar is full of sporting events, music festivals, historic commemorations, religious feasts, and national holidays. All are windows on island life not open to visitors at other times of the year. You can watch the fun from the sidelines or join the parade, sing along with the music, and try the dances. And if you bring your camera, you'll run out of film before you run out of subjects to photograph.

JUNKANOO, A NATIONAL FESTIVAL

Of all the festivals, none compares to Junkanoo, an exuberant Bahamian celebration full of color and creativity, humor, rhythm and music, dance, fun, and festivity. The national extravaganza traces its origins to the West African dance and mask traditions kept alive throughout the West Indies by slaves brought to the New World in the seventeenth and eighteenth centuries. After emancipation in the early nineteenth century Junkanoo was suppressed by religious zealots,

both black and white. It had nearly died out when it was revived in the 1970s as part of the effort to preserve the Bahamas' multifaceted heritage.

Now, once again, Junkanoo is part of the Bahamian tradition reflected in the art, dance, and music. It has been taken into the schools, where the construction of costumes is part of the curriculum, and sent abroad by the musicians and entertainers, where it is receiving international recognition.

Junkanoo is the Bahamian version of Carnival, with parades, costumes, and music, but unlike traditional Carnival, it is held at the end of the year and the start of the new one. The first Junkanoo parade starts at daybreak on December 26, Boxing Day, a public holiday stemming from British tradition. Bahamians and visitors who feel the spirit don brilliant costumes and parade through downtown Nassau to the clatter of cowbells, horns, whistles, and the driving beat of African drums. Prizes are awarded to those with the most unusual and elaborate costumes—all made from cardboard and strips of paper laid down in tight layers. Every display must be able to be carried by one person; nothing on wheels is allowed.

Participants and viewers need to be on the street before daylight—it's all over by 8 A.M. (Photographers need fast film as the light is still low at parade time.) Bleachers are set up in the judging area on Bay Street west of Rawson Square, and the judging takes places from 6 to 7 A.M. Costumes that do not win are often dumped in the street and make fine souvenirs.

The celebration is repeated on New Year's Eve after the private parties at homes and hotels wind down and the streets begin to fill with late-night revelers. It lasts through New Year's Day. But visitors do not have to wait to the year's end to see Junkanoo. They can sample it at some nightclub and folkloric shows and other celebrations throughout the year and visit the Junkanoo Expo by the port, where many of the winning costumes are displayed.

GOOMBAY, A SUMMER FESTIVAL

Goombay Summer Festival is a series of special events for visitors featuring the music of Junkanoo and Goombay. Different events give visitors an opportunity to experience the Bahamians' Bahamas with their music and dance, culture, crafts, and cuisine.

Goombay has several derivations and has come to have several meanings. Historically, it referred to the drumbeats and rhythms of Africa brought to the Bahamas by slaves and free blacks. The term was used during the ring-play and jump-in dances when the drummer would shout *Gimbey* at the beginning of each dance.

Today, Goombay is used to refer to all Bahamian secular music, especially that using the traditional goat-skin drum, a barrel-shaped drum made from wooden kegs with goat or sheep skin covering one end, positioned between the legs and played with bare hands. The word *Goombay* is still used in West Africa, especially by Ibo tribes, who have a similar drum they call Gamby.

OTHER FESTIVALS AND EVENTS

Independence Week in early July is another holiday filled with festivities, parades, and fireworks to celebrate the independence of the Commonwealth of the Bahamas. It culminates on Independence Day, July 10, with fireworks at Clifford Park.

Emancipation Day, the first Monday in August, is a public holiday which commemorates the abolition of slavery in 1834. It is followed on Tuesday by Fox Hill Day. In the old days, Fox Hill was isolated from Nassau; hence, the residents did not learn about the Emancipation until later. And so, symbolically, they celebrate on the second day.

October 12, Discovery Day, is a public holiday with special meaning in the Bahamas. It was on a Bahamian island, which the native Lucayan Indians called Guanahani, that Christopher Columbus landed in 1492. Columbus renamed the island San Salvador.

Another October highlight is the formal opening of the Supreme Court when the chief justice, dressed in the traditional robe and wig, is escorted by the commissioner of police to inspect the Police Honor Guard while the famous Police Band strikes up the band. An equally colorful event with pomp and pageantry is the formal opening of Parliament, usually in February.

The Christmas festivities begin in mid-December with an annual candlelight procession staged by the Renaissance Singers. The group performs at Government House ballroom and the Dundas Centre for the Performing Arts with a repertoire ranging from Renaissance classics to modern spirituals. For information on tickets, contact the Ministry of Education, Division of Cultural Affairs (Tel. 322–8119). Although the performances are usually sold out early, the ministry makes an effort to accommodate visitors.

FREEPORT

GRAND BAHAMA ISLAND

When American financier Wallace Groves began to turn his dream into reality in the 1950s, Grand Bahama Island, 60 miles from Florida, was little more than limestone, pine trees, and brush. From the money he earned lumbering the pine, he began developing the island. Today Freeport, as it is better known, is the second largest town and largest industrial area in the Bahamas and a major international resort.

Freeport spent the 1960s in the limelight, particularly after Cuba went by the board as an American playground, but by the 1970s it had lost much of its luster. The recession, worldwide economic problems, and competition from new resorts in Florida and elsewhere resulted in a setback for Freeport.

A renaissance began in 1984 with the multimillion-dollar renovation of the Princess Hotels and Casino. This was followed the next year by the $40-million facelift and expansion of the 500-acre Lucayan Beach Hotel and Casino, which had been closed since 1976. Port Lucaya, a shopping and entertainment complex, was added along with the "Dolphin Experience" attraction.

Freeport also got another boost when it became a popular cruise stop, especially for short cruises from Florida. These cruises bring more visitors to the island in a month than many islands see in a year. And, on a smaller scale, there is as much for them to enjoy here as in Nassau. The island has an active People-to-People program similar to that in Nassau, as well as a large variety of restaurants, two glittering casinos, a famous international shopping bazaar, and six golf courses.

IN BRIEF

LOCATION: Grand Bahama Island is about 80 miles from end to end. The cruise ship port, situated on the south coast at the mouth of Hawksbill Creek, is about five miles from the town of Freeport where the Bahamas Princess Hotel and Casino, its golf courses, and the International Bazaar are located. Another five miles east along Sunrise Highway takes you to the Lucayan residential and resort area where major hotels front expansive white sand beaches on the south shore and offer an array of water sports.

TRANSPORTATION: Metered taxis are available at the port, downtown Freeport, and at hotels. Rates are supposed to be fixed at $2 flag-fall and 20 cents each one-fifth mile for one or two passengers; $2 for each additional passenger.

If you plan to engage a taxi for sight-seeing, you should negotiate the price in advance. Rates are $12 per hour for a five-passenger car; $15 for larger ones. Also, you should be aware there are free-lancers who are not legal taxis and who will charge whatever they think they can get. Look for taxis with a "Bahama Host" sticker on the windshield. They are reliable and the best informed.

Town buses or jitneys (65 cents) run during the day from town to Lucayan and West End. However, as a cruise passenger with limited time, you are better off hiring a taxi or renting a car if you want to visit either end of the island.

CAR RENTALS: To rent a car with a credit card, you must be 21 years or older; without the card, 25 years or older. Americans may use U.S. driver's licenses for up to three months. Car rentals are available from several locations in town and at major hotels. When you have reserved a car in advance with Avis, Hertz, or National, they will deliver your car free of charge to the port. Expect to pay $50 and up for a subcompact with unlimited mileage. Jeeps are available too.

Avis, Tel. 352–7666;

Courtesy Car, Tel. 352–5212;

Hertz, Tel. 352–9250;

National, Tel. 352–9300;

Star Rent a Car, Tel. 352–5953

And remember, Bahamians drive on the **LEFT.** You will need a map and a good sense of direction because even new maps are not up-to-date. Do not hesitate to ask anyone for directions.

MOPEDS/BICYCLES: You can rent a bike at the International Bazaar in Freeport. A valid driver's license and a helmet supplied by the rental agency are compulsory. Prices are about $30 per day. To repeat, *DRIVING IS ON THE LEFT.*

SHOPPING: Freeport has as much shopping appeal as Nassau. The *International Bazaar,* housing dozens of boutiques with merchandise from all over the world, set the standard for other tourist destinations when it first opened in the 1960s. It has since been expanded to hold about 75 shops where you can buy anything from $2 T-shirts to $2,000 emeralds. Among the familiar names are Columbian Emeralds, Fendi, and Little Switzerland. Other shopping centers in the Freeport area are Town Centre and Churchill Square.

Next to the International Bazaar, *The Perfume Factory,* which houses *Fragrance of the Bahamas,* is set in a replica of an old Bahamian mansion, where various scents for ladies and gents are made. Guides dressed in period costumes give visitors a tour and explain how the essences, made only fromnatural plants, are blended into perfumes and other products. There are six standard fragrances, and you can also create your own scent, which will be officially registered in your name. Perfumes, lotions, and T-shirts are available for purchase. The fragrance Guanahani—the original name of San Salvador, where Columbus made his first landfall—was created in 1992 to mark the Quincentennial.

Port Lucaya, a waterside shopping, entertainment, and water-sports complex in the heart of the Lucayan resort area, has over 40 stores, snack bars, and restaurants in attractive, colonial-style buildings. "Celebration Circle," the entertainment center, features steel bands, reggae groups, and other entertainment.

Many of the best-known Nassau stores have outlets in Freeport and Lucaya. Generally, shops are open Monday through Thursday, 9:30 A.M. to 3 P.M., and Friday to 5 P.M. However, some shops stay open to 6 P.M., and others, such as Oasis, which sells perfumes, toiletries, and jewelry, are open until 10:30 P.M. Some stores open on Saturday morning; the straw market and pharmacies open on Sundays.

BEACHES AND WATER SPORTS: Grand Bahama has some of the finest beaches in the Bahamas. Among the best with hotels and facilities is Xanadu Beach, south of the Princess Hotel complex, five miles from the port; and Lucayan Beach, 11 miles east of the port. If you prefer an undeveloped beach with miles of sand all to yourself, head toward West End. Several minor roads between Harry's American Bar and Buccaneer lead to lovely beaches. The Lucayan National Park on the south coast is a drive of about 30 minutes from town. Freeport also has terrific fishing, sailing, and windsurfing at prices generally less than in Nassau. All beachfront hotels have windsurfing equipment.

Freeport's facilities for scuba and snorkeling are not only the best in the Bahamas, they are among the best in the world. It is home base for *UNEXSO, Underwater Explorers Society* (Box F–2433; Tel. 373–1244; 800–922–3483). Their facility, adjacent to Port Lucaya, offers eight levels of instruction and includes an 18-foot deep diver training pool and pro shop. The facility also has a recompression chamber.

An introductory lesson with equipment, three hours of professional instruction, and a dive with your instructor on a shallow reef trip costs $79. There is a daily snorkeling trip for $15. For experienced divers, the society has three dive trips daily, including night dives. A three-dive package with all gear is $75.

THE DOLPHIN EXPERIENCE: UNEXSO has six Atlantic bottlenose dolphins as part of a program to observe how the animals interact with humans under highly controlled circumstances. The dolphins are also released to the open sea daily to swim with scuba divers on the coral reef. Offered in its short form several times daily, the Experience starts with a briefing for participants and is followed by a 20-minute session at the nature reserve created for the Dolphin Experience. Here, a small number of people at a time are allowed to wade into a shallow holding pen to stroke the dolphins while the animals swim in and out on whistle signals from the guide. Cost is $30 adult; no charge for children five years and under.

Although the management does not encourage this activity, it advertises that you can arrange—in advance—to swim or snorkel with the dolphins in the reef-protected waters near the reserve. Cost is $85.

TENNIS: Tennis, too, is popular and readily available at the *Bahamas Princess Resort and Casino,* with 12 courts and the most convenient location to the port. Rates are very reasonable.

GOLF: Freeport has almost half the golf courses in the Bahamas. Those nearest the port are the pair of championship courses at the *Bahamas Princess Hotel and Golf Club* (Tel. 352–6721). The Emerald Course (6,679 yards, par 72) designed by Dick Wilson has 84 bunkers and is considered the toughest on the island; the Ruby Course (6.750 yards, par 72) was designed by Joe Lee. Greens fees are $58 for hotel guests, $63 for non-guests with shared cart in winter, $46 and $51 in summer, for 18 holes; $20 club rental.

Lucayan Golf Course (Tel. 373–1066; 6,488 yards, par 72) is a 15-minute drive from the port. Also designed by Dick Wilson, the layout, noted for its fast greens, has several par fives over 500 yards long. Greens fees and shared cart are $44 in winter, $23 in summer for 18 holes; $22 and $21 for 9 holes. $20 club rental per set.

Some cruise lines have golf packages or will make arrangements for play for passengers. If not, you should call ahead for reservations. For cruise passengers who are planning to overnight here, some hotels have golf packages.

HORSEBACK RIDING: *Pinetree Stables* (Beachway Drive; Tel. 373–3600) offers trail rides three times daily, except Mondays.

INFORMATION: The Tourist Information Centre is located in the Sir Charles Hayward Library (Tel. 352–8044), and there are booths at Freeport Harbor (Tel. 352–9651), at the airport (Tel. 352–2052), and in the International Bazaar. The offices are open 8:30 A.M. to 5 P.M., Monday through Saturday.

EMERGENCY NUMBERS:

Medical Services: Rand Memorial Hospital, Tel. 352–6735

Police: Freeport, Tel. 911

Ambulance: Freeport, Tel. 352–2689

SIGHT-SEEING

In contrast to its high-living, high-stakes image, Freeport has several attractions that tell its history and highlight its tropical variety.

GARDEN OF THE GROVES This ten-acre park and botanical garden, named for Freeport's developer, is one of the loveliest spots in Freeport. It has footpaths through exotic tropical gardens with ponds and pretty waterfalls and places to sit to enjoy the peace and tranquility of the setting. At the entrance is the Grand Bahama Museum (Tel. 373–5668), a small museum with exhibits of Lucayan artifacts, a reconstructed Indian burial site found in one of the mysterious water-filled caverns that honeycomb the island and probably gave rise to the Fountain of Youth myth that led Ponce de León here in 1513.

The museum has a model of the Pine Ridge lumber railway, the early harbor, and a settlement house that was reconstructed out of Freeport's first airport terminal; a bush medicine garden; a thatch exhibit; and colorful costumes of Junkanoo. The Freeport Story, from the dream of Wallace Groves in 1955 to the three decades of development, is also displayed. Admission is $5 for adults; none for children up to ten years of age.

LUCAYAN NATIONAL PARK Located 25 miles west of Freeport near the former U.S. Army Missile Tracking Base, the Lucayan National Park (Tel. 352–5438) is about a 30-minute drive from downtown. The 40-acre park, opened in 1985, is situated on land donated to the National Trust by the Grand Bahama Development Company and is composed of four different ecological zones. The park, designed by Freeport planner Peter Barratt, has a 1,000-foot-wide beach with some of the highest dunes on the island. Gold Rock Creek, which is bounded by extensive mangroves, flows through the park to the sea. Among the flora are coca plums, seagrapes, sea oats, and casuarinas. Another area has Ming trees, wild tamarind, mahogany, and cedar trees.

The park is also the entrance to one of the world's longest charted cave systems, but access to the caves is restricted to scientists and archaeologists who must have permission from the National Trust. Lucayan Indian relics have been found inside the caverns.

There are footpaths and raised wooden walkways over the mangroves to the beach and a map on display at the car park. Further information is available from the Rand Nature Center. The area is popular with birdwatchers, but the main reason to visit this area of the island is the lovely, untouched beaches.

RAND MEMORIAL NATURE CENTER (P.O. Box F–2954, Tel. 352–5438) Located 3 miles from the International Bazaar, the center, which is also the headquarters of the Bahamas National Trust, comprises 100 acres of tropical plants, trees, birds, and butterflies and is home to hundreds of species of plants and approximately ninety-six species of birds. A preserve for the native pine forests that once covered the island, it contains many species endangered by the island's continuing development.

An hour-long walking tour along winding trails provides an opportunity to see and photograph tropical flora, including many species of wild orchids and a great variety of birds. At the end of the trail, surrounded by numerous flowering exotic plants, is a pond that is home to a small group of flamingos. Hours: Mon.–Fri., 9 A.M. to 4 P.M.; Sat. to 1 P.M. Admission: $5 adults; $3 children ages 3 to 12. Guided tours are available.

BOAT EXCURSIONS Snorkeling trips, picnic trips, and sunset party cruises are available from *Pat & Diane* (Tel. 373–8681) and *Reef Tours* (Tel. 373–5880), all departing from Port Lucaya. The latter also claims to have the largest glass-bottom boat on the seas. It departs daily from the Port Lucaya marina at 10:30 A.M. and 12:30 and 2:30 P.M. on reef cruises. Prices range from $17 to $35, depending on the time of day, length of cruise, and amenities offered.

The Deepstar Submarine (Tel. 373–7934), based in Lucaya, is a new adventure in the first submarine with a completely transparent acrylic hull, which provides passengers with a panoramic view of the magnificent underwater environment. The vessel goes to depths of between 70 and 100 feet, and carries 45 passengers on a two-hour voyage. Operated by Comex Submarines Ltd., the Deepstar departs three times daily from the UNEXSO dock in Port Lucaya onto a ferry that takes them to the *Deepstar.* Cost: $49 adults, $41 children.

DINING AND RESTAURANTS IN FREEPORT

Like Nassau, Freeport has a great variety of restaurants, including inexpensive ones specializing in Bahamian dishes. The International Bazaar, Port Lucaya, and large resorts also provide many choices.

Fatman's Nephew offers patio dining on Bahamian specialties such as cracked conch. Popular in the Lucayan area on Taino Beach are the *Surfside Restaurant,* a rustic seaside tavern known for minced lobster, and *The Stone Crab,* which specializes in lobster and steaks.

On the more expensive side, *Pier One,* just west of the port, has a rustic setting where every table has a pretty view of the sea. The specialty is fresh seafood, particularly fresh oysters and the catch of the day, and there's calypso entertainment most of the time.

Every Wednesday evening a native fish fry dinner is held at *Smith's Point,* a small beachside settlement. Visitors dine on fresh seafood and can meet local residents. It's not an advertized event, but local taxi drivers know about it. Cost is about $6 per person.

Nightlife centers around the large hotels. Princess Casino Show has two shows, nightly except Monday, at 8:30 and 10:45 P.M.

A DRIVE AROUND GRAND BAHAMA ISLAND

To explore the less commercial side of Grand Bahama, a drive of 21 miles to West End will take you to the oldest settlements and some of the quieter corners of this surprising island.

If you are driving from the port or town head west on Queens Highway to Hawksbill Creek, where there are large piles of conch shells and where Abaco fishermen unload their catch. Continue along Fishing Hole Road to Eight Mile Rock, the largest native settlement on the island, aptly named for the 8 miles or so of rocky shore on its south coast. The colorful village of brightly painted wooden houses was settled around 1830. The picturesque *St. Stephens Anglican Church,* built directly on the sea, dates from 1851.

Queens Highway continues to Seagrape, another tiny hamlet with a reputation for making the best bread in the Bahamas. The next town is Holmes Rock where the *Hydroflora Gardens* are growing hydroponic tomatoes, cucumbers, and other vegetables. As you near West End, you pass the saltwater Pelican Lake and Bootle Bay.

West End, hugging the water's edge at the westernmost tip of Grand Bahama Island, is less than 60 speedboat miles away from the Florida coast. It is the oldest settlement on the island and has had at least two fast but fleeting booms—during the American Civil War as a base for southerners running ammunition and supplies through the Yankee blockade to Confederate forces, and during Prohibition when the likes of Al Capone found it a convenient shipping point for liquor from Europe.

After 1933, West End went back to being a sleepy fishing village, attracting such occasional deep-sea fishermen as Ernest Hemingway. Nothing else much happened until Billy Butlin of British resort fame built one of his holiday retreats, but it never had quite the success of its English seaside counterparts. It was followed by a Jack Tar Village, which also enjoyed a period of success but is now closed.

The road into town takes you by tiny wooden stalls beside mounds of conch shells where you can stop to watch one of the local fishermen prepare his day's catch for tomorrow's market. There's an old church built in 1893 and the *Star Hotel* (Tel. 346–6207), the island's first, built in 1946. The rickety wooden building, no longer a hotel, has a new lease on life. It is being renovated by the grandchildren of the original builder and, at present, houses a bar and a restaurant serving local food.

On your return trip, if you haven't lingered too long, you might stop at *Harry's American Bar* at Deadman's Reef. It's famous for sunsets and Harry's Hurricane—and if you take in too much of either, you are likely to miss your boat.

East End Adventures (242–373–6662): One of Grand Bahamas' newest additions are ecological excursions to the east end of the island, operated by two local residents, Tiffany Barrett and Clarence Bellof. You are picked up in early morning by Jeep for a drive to the east end to McLean's Town where you take a short boat ride to Sweeting's Cay—near yet remote—where you have a glimpse of local life and enjoy a drinks, a Bahamian picnic lunch, and swimming and snorkeling at a sublimely beautiful deserted beach. Cost is $100 per adult, $50 per child under 12.

THE FAMILY ISLANDS

The Other Bahamas—the hundreds of islands, islets, and cays which make up the Bahamas archipelago—are known as the Out Islands (meaning out beyond the main center of Nassau). They are the serene hideaways of our dreams, where endless miles of white and pink sand beaches are surrounded by gin-clear waters and where life is so laid back, ten people make a crowd. Only about three dozen islands have permanent settlements.

No cruise lines offer year-round cruises, but several ships occasionally call at one or two locations, and most ships on three- and four-night Bahama cruises from Florida stop for the day at one of the typical uninhabited islands. These are leased from the Bahamas government for an extended period of time and outfitted with the facilities and amenities to give their passengers a comfortable and fun-filled day at the beach.

THE ABACOS At the northern end of the Bahamas archipelago, a group of islands and cays is strung in boomerang fashion for 130 miles, coupling the Sea of Abaco, whose sheltered waters offer some of the Bahamas' best sailing. Two main islands, *Little Abaco* and *Great Abaco,* are joined by a causeway.

Walker's Cay, a well-known fishing resort, lies off the north tip of Little Abaco; Hole in the Wall at the south end of Great Abaco was a strategic location throughout the eighteenth century for guarding the shipping lanes to Nassau.

Marsh Harbour, the capital and main hub of the Abacos, is the third largest town of the Bahamas and one of the main boat-chartering centers of the Caribbean. It has a resident population of about 1,000 and an airport. Its small resorts are operated by native islanders or American and Canadian transplants. Guests dine on fresh fish and homemade island specialties, and enjoy lazy, sunny days sailing, snorkeling, windsurfing, or doing lots of nothing.

Wallys (on the main road at the edge of town; Tel. 367–2074) is a restaurant/bar in a pretty, pink, attractively furnished villa with a veranda overlooking a flower-filled lawn and the sea. The popular bar is known for its special tropical drinks; the restaurant serves lunch. There is also a boutique.

On nearby Elbow Cay, colonial Hope Town is one of many old settlements in the Bahamas that look like New England villages with palm trees. It is situated on a picture-postcard harbor complete with a candy-striped lighthouse and can be reached by ferry from Marsh Harbour. *Wyannie Malone Museum* (Tel. 366–0311), set in one of the island's oldest houses—it seems almost like a dollhouse, it is so small—is devoted to the island's history. In 1991, it won the American Express Heritage Award as an outstanding example of a small community's effort at preservation.

Of the Loyalists from New York who came in 1783 to join the English settlers living in the Abacos, some stayed at New Plymouth, another Cape Cod village in the tropics, on Green Turtle Cay. For many years it was the largest settlement and capital of the Abacos. In recent times, the old fishing village has become something of an artist colony whose members were attracted by its beauty and serenity and by two native sons—Alton Roland Lowe, a historian and one of the Bahamas' leading landscape artists, and James Mastin, an outstanding sculptor—who led the way.

The *Albert Lowe Museum,* created by Alton Lowe in honor of his father, who was a noted carver of ship models, is devoted to the history of the Abacos and to shipbuilding. It occupies a pretty Victorian house on the main street, a short walk from the town dock. Lowe's paintings, most of which depict local island subjects and settings, and Mastin's works are on view, and prints are available for sale.

A few steps from the museum on the same street is the *Memorial Sculpture Garden,* Mastin's contribution to the island. Opened in 1983 for the bicentennial of the island's Loyalist settlements, the bronze statues represent the people who shaped the history of the Bahamas down through the centuries from the first settlers to the present. The busts are placed around a central monument of two women—one white, one black—representing the Loyalists, plantation owners who fled the American Revolution with their slaves and were the earliest settlers.

Almost as famous as the artists is *Blue Bee Bar,* whose walls and ceiling are covered with thousands of business cards from around the world. Miss Emily, as Emily Cooper, the former proprietress was affectionately known, is credited with creating the Goombay Smash, a famous tropical drink served in bars throughout the Bahamas—although this churchgoing lady was a teetotaler and never tasted her famous drink. Now, the bar and its traditions are carried on by her daughter. The town also has several tiny hotels situated in houses dating from the eighteenth century. These nestle between the neat white clapboard cottages trimmed with pink, blue, yellow, or green and set in flowering gardens. The neighboring island of Green Turtle Cay, another popular boating center, can be reached by small ferry.

Less than an hour's drive west of Marsh Harbour through forested land is Treasure Cay, where *The Day of the Dolphin* with George C. Scott was filmed. Legend has it that 17 Spanish treasure galleons sank here in 1595. Some have been found; exploration for the others continues. In 1962, two entrepreneurs—one British, one American—developed a self-contained resort, Treasure Cay Beach Hotel and Villas, on 1,500 acres along a three-and-a-half-mile, half-moon beach of powdery sand washed by aqua seas.

Another island south of Marsh Harbour is Man-o-War Cay, famous for its boat builders who craft their vessels by hand. The cay has no cars, but in recent years progress has brought golf carts, which many of the American retirees who populate the island use to get around. One of Man-o-War Cay's enterprising natives has turned the family's sail-making tradition into a prosperous cottage industry producing sturdy tote bags, hats, and a variety of other products that are particularly prized by yachtsmen.

ANDROS A 30-minute flight west of Nassau will bring you to Andros, the largest island of the Bahamas and one of the least developed. The interior of the island is covered with pine forests interspersed with mangroves; other parts are mud flats or barren. Off the east coast of Andros lies the Barrier Reef, over 100 miles long, the third largest in the world. Just beyond is the Tongue of the Ocean, a depression that plunges as deep as 6,000 feet at the north end. These natural phenomena attract

divers and sportfishermen from around the world. Andros also calls itself the bonefishing capital of the world. Among the resorts, *Small Hope Bay Lodge* at Fresh Creek was the first organized diving resort in the Bahamas.

BERRY ISLANDS The group of about 30 islands with total land area of only 14 square miles is located between New Providence (Nassau) and Grand Bahama Island (Freeport). Most are uninhabited, and several are popular stops for cruise ships whose passengers spend the day on "their" island, enjoying the beaches and swimming and snorkeling in clear water. Their lovely little harbors, coves, and protected waters make them popular with yachtsmen.

THE BIMINIS South of Freeport where the Bahama Banks meet the Gulf Stream are the Biminis, the Bahamian islands only 50 miles from Florida. Ernest Hemingway was a frequent caller, and his old haunt, *The Compleat Angler,* a wooden frame hotel and bar, displays his paintings and writings from 1931 to 1937. Adam Clayton Powell, the flamboyant Harlem minister and congressman, made Bimini his second home. Long before either of them, however, Ponce de León stopped here in his search for the Fountain of Youth. No less than four places commemorate his landing.

The group is divided into the North Biminis and South Biminis and, along with Cat Cay, are among the prime game fishing centers in the Western Hemisphere. Because of their proximity to the Gulf Stream, Bimini waters teem with sea life. Vestiges of old ships in Bahamian waters number in the hundreds. Among the most famous is the *Sapona,* which lies between South Bimini and Cat Cay. Built by Henry Ford around 1915, the ship served as a private club and is said to have been a rum-runner's storehouse in the 1920s when it was blown ashore by a hurricane in 1929.

The main settlement is Alicetown on North Bimini. You can walk or bike around most of the island in an hour or so. Although the island takes on something of a rowdy party atmosphere in the evening (the fishing crowd at one of their favorite bars), during the day it is a sleepy little place, pleasant for picnicking and lazing on the beach. The best beach is the mile stretch of sand opposite a Cape Cod-type cottage called the Anchorage, which Hemingway used as his setting for *Islands in the Sun.* Another pretty beach shaded with graceful pine trees lies north of town and is reached by a path at the end of the paved road to Bimini Bay. Its calm waters are delightful for swimming and snorkeling.

CAT ISLAND West of the Exumas lies Cat Island (not to be confused with Cat Cay). It is covered with forested, rolling hills that soar to the great height of 204 feet—the ighest natural point in the Bahamas. Once prosperous ith sugar plantations of the Loyalists who had fled the merican Revolution, Cat Island is largely untouched day and is best known as the childhood home of actor idney Poitier. Its four tiny hotels and wide white beach- s are made for ardent escapists.

LEUTHERA First-time visitors to the Other Bahamas ften select Eleuthera because of its combination of far- way tranquility, the pretty setting of pastel-painted ouses surrounded by gentle green hills, and its 300 ears of history. It also has comfortable, unpretentious otels, good dining and sports facilities, and more roads nd transportation than the other islands. The island is imous for its pink sand beaches.

Situated 60 miles east of Nassau, Eleuthera is a 110- nile skinny spine never more than 2 miles wide, except r splays at both ends. It has six official ports of call and nree airports with direct flights from Nassau, Freeport, ort Lauderdale, and Miami.

Eleuthera has three of the Bahamas' oldest and pretti- st settlements: Governor's Harbour, the main town near ne center of the island and the hub of commercial activ- y, over 300 years old; Dunmore Town on Harbour sland; and Spanish Wells.

Harbour Island, almost touching the northeastern tip f Eleuthera, is one of the most beautiful spots in the ahamas and the site of Dunmore Town, its original apital and now a tranquil village of neat old houses and ower-filled lanes. A high green ridge dotted with pink nd white colonial homes separates the seventeenth- entury village from a 3-mile beach of pink, powdery and, whose color comes from the coral. The island has ight small hotels.

Spanish Wells, located off the northern end of leuthera, is a popular fishing and yachting center. It ets its name from the Spaniards who came ashore here replenish the freshwater supplies of their ships after naking the long voyages between the Old and New Vorlds.

The southern part of Eleuthera is slated for major evelopment to create a new resort center that is low- ey, tasteful, and ecosensitive, in line with the Bahamas' olicy of encouraging development that is compatible vith the environment.

PRINCESS CAY: The "private island" used by Princess ruises for most of its Caribbean itineraries is a recre- tional facility spread along a lovely beach at the south- rn tip of Eleuthera. Here, Princess has developed xcellent facilities for a-day-at-the-beach for its passen- ers, offering a wide range of water sports, beach ames, guided nature walks, several bars, a boutique, mall markets for local Bahamian crafts, and local ntertainment. Lunch is served at a large pavilion to all

passengers who chose to spend the day at beach. Continuous tender service is provided by the line between the ship and the beach.

THE EXUMAS From 35 miles south of Nassau, the Exumas spread southeast over an area of 130 square miles. The group is particularly popular with yachts- men who say the variety of color and subtle shades of the waters around the Exumas have no equal. Snorkelers and divers sing their praises, too. The *Exuma Land and Sea Park* is a preserve accessible only by boat.

George Town, the capital, is a quiet village of 800 peo- ple and several small hotels. Across the bay is Stocking Island whose lovely stretches of white sand beach are rich with seashells. About a dozen resorts are dotted through the Exuma chain, as are hundreds of beaches and coves. This sea-lover's mecca becomes busiest in April, when the islands host the annual Out Islands Regatta, the Bahamas' most prestigious sailing race.

INAGUA The Bahamas' third largest island is one of the least visited. Flamingos outnumber people 40,000 to 1,000. The 287-square-mile *Inagua Park* is the largest flamingo preserve in the Western Hemisphere. *Union Park* is a reserve for giant green turtles.

SAN SALVADOR Situated east-southeast of Nassau and directly east of Cat Island, San Salvador is the island "where it all began," so to speak. Although the island had been neglected, it received a great deal of attention in 1992 when the Bahamas celebrated the Quincentennial as the site of Columbus's first landfall in the New World. The island has four monuments commemorating Columbus's first landfall. (The land- ing site has been disputed as much as the landing!)

The San Salvador Museum has a new home in a reno- vated building that was originally constructed in the early nineteenth century and served until 1966 as a courthouse, a jail, and the Commissioner's Office. The building was restored by the Kiwanis Club of San Salvador with help from other service clubs and private groups. The exhibits are arranged in four groups: Columbus, 1492; The Lucayans, A.D. 600–1492; San Salvador, 1492–1838; and San Salvador in the late- nineteenth and twentieth centuries. The Lucayan exhibit has a map that shows the forty-eight known Indian archaeological sites on San Salvador.

San Salvador has a Club Med, which the Bahamian government hoped would bring new life and tourism development to the island, but it hasn't happened yet. There is a small hotel, *Riding Rock Inn,* near Cockburn Town, the main village. The island is prized by scuba enthusiasts because it is almost virgin territory. Both Club Med and the Riding Rock cater to divers.

AIRLINES SERVING THE FAMILY ISLANDS

Bahamasair (800–222–4262) serves all the airport centers of the Out Islands from Nassau. Same-day connections from U.S. and Canadian gateways are available to Abaco, Andros, Bimini, Eleuthera, and Exuma. Several small airlines offer service to the main Out Islands from Florida.

Key West

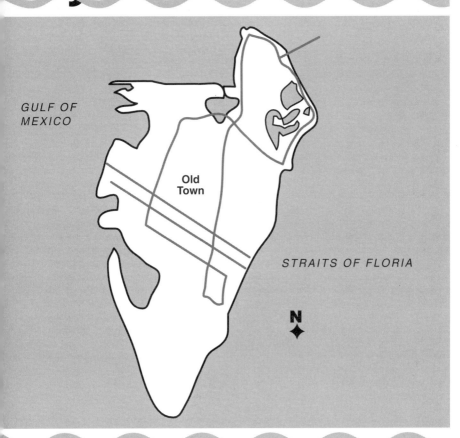

GULF OF
MEXICO

Old
Town

STRAITS OF FLORIA

N

AT A GLANCE

CHAPTER CONTENTS

AMERICA'S FIRST CARIBBEAN ISLAND

Key West is a state of mind as much as a place. Earthy and stylish at the same time, the nation's southernmost town is one of the most delightful places in the world—one-of-a-kind and infectious. Decades of writers, artists, and loads of eccentrics have made it that way—none more famous than Ernest Hemingway, Tennessee Williams, and nature artist John James Audubon. One gave it his lust for living; another, his flair for eccentricity; and the other, a cause for preservation. Combined, they set the stage for the theater that is Key West.

In recent years, Key West has become one of cruising's most popular ports of call, visited by 14 cruise ships at last count. And why not? It's one of the country's most interesting and charming towns—easy, convenient, and ideal for a day's visit. Cruise ships dock almost at the heart of Old Town, the oldest and most interesting part of Key West, and within walking distance of major attractions, shops, and restaurants.

In the 1920s and 1930s, before Key West had become a popular vacation destination, it barely qualified as a stopover on the way to Havana. Passengers in New York would board a train called the Havana Special, and on arrival in Key West, transfer from the train to their ship without leaving the pier for the overnight voyage to Cuba.

Key West began its transformation from a small, historic southern town to a major international resort in the 1950s and 60s, attracting artists, writers, and people from the fashion world. But even with the changes, it kept its traditional resident communities—Cuban-Americans (from the time of the Spanish-American War), blacks (who came even earlier as freemen, runaway slaves, shipwreck survivors), and Conchs and long-time residents whose forebearers came as traders, merchant seaman, wreckers, and fishermen. (No one can say how many generations of living on the island it takes to be considered a Conch; the Old Island Restoration Foundation maintains that anyone born in the Keys is a Conch.)

In any case, the mix of artists and shrimpers, rednecks and blacks, yuppies and blue collar, gays and straights, writers, hippies, expatriates, and escapists from all over, has given Key West an unusual combination of style and luxury and working-class simplicity (at least, until recently). Key Westers think of themselves as far removed from the Upper 48—and they are.

Key West has a long history of rags to riches. It was discovered by early Spanish explorers who, it is said, found piles of human bones on the island and called it *Cayo Hueso* (Island of Bones). History has not learned to whom these bones belonged, but the assumption is they were one of the Indian tribes, the Caloosa or Seminoles, who roamed the Keys.

Throughout the seventeenth and eighteenth centuries Key West, along with all the Keys, was the lair of pirates who preyed on Spanish galleons ladened with gold, silver, and gems from Mexico and South America that had to pass through these waters on return to Spain.

In 1822, the island was sold by a Spaniard to John Simonton, an American businessman, for $2,000, and the American flag was raised in the vicinity of Mallory Square the same year. Over the next fifty years the population quadrupled to almost 3,000 and was made up of New England merchant-seamen and white Bahamian traders, most of whom were engaged in the wrecking business—the very profitable enterprise of salvaging goods from ships that hit the reefs fronting the Keys. It was not uncommon for wreckers to cause such mishaps purposely by posting false signal lights for approaching ships during storms.

The construction on a lighthouse in the 1850s put a big dent in their business and Key West had to wait for its next boom—first, from sponging, and then from cigar making. Both were attributed to the influx of Cubans in the last quarter of the century. Once again, the town flourished and was said to have been the richest town per capita in the country. But by the 1930s the town was down on its luck to such an extent that 80 percent of the town's 12,000 people were on welfare.

World War II and the U.S. Navy brought life back to Key West, only to be abandoned after the war. President Truman visited Key West in 1946 and continued to return frequently while he was chief executive, bringing the town a certain amount of attention. Hemingway had been living there since 1931 and Tennessee Williams came frequently in the 40s, encouraging his literary friends to join him. By the late 1950s and for the next decade, investment filtered in slowly, but it was not until the 1980s, when Key West became fashionable and restoration of the Old Town, which had started in the 1970s, was well under way, that real estate prices skyrocketed and the boom was on again.

Key West is small and easy to find your way around and it has something for everyone—historic sites enhanced by their colorful past, unusual architecture, and the famous writers and artists who lived and worked here; funky as well as smart shops, restaurants, bars, and entertainment; sports, including snorkeling and diving on the only coral reef offshore the ontinental U.S., and of course, the famous Key West unsets, not to mention Key lime pie and margaritas.

Key West is both an island and a city, with a population of less than 50,000 residents that is swollen by over a million tourists annually. Closer to Cuba then to Miami, Key West, with its graceful palms and masses of bougainvillea, its tropical climate and easy living ambience, seems as Caribbean as any of the islands bathed by that sea.

Key West will probably remind you of New Orleans in more ways than one. Conch, like creole in New Orleans, refers to people, food, and a style of architecture. As you will quickly learn, the Conchs are proud of their name. In 1882, they even declared Key West the Conch Republic and seceded from the Union—but that's another story.

Local lore says the name conch (pronounced konk) comes from the seventeenth century when the Eleutheran Adventurers, a group from Bermuda that had established a colony in the Bahamas, fled to Key West after the British tried to tax them, declaring they would "eat conchs" before paying taxes to the Crown. As enduring as the conch, some might muse, has been the legacy of piracy—reflected not only in real estate prices but in the town's anything-goes attitude, relishing the unexpected and keeping rules only to break them.

FAST FACTS

POPULATION: Key West has about 50,000 permanent residents, and the population doubles or triples with the number of tourists at almost any time of the year, but particularly during the winter season.

CLIMATE: Balmy weather almost year round. Temperatures average 75°F in January and 82°F in summer. Short tropical rains come often in the fall and spring, but rarely last more than a few minutes.

CLOTHING: Tropical-casual. Seldom do men wear ties. A sweater or jacket is needed in the shade in the winter and almost anytime for air-conditioning.

CURRENCY: U.S. dollar. Travelers checks and credit cards are widely accepted.

CUSTOMS REGULATIONS: Cruise passengers are admitted without formalities (you're still in the U.S.), but it is wise to

carry a passport, birth certificate or driver's license, or voter's registration card for identification.

ELECTRICITY: 110 volts, 60 cycles.

LANGUAGE: English with a twang.

POSTAL SERVICE: The post office is located on Whitehead at Fleming Street, five blocks south of the pier.

PUBLIC HOLIDAYS: All U.S. holidays plus a few special local ones. (See Celebrations later in this chapter.)

TELEPHONE AREA CODE: 305.

AIRLINES: American/American Eagle, Comair/Delta, Gulfstream, and USAir Express have frequent flights daily from Miami International.

INFORMATION:

Key West Chamber of Commerce, 402 Wall Street/Mallory Square; Key West, FL 33040; Tel. 800–LAST KEY, 305–294–2587.

The office has maps, brochures, and information on self-guided walking tours.

Hours: Mon.–Fri., 8:30 A.M.–5 P.M.; Sat. and Sun., 9 A.M.–5 P.M.

Old Island Restoration Foundation, Hospitality House, Mallory Square, Box 689; Key West, FL 33041; Tel. 305–294–9501.

BUDGET PLANNING

Key West is as expensive as you want to make it. Fortunately, your feet can get you around town to almost all the main attractions. There are bikes and mopeds for rent and public buses, as well as car rentals for those who want to get out of town. If you are on a tight budget, you should plan your sight-seeing because the museums, historic homes, and other attractions charge admission—$5 to $10 for adults and half the amount for children. There are restaurants in every price range and souvenirs from $5 T-shirts to $5,000 paintings.

PORT PROFILE: KEY WEST

LOCATION/EMBARKATION: The port in Key West is located in the northwest corner of the island. Downtown, known as Old Town, stretches directly behind the dock to the south and east. Duval Street, the main thoroughfare of Old Key West, runs for about a mile from the dock to Southernmost Point, and in a bit of hyperbole, is called the longest street in the world because it runs from the Gulf of Mexico to the Atlantic Ocean. Most cruise ships anchor at the piers fronting Old Town, but the megaliners dock at a new facility on the west side of town and their passengers are transported to Mallory Square by the Conch Train. (You are not allowed to walk it, even if you want to, as the area is still under the Navy's jurisdiction.)

Walk in any direction from Front Street or up Duval Street and you will find something of interest. It's hard to get lost as the center of town is only about ten blocks square, laid out in a grid and easy to follow with maps available at the Key West Chamber of Commerce on Wall Street by Mallory Square.

FACILITIES: Key West has the feel of a tropical port with the added advantage of good transportation, communications, and technical facilities not always available in the Caribbean.

LOCAL TRANSPORTATION: Taxis are readily available, but you do not need them unless you have trouble walking. In that case, you might want to use public buses or take one of the town tours offered by the Conch Train or Old Town Trolley (see details under Shore Excursions). All major car rental companies are represented here. Due to the heavy demand during the peak winter season, you would be wise to make reservations from home before departing on your cruise through a rental company's 800 number.

BIKES: Bikes are the best way to get around Key West. The island is only a mile wide, seven miles long, and entirely flat. Rentals are available from *The Bike Shop* (1110 Truman Avenue at Varela Street; Tel. 294–1073) and *Moped Hospital* (601 Truman Avenue at Simonton Street) and most hotels.

AUTHOR'S FAVORITE ATTRACTIONS

WRITER'S WALK
STROLL ON DUVAL STREET
OLD TROLLEY TOUR
KAYAKING IN THE BACK COUNTRY
DIVING OR DEEP-SEA FISHING

SHORE EXCURSIONS

Conch Tour Train (Mallory Square/Front Street, Tel. 305–294–5161), $15 adults; $8 children. A leisurely hour-and-a-half-orientation to Key West with running commentary by the driver/guide on dozens of sites en route. The train is made up of three or four open-sided cars pulled by a truck disguised as a caboose. With the tour ticket, you receive some discount coupons. Some driver/guides are better than others, adding interesting tidbits along the way; others sound like an endless recording, rattling off information too fast to understand or retain. (You can easily take the tour on your own; tours depart from the Conch Train's depot about every 30 minutes throughout the day.)

Old Town Trolley (Mallory Square/Wall Street, Tel. 305–296–6688; $15 Adults; $6 children). Trolley cars similar to those in San Francisco (except that they are motorized) have the same owners as the Conch Train and offer a similar tour—but with one important advantage. Passengers may get on and off the trolley at any stop along the route, making it a more useful facility for those who want to explore a particular area of the town. (You can easily take the trolley on your own; tours depart about every 30 minutes from their depot and like the train, some guides are better than others.)

Conch Train/Trolley, Aquarium, and Shipwreck Historeum (2.5 hours; $28 per person). After an island trolley or train tour, participants visit Key West Aquarium for a self-guided tour of about 45 minutes and the Shipwreck Historeum, where actors and exhibits bring to life the colorful history of Key West's wrecker days. (Aquarium and Shipwreck Historeum, both by Mallory Square, can be visited on one's own.)

Island City Strolls (Island City Heritage Trust, Box 56, Key West; Tel. 305–294–8380; $15). A variety of scheduled walking and biking tours, led by author/historian Sharon Wells, depart daily at 10 A.M. from Nancy's Secret Garden (see later in chapter) and four days weekly at 4 P.M. from the Bike Shop (1110 Truman Avenue), taking in historic, cultural, and natural attractions en route.

Key West Nature Bike Tour (Inquire with Lloyd Mager, Tel. 305–294–1882). Mager leads a two-hour bike trip with a lesson in Key West history, architecture, and flora, daily except Mondays, departing at 9 A.M. from the Moped Hospital (601 Truman Avenue at Simonton Street). Cost: $15 per person, plus bike rental.

Pelican Path (Old Island Restoration Foundation, Hospitality House, Mallory Square; Tel. 305–294–9501). A carefully laid-out, self-guided route leads past many of Key West's landmarks and famous old houses in Old Town. A folder with a good map of the route and brief descriptions of the houses, prepared by the Old Island Restoration Foundation, is available from its office. The few landmark houses open to the public charge admission. The tour is of particular interest to architecture and history buffs. The Foundation also offers guided house and garden tours during the winter season, usually for about $10 per person.

Writer's Walk (Key West Literary Seminar, 419 Petronia Street; Key West 33040; Tel. 305–293–9291; fax 305–293–0482; $10). An hour or so mile-long tour of literary Key West, led by a Literary Seminar member, is offered at 10:30 A.M. on Saturday from Heritage House and on Sunday from Hemingway House during the winter season, and by request the rest of the year. The majority of houses are private residences not open to the public. A stop is made at Casa Antigua, Hemingway's first Key West residence. Ticket provides discounts on entrance fees to Heritage House and Hemingway House.

Catamaran Sailing and Snorkeling (3 hours, $39 adults, $20 children). A 65-foot catamaran sails to the continental United States' only living coral reef, which lies seven miles southeast of Key West. Snorkeling equipment, floatation devices, and instruction are included. The boat has changing facilities and freshwater showers. Complimentary soft drinks, beer, and wine are served. Children under 12 years cannot participate in the snorkeling.

Coral Reef Glassbottom Boat (2 hours, $20). The boat travels 7.5 miles out to the only living coral reef in the continental U.S. for participants to see the colorful fish and dramatic corals.

Key West Scuba (3 hours, $66). For certified divers, Padi five-star instructors offer full range of services for diving on one of two sites: the Sambos, a collection of three shallow reefs 15–40 feet deep, each 1.5 to 2.5 miles apart and richly populated with reef fish; or an artificial reef formed by the 187-foot Cayman Salvager, sunk in 1985. Equipment is included. (See Sports section later in this chapter.)

Key West Seaplane Service (5603 College Rd.; Tel. 305–294–6978; fax 305–294–4660). Seaplanes fly to the Dry Tortugas and Ft. Jefferson National Park, 70 miles into the Gulf of Mexico, where you can spot marine life, ship wrecks, and Mel Fisher's treasure site and enjoy swimming, snorkeling (free gear), bird watching, and sight-seeing.

KEY WEST ON YOUR OWN

Key West, where a bit of Cape Cod meets New Orleans and mingles with the Caribbean, is a place to savor the atmosphere rather than to absorb the sun. There's no place quite like it. How you spend your time largely depends on your interest. There's historic Key West, architectural Key West, and literary Key West. There are forts, art galleries, museums, funky shops and chic boutiques, sidewalk cafes and legendary pubs, golf, diving, fishing, kayaking, and more. Indeed, Key West has more attractions and diversions than you could possibly do in one day, but the one thing the island does not have is good beaches.

Key West's Historic District has over 3,000 buildings constructed prior to 1900. Many are still privately owned by the families who built them; others have been made into stores, art galleries, inns, and museums and are windows onto the town's fascinating history and the people who have made it so special. Hemingway House, where the author wrote *For Whom the Bell Tolls* and other masterpieces, is a National Historic Landmark. His favorite bars are still among the most popular spots in town.

For a quick overview, take a train or trolley tour, passing along tree-shaded streets lined with gingerbread-trimmed houses and Victorian mansions. Then, to get the real feel of Key West, walk—amble is a better description—in Old Town. A stroll on Duval Street will help you measure the town's pulse. You can cross the entire island on Duval or Whitehead street (a little over a mile) in 30 minutes, but then, it can also take three hours. You will want to window shop, stop at a bar or sidewalk cafe, chat with some of the town's friendly, funky characters, buy a souvenir or a work of art, and visit a museum or historic house. Stop by the Key West Chamber of Commerce or Hospitality House, both at Mallory Square, for maps and information.

MALLORY SQUARE AND VICINITY

Mallory Square (1) on the island's northwest corner at the foot of Duval Street, a short walk from the pier, was the heart of Key West in the old days, and it's the center of activity for visitors today. The old buildings beside the square once quartered the trades (read wrecking) that made Key West rich; now, they house shops, restaurants, bars, and museums. You will need some imagination to picture the setting in seafaring days, as the square itself has been reduced to a small area by the sea where sunset devotees come to watch the nightly show; the rest is a parking lot.

On the east side of the square in a building dating from 1850 is the *Waterfront Playhouse* (Tel. 294–5015), home of the Key West Players, now in its 57th season. On the west is *Hospitality House,* the headquarters of the Old Island Restoration Foundation, in a Conch house dating from the late nineteenth century. And behind it on Wall Street is the *Chamber of Commerce,* in a former warehouse. Wall, Front, Whitehead, Greene, and Duval streets—with many of Old Town's main attractions—parallel or lead off the square. Most sight-seeing excursions start from here.

Key West Aquarium (1) (1 Whitehead Street; Tel. 296–2051). Exhibits of Atlantic marine life are a hit with kids, especially watching sharks and turtles being fed by hand. Hours: Daily 10 A.M.–7 P.M. Admission: $6.50 adults; $3 children 8–15; under 7, free; frequent guided tours between 10:30 A.M. and 4:30 P.M.

Key West Shipwreck Historeum (1) (Wall and Front streets; Tel. 292–8990). One of the island's newest museums offers an excellent presentation of the Keys' famous—and infamous—wrecking era with artifacts from the *Isaac Allerton,* said to have carried the richest manifest of any ship of her day when she went down in 1865. Key West's colorful history is bought to life by actors and exhibits that help viewers understand the times that revolved around shipping and the town that originally built its fortune rescuing survivors of shipwrecks and reaping rich rewards from the cargoes they salvaged.

The building has a 65-foot observation tower, similar to those used in olden days to spot ships and now offering visitors a great view of the harbor, Old Town, and its surroundings. Hours: Daily 9 A.M.–6 P.M. Admission: $7.50 adults; $3 children. If you only have time for one historic museum, this would be the one to select.

On the corner at Front Street, the *Key West Art Center* is a nonprofit artist cooperative, housed in a late nineteenth-century wooden structure that was used in the 1930s under the New Deal for the W.P.A. Art Project headquarters.

MAP LEGEND FOR OLD TOWN, KEY WEST

1. **Mallory Square/Wall and Front streets**
   Key West Aquarium
   Waterfront Playhouse
   Hospitality House/Old Island Restoration Foundation
   Chamber of Commerce
   Key West Shipwreck Historeum
   Key West Art Center
   Clinton Square Market/Naval Coal Depot
   U.S. Customs House
2. **Mel Fisher's Maritime Heritage Museum**
3. **Audubon House and Tropical Gardens**
4. **Little White House**
   Kelly's Caribbean/PanAm
5. **Heritage House**
6. **Sloppy Joe's**
7. **The Wrecker's Museum/The Oldest House**
8. **St. Paul's Episcopal Church**
   La Concha
9. **Fast Buck Freddie's**

   Jimmy Buffet's Margaritaville
   San Carlos Opera House
   Ripley's Believe It or Not Odditorium
10. **Monroe County Courthouse/Post Office**
11. **Blue Heaven/Bahama Village**
12. **Hemingway House**
13. **The Lighthouse and Military Museum**
14. **Southernmost Point**
    Harris House/Southernmost Home
15. **Curry Mansion Inn**
16. **Casa Antigua**
17. **Donkey Milk House**
18. **Octagon House**
19. **Monroe County Public Library**
20. **Gingerbread House**
21. **Windsor Compound**
22. **Burton House**
23. **Secret Garden**
24. **Tennessee Williams House**
25. **Fort Zachary Taylor**

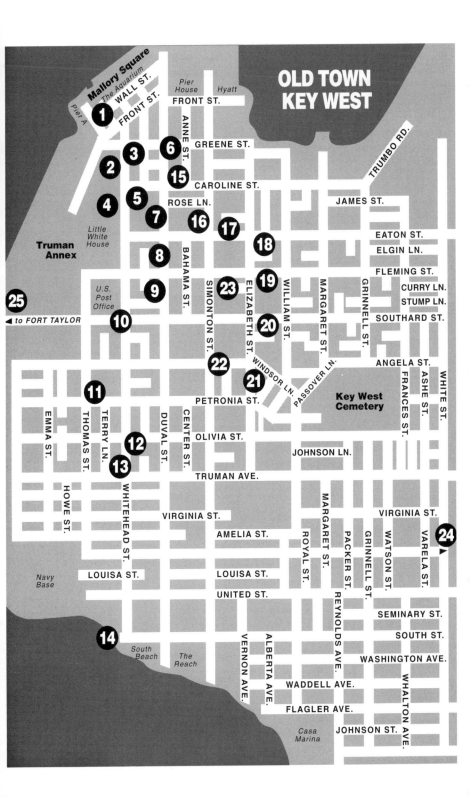

OLD TOWN KEY WEST

Mallory Square
The Aquarium
WALL ST.
FRONT ST.
Pier A

Pier House
Hyatt

FRONT ST.

ANNE ST.
GREENE ST.

CAROLINE ST.

ROSE LN.

BAHAMA ST.

Little White House

Truman Annex

U.S. Post Office

to FORT TAYLOR

JAMES ST.

TRUMBO RD.

EATON ST.
ELGIN LN.
FLEMING ST.
CURRY LN.
STUMP LN.
SOUTHARD ST.

SIMONTON ST.
ELIZABETH ST.
WILLIAM ST.
MARGARET ST.
GRINNELL ST.

WINDSOR LN.
PASSOVER LN.

ANGELA ST.
FRANCES ST.
ASHE ST.
WHITE ST.

Key West Cemetery

PETRONIA ST.

EMMA ST.
THOMAS ST.
TERRY LN.
DUVAL ST.
CENTER ST.

OLIVIA ST.

JOHNSON LN.

TRUMAN AVE.

HOWE ST.
WHITEHEAD ST.

VIRGINIA ST.

AMELIA ST.

MARGARET ST.
ROYAL ST.
PACKER ST.
GRINNELL ST.
REYNOLDS AVE.
WATSON ST.
VARELA ST.

VIRGINIA ST.

LOUISA ST.

LOUISA ST.

UNITED ST.

Navy Base

SEMINARY ST.
SOUTH ST.
WASHINGTON AVE.

South Beach
The Reach

VERNON AVE.
ALBERTA AVE.

WADDELL AVE.

FLAGLER AVE.

JOHNSON ST.

WHALTON AVE.

Casa Marina

Next to the Aquarium, the *Clinton Square Market* was formerly a naval storehouse dating from 1861, and is now the town's oldest brick building. Today, it houses a group of attractive specialty shops. Next to it, the massive *U.S. Customs House,* dating from 1891, is said to be the only structure in Florida in Romanesque Revival style. Used for various government agencies over the century, it was put on the National Register of Historic Places in 1973 and is now being renovated by the Key West Art and Historical Society as a museum.

Front Street, as the name implies, fronted the harbor in olden days and was the main commercial street, with banks, trading offices, bars, and flophouses for the merchant seamen. Apparently, one of the most raucous, the Havana-Madrid, was a tavern and striptease joint; it's namesake today is a seafood specialty restaurant at 410 Wall Street.

Mel Fisher's Maritime Heritage Museum (2)

(200 Greene Street; Tel. 294–2633). A visit to this museum with the discoveries by America's most noted shipwreck sleuth, Key West's own Mel Fisher, can turn anyone into a hopeful treasure-hunter. In 1985, after many tries, Fisher found the *Nuestra Senora de Atocha,* a seventeenth-century Spanish galleon that went down in 1622 only 45 miles west of Key West, with an estimated $400 million in gold and silver. On display is a copy of the ship's manifest, heavy gold crosses and chains, emeralds, coins, weapons, and other artifacts recovered from the sunken treasure. Much more is in storage and on the seabed where it will stay. Other displays are from the *Santa Margarita,* another Spanish treasure ship. Hours: Daily 10 A.M.–5 P.M. Admission: $7 adults; $1 children 6 to 12; under 6, free.

To the west of the museum is Clinton Square, with a small garden and gate leading to the Little White House; the main entrance to President Truman's winter retreat is farther south on Whitehead Street.

Key West Cigar Factory (Pirates Alley) is the last of a once major industry in Key West brought here by Cubans in the late nineteenth century. In a setting of old equipment and furnishings that has not changed in a century, two people demonstrate the old method of hand-rolling cigars. There are several other cigar stores in town; most now have their factories in the Dominican Republic.

Audubon House and Tropical Gardens (3)

(205 Whitehead at Greene Street; Tel. 294–2116). Built in 1830 for Captain John H. Geiger, a skilled harbor pilot and master wrecker, the house is typical of Key West architecture of the period and is surrounded by lush gardens. When nature artist John James Audubon visited Key West in 1832 to hunt and sketch local birds, tradition has it that he stayed at Geiger's home, although there is apparently no historical record to substantiate the claim.

Nonetheless, more than a century later, Key West native son and prominent Miami businessman Mitchell Wolfson acquired the Key West landmark, restored it, and dedicated it as a public museum, to be named Audubon House. The restoration is credited with sparking a preservation trend in the mid-1970s, led by a pair of Old Town merchants who teamed up to renovate 15 buildings along the 600 block of Duval Street. Today, the downtown restoration is nearly complete, with the renovated buildings and homes housing smart boutiques, art galleries, restaurants, and pubs.

Audubon House, run by the Florida Audubon Society, has been elegantly furnished with antiques of the period. The original furnishings probably came from the salvaged cargo of wrecked ships, as was customary at the time, and would have originated in far-flung places around the globe. Some of Audubon's most famous engravings, such as the Roseate Spoonbill, hang on the walls, and in the garden is the Geiger tree used as a background by Audubon for his engraving of the white-crowned pigeon, which he named the Key West pigeon; it was one of 18 species new to Audubon. A fine collection of porcelain birds by Dorothy Doughty is also on display. The museum offers a videotape presentation of Audubon's *Birds of Florida.* The entrance is through the museum's store, where you can buy Audubon posters and books. Hours: Daily 9 A.M.–noon and 1–5 P.M. Admission: $7.50 adult; $2 children 6 to 12; under 6, free.

Little White House (4)

(111 Front Street; Tel. 294–9911). After his first visit in November 1946, Harry Truman became enamored of Key West and returned frequently throughout his presidency, making the estate his presidential vacation retreat. The house, built by the Navy in 1890 for a naval commandant, is now a museum with Truman memorabilia. Hours: Daily 9 A.M.–5 P.M. Admission: $7 adults; $3 children. A guided tour is given about every 15 minutes.

(Incidently, the sign on the entrance gates at Whitehead and Caroline streets is misleading, appearing to indicate that the white house immediately inside the gates was Truman's pad. It was naval officer quarters built in 1904 and recently renovated. The Truman house is farther west.)

The 44-acre Truman Annex extending south along Whitehead Street was part of the former U.S. Naval Base, bought a few years ago by private developers who created a luxury residential and resort community. The Hilton Hotel, opened in early 1996, anchors the north end and has retail shops, restaurants, a deep-water marina, a beach club, and condos. The hotel faces Sunset Island (formerly known as Tank Island), which has beach facilities. Frequent ferry service is available from the hotel. Hyatt Hotels' first time-share venture is also there.

As noted earlier, the gates on Whitehead Street face Caroline Street, an interesting block for detouring to Duval Street. Those with a keen interest in Key West architecture or its literary and theatrical luminaries might prefer to continue on Caroline to the landmarks (15) to (23) on the map.

On the corner across from the Little White House gates is *Kelly's Caribbean* (301 Whitehead Street), a garden restaurant in the former building of Aero-Marine Airways, which provided mail service between Key West and Havana in the 1920s. The building once occupied the site where Pier House is today; it became the headquarters of Pan American World Airways after the airline launched its service to Havana in 1928, ushering in the new era of international passenger air travel. Kelly's belongs to actress Kelly McGillis of *Top Gun* and *Witness* fame.

Heritage House (5) (410 Caroline Street; Tel. 296–3573). Built about 1834—but it's not clear by whom—it was owned by George Carey, a liquor merchant who expanded the house in 1844 for his bride, adding the front rooms and porch. The house remained in the family for almost a century and was altered many times. In 1934 it was bought by Jessie Porter Newton, one of the driving forces behind Key West's preservation efforts. She renovated the house and added a garden and swimming pool in place of the cookhouse and cistern, and another room (called the Chinese porch) decorated with Asian art and antiques. More recently, she built a second house for herself, hidden in the trees at the rear of the property, and turned the old house into a museum brimming with furniture and collectibles from the four corners of the globe.

Miss Jessie, as the guides refer to her, was a longtime friend of Robert Frost, who visited Key West frequently in the 1940s, staying first in a rental house at 707 Seminole Avenue and at Casa Marina, until he took up semi-residence in the small, tin-roofed cottage at the rear of Miss Jessie's house, where he spent 14 winters. Hours: Daily 10 A.M.–5 P.M. Admission: $6 adults; $3 children 3 to 14. Guided tours of the Heritage House are available but the Frost cottage is not included, as it is often used for literary meetings and seminars. A Robert Frost Poetry reading and seminar is held in March.

On the corner of Caroline and Duval stands one of the town's largest houses, built in the last century for Dr. J. Y. Porter, Florida's first Public Health Officer, credited with significant research on yellow fever. The building now houses several art galleries.

DUVAL STREET

Key West's famous Duval Street, named for the first governor of the Florida territory, is the main drag of Old Town, awash with bars, shops, art galleries, and old houses with a slice of history at every address. The street from the north end at Mallory Square to the south end at the Southernmost House has been invaded by T-shirt and knickknack shops, but happily there are plenty of other stores with attractive art, object d'arts, restaurants and sidewalk cafes, and clothing boutiques to make it interesting and easy to combine a shopping expedition with a stroll through history.

Sloppy Joe's (6) (201 Duval Street) was one of Hemingway's favorite haunts and is still a mecca for Hemingway fans. Owner Joe Russell, a Key West boatman, was immortalized by Hemingway as "Freddie" in *To Have and Have Not*. In 1937, when the rent on Russell's Greene Street location (the original site) was to be raised, Joe moved his bar to Duval Street in the middle of the night. Note the painting on the south wall by the bar; it shows a young Hemingway with a typewriter and Sloppy Joe wearing the crown of grapes and sitting at a table surrounded by friends—a rough bunch known as "The Mob." The painting was done by an artist in the W.P.A. Arts Project.

When Hemingway left Key West to live in Cuba, he stored some of his belongings in a back room here. In 1962, after his death, Mary, Hemingway's last wife, discovered among those belongings the original manuscript of *A Farewell to Arms* and *To Have and Have Not,* and even some uncashed royalty checks.

Full and noisy from morning to night, no tourist to Key West would think their visit complete without a stop here. If you want a souvenir from the country's most famous bar, the adjoining T-shirt shop probably does as much business as the bar.

The Wrecker's Museum/The Oldest House (7) (322 Duval Street; Tel. 294–9502). Built about 1829, it claims to be the oldest house in Key West and was the home of Capt. Francis B. Watlington, a merchant seaman and wrecker. Key West's piracy and wrecking days are told through pictures, old documents, and ship models; the furnishings reflect the family life of a sea captain of the time. The kitchen in the back is separate from the house, as was characteristic in those days. Hours: Daily 10 A.M.–4 P.M. Admission: $4 adults; 50 cents children.

St. Paul's Episcopal Church (8) (401 Duval Street). Begun in 1832, the present church is the fourth on the site. Among its many moments in history, it was seen in Tennessee Williams's film *The Rose Tattoo.*

La Concha (8) (430 Duval Street; Tel. 800–745–2191, 296–2991). It's a Holiday Inn unlike any other in the chain. Opened in 1926 at a time when Key West, then a major port and link for tourists en route to Havana, needed a first-class hotel, La Concha quickly became the social center of the town. The seven-story building was—and still is—the tallest building in Key West, with fabulous new features such as rooms adjoined by baths, hot and cold running water in all rooms, an elevator, telephone booths, a haberdashery, a bakery, and a bank.

Now listed in the National Register of Historic Places, the hotel has seen a great deal of history. Here in 1927, Juan Trippe, founding president of Pan American World Airways, formally announced the start of passenger service between Key West and Havana, launching international air travel. Hemingway, a guest and frequent patron of La Concha's Duval Street bar, included the hotel in his *To Have and Have Not.* And Williams wrote much of *A Streetcar Named Desire* while he was staying here in 1947.

The hotel's fortunes and misfortunes paralleled those of the town's and, during the 1930s, both fell on hard times. The hotel was sold and resold several times and suffered from hurricane damage and neglect. By the time Atlanta architect Richard Rauh was brought in to rescue it, the hotel had been badly vandalized and was boarded up. In 1986, after a multimillion-dollar renovation, the hotel reopened and quickly took its place once again as the belle of Duval.

Fast Buck Freddie's (9) (500 Duval Street; Tel. 294–2007) is Key West's answer to Bloomingdale's. Those who are old enough to remember will immediately recognize the exterior as a former Kress Five & Dime store, built in 1913, but inside, it is a chic emporium. The building is shared with *Jimmy Buffett's Margaritaville,* the store and restaurant of Key West's most famous citizen (after Hemingway) who got his start here. And he does show up here from time to time.

San Carlos Opera House (9) (516 Duval Street). Restored in 1990, the building is the third on the site and has served the Cuban community since 1871, when the first structure was dedicated. It is used as a center for music, plays, and other cultural activities.

Ripley's Believe It or Not Odditorium (9) (527 Duval Street; Tel. 293–9694). The fun house museum, based on the works and collection of Robert Ripley, is set in the renovated Strand Theater, a former movie house with a fanciful facade built in the 1930s as one of the W.P.A. projects to employ local artists and work-

ers. Hours: Daily 10 A.M.–11 P.M. Admission: $9.95 adults; $6.95 children 4–12, plus tax.

If you continue south on Duval Street, the walk from Southard Street to the ocean becomes an art and shopping excursion more than a sight-seeing one, as many of the best art galleries and boutiques are in these blocks.

Alternatively, you could turn west on Southard, one block to Whitehead, where you will find the Post Office to your right and the Monroe County Courthouse (10) at Jackson Square to your left. The Green Parrot Bar, a watering hole popular with locals, has held down the corner of Whitehead and Southard since 1890. Straight ahead, Southard Street continues to Fort Taylor (25).

Blue Heaven (11) (Thomas and Petronia streets). If it's lunch time, you may want to detour another block south to Key West's most written-about restaurant/art gallery in the heart of Bahama Village, the town's oldest black neighborhood.

Bahama Village historically was made up mostly of Bahamians and Cubans of African origin and has had various names—La Africana in the 1880s, Jungle Town in the 1950s and 60s, and now Bahama Village. Indeed, a ceremonial arch with the Bahamian coat-of-arms mounted over Petronia Street at Duval proclaims it thus. The area is something of a hodgepodge architecturally and culturally, with tiny houses, narrow lanes, churches, funky art galleries, and men sitting under shade trees playing dominos—a picture one is likely to see in any barrio south of Miami. Although some restoration has been done, enough of the neighborhood's character remains to get the feel of Key West in another era.

Blue Heaven, which dates back to 1884, has had quite a past—as a pool hall, ice-cream parlor, dance hall, bordello, and artists' studios. Hemingway used to referee boxing matches in an outdoor arena under the Spanish lime tree, and young black boxers like "Iron Baby" Roberts and "Battlin Geech" Kermit Forbes sparred with him on Fridays. Apparently, cockfights were frequent too, as there's a "Rooster Graveyard" with tombstones intact in the northeast corner.

At the back of the outdoor restaurant, set under enormous shade trees and showers of bougainvillea, stands a water tower dating from about 1920; it was moved here from Little Torch Key, where it had been used for the men building the Flagler Railroad that once brought mainlanders to Key West on the Havana Special.

On the ground level, a tiny gift stall sells Blue Heaven T-shirts and handcrafted silver jewelry, and at *Wrapunzels,* wrapper Sam Bones uses beads to make unusual hair creations and jewelry. Stairs lead to the *Itoki Gallery* on the upper level, featuring West Indian art and artwear and billing itself as the smallest art gallery in Key West. Artist/proprietor Suzanne Pereira, who has an interest in the culture and folklore of Latin America, named the gallery after a Central American goddess figure that is half woman and half scorpion.

The second floor of the Blue Heaven building was once a dance hall and bordello, as the doors with wooden slots (so customers could peek at the girls) attest. It now houses the *Bordello Gallery,* a co-op of local artists. Among them, Jim Sherrington does scrimshaw pieces exploring nautical and mythological themes. Angela and Charles, a husband/wife team, collaborated on handpainting some of the "coolest bicycles in Key West." Angela also makes jewelry using local woods and seed pods, and you are invited to try out some of Charles's handmade musical instruments. The gallery also displays paintings, photography, furniture, and decorative objects by local and visiting artists.

Oh, yes, the food. It's as eclectic as the setting, and quite good, and you can't beat the price. Several handsome roosters strutter about under foot, stopping from time to time to crow. But it's the fresh flowers on the tables in this chicken patch that's the pièce de résistance.

Hemingway House (12) (907 Whitehead Street; Tel. 294–1575): The large house suggesting Spanish colonial design is set back from the street in lush tropical gardens. Built by a Connecticut merchant in 1851, it is now a national historic landmark and museum and one of Key West's most unusual structures. Constructed of native rock hewn from the grounds, the house has features unusual for Key West, such as arched windows with shutters and a second floor wrap-around veranda with an iron balustrade that would seem to fit in New Orleans more than Key West.

Hemingway bought the house in 1931 and added a swimming pool, the first in Key West. He lived here for two decades, during which he did much of his greatest works, including *For Whom the Bell Tolls, Death in the Afternoon, The Green Hills of Africa, Snows of Kilimanjaro, To Have and To Have Not,* his play *The Fifth Column,* and many short stories. It was his most productive period, when he was idolized and imitated by writers the world over. Hemingway sold the house shortly before his death in 1961.

The gardens are beautiful, but the house is disappointing—sparely furnished with almost none of the furnishings having belonged to Hemingway except a collection of his childhood books in a glass case on the second floor and some family photographs. There are numerous cats which tour guides say are descendants of Hemingway's cats, but that's questionable. Hours: Daily 9 A.M.–5 P.M. Admission: $7.50 adults; $2 children 6 to 12. Guided tours start about every half-hour.

Hemingway is said to have kept a rigorous schedule, up before sunrise and writing until noon in his study in the loft of the pool house, joined to the main house by a catwalk. He would spend the remainder of the day fishing with his friends and some local fisherman on his 40-foot boat, *Pilar.*

Much of Hemingway's life was also centered at *Sloppy Joe's,* his favorite bar, originally located on Greene Street (see earlier description). There, Key West's most famous writer had a reserved bar stool where he enjoyed his daily ration of booze. There, too, Hemingway saw for the first time Martha Gellhorn, whom he later married.

The bar is still there but is known as *Captain Tony's Saloon* (428 Greene Street; Tel. 305–294–1838). Although Tony Tarracino, the former owner and mayor of Key West, no longer owns it, the colorful bar, which claims to be the oldest in town, has changed little since Hemingway's day. The ceiling is covered with thousands of calling cards and almost as many bras, and a motley crew of loyal patrons occupy the bar stools, talking and vaguely listening to the entertainer plucking a guitar.

Key West keeps the novelist's image alive with Hemingway Days, a week-long festival marking the author's birthday on July 21 with a Hemingway Look-Alike Contest, writer's workshop, and other activities.

Key West Lighthouse (13) (937 Whitehead Street; Tel. 294–0012). Across the street from the Hemingway House, a 110-foot lighthouse, built in 1847, marked the water's edge in those days. It is still the best location for a panoramic view of the Key West, with the Atlantic Ocean on the east and the Gulf of Mexico on the west. There are 88 steps to the balcony and another 10 steps to the light station.

The *Lighthouse Military Museum,* in a small building on the south side of the compound, has interesting exhibits of old military uniforms, ship models, and other seafaring paraphenalia. Hours: Daily 9:30 A.M.–5 P.M. Admission: $5 adults; $1 children 7 to 12.

(Truman Avenue, which you will cross when you continue south, is the southern terminus of U.S. 1.)

Southernmost Point (14), a red, black, and yellow marker at the end of Whitehead Street, is a Key West landmark, establishing the spot as the most southerly in the continental United States. It also indicates that Cuba is 90 miles away. In the past, a more portable sign—irresistible to souvenir hounds—was here until the townsfolk got fed up with having to replace it.

They could hardly have thought up an uglier monument than the present one, yet no one passes here without stopping to take a picture.

As you will discover, all the surrounding streets have places claiming to be the "southernmost" hotel, motel, guesthouse, café, laundry, church, etc. Harris House, the large home occupying most of the block at South and Duval streets, claims to be the Southernmost House. Built for a judge around 1905, it was a fashionable restaurant frequented by Tennessee Williams and his friends in the 1950s. It is now a private residence.

(From here, you can return via Duval Street and the art galleries; or, if you decide to skip the Southernmost Point, from the Hemingway House you could return to Duval as far as Angela Street and pick up the walk from Number (15) to (23) in reverse order.)

CAROLINE STREET AND BEYOND

For literary, theater, and architecture buffs, the streets east of Duval from Caroline to Angela have some of the finest houses in Key West. Most are private residences, but some have been converted to inns and stores and many are the homes and haunts of famous writers, playwrights, and celebrities who have lived in Key West all or part of the year.

Curry Mansion Inn (15) (511 Caroline Street; Tel. 294–5349; 800–253–3466). The elaborate Victorian house was built by Milton Curry, Florida's first millionaire, who made his fortune as a wrecker.

The rear of the house is part of the original structure built in 1855; the front part was added in 1899 when Curry married. The wide porch surrounding the house on three sides is one of its best features; the elegant design and details here and under the eaves are of special interest. The mansion was restored by the present owners, beginning in 1974, and includes the kitchen where the first Key lime pie is said to have been baked. The guest wing, added in 1989, houses the bed-and-breakfast inn with 15 rooms, each with private baths.

Among the many interesting features to note is the 1853 Chickering grand piano in the music room, which belonged to Henry James and came from his home in Newport. In a glass case in the library, you can see Ernest Hemingway's favorite big game gun, a Westley Richards .577, with which he was often photographed. In the dining room, the gold-colored tableware is meant to suggest the original solid gold Tiffany service for 24 that Curry had made. Some pieces are on display at the Audubon House. Daily tours: $5 adults.

Across the street (where there's a jewelry store) was the site of the *Tradewinds Club* in which Tennessee Williams stayed.

Casa Antigua (16) (312 Simonton Street at the corner of Rose Lane) was Hemingways' first Key West pad and the place where he wrote most of *A Farewell to Arms.* Papa and his wife, Pauline, came to Key West in 1928 by ferry from Cuba after a voyage from France, having heard about the island from writer John Dos Passos, who joined them later. Key West's freewheeling atmosphere in 1929 is described by Dos Passos in his autobiography, *The Best of Times.* Casa Antigua was once an inn; now the large building is a private residence separated by a fabulous tropical garden and swimming pool from the owners' craft store, *Pelican Poop,* at the front.

Donkey Milk House (17) (613 Eaton Street; Tel. 296–1866). Built in the 1860s and occupied by the same family for over 120 years, the house was saved from the Great Fire of 1886 by a U.S. Marshall who dynamited the nearby structures along Eaton Street. It is a good example of the architectural style known as Classical Revival in Key West and won an award in 1992 for its restoration.

There's a century-old Cuban rainwater vessel out front, now filled with plants; inside, the floors have Spanish tiles and hand-decorated ceilings dating from 1890. The owners live in the 10-room house filled with fine period furniture and open it to the public as a house museum. There is a small antiques shop on the first floor. Hours: 10 A.M.–5 P.M. Self-guided tours: $5.

Octagon House (18) (712 Eaton Street), a wood frame house built at the turn of the century by Richard Peacon, a grocery store owner, has been given its name because of its unusual multi-sided structure. Angelo Donghia, one of the best-known interior decorators of the 1960s, bought the house in 1974 for $45,000 and renovated it. Six year later, fashion designer Calvin Klein paid the princely sum of $975,000 for it—the highest amount ever paid for a Conch house up to that time. Now on the National Register of Historic Places, it recently sold for a reported $1 million.

On Peacon Lane, a small street facing the Octagon house, an abode at 328 Peacon Lane is said to be the least altered of any Key West home. The kitchen in the rear is detached from the house, a precaution against fire seen in the design of houses in olden times. In the 1970s Henry Faulkner, an artist and every inch as much an eccentric as his friend Tennessee Williams, lived here with his goat, Alice, which he often dressed up and took to parties. The house is now owned by the son of Bertolt Brecht.

Monroe County Public Library (19) (700 Fleming Street) in an art deco–style building houses a wonderful collection of old photographs, local historical documents, and genealogy records that researchers and other interested parties are welcome to use. The west side of the building opens onto a garden festooned with palms, acquired as a result of a benefactor who donated the money specifically for them.

Across the street, the twin Victorian houses (701 and 703 Fleming Street) with wrap-around verandas were dilapidated when Jerry Herman of Broadway fame bought them in the early 1980s. After a superb two-year restoration, Herman sold the corner house and lived at the other. Herman's best-known hits were *Aunti Mame, Hello Dolly!* and *La Cage aux Folles.*

Down the street, *Fausto's Food Palace* (522 Fleming Street) calls itself a social center and the town's oldest grocery store; and *Key West Island Bookstore* (513 Fleming Street) is the town's best for books on Key West and those by writers associated with the town.

Gingerbread House (20) (615 Elizabeth Street at Baker's Lane) has so much filigree trim it could be called the Wedding Cake House. The name would be appropriate because it was built in the 1880s by Benjamin Baker, a lumber-mill owner and builder, as a wedding present to his daughter. The house, which won a Preservation Award in 1995, was so well built that during a tornado in 1972, the structure was lifted 7 feet off its foundation but not damaged.

Around the corner the small, dark wood house at 709 Baker's Lane was the home of James Herlihy, author of *Midnight Cowboy* and *Blue Denim,* among others, in the late 1960s. He, too, was a good friend of Tennessee Williams. Note the stained-glass window above the front door.

Windsor Compound (21) (713–727 Windsor Lane). At several locations in Key West, groups of adjoining dilapidated houses have been renovated as residences for writers. The Windsor Compound has served as the winter residence for such important writers as 1993 Poet Laureate Richard Wilbur and Pulitzer Prize–winner John Hersey, who wrote *A Bell for Adano* and *Hiroshima,* among others.

Farther along at Margaret and Angela streets is the *Key West Cemetery* where burials are in above-ground tombs, as in New Orleans. The cemetery is famous for some of the inscriptions on the tombstones; the one most often cited reads, "I told you I was sick." Some of the deceased were buried with their pets. The gates close at sunset.

Burton House (22) (608 Angela Street). Philip Burton, a playwright, author, and Shakespearean scholar, served as headmaster at the Port Talbot School early in his career and became the foster parent of actor Richard Burton. The elder Burton bought the Key West cottage in 1974 and lived there until his death in 1995. Elizabeth Taylor was a frequent visitor.

Secret Garden (23) (One Free School Lane; Tel. 294–0015). Immediately after 521 Simonton (across the street from the Heron Hotel) is Free School Lane, which leads to the entrance of Nancy Forrester's Secret Garden, the largest private tropical garden in Key West and jungle-thick with enormous trees, flowers, and birds. Walking tours led by historian Sharon Wells and other guides depart from here daily at 10 A.M. (Tel. 294–8380).

Tennessee Williams House (24) (1431 Duncan Street). The famous playwright visited Key West for a few months in 1941 where he finished *Battle of Angels* and returned frequently for visits. In 1951, he bought a modest house and had it moved from Bahama Street, a lane just east of Duval, to Duncan Street about a mile to the east, for greater privacy. The one-story white-frame cottage with red shutters was his home for three decades until his death in 1983. During those years he won two Pulitzers—for *A Streetcar Named Desire* and *Cat on a Hot Tin Roof.* Among the other plays he wrote here were *Night of the Iguana* and *The Rose Tattoo,* which was later filmed in Key West with some of the scenes shot at Williams's house. The swimming pool has a mosaic tile rose tattoo on the pool floor.

Williams enjoyed playing the role as Key West's most famous celebrity during the 1950s and 60s, appearing regularly at parties and bars and entertaining Gore Vidal, Truman Capote, and other famous friends. Williams, who was 30 years old when he first came to Key West, has been quoted as saying that he came because he "liked to swim and because Key West was the southernmost place in America."

Tennessee Williams Fine Arts Center (Tel. 294–6232) at Florida Keys Community College on Stock Island was built in Williams's honor. The center stages plays, dance, films, and concerts during the winter season.

Fort Zachary Taylor (25) (Tel. 292–6713). On the southwestern end of the island (about a 10-minute bike ride from Mallory Square) stands a trapezoid-shaped fort, which was begun in 1854 and finished in 1875, 21 years later. During the Civil War it was controlled by Union forces, who used it as a base for blockading Confederate ships. Buried under tons of sand and largely forgotten, it was restored in the 1960s, mainly through the efforts of historian Howard England. The fort has a large collection of Civil War artifacts. The grounds of the fort are a park with a large manmade beach and picnic areas, popular with families. Hours: Daily 8 A.M. to sunset; Admission: $3. Free tour of the fort at 2 P.M.

THE OTHER KEY WEST

Three miles from the pier and Mallory Square at the eastern end of the island along U.S. 1 is another Key West, as different as the 150 years that separate them. A city bus connects the two, but unless you have a particular fondness for shopping centers, you need not bother.

East Martello (3500 South Roosevelt Boulevard, next to Key West International Airport). The historic brick and masonry Civil War fort is a National Historic Site. The East Martello Museum and Art Gallery, located in the tower, holds a large collection of artifacts from the Keys and Key West. The second wing gallery features exhibitions that change monthly during the season. Hours: Daily 9:30 A.M.–5:30 P.M. $3 adults; $1 children.

Thomas Riggs Wildlife Refuge (South Roosevelt Boulevard; Tel. 296–6346 or 294–2116). Bird-watchers and nature lovers will find the spot a refuge away from the crowds. An observation platform provides views of Key West's historic salt ponds and a chance to see heron, ibis, osprey, and small wading birds. Phone ahead to be sure the reserve's gates are open.

SPORTS

GOLF: *Key West Resort Golf Course* (6450 East College Road; Tel. 305–294–5232). The 18-hole course (6,500 yards, par 70) is located on Stock Island about three miles east of the pier. Call for tee times, carts, and club rental information.

FISHING: Key West offers good deep-sea fishing in the Atlantic and bonefishing in the shallow water backcountry on the north and west side of the Keys. Dozens of private sportfishing boats offer excursions on an individual or charter basis. Check out *Capt. Bill Wickers' Charter Boat Linda D* (City Marina; Tel. 800–299–9798); *Yankee Cruise & Fishing* (Lands End Marina, Margaret Street; Tel. 800–634–0939); or *The Galleon* (617 Front Street; Tel. 296–7711, 800–544–3030), a marina and water sports center. Half- and full-day charters are available.

DIVING: The water sports center at the *Hyatt Key West* arranges diving and snorkeling excursions. *Key West Pro Dive Shop* (3128 North Roosevelt Boulevard; Tel. 800–426–0707, 296–3823) has daily excursions for snorkelers to advanced divers; instruction and equipment are available.

SAILING AND KAYAKING: *Sebago Catamarans* (328 Simonton Street; 305–292–5687) offers catamaran sailing with snorkeling and kayaking or fishing. Excursions depart at 9 A.M. and 1 P.M. from Key West Bight at the east end of Front Street.

BEACHES: If you really prefer a day in the sun, Smathers Beach (South Roosevelt Boulevard) is a 3-mile stretch favored by sporty types. It's body-to-body during college spring break. Water sports equipment is available for rent. Higgs Beach (Atlantic Boulevard) is popular with gay men. There are shaded picnic tables and a snack stand.

Close to the port on the gulf, the Hyatt Key West has a postage stamp beach and a pretty swimming pool. If you call in advance and plan to have lunch at their attractive restaurant, *Nicola,* you are not likely to be turned away for a swim.

NATURE IN THE WILD: The north/northwest side of the Keys, known as the backcountry, is a region of shallow flats and mangroves which, for the most part, lies along the north side of U.S. 1. Not easily navigable or accessible to major boat traffic, the area is largely untraveled, unspoiled, and rich in plant and animal life. Kayaking is ideal for excursions here, and tours are available with guides eager to share their knowledge about the Keys' environment. Wildlife abounds; kayakers frequently spot roseate spoonbills, osprey, great white herons, and even bald eagles. The flats support small lobster, young reef fish, turtles, stingrays, and big predators like shark and barracuda.

SHOPPING

ART AND ANTIQUITIES: Key West has a lively art community and more than three dozen art galleries showing their works; most are on or near Duval Street and feature almost every kind of art. *Key West Art Center* (301 Front Street; Tel. 305–294–1241) is a nonprofit artist cooperative housed in a turn-of-the-century structure where members, who must be local property owners, showcase their work. On alternating Thursdays, the center presents a public forum on a wide range of practical topics.

Guild Hall Gallery (614 Duval Street; Tel. 305–296–6076) is a cooperative of local women artists. *Gingerbread Square* (1207 Duval Street) is the oldest private gallery in Key West and represents many of the best artists. The Key West Art Gallery Association publishes a brochure with a map and brief descriptions of the specialty of each of its twenty-two members.

CANDY AND COFFEE: *Baby's Place Coffee Bar* (1111 Duval Street; Tel. 800–523–2326, 292–3739) bills itself as the Southernmost Coffee Roasters in America and sells 50 kinds of coffee from around the world. For those with a sweet tooth, *Jim Garrahy's Fudge Kitchen* (Clinton Square) has Key lime fudge, which you can watch being made in the afternoon and try a free sample; or, buy a slice for about $10 a pound. *Key West Candy Store* (817 Duval Street; Tel. 305–293–8505) also has Key lime fudge.

CLOTHING AND GIFTS: *Bird in Hand* (400 Front Street) features a great variety of crafts by local artists. *Cavanagh's* (520 Front Street) is something of a decorator's dream with everything from unusual rugs to Chinese porcelain and just as unusual clothing and jewelry. *Club West Casual Wear* (Clinton Square Market) has stylish, easy-to-wash cotton sportswear for great low prices.

Key West Aloe (524 Front Street) makes a full line of skin and body care products; *Baskets,* which is part of the store, makes up spice, candle, herb, and many other types of pretty gift baskets. *Key West Island Bookstore* (513 Fleming St.) has the best selection on books on Key West and its well-known writers. *Kokopelli* (824 Duval Street) features art, jewelry, pottery and object d'art from the American Southwest. *Kudo* (1208 Duval Street; Tel. 294–3771) specializes in African art and rugs.

DINING AND RESTAURANTS

Asia Buffet (221 Duval Street; Tel. 305–292–0090) offers a more-than-you-can-eat inexpensive lunch and early dinner buffets.

Blue Heaven (729 Thomas Street; Tel. 296–8666) serves Caribbean and vegetarian soul food in an outdoor setting with huge shade trees overhead and roosters under foot. (See #11 above for description). Inexpensive.

Cafe Marquessa (600 Fleming Street; Tel. 305–292–1244) is one of Key West's top restaurants for sophisticated island fare in a chic setting. Moderately expensive.

Café des Artistes (1007 Simonton Street; Tel. 305–294–7100). Top French restaurant. Expensive.

El Siboney (900 Catherine Street; Tel. 305–296–4184) has won the hearts of locals for Cuban dishes, but I found only the black bean soup and price worth the long walk. Inexpensive.

Jimmy Buffett's Margaritaville (500 Duval Street; Tel. 305–292–1435). Enjoy "cheeseburgers in paradise" with a front-row seat on Duval for the passing parade. Music in the afternoon and evening. Moderate.

Louie's Backyard (700 Waddell Street; Tel. 305–294–1061) has been on everyone's favorite list for ages, no matter how disinterested the waiters in providing good service. But then, there are great views of the Atlantic. Moderately expensive.

Nicola Seafood (Hyatt Resort & Marina, 601 Front Street) overlooking the Gulf of Mexico has a new menu of lunch treats with a Caribbean flavor. A champagne brunch is a Sunday special. The poolside *Scuttles* offers tropical drinks and light dishes, and you don't have to leave your lounge chair. *Nick's Bar & Grill,* upstairs from Nicola's, is delightful for cocktails or dinner with a spectacular view of the sunset.

Pepe's Café & Steak House (806 Caroline Street; Tel. 305–294–7192) has served breakfast, lunch, and dinner for eons at surprisingly low prices. In season, Apalachicola Bay oysters are a specialty.

Pier House (One Duval Street; Tel. 296–4600) is famous for its seafood, margaritas, and sunset location. Moderately expensive.

Yo Sake (722 Duval Street; Tel. 305–294–2288). Sushi with a tropical touch under a billowing white canvas. Moderate.

ENTERTAINMENT

After the sun goes down, Key West's nightlife lights up all over town with comedy and combos–rock, pop, reggae, soul, Cuban, country, and more. Key West even has its own brand of music—Conchtown rhythm—a mix of New Orleans jazz and calypso.

Unfortunately, cruise ships must leave their dock by 6 P.M.—that's part of the agreement the lines made with the city. But you don't have to miss out on all the fun, as some places like *Rick's* (208 Duval Street; Tel. 296–4890) and *Jimmy Buffett's Margaritaville* (500 Duval Street; Tel. 292–1435) get started with music in the afternoon, and others like *Sloppy Joe's* (201 Duval Street; Tel. 294–5717) never seem to stop.

The *Wine Galley* (1 Duval Street; Tel. 296–4600), a piano bar at the Pier House usually presided over by Bobby Nesbitt, who has a way with Cole Porter, and *Havana Dock,* upstairs from the Wine Galley, with a wide deck that's packed at sunset, are close enough to the pier that you could make a mad dash to your ship just before the gangway goes up.

CELEBRATIONS

January–April: Old Islands Days highlight the Keys history and culture with Key West's House & Garden Tours; Art Fest; Literary Seminar; and others. A calendar of events is available from the Chamber of Commerce (Mallory Square/Wall Street).

April: A ten-day festival in late April celebrates the Conch Republic Independence, when in 1882, Key West declared war and seceded from the Union.

July: Hemingway Days is a week of activities to celebrate the birthday of Ernest Hemingway on July 21. The seven-day festival, rich in nostalgia for Hemingway buffs, includes a Hemingway Look-Alike, short story, and storytelling contests, a writer's workshop and conference, a radio trivia quiz, and more.

October: Fantasy Fest, a ten-day event in late October embracing Hallowen, is Key West's answer to New Orleans' Mardi Gras, with food fests, street fairs, concerts, an arts-and-crafts show, and more. There are a Pretenders-in-Paradise Costume Contest, Pet Masquerade and Parade, and other activities capped by Saturday night's Twilight Fantasy Parade with fancy floats.

THE SUNSETS

Key West abounds with wonders—natural and manmade—but its famous sunset is something of both. Daily as sunset nears islanders joined by tourists, young and old, arrive at Mallory Square pier. (Hotel desk clerks watch for the exact second the sun is to set and alert guests so they can go barreling down to see it.) Soon the place is alive with entertainment: Jugglers here, tumblers there, foot-tapping music all around; a unicyclist wriggling free of a straitjacket; a gaily dressed young woman beating out a tune on a washboard. There is applause not only for the entertainers but the entire celebration. The applause grows louder when the Key West sun—that massive fireball symbolizing life—falls below the horizon.

Jamaica

MONTEGO BAY, OCHO RIOS, PORT ANTONIO, KINGSTON

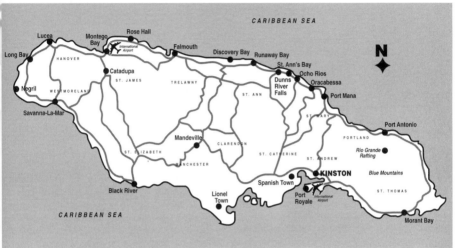

AT A GLANCE

CHAPTER CONTENTS

THE QUINTESSENCE OF THE TROPICS

How easy it is to fall in love with Jamaica! Awesome blue-green mountains frame its white sand beaches and turquoise waters and cool the air of the tropical sun. Voluptuous hillsides decorated with brilliant flowers, forests alive with vivid birds, trees laden with exotic fruits, rushing waters, laughing children, gentle people whose voices lilt as though they were singing—these are the charms with which this Caribbean beauty seduces her admirers.

Jamaica, situated 90 miles south of Cuba and an hour-and-a-half flying time from Miami, is the third largest island in the Caribbean and covers 4,411 square miles. Those who think of her simply as another Caribbean island are often surprised by their sense of being in a big country.

The impression comes in part from the thickly forested mountains, which rise to 7,402 feet at their peak and cut the north coast from the south. A further sense of space comes from the land's diversity and richness. Over 126 rivers flow down the mountainsides; the tropical landscape nurtures 3,000 species of plants, including 600 unique to the island, and hundreds of birds. Indeed, Jamaica's name is derived from the ancient Arawak *Xaymaca*, meaning land of wood and water.

A third, but more elusive, reason for Jamaica's aura of a big country is its distinctive culture, built layer upon layer from the Spaniards who first plundered and victimized the original Arawak inhabitants to the English who colonized and exploited it, to the Africans and Asians who worked the plantations or fled to freedom behind the mountains of the interior. Levantine traders, Christian missionaries, Rastafarian cultists, movie stars, polo players, novelists, Black Power advocates, Third World activists, and pop music superstars are all threads in its richly textured tapestry.

Jamaica's capital, Kingston, is situated on the south coast on one of the best natural harbors in the Caribbean. It is the commercial, cultural, and administrative center of the country, but not the tourist one. The tourist's Jamaica stretches more than 100 miles along the north coast from Negril on the west to Port Antonio on the east. It is dotted with resorts of all styles where it's easy to be lazy under a bright Caribbean sun or be active with tennis, golf, horseback riding, scuba, and a dozen other sports. More adventurous tourists climb the majestic Blue Mountains, camp along less-traveled

coasts, and explore the river valleys and tiny villages of the interior. Near the coast, mountain streams rush headlong to the sea or converge in waterfalls under umbrellas of thick foliage and brilliant flowers—settings that are the quintessence of the tropics as visitors imagine them.

THE JAMAICAN DISCOVERY

Jamaica's history is as vivid as its landscape. It was first sighted by Christopher Columbus on his second voyage in 1494, whereupon its beauty led him to describe it as "the fairest isle that eyes have seen" and to name it Santa Gloria. Unfortunately, the island was to become the scene of his most inglorious days.

On Columbus's fourth and final voyage two of his ships were so badly damaged off the coast of Santa Gloria that he had to beach them at a protected cove that today is identified as St. Ann's Bay. Here, Columbus spent a year awaiting rescue by other Spanish expeditioners in nearby Hispaniola. After his return to Spain, Columbus, having fought a long battle with the Spanish Crown to retain the land and titles promised him, was granted Jamaica as part of his family domain. To this day, Columbus's heirs carry the title of El Marquis de Jamaica.

After Columbus's death in 1506, his son Diego became the Governor of the Indies; from Santo Domingo he sent Juan de Esquivel, a former lieutenant of his father's, to Jamaica to establish a colony. Under him the town of *Sevilla la Nueva*, or New Seville, was laid out in 1509, and other settlements were made along the coast, particularly in the south, which the Spaniards found to be healthier. In 1523 they established Villa de la Vega, and twelve years later, abandoning New Seville, they moved their capital to the south coast. It was renamed St. Jago de la Vega; later, the English called it simply Spanish Town.

ARRIVAL OF THE BRITISH

By 1655 when the British seized control of the island, the Spaniards had already annihilated the native Arawaks—estimated to have numbered between 60,000 and 100,000—through enslavement or disease and had replaced them with African slaves. The Spaniards fled to nearby Cuba, but their slaves took to the mountains and continued fighting; they became known as the Maroons, from the Spanish *cimarron,* or wild. The British were unable to defeat them and finally made an agreement enabling the Maroons to stay in the mountains with a certain autonomy in exchange for peace.

Unfortunately, British rule was no better than the Spanish. Rather, the island became the base for the most famous and infamous pirates of the century who operated with the blessings of the Crown to such an extent that Henry Morgan, one of the most notorious, was actually knighted and made a lieutenant governor of Jamaica. Port Royal, on a spit of land west of Kingston airport, became such a scandalous pirate's port that it earned the title of "the wickedest city in Christendom."

From a pirates' lair, Jamaica became an eighteenth-century center of the Caribbean slave trade where, it is said, as many as a million Africans were sold to the owners of sugar plantations that had been developed throughout the region. The British also turned it into a sugar colony of enormous wealth.

THE ROAD TO NATIONHOOD

By the nineteenth century, Jamaica had become Britain's most important Caribbean colony, economically. Great plantations of sugar, tobacco, and indigo, and later bananas, created enormous wealth for their owners—often absentee landlords living splendidly in England. There were uprisings by slaves and rebellions by freedmen—the separate mulatto class that had resulted from the unions between white men and black women.

In 1834 slavery was finally abolished, but that was only the first battle. For the next century, every attempt by the freed slaves to improve their lot and to have a voice in government was dealt with harshly by the British governors in charge. A naive effort led by a Baptist deacon and small farmer, Paul Bogle, in 1865 at Morant Bay met such vicious reprisals that the governor was recalled. Soon after, Jamaica was made a Crown Colony.

By the 1930s after the Depression had taken its toll in Europe and the Americas, Jamaica's struggle for freedom and independence entered its last phase, bringing to the limelight two men whose influence is still felt today. Alexander Bustamante was a leader of the trade union movement, founder of the Jamaica Labour Party, and the first prime minister. Norman Manley, a prominent lawyer, was the founder of the People's National Party and father of the nationalist movement; he also served as premier. In 1944, Britain accepted a new constitution based on universal suffrage and in 1962 granted the country independence.

For almost a decade Jamaica enjoyed a honeymoon as the darling of the Caribbean for winter vacationers. Investment money poured in, and resorts mushroomed along the north coast. Bauxite, which is used to make aluminum, was found in commercial quantities and its mining brought new wealth.

But in the 1970s, the wave of unrest that had swept across America in the 1960s washed ashore in the Caribbean. Norman Manley's son Michael, who proved to be as charismatic as his father, sought to chart a new course, and Jamaica became the focal point of radical change. By then, too, the oil crisis and worldwide inflation were taking their toll. Before long, Jamaica, the pampered adolescent, had become a lawless teenager, and in her search for identity and direction alienated most of her friends, frightened away her suitors, and mismanaged her wealth to the point of destitution.

By October 1980, enough Jamaicans had concluded that their country's youthful excesses had gone far enough, and they voted in the government of Edward Seaga. Almost overnight the atmosphere changed; confidence was reestablished, and the American-born and Harvard-educated Seaga—with some help from his friends—got Jamaica back on track. In 1989, Manley was returned to power and, having by his own admission learned from past mistakes, steered the country on a more moderate, prudent course. Now, his successors are continuing the task of building a new Jamaica.

LASTING ACHIEVEMENTS

Although Jamaica's road to nationhood has hardly been filled with sunshine, the country radiates creativity and artistic fervor and can point to a long list of accomplishments by its multifaceted society. In addition to the quarter million slaves who were retained in Jamaica to work the sugar plantations, the colony was a trading center that attracted large numbers of Europeans and traders from the Mediterranean. After slavery was abolished, a new wave of Asians arrived as indentured workers. Thus over the centuries Jamaicans became a thorough mixture of races, nationalities, and cultures from which has grown one of the Caribbean's most dynamic societies, influential throughout the West Indies in music, dance, and art.

For starters, Jamaicans have enriched the English language and made it sing with a soft lilt. And they have made music. Reggae, one of the most influential rhythms of the pop scene today, was born in Jamaica. It, too, is a mixture of folk, soul, and rock. The annual Reggae Sunsplash, a summer music festival, attracts musicians and fans by the thousands from around the world. In the arts, Jamaica has its own national dance company, national theater, national pantomime troupe, national choral group, national art gallery, and national crafts institute.

In a country so rich with history and natural beauty, so full of fun and pleasures, it will be hard to decide what to do during your visit. You cannot see Jamaica in a day or even in a month, but if you take full advantage of your time in this extraordinary port of call, you will come away with some idea of why it enchants even the most blasé of men like Noel Coward; beguiles suitors as different as Errol Flynn and Johnny Cash; and looms so large on the Caribbean landscape that only excessive images seem to capture the whole of it.

FAST FACTS

 POPULATION: 3 million; 800,000 people live in Kingston and its surrounding metropolitan area.

 MAIN CITIES: Kingston, Montego Bay, Ocho Rios, Port Antonio, Mandeville, Negril.

 CLIMATE: Jamaica has no winter. Year-round, temperature along the coast hovers around 80°F but can go as low as 70–75°F between December and March, and up to 90°F from July through September. The rainy seasons are May–June and September–October, with short tropical downpours. Cool breezes from the sea keep the days pleasant; mountain regions can be chilly in winter months.

 CLOTHING: Lightweight tropical clothing is best year-round, but beachwear, especially scanty bathing suits (on either sex!), is not acceptable any place but at beaches and beachside hotels. You should wear a shirt or cover-up while strolling in town. Jamaicans find a too-casual appearance offensive. In winter, be sure to pack a light sweater or jacket as evenings, even on the coast, can be chilly.

 CURRENCY: Jamaican Dollar (JDS or JD$). The current exchange rate is US $1= about JD $40. Upon arrival, visitors must convert their U.S. or Canadian money into Jamaican dollars at banks or exchange bureaus, cruise ship piers, airports, or hotels, and obtain a receipt. You need an official receipt to reconvert your unspent Jamaican money. Major credit cards can be used in most hotels, shops, and some restaurants.

 CUSTOMS REGULATIONS/DEPARTURE TAX: Cruise passengers who disembark in Jamaica and return to the United States by plane must pay a JD $500 or US $15 departure tax. U.S. Customs will confiscate any fruits, vegeta-

bles, or plants from Jamaica. The only exception is flowers sold in departure lounges at the airports that have been specially packaged by the Ministry of Agriculture.

 ELECTRICITY: 110–120 volts; 50 cycles.

 ENTRY FORMALITIES: No visas for U.S. and Canadian citizens; however, a passport or birth certificate with valid photographic identification is required for proof of citizenship, and a valid driver's license is necessary for car rental identification.

 LANGUAGE: English is the official language and spoken with a melodic lilt that is sometimes difficult to understand. Jamaicans also have a patois, incomprehensible to foreigners, and their colorful speech is peppered with a plethora of words and idiomatic expressions dating back to English settler days.

 POSTAL SERVICE: Every port has a conveniently located post office where you can buy colorful Jamaican stamps as souvenirs or mail postcards and letters. (You can also mail them from your ship.)

 PUBLIC HOLIDAYS: January 1, New Year's Day; Ash Wednesday; Good Friday; Easter Monday; May 23, Labor Day; third Monday in October, National Heroes Day; first Monday in August, Independence Day; December 25, Christmas; December 26, Boxing Day.

 TELEPHONE AREA CODE: 809. Each of the main towns—Montego Bay, Ocho Rios, Kingston, etc.—has one or more different prefixes (92, 93, 94, etc.) + five digits.

 TIME: Same as U.S. Eastern Standard Time, but Jamaica does not switch to Daylight Saving Time and is therefore one hour behind Eastern time from April through October.

 VACCINATION REQUIREMENT: None.

 AIRLINES: *From the United States to Montego Bay and Kingston:* Air Jamaica, American, Continental, Northwest, USAir, and TWA. *From Canada:* Air Canada. *Intra-Island:* Air Jamaica Express serves Montego Bay, Kingston, Negril, Ocho Rios, and Port Antonio. Timair provides intra-island charters and air-tours.

INFORMATION:

In the United States, Jamaica Tourist Board Offices:

New York: 801 Second Ave., 20th Floor; NY
10017; Tel. 212–856–9727; 800–233–4582;
fax 212–856–9730

Chicago: 500 North Michigan Avenue, Suite
1030; IL 60611; Tel. 312–527–1296;
fax 312–527–1472

Coral Gables: 1320 S. Dixie Hwy., Suite 1100; FL
33146; Tel. 305–665–0557; 800–233–4582;
fax 305–666-7239

Los Angeles: 3440 Wilshire Blvd., No. 1207; CA
90010; Tel. 213–384–1123;
fax 213–384–1780

In Canada:

Toronto: 1 Eglinton Ave. East, Suite 616, Ontario
M4P 3A1; Tel. 416–482–7850;
fax 416–482–1730

In Port:

Black River: Hendriks Building, 2 High St.
(Black River P.O.); Tel. 965–2074;
fax 965–2076

Kingston (Main Office): I.C.W.I. Building, St.
Lucia Ave., New Kingston; Tel. 929–9200;
fax 929–9375

Montego Bay: Cornwall Beach; Tel. 952–4425;
fax 952–3587

Negril Adrija Plaza; Tel. 957–4243;
fax 957–4489

Ocho Rios: Ocean Village Shopping Center;
Tel. 974–2582; fax 974–2559

Port Antonio: City Centre Plaza; Tel. 993–3051;
fax 993–2117

BUDGET
PLANNING

AND OTHER PRACTICAL TIPS

Jamaica is one of the Caribbean's best vacation buys.
The favorable exchange rate means many local goods,
services, and dining experiences are excellent values.
Some things, however, can be expensive; the pattern for
what's cheap and what's expensive is uneven. As a rule,
anything that is imported—wine, cars, etc.—is expensive due to steep import duties; but locally made products—rum, beer, crafts, etc.—are cheap.

Car rentals are expensive—averaging US $54 to $70
for the smallest economy car, plus $10 to $15 per day
for insurance. Gas is also very expensive. Driving is on
the LEFT.

Taxis are expensive, but when shared with friends or
other passengers, they are the best and most economical way to see the island. When you hire a taxi, you usually get a first-rate tour guide and raconteur who will
enrich your visit with stories and pithy insights, especially if you enter into the spirit of the occasion with
conversation that shows your interest in Jamaica.

Members of JUTA (Jamaica Union of Travellers
Association) are trained drivers licensed by the government to transport visitors; their rates are set by the government. There are also unmetered city taxis. When
negotiating with a driver, be sure to agree on the price
before you get into the vehicle. Don't be shy. Ask how
much your intended time or tour will cost; add a 10
percent tip at the end (if you have been pleased with the
service).

Do not buy cheap crafts on impulse; look around first,
as there are considerable differences in quality and variety. And don't be afraid to bargain with crafts people;
they expect it. As a strategy for bargaining: you will be
amazed how fast the price drops when you start to walk
away. And don't be intimidated by the large numbers of
"higglers," as the women street vendors are known, that
greet you. If you have no interest in buying, say a polite
"No thank you, not today," and keep walking.

Eat in local restaurants featuring Jamaican cuisine,
which is unusual, delicious, and reasonably priced. In
contrast, meals and drinks at large resorts can be three
times the cost as local restaurants. Wine and drinks of
imported spirits are expensive. Bring plenty of film. It is
very expensive in Jamaica—over twice what you would
pay at home—and often hard to find.

If the goal of exploring on your own is to have a closer look and touch of Jamaica than you can get from a
tour bus, you might find these tourist "dos" and
"don'ts" helpful.

The Jamaicans are Jamaicans and very proud. Please
don't refer to them as "the natives." Nor are they happy
to have strangers shove cameras in their faces. If you
want to take candid shots, be discreet. If you want a
portrait, ask with a smile. It's easy to chat and make
friends with Jamaicans. Some are delighted to have
their pictures made; others do not like it.

As important as a 10 percent tip may be, a "good
morning," "thank you," and a smile are valued even
more. Older Jamaicans, particularly, are almost courtly
in their manner, and they very much appreciate your
courtesy. Jamaicans have a delightful sense of humor.
You can often get rid of a Jamaican peddler with humor
faster than with anger.

Don't leave valuables unattended on the beach, and
on crowded streets watch your handbag and wallet as
you would in any U.S. city. In spite of what you may have
heard about *ganja,* the Jamaican marijuana, drugs are

illegal in Jamaica. Foreigners are not immune from arrest and imprisonment if caught with drugs.

CRAFTS AND DUTY-FREE SHOPPING

Jamaica has never been considered a mecca for serious shoppers, but there are some unusual buys, especially in certain crafts and food products. Items to buy fall into two categories: those produced on the island and duty-free imports, which can run up to 30 percent lower than U.S. prices.

In Montego Bay the best shops are in the hotel district around Doctor's Cave and boutiques in deluxe hotels. Most in the city center are not worth your time, except for record stores. In Ocho Rios, there are two shopping plazas—*Island Center* and *Taj Mahal*—less than a mile from the harbor. They have duty-free shops, souvenir stores, and clothing boutiques.

ART AND ARTISTS: The most outstanding and desirable Jamaican products are original paintings and sculpture by contemporary artists who do not mass-produce their work. The best have achieved international recognition and are a source of national pride to Jamaicans. Among the most respected names are the late Edna Manley, mother of former prime minister Michael Manley, noted for her sculpture; forties artists John Dunkley and Henry Daley; and the late Kapo, the best known of the intuitive artists.

To learn about current exhibitions during your visit, contact the Jamaica Tourist Board offices. The art galleries on the north coast selling original Jamaican art and sculpture include, in Montego Bay, *Gallery of West Indian Arts* (One Orange St.), whose owner is responsible for creating a new art in the brightly painted, whimsical carved animals now found in gift shops around the island; *The Bay Gallery* (St. James Court), which holds exhibitions throughout the year. In Ocho Rios, *The Frame Centre* (Island Center); and *Harmony Hall* (Highway A-3, four miles east of Ocho Rios), which is one of the country's leading galleries, dedicated particularly to discovering and promoting promising young Jamaican artists. The largest number of galleries is in Kingston.

BOOKS/NEWSPAPERS: United States newspapers are available at hotel newsstands, usually a day late. Hotel shops are also the best place to find books on Jamaica and Jamaican cookbooks. In Ocho Rios, *Ocean Village Shopping Center* has a book and sundry shop, and several stores in new Island and Taj Mahal centers carry books on Jamaica.

CLOTHING AND FABRICS: Jamaica produces some attractive men's and women's tropical sportswear. Colorful silk-screened fabrics made into daywear and eveningwear can be found at better quality boutiques in the new shopping center at *Half Moon Bay Hotel*, east of Montego Bay and at *Swept Away* resort in Negril. The most recent addition, Reggae to Wear, makes casual dresses with a '90s look from Balinese and Indian fabrics with great designs and affordable prices in the $30 to $60 range. The clothing is widely available at hotel boutiques in Montego Bay and Ocho Rios.

Jamaica has a crop of young designers creating bathing suits and resort and daywear for the country's young professionals. Designer Michelle Haynes (Caribbean Clothing Co., 13 Oxford Terrace, Kingston 5; Tel. 809–929–0314), is the name behind Mijan, an inexpensive line of women's casual knitwear and the best known, most widely distributed. Among her latest creations are Mijan Interlocks–resort and leisurewear ideal for travel. "Interlock" is a double-stitch cotton and polyester knit that needs no ironing; and it's also a wardrobe of tops, bodysuits, skirts, jackets that can be worn together to create endless ensembles, ready to go anywhere at anytime. Mijan fashions can be purchased at Cactus Collection or Mingles in Ocho Rios and at specialty shops in Couples, Breezes Jamaica, Half Moon, and other resorts.

CRAFTS: Shopping for Jamaican crafts and products can be fun if you are not deterred by insistent hawkers. A great deal of the straw work is similar to that found in other Caribbean markets. Other products, particularly spices, woodcraft, and dolls are more distinctive. Prices are lower at markets and from street vendors than in shops, especially when you bargain, but the quality is generally better in hotel gift shops and specialty stores such as *Things Jamaican.* The Montego Bay and Ocho Rios Craft Markets have almost identical merchandise, making up in quantity and cheap prices what they lack in quality. There are huge selections of straw hats, baskets, placemats, floor and beach mats; carved statues, animals, bookends, trays, bowls, and masks; and T-shirts of every description.

The best wood products are fashioned from mahogany and mahoe, the national tree, a variegated hardwood with a blue tint. These are most attractive when they are combined with a variety of woods into such products as trays and jewelry boxes. In Montego Bay, the best workmanship can be found in products at *Things Jamaican* and *Greenwood Great House gift shop;* in Ocho Rios, at *Harmony Hall* and *Coyaba Garden Gift Shop.*

The latest woodcrafts to blossom are whimsical, brightly painted animals carved from wood. They started with Liz DeLisser, an artist and owner of the

West Indian Art Gallery in Montego Bay, who is credited with discovering the brilliant self-taught woodcarver Obed Palmer and a dozen other carvers in the Trelawny parish village of Bunkers Hill. The craftsmen turn out an array of whimsical-looking animals, from lions to doctor birds and parrots, and paint them in the colorful and unlikely colors of Carnival—a pink-whiskered lion with red or green dots, a blue alligator with orange and pink scales, etc. The figures represent a new form of Jamaican intuitive art; they are carved from Jamaican cedar, which resists cracking and termites but is easy to carve. The gallery helped Palmer finance the workshop next to his home, and DeLisser has added her colorful artistry, helping to make the animals enormously popular. Now they are produced for shops throughout Jamaica and in other Caribbean islands; they have even been featured at Bloomingdale's in New York.

From mid-November to mid-December, crafts fairs and Christmas bazaars are held frequently and are good places to find unusual gifts for Christmas presents, such as savory jams and pickles, handmade dolls, aprons and some clothing, and original art at very reasonable prices.

GROCERIES: A variety of Jamaican food products make excellent gifts to take home. In supermarkets and hotel gift shops, you can find *PickaPeppa,* a delicious spicy sauce similar to a barbecue sauce; Hellfire, another savory sauce; local spices such as pimento (allspice), curry powder, ginger, and jerk pork seasoning; and jams and preserves.

Some labels to look for are *The Gift Affair* (Tel. 978–2781), a packager of cottage industry producers of Jamaican candied fruit, jams, cakes, and spices; *Beenybud and Friends,* which packages Jamaican spices; *Bromley's Spice and Sizzle* for jars of jerk seasoning; *Busha Browne* for jars of chutney and spicy fruits; and *Ital Herb Farm,* whose packaged herbs sell in New York stores for double the price.

Jamaican coffees are among the world's finest; pure Blue Mountain coffee, however, is also the most expensive. Blends and other brands, including High Mountain, are less costly. They are priced most reasonably at grocery stores, but NOT at shopping center or airport boutiques. In Montego Bay, *Wesmore Supermarket* is open daily until midnight; another supermarket can be found at Overton Plaza (Union Street).

JEWELRY: Gemstone jewelry, including coral agate from Jamaican riverbeds, black coral, and other semi-precious stones in handwrought settings, is available at *Blue Mountain Gems* (Holiday Village, Montego Bay) and other craft shops. However, workmanship and design are unsophisticated. Duty-free stores have gold, pearls, and famous-make watches, but do not expect any of it to compare to the selections found in ports famous for shopping, such as Nassau or St. Thomas.

LIQUOR AND LIQUEURS: Among the best local products are Jamaica's fine rums and liqueurs. Appleton and Myers rums are bargains at US $5 or $6 per bottle, as is Tia Maria, the country's famous coffee liqueur. Lesser-known flavors are Rumona, Sangster's Ortanique, Blue Mountain Coffee liqueur, and a wide range of fruit-based rums.

PERFUMES: *Parfums Jamaica* (11 West Kings House Road, Kingston 10) makes a variety of fragrances for men and women; they are sold in hotel shops and specialty stores. They are nicely packaged, inexpensive, and make attractive gifts.

Duty-Free Shopping

Procedures for duty-free shopping in Jamaica permit you to take all purchases with you except liquor and tobacco products, which must be delivered in-bond to your ship. In case you are asked, you must be able to prove you are a visitor.

Duty-free stores offer the standard brands of perfumes, gold jewelry, china, and similar products available in other duty-free ports. Shops with the best and most attractive selections are found at large hotels and resorts, such as the shopping center at Half Moon Club in Montego Bay. Some other stores you might visit are *Chulani, India House,* or *Presita* (City Center, Montego Bay; Taj Mahal, Ocho Rios) for cameras and electronic equipment; *The Royal Store* and *Indian Shop* (downtown Montego Bay and Ocho Rios shopping centers) for china and crystal; and the *Swiss Stores* (Half Moon Club, Montego Bay; Ocean Village, Ocho Rios) for watches and fine jewelry.

 ## Cuisine and Dining

Of all the islands you might visit during a Caribbean cruise, Jamaica is one waiting for those with an inquisitive palate. The country's unusual and exotic national dishes are found no place else in the region. The taste of Jamaica is an experience that inspires the African expression *nyam,* meaning to eat happily and heartily.

For a morning refreshment, pick an odd-looking fruit from a street vendor balancing her supply in a colorful basket on her head. (She will also be a wonderful portrait in your camera lens—especially when you please her by making a purchase.) Jamaica is a cornucopia of tropical fruits and vegetables: ortanique (orange-tangerine hybrid), mango, soursop, star apple, and otaheite apple are a few of the delicious ones awaiting you.

The traditional breakfast dish is *saltfish and ackee.* Ackee is an unusual fruit that looks like red peppers growing on a tree, but when ripe, bursts open to reveal large black seeds covered with yellow lobes. The lobes are boiled, blended with onion, pepper, bacon, and salted cod. This mixture is often served with boiled green banana, johnny cakes (fried flour dumplings), and bammies (cassava cakes). The flavor and texture of ackee suggest scrambled eggs and blend well with the fish.

For lunch and dinner, Jamaican soups are rich and bold enough to make a meal alone. The tastiest are *pumpkin soup* (hot or cold); *red bean soup;* and *pepperpot,* a hearty blend of callaloo (spinach-like greens), crab, pork, coconut milk, root vegetables such as yam, and seasonings. Callaloo, yams, yucca, or cassava are among the most common ingredients of Caribbean cuisine, but each island has its own special treatment.

Among the most popular dishes are *escovitched fish,* snapper or small reef fish fried whole in a spicy sauce of onions, hot peppers, green peppers, and tomatoes; *rundown,* which is mackerel or salted cod boiled in coconut milk and eaten with a mush of onions and peppers; and *stamp and go,* crisp codfish fritters eaten with a meal or as finger food.

Jerk pork or *jerk chicken* is to Jamaica what barbecue is to Texas—only different. The meat is cooked slowly for hours over an open fire of the pimento (allspice) tree wood, permeating the meat with the particular flavor. *Jerking,* as this method of preparation is known, is a specialty of the Port Antonio area, and ten years ago there was only one jerk place on the entire north coast. Now they are everywhere—a testimony to its great popularity with visitors and Jamaicans alike.

Seafood is plentiful in Jamaica, including local peppery shrimp from the Black River area, lobster, land crabs, and a variety of fish from grouper to wahoo. But of all the selections smoked marlin is fabulous—more delicate and delicious than smoked salmon. Like jerk pork and chicken, it is cooked slowly over a pimento wood fire, giving it an unusual flavor. This specialty is made by *Valhalla Farms* (9 St. James Street, Montego Bay), among others, and appears on some restaurant menus. You can also buy it packaged in some supermarkets.

For beverages, Jamaica's Red Stripe beer is the perfect complement to local cuisine. There's Dragon Stout, too, and a variety of liqueurs. Ting, a grapefruit juice soda, is wonderfully refreshing.

SPORTS AND ENTERTAINMENT

Jamaica has some of the best sports facilities in the Caribbean for golf, tennis, horseback riding, and aquatic adventures. If you had the time, you could hike through forests in the Blue Mountains, raft down the Rio Grande in Port Antonio, troll for blue marlin and other game fish a few miles offshore, and practice the equestrian arts at Chukka Cove at St. Ann's Bay.

If your cruise ship does not offer packages or make arrangements for your desired sport and you must do it yourself, a word of advice: call ahead or ask your travel agent to make reservations in order to guarantee space. This is especially important during the peak season from December through April, and particularly for golf, diving, and deep-sea fishing charters.

The three-leg, blue marlin tournament—an event which showcases Jamaica as a premier marlin location, starts in early September with a five-day international meet sponsored by the Montego Bay Yacht Club; a second leg two weeks later in Ocho Rios; and a third in Port Antonio in early October. For spectator sports, cricket is king here and the national passion of many West Indians.

NIGHTLIFE, CULTURAL EVENTS, AND FESTIVALS

Although there are no casinos (only slot machines in some hotels) or glitzy cabaret shows in Jamaica, there is plenty of after-dark entertainment, from beach parties to concerts and special events featuring authentic Jamaican folkloric dancing, music, and local food. Most nightspots do not open until 9 P.M. or really get going until midnight. To learn what's happening, check the tourist tabloids, distributed free at hotels and restaurants.

Two popular Jamaican evening events highlighting the indigenous culture are held in each of the major resort centers. In Montego Bay, *A Night on the Great River* is a torch-lit boat ride to an island upstream on the Great River where participants enjoy drinks, dinner, a folkloric show, and dancing in a recreated Arawak village. In Ocho Rios, *A Night on the White River* and the weekly *Dunn's River Beach Party* are variations on the same theme.

Jamaicans have a wonderful expression for "feeling happy and alive," which they sum up with one patois word, *irie.* Any event can turn into a festival, whether it's a long weekend during a public holiday or a gathering of friends for a special event. But in the true sense of festival, Jamaica's vibrant culture, lively spirit, and love of music are most visible and infectious during Carnival in April, Independence Week celebrations in August, and Junkanoo at Christmas.

Junkanoo is a sort of Carnival celebrated with lots of music, parties, and street parades highlighted by colorfully costumed participants, masked dancers, and musicians. It takes place between Christmas and the New Year and arises from the tradition during slavery when Christmas was the only day in the year the slaves were allowed to celebrate.

Carnival, which started in Jamaica in 1990 with guidance from experts who stage the famous Carnival in Trinidad, borrows the traditions from Trinidad but has acquired more of a Jamaican character with each passing year. The main venue is Kingston, with mini-versions in the resort centers on the north coast.

The prelude to Independence Day in August starts in July with a month-long agenda of Jamaica's best talent in the arts, including dance performances, art exhibits, culinary fairs, and concerts. The country's far-flung sons and daughters return en masse from overseas to celebrate, and visitors are encouraged to join in.

Annually in August, the internationally famous *Reggae Sunsplash,* featuring top local and foreign reggae artists, is held in the Montego Bay–Ocho Rios area. The five-day event is attended by thousands of music lovers from Jamaica and around the world.

INTRODUCTION TO MONTEGO BAY

Whether they arrive by cruise ship or by air, most visitors' first glimpse of Jamaica is Montego Bay, the country's second largest town and center of tourist development for five decades. Immediately behind the town and coast rise green-clad mountains with whitewashed houses and flowering gardens in the kind of setting that has earned Jamaica its lush, tropical image.

Even though MoBay, as it is known, looks new, the town was first developed two centuries ago as a port—one of several on the north coast—from which sugar was shipped to Europe and other markets. Something of its past is retained in restored old buildings that house attractive restaurants and shops and historic mansions that are museums or hotel centerpieces.

Freeport, where your ship docks, and the entire waterfront area from the pier to Doctor's Cave beach are the result of government and private urban development on land reclaimed from the sea. In addition to giving Montego Bay a new harbor, this has restored and expanded the beach areas to as much as ten times their size three decades ago. The town of Montego Bay divides conveniently into two parts: the town center or western portion, which is the first part you reach coming into Montego Bay from the port, and the tourist district or eastern side.

The town center is the business district, which includes banks, professional offices, stores, and some historic landmarks as well as industrious street salesladies, called higglers, who peddle their produce and products in the marketplace. Here, too, pushcart vendors sell snacks, cold drinks, and ice cream to the loudspeaker blare of reggae and calypso from streetside record shops. The scene might not be for everyone, but it certainly *is* Jamaican.

The eastern section of town (approximately mile from the Montego Bay Craft Market at Market and Harbour streets) comprises the original tourist area of older hotels, congenial meeting and eating spots, and a wide assortment of shops. If you want nothing more than a golden day on Doctor's Cave Beach and a chance to sample Jamaica's water sports, you won't have to travel any farther than this area of town. Most hotels, restaurants, and dozens of shops and craft vendors are located along the main coastal arteries of Gloucester and Kent avenues; a few are perched on the hillside overlooking the town.

Dining choices range from finger-food sold by sidewalk vendors to Continental fare at chic resorts. At *The Pork Pit,* now located in the hotel area known as The Strip, you can have your first adventure in Jamaican food by trying *jerk pork* or *jerk chicken,* a popular Jamaican specialty.

The touring area of Montego Bay and its nearby attractions covers a 40-mile coastal stretch between Falmouth, 23 miles to the east, and Tryall Golf and Beach Club, 15 miles west of the town. How far to travel and how much to see will largely depend on which attractions—grand plantation houses, lavish gardens, the beach, or sports—have the strongest appeal to you.

East of Montego Bay along a coastal road leading to Ocho Rios, there is a series of luxury beach resorts and two of the most splendid plantation houses or "great houses" in Jamaica, both dating from the eighteenth century. West from the pier for 10 to 12 miles, you come to the fashionable resorts of Round Hill and Tryall Golf and Beach Club, whose centerpiece is an eighteenth-century plantation house. Farther west, the road leads to Negril, famous for its 7-mile stretch of beach and laid-back life-style.

PORT PROFILE: MONTEGO BAY

EMBARKATION: The cruise ship dock is three miles west of downtown in the Freeport area of Montego Bay Harbor, a deep-water pier with eight berths. Four cruise ships can dock at a time; the other berths are used for cargo ships. No special identification is required; passengers may go to and come from their ships freely. A fleet of JUTA cabs, minibuses, and other ground transportation is on hand to take passengers the short ride to town or on tour. A Jamaica Tourist Board information booth is in the terminal to assist visitors. There are phones and shops; on the west side of the port is the Montego Freeport in-bond shopping area which has duty-free stores—that's why it is called "Freeport." China, watches, and other items typical of duty-free shops are available. In general, the merchandise is poor. Also, there is an additional charge of 5 to 10 percent for the use of credit cards.

LOCAL TRANSPORTATION: *Taxis:* JUTA (Jamaica Union of Travellers Association), the government-licensed and -approved fleet, are reliable and have something of a monopoly at the docks. Remember, you can share the cost of a taxi with up to three people. A shuttle from the pier to MoBay city center costs $2 per person; to Doctor's Cave Beach, US $3 per person; east to Half Moon Club, $20; west to Tryall Resort and Golf Club, $30. A sign in the Terminal building lists all prices of taxis and tours to major destinations. No public buses leave from the piers.

Soon Come Shuttle: The latest addition–and the best bargain in Jamaica–is the "Soon Come Shuttle." The service consists of four brightly colored small buses that run on designated routes along the hotel district known as The Strip, where most of the restaurants, bars, and shops catering to tourists are located, and as far as Sea Castles, about 10 miles east of town. A ride costs US $1–2 per ride, depending on the route. Operated by Air Jamaica Tours in conjunction with the two main taxi organizations and 130 hotels, bars, restaurants, shops, water sports operators, and other tourist enterprises in Montego Bay, the shuttle is meant to help visitors have a fun-filled holiday during their stay in Jamaica. The group publishes a newsletter with information on music, sports, and other activities taking place during the month and a colorful map showing all the stops on the routes. The stops are also designated by the Soon Come Shuttle logo–a friendly, brightly colored parrot.

To rent motorbikes, you will need to take a taxi from the pier into town, where you can rent bikes and mopeds from *Montego Bay Bike Rentals* or *Montego*

Honda (21 Gloucester Avenue; Tel. 952–4984). Rates are about US $30 to $40 per day for scooters; US $35 per day for motorcycles, plus a $300 deposit which is refunded upon return of the vehicle in good condition. Driving is on the **LEFT**. It is imperative that you be an experienced driver. Jamaican drivers go slightly mad behind the wheel of a car and think the entire road is theirs—blind curves and all!

CAR RENTALS: *United Car Rentals* (49 Gloucester Avenue, Montego Bay; Tel. 952–3077) offers reasonable rates by Jamaican standards and has pickup service at the port if you call. As an example of prices, *Island Car Rental)* in Montego Bay charges for a subcompact, standard shift, US $65; automatic, US $71; air-conditioned, US $77. Rates include gas, unlimited mileage, and insurance, which is compulsory. If you do not have a major credit card, you must leave a large deposit.

Major rental companies such as Avis and Budget are located at Sangster International Airport east of town (about 5 miles from the pier). If you want to rent from one of them, it is better to go directly to their airport offices. Although the companies have pickup service at the pier when you reserve in advance, there could be a long wait, as rental companies are inclined to deal with their airport traffic first. Remember, driving is on the **LEFT**. Avis, Tel. 952–4543; Budget, Tel. 952–5061; Affordable, Tel. 952–4975; National, Tel. 952–2769.

EMERGENCY NUMBERS:

Medical Service, Dial 110 or Cornwall Regional Hospital, Tel. 952–5100;

Police Department, Dial 119;

Ambulance, Dial 110

SERVICE CLUBS: *Rotary* meets for lunch at Sandals Royal, Tuesday, 12:45 P.M.; *Kiwanis* at Wexford Court Hotel, Thursday, 1–3 P.M.; *Lions* at Seawind Hotel, second and fourth Thursday, 12:30 P.M.

INFORMATION: The Jamaica Tourist Board's main office at Cornwall Beach (Tel. 952–4425) has extremely courteous and helpful staff and literature on local tours and attractions.

AUTHOR'S FAVORITE ATTRACTIONS

CORAL SEE SEMI-SUBMERSIBLE
GOLF, HORSEBACK RIDING, OR TENNIS
DAY TRIPS: ROSE HALL GREAT HOUSE; APPLETON EXPRESS
MEET THE PEOPLE
SUPERMARKET SHOPPING FOR JAMAICAN PRODUCTS

MONTEGO BAY SHORE EXCURSIONS

Cruise ships offer passengers many tour options and often have reduced rates for children. We have selected the most interesting, unique-to-Jamaica tours or those designed for a special interest. These excursions can be taken on your own by hiring a taxi or renting a car or by going on a tour. The choice between taking an organized tour or following independent travel should not be based on cost but on preference. Descriptions of places visited are given elsewhere in the chapter. The following prices are based on JUTA's published fees and may vary by a few dollars from one tour company to another.

Great House Tour: 4 hours, US $20 per hour for 1–4 persons by car. Cruise ship shore excursion, US $37 for 3 hours. This half-day trip combines a tour of Montego Bay, a drive east of town passing Half Moon and Rose Hall Beach Hotels, and a visit to the beautifully restored eighteenth-century Rose Hall Great House, home of the legendary White Witch. (See Plantation Tours later in the Montego Bay section for other options.)

Scuba Diving: 3-hour resort course for noncertified divers, US $60. It includes equipment and instruction at a hotel pool, followed by an open-water dive with instructor. For certified divers, MoBay has good licensed dive operators. You may need to make your own arrangements in advance, although more cruise ships are starting to offer diving excursions. Most morning trips are four-hour, two-tank dives that depart between 8:30 and 9 A.M.; afternoon trips are two-hour, one-tank dives that leave at 2 P.M.

Martha Brae River Rafting: 4 hours, US $36 per person with rafting. Cruise ship excursion, US $54. A mile upstream on the Martha Brae River, 23 miles east of Montego Bay, you board a 15-foot bamboo raft, skillfully maneuvered by a Jamaican helmsman, for a relaxing hour's meander downstream through lush riverside vegetation.

Negril Beach Tour: 8 hours, US $23 per person. A two-hour motorcoach drive west of Montego Bay through some of Jamaica's loveliest coastline to Negril, a resort with a 7-mile beach of Caribbean beauty. The tour is for those who put tranquil beaches at the top of their priorities.

Custom-Built Tours: The Touring Society of Jamaica, (Boscobel Post Office, St. Mary; Tel./fax: 809–975–7158) has excursions focusing on nature, birds and gardens, and art and architecture. See Ocho Rios Shore Excursions later in this chapter.

Coral See Semi-submersible: 1 hour; $35 per person. See description in Sports—Snorkeling/Diving section later in this chapter.

Golf See Sports section later in the chapter. As a cruise ship shore excursion, golfing at Half Moon Bay, 12 miles east of Montego Bay, is US $95 for 9 holes; $150 for 18 holes.

Day Cruises: up to 4 hours, about US $35 to $45 per person. Several party cruises depart from *Pier One Marina* (Howard Cook Hwy.) on a variety of boats and include reef snorkeling, light lunch, and drinks.

Airtours by Timair, Ltd. See Jamaica from the air with ex-British Airways pilots, leaving from Sangster International Airport (Montego Bay; Tel. 952–2516). Island flight-seeing costs about US $75 per person and must be arranged in advance.

MONTEGO BAY ON YOUR OWN

A WALK AROUND MONTEGO BAY

*M*ontego Bay is not a walker's joy in the way Nassau and Old San Juan are, as there is little of its historic past left to see. Yet the old town is not without interest, particularly for people watchers. Start with a brief taxi tour of Montego Bay to decide which part of town, if any, to explore on foot. Montego Bay is a maze of streets, particularly in the area of Fort and Gloucester streets, and can be confusing. Fort Street turns into Queen's Drive and curves up a hill to inland hotels and restaurants overlooking the bay. It's not a walk but a hike and it's hard-going under the warm Jamaican sun. We don't suggest it.

FORT MONTEGO At the roundabout on Harbour Drive (one block south of Howard Cook Highway) at the base of Miranda Hill are the ruins of Fort Montego, built in 1752, which still has 3 of its original 17 cannons pointed seaward. To the south, all roads merge into St. James Street (sometimes shown on maps as Barnett Street), the main road through downtown that leads to Sam Sharpe Square, the town square.

SAM SHARPE SQUARE The square, a miniature version of the Parade in Kingston, is named for Jamaican hero Sam Sharpe who was hanged by the British for leading a slave revolt in 1831. It has become traditional in recent years for candidates for national political office to launch their campaigns here. The square is centered around a white-painted, bronze fountain dating from the early 1900s. On the south side, a tableau of five bronze statues by Jamaican sculptor Kay Sullivan depicts Sharpe, Bible in hand, preaching to his followers. At the southeast corner, a very small eighteenth-century building called "The Cage" was once a prison for runaway slaves. It now houses a travel agency.

THE TOWN HOUSE Church Street, which crosses St. James Street on the west of the square, has two fine old buildings. The Town House is a Georgian structure built as a private residence in 1765 by David Morgan, a wealthy merchant. It has been a church manse, a Masonic Lodge, a warehouse, and a lawyer's office, and it has served as Montego Bay's first synagogue. In 1967, the building was bought by Nigel Pemberton, the present owner, from a group headed by Lady Sarah Churchill; and in the same year, Paul Aycock of Knoxville, Tennessee, and a group of his friends converted the cellar into a restaurant, *The Townhouse.*

ST. JAMES PARISH CHURCH Across from the Town House is the beautifully restored St. James Parish Church, established in 1782, which contains ornate monuments erected by wealthy sugar barons. Several nearby streets have nice old balconied houses, which may be interesting to photograph.

GALLERY OF WEST INDIAN ART One Orange Street. Gallery owner and artist Liz DeLisser is credited with discovering the brilliant self-taught woodcarvers of Bunkers Hill, who turn out an array of whimsical-looking animals and paint them in the vibrant colors of Carnival, creating a new form of Jamaican intuitive art. (See earlier description under Jamaican Crafts.)

GEORGIAN COURT Another block south, at Two Orange Street, two restored eighteenth-century townhouses, connected by a courtyard, hold a restaurant and art gallery.

One block east at Union Street you can turn south to the City Center, a group of duty-free shops with a limited but well-priced selection of standard goods and souvenir shops with low-quality merchandise. Unless you are an incurable shopper, your time can be better spent elsewhere. One exception is record stores that carry reggae and other West Indian recordings.

MONTEGO BAY CRAFTS MARKET You should return to the roundabout at the foot of Market Street and the Crafts Market. You can easily spend an hour or so poking around the dozens of craft stalls and haggling with vendors, but you will quickly discover that most of the stalls sell the same merchandise, and unfortunately very little is of high quality. The stall keepers will vie insistently for your attention, but do not feel under any pressure to buy. Here, you can have a tropical print shirt tailored in a few hours. There is a refreshment stand with shaded tables where you can take a break from your walk.

WALTER FLETCHER BEACH East of the market, Walter Fletcher Beach, a large public park, has good facilities, tennis courts, and many vendors. There is a small entrance fee.

THINGS JAMAICAN Before you continue farther east, detour to Fort Street (a one-way street running west and parallel to Gloucester Avenue) to *Things Jamaican,* the store of the government-sponsored cooperative of crafts people. The quality of the crafts is superior—and slightly more expensive—than crafts in the market.

A DRIVE AROUND MONTEGO BAY

A taxi tour of Montego Bay and its environs should be about US $75 for half a day or US $150 for a full day for up to four people; agree on the price before you depart. As an alternative, especially for those who like being on their own, you could create your own itinerary by using the "Soon Come Shuttle" (see description under Local Transportation earlier in this chapter). The shuttle bus travels along main routes, stopping in front of or near many locations described in the drive east of Montego Bay and in the Walkabout section above.

RICHMOND HILL To get your bearings, Richmond Hill Inn offers a splendid panoramic view of Montego Bay. You will come back down from that lofty perch along Union Street, through the downtown marketplace area. Before turning onto Gloucester Avenue to continue to the eastern beach and hotel strip, you pass the sprawling Montego Bay Crafts Market.

DOCTOR'S CAVE BEACH One mile east on Gloucester Avenue, a main thoroughfare, brings you to Doctor's Cave Beach, the heart of the tourist area. A short distance beyond is Cornwall Beach, where the Tourist Board's office is located. There are a bar and snack counter, water sports, changing facilities, and entertainment. There is a small entrance fee.

A DRIVE EAST OF MONTEGO BAY—
GOLF, GREAT HOUSES, AND RAFTING

If you rent a car rather than hire a taxi and guide, you should familiarize yourself with a good map first. Maps published by the Jamaica Tourist Board are available from the board's information offices. Be especially careful when driving through busy own streets. The pedestrian is always right. And remember, driving is on the LEFT.

Heading east on Gloucester Avenue, you must turn right onto Sunset Street, which will lead you to a series of roundabouts and Sangster International Airport. The road that passes the airport is the main coastal road, A-1. Two miles beyond the airport the highway passes several resorts in the Rose Hall area and the Holiday Village Shopping Center, a cluster of duty-free shops and other stores selling low-quality goods. Farther along you pass the all-inclusive resort village *Sandals Royal,* similar to Club Med but for couples only.

HALF MOON BEACH After another mile or so, you reach the *Half Moon Club,* one of the leading hotels in the Caribbean. It is set on 400 acres of landscaped gardens fronting a mile-long beach—the prettiest and longest in the area—and has an 18-hole championship golf course and one of the largest tennis complexes in Jamaica. The *Seagrape Terrace* is popular for lunch and there's a delightful bar by the beach. *The Sugar Mill,* another restaurant, overlooks the golf course. The Arcade has sophisticated boutiques and duty-free shops, as does Half Moon's new shopping complex adjacent to the east end of the property. The hotel's sports and restaurant facilities are available to nonguests, but you should make reservations in advance, as the hotel enjoys a very high occupancy year-round.

Another mile or so will bring you to *Wyndham Rose Hall Beach Hotel and Golf Club* which also has an 18-hole championship golf course and other sports facilities available to day visitors on prior arrangement.

ROSE HALL GREAT HOUSE About halfway between Half Moon Beach and Wyndham Rose Hall is Jamaica's most famous plantation house, Rose Hall Great House, a restored mansion with a majestic setting on a hillside overlooking the sea. Built around 1770 by John Palmer when he was the queen's representative for the Parish of St. James, the mansion was acquired in the 1960s by American millionaire John Rollins, a former lieutenant governor of Delaware, in the purchase of a huge tract of land for development. The plantation house was partially damaged in the 1831 slave uprising and unoccupied for over a century; it was a ruin when Rollins acquired it. He spent several million dollars to restore it as a museum and furnish it with art and antiques to recreate the grandeur of an eighteenth-century plantation house.

Named for Palmer's first wife, Rose, the mansion is even better known for the legends that surround his fourth wife and last mistress of the house, Annie, although there is little foundation for them in fact. Known as the White Witch of Rose Hall, Annie Palmer, whose ghost was said to haunt the estate after her murder by an unknown hand in 1833, was a beautiful English woman tutored in the black arts by a Haitian priestess. According to the legend, she poisoned one husband, strangled another, murdered a third, and handed out similar fates to a gaggle of lovers (often picked from among her slaves) before meeting her end—and she was only 29 years old! Hours: 9 A.M. to 6 P.M. daily. Admission: US $15 with a tour by colonial-costumed guides, who embellish the stories of the haunted house with some imagination of their own.

CINNAMON HILL Another side road past Rose Hall and the walled burial plot of the Moulton Barrett fami-

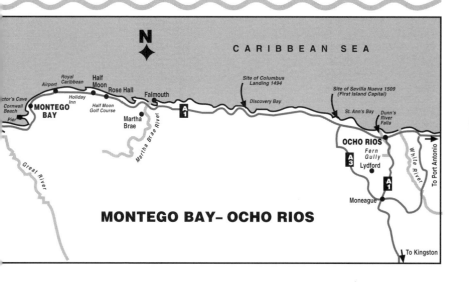

ly leads to *Cinnamon Hill Great House,* the home of relatives of English poet Elizabeth Barrett Browning. The Barrett family was one of the largest plantation owners in Jamaica. The house has been restored and belongs to American country-and-western star Johnny Cash, who visits Jamaica frequently. It is not open to the public, but golfers who play the Wyndham Rose Hall Golf Course pass the mansion on the 14th hole.

GREENWOOD GREAT HOUSE Continuing east on Highway A-1, four miles past Wyndham Rose Hall Beach Hotel and White Witch Riding Stables, a turnoff on the right leads to another Barrett mansion, occupied continuously since it was built in the late 1700s by Sir Richard Barrett, a cousin of the English poet. In the 1980s it was restored and furnished with antiques by its present occupants and owners, Bob and Ann Betton. The most interesting aspect of the house is the Bettons' collection of antique musical instruments. Several pieces of furniture belonged to the original Barrett owners. From the second-floor balcony there is a spectacular view of the north coast as far as Discovery Bay, 35 miles away. There is a bar in the former kitchen and a gift shop. Outside in the garden is a collection of old carriages. Hours: 9 A.M. to 6 P.M. daily. Admission: US $10 adults, $5 children; includes a tour.

GOOD HOPE One of the most beautiful greathouses, Good Hope was recently renovated as a small, exclusive inn. Several packages are available: House tour and lunch, $40; tour and tea, $30; tour and one-and-a-half-hour horseback ride, $75. Phone 809–954–3289 for arrangements. (Although these are the most famous historic houses, the north coast of Jamaica has a wealth of lovely old homes and historic buildings. In her book, *Jamaican Houses: A Vanishing Legacy,* artist Anghelen Arrington Phillips includes fine sketches of 40 such structures.)

FALMOUTH Built as the capital of Trelawny Parish at the height of the area's sugar-growing prosperity, Falmouth, 23 miles east of MoBay, has a significant group of historic structures dating from the late-eighteenth century. Today, the town is part of the National Trust and preserves Jamaica's Georgian heritage. The most significant buildings are on Market Street west of Water Square. *The Barrett House* (One Water Street), was the townhouse of the Cinnamon Hill Barretts and built in 1779. The *Post Office* is a particularly well-proportioned structure with fine details; and the brick house at 21 Duke Street is considered the best example of the early Georgian style. Falmounth has been used several times as a movie set.

MARTHA BRAE RIVER Falmouth is near the Martha Brae River, the town's water source and the venue for a river rafting excursion. Signs on the highway point to the turnoff to the *Rafter's Village,* a mile upriver, where the raft trip begins. There are a restaurant, bar, swimming pool, and boutique. The raft trip operates from 9 A.M. to 4 P.M. and takes one-and-a-half hours; you are driven back to the village at the end of the trip. Cost: US $37 for two people.

A DRIVE WEST OF MONTEGO BAY— NATURAL AND MANMADE SPLENDORS

ROCKLANDS BIRD SANCTUARY From the pier the drive west on Highway A-1 takes about two hours to Negril. A detour at Reading takes you to the Rocklands Bird Sanctuary and Feeding Station, home to large numbers of hummingbirds and many other bird species. The hummingbird species known locally as the "doctor bird" is Jamaica's national bird. You might prefer to stop on your return at feeding time—3:30 P.M.— when you can have the tiny birds eating out of your hand. Admission $5, and includes a guided tour along a nature trail.

Beyond Reading, you pass some elegant homes, many owned by foreigners who winter in Jamaica. The road crosses the *Great River* where visitors can enjoy river rafting by day and in the evening, a torchlit cruise upriver to a landing for a Jamaican dinner and entertainment. During the summer months, after heavy rains, the excursion does not operate. To inquire, Tel. 952–5047.

ROUND HILL After crossing the parish boundary into Hanover at the Great River, you will see the entrance to Round Hill Hotel marked by gateposts. Set on a small peninsula of 98 acres in beautifully terraced gardens overlooking a private beach, the resort is one of the most exclusive and expensive in Jamaica. It was developed in 1953 by Jamaican entrepreneur and later director of tourism John Pringle with a group of investors who included Noel Coward and Oscar Hammerstein. Hugging the cove in stair-step fashion are the villas, each built to the design of its owner, and most with private pools and gardens festooned with brilliant flowers.

TRYALL GOLF AND BEACH CLUB Four miles farther west is the magnificent 2,200-acre sprawl of *Tryall Golf and Beach Club,* created in a fashion similar to Round Hill. The main house, an eighteenth-century estate house, and 43 palatial private villas are perched on a hillside; the rolling terrain of an 18-hole championship golf course, with an aqueduct and nineteenth-century waterwheel, serves as a backdrop for the villas while flowering gardens, the Montego Bay coast, and the sea provide their picture-window views. In addition to the wealthy homeowners who come for the winter season, both resorts have long attracted an array of international luminaries and celebrities.

KENILWORTH Beyond Sandy Bay to the west is the Kenilworth Estate, the finest sugar estate ruins in Jamaica. The factory buildings, impressive stone structures with Palladian windows and arched doorways, lie a mile south of the main road.

LUCEA Another 25 miles west is Lucea, once the main port and center of life for this corner of Jamaica during the heyday of the sugar plantations. Today it is an agricultural center for banana cultivation and molasses production. The town has several historic buildings, the most significant of which is the early nineteenth-century *Courthouse*. In the restoration the cupola was redesigned and enlarged to fit the clock whose face measures almost five feet. As the story goes, the clock was shipped to Jamaica by mistake and had been intended for the island of St. Lucia, a thousand miles away!

NEGRIL Hotels and tourist facilities have been added to Negril in large numbers since it was discovered by the flower children of the sixties, when it was a small village. However, its natural beauty has been saved somewhat because no building can be constructed higher than the tallest tree. Negril is particularly popular for scuba and windsurfing; there's also tennis, horseback riding, and an 18-hole golf course. The nearby region is full of lore and legend dating from the sixteenth and seventeenth centuries, when this coast was a pirate's haven.

OTHER SIGHT-SEEING OPTIONS

APPLETON EXPRESS: Formerly a train dubbed the Catadupa Choo Choo, the excursion is now taken by a bus that travels south of Montego Bay, 40 miles deep into the mountains to the Cockpit Country, which was once the region of the Maroons, the runaway slaves and freedmen who fought the British to a truce that allowed them self-government. The bus makes half-day or all-day trips, depending on the day of the week, departing between 8 and 9 A.M. and stopping at several small villages. At Cambridge villagers sell hand-carved birds and woven baskets; at Ipswich Caves passengers can visit caverns; and in Appleton passengers picnic by a mountain stream and tour the Appleton Rum factory.

SEAFORD TOWN: In 1835, 532 Germans from Hanover and Weserbergland arrived in Jamaica as indentured laborers. Of the group 251 were to form the township of Seaford, a 500-acre plot given by Lord Seaford from his 10,000-acre estate. After emancipating the slaves, the British colonial government made a policy of bringing European peasants to the island, ostensibly to create thriving communities that would act as both models and employers for the former slaves. But in fact, the new immigrants were to populate the countryside with whites and help keep the peace. The scheme was

never a success, and the people who suffered most were the immigrants who had been lured to the tropics by promises of land and a new life in paradise.

In Seaford Town, disease, malnutrition, and migration to the United States reduced the population to 100 within three years. Originally the settlers were to be given title to the land after 5 years; it took 15. Nonetheless, in the next 150 years the survivors scraped out a small living as farmers and became completely integrated into the mountain life of Jamaica. Among those in the first group was a teacher and minister who taught the children to read and write and began a church which gave the settlement a sense of community that continues today.

In 1978 one of the recent ministers, Father Francis, completed the *Seaford Town Historical Mini-Museum*, which tells the story of the immigrants and traces each of the family trees. In the same year, *St. Boniface Industrial Training Centre* was opened with the help of the German and Jamaican governments and German Catholic church. The center is a trade school for over 100 boys and girls from throughout Jamaica. *Mission Medical Project,* opened in 1981, provides a doctor and nurse for the area; a health center was added in 1984.

HILTON HIGH DAY: A visit to Seaford Town is one of the stops on the tour offered by Hilton Plantation, which is situated on 40 tropical hillside acres about 20 miles south of Montego Bay near Catadupa and Seaford Town. The excursion is organized by Norma Hilton Stanley, who returned to her native Jamaica after many years of living in the United States, and has a genuine desire to show visitors the "real" Jamaica.

The trip leaves Montego Bay at 8:30 A.M. (passengers with prior arrangements are picked up from the cruise ship pier) for a drive up the mountainside to Mrs. Stanley's home, where you enjoy a Jamaican breakfast and a tour of the grounds with an explanation of tropical fruits, vegetables, trees, and flowers; it continues with a visit to Seaford and concludes with a Jamaican lunch at the homey retreat. The food is fresh and grown on the land and includes roast pig, the main dish of the luncheon. The tour returns by a different route through the Cockpit Country and is back in Montego Bay by 3:30 P.M. The Plantation Tour, including round-trip transportation and two meals, costs US $50. Anyone touring the countryside on their own can have lunch and the Hilton Plantation tour for $20 per person. Booking office: Beach View Plaza, Tel. 952–3343. In recent years a dozen or more similar plantation tours have become available–different ones offered by various cruise lines. For example, Croydon Plantation (6 hrs.; $67 adults, $44 children), and Lethe Plantation (4 hrs.; $46) are offered by Princess Cruises.

MEET THE PEOPLE: The Jamaica Tourist Board has a Meet-the-People program through which visitors have the opportunity to spend time with a Jamaican host or hostess with whom they may share a common interest. It gives visitors a close look at the life-styles and culture of the country. You can ask to participate at the Tourist Board's Montego Bay office at Cornwall Beach. To ensure that someone with your particular interest is available, contact the U.S. office of the Jamaica Tourist Board nearest you in advance.

 **RESTAURANTS**

Marguerites and Margueritaville (Gloucester Avenue; Tel. 952–4777). Long one of MoBay's most popular restaurants, it reopened recently under new ownership and has become *the* place to dine in town day or night. There are two restaurants: *Marguerites* is the expanded former restaurant with indoor/outdoor terrace dining overlooking the sea and fabulous cuisine. Seafood is the specialty, but there are many other selections of creative, Caribbean-inspired dishes, pastas, and great desserts. It's a bit pricey for Jamaica but worth it.

The second restaurant, *Margueritaville,* has several levels: one houses a casual, moderately priced sports bar serving sandwiches and snacks and a boutique; another features an open-air disco with live entertainment; and on the top level you'll find a wild-ride slide that winds three stories down to the sea. There's also a water sports center for snorkeling and diving. Margueritaville is also a stop on the Coral See, a semi-submersible and one of Montego Bay's newest attractions, which takes passengers on excursions in the Montego Bay Marine Park.

Norma's at the Wharf House (Reading by the sea; Tel. 979–2745). Situated in a private home, the restaurant is the creation of Norma Shirley, who has a loyal following among Jamaica's movers and shakers at her Kingston restaurant. Menus have an eclectic selection of Norma's creations, which use local products in a sophisticated way. Lunch (moderately expensive) and dinner (very expensive) are served daily except Monday.

The Pelican (Gloucester Avenue; Tel. 952–3171), the long-time favorite for Jamaican specialties, remodeled its interior with fancier decor and increased prices, but it's clean, comfortable, and convenient. Moderately expensive.

The Pork Pit (off Gloucester Avenue, near Doctor's Cave Beach) is an open-air barbecue pit serving some of Jamaica's best jerk meats and fish. Jerk, cooked slowly on a wood fire all morning, is ready by 1 P.M. and can be eaten here or carried out. Inexpensive.

Reading Reef Club (Reading; Tel. 952–5909). Located in a small hotel of the same name, about . miles west of the port, this restaurant is owned by New Yorker Joanne Rowe, whose specialties are pasta and homemade pastries but whose menus have fresh fish and produce from Jamaica. Moderately expensive.

The Sugar Mill (Half Moon Club/golf annex, Rose Hall; Tel. 953–2314) has an elegant setting on a garden terrace with Continental emphasis but Jamaican selections as well. Open for lunch and dinner. Expensive.

The Town House (Church Street; Tel. 952–2660), long time MoBay favorite, has a historic eighteenth-century townhouse ambience that far exceeds its culinary achievements. Expensive.

 **SPORTS**

BEACHES/SWIMMING: The most popular beach in town is *Doctor's Cave Beach,* 3 miles east of the cruise ship dock. It has water sports concessions and refreshment stands on the premises. There are changing areas and showers. A small entrance fee is required.

One of the best-kept secrets in Montego Bay is the nude beach at *Seawind Beach Resort,* near the cruise ship dock. It's a private beach for the hotel's guests, but if you inquire at the front desk and ask to have lunch and use of the beach, you normally will receive permission.

BOATING: For day sails, snorkeling cruises, and boat charters contact *Pier One* (Howard Cook Highway opposite Craft Market; Tel. 952–2452). Other charter and boat trips are available from *Seaworld Resorts Ltd.* (Cariblue Beach; Tel. 953–2180).

DEEP-SEA FISHING: A half-day charter, with bait and tackle provided, for blue marlin, tuna, dolphin, and wahoo costs US $300 to $450. Contact *Stanley's Bay Marina* (near Ironshore, east of Montego Bay; Tel. 952–3859) and *Seaworld Resorts Ltd.* (Cariblue Beach; Tel. 953–2180). Free pickup is provided. Cruise ships can arrange them. Cost: $125 per person for minimum of four people for a four-hour excursion.

GOLF: For beauty, variety, and challenge it would be hard for any place in the Caribbean to surpass golfing in Jamaica. There are courses within reach of major tourist centers, but for serious golfers, Montego Bay, with four championship courses, is the undisputed headquarters. Call for starting times. All locations have clubhouses, restaurant/bars, and pro shops with clubs for rent.

East of MoBay in the Rose Hall area, the best course is the 18-hole championship layout by Robert Trent Jones at Half Moon Club (7,143 yards, par 72; Tel. 953–2211). Opened in 1961, it is characterized by lush green rolling hills overlooking the sea. It has putting greens, a practice range, pro shop, and clubhouse restaurant. Greens fees: US $85 for nonguests; cart fees are $24.

Wyndham Rose Hall Beach and Country Club (6,930 yards, par 72; Tel. 953–2650; 800–822–4200) has the most unusual course. The front nine stretch over gentle hills by the sea, but the back nine climb up and around steep hills and are as interesting as they are difficult. The 15th hole has a waterfall as its backdrop; the 9th and 16th holes are laid out around the ruins of an eighteenth-century aqueduct; and the 14th plays alongside Cinnamon Hill Great House, the home of singer Johnny Cash. Greens fees: US $60 for 18 holes.

About 12 miles west of the pier, the 18-hole championship course of *Tryall Golf and Beach Club* (6,680 yards, par 71; Tel. 952–5110) is considered the island's best, in terms of layout, play, and scenery. Greens fees: $125 plus 12.5 percent tax for nonguests. The course is often closed to nonguests in winter; inquire in advance of your cruise.

HORSEBACK RIDING: Available by reservation at *Rocky Point Stables* (Half Moon Club; Tel. 953–2211) and *White Witch Stables* (Rose Hall; Tel. 953–2746). A trail ride of one-and-a-half hours costs $40; a somewhat longer one that includes a ride by the sea is $50.

SNORKELING/SCUBA: The shallow reefs and drop-offs of Jamaica's north coast offer good diving over unusual underwater sites whose highlights are tunnels, crevasses, mini-walls, and what Jacques Cousteau once called "some of the most dramatic sponge life in the Caribbean." Each dive operator has different names for the sites selected.

DO NOT dive or snorkel with "freelance" guides soliciting business along the beach. Use only established operators, where you must show your certification card or take a scuba resort course before you can don tanks. *Resort Divers* (Island Plaza, second floor; Tel. 974–5338) is a PADI operator based in Ocho Rios but with shops in six locations on the north shore; it handles beginners and novices as well as certified divers. An introductory course is US $60; one-tank dive, US $30; two-tank, $55, including equipment. Snorkeling costs about US $20 per trip with equipment.

Some other licensed operators are *Seaworld Resorts Ltd.* Cariblue Beach, Rose Hall; Tel. 953–2180) and *Poseidon Nemrod Divers* (Reading Reef Club, Negril Highway; Tel. 952–3624).

MONTEGO BAY MARINE PARK A 15.3-square-kilometer shoreline preserve on the east side of Montego Bay is Jamaica's first Marine National Park. The preserve is home to mangroves, seagrass beds, and coral reefs and boasts some of the greatest coral diversity in the western Atlantic. In recent years, these marine habitats

have been severely disturbed by increased tourism, over-fishing, and pollution. The marine sanctuary, together with the Blue Mountain National Park, is part of a pilot project financed in part by aid from the United States.

Now, for the first time, those who do not dive can enjoy the marine park from the comfort of a semi-submarine, the *Coral See*. It is quickly being added to cruise ship shore excursions, but if your ship does not have it yet, you can inquire from *Moboy Under Sea Tours*, Tel. 950–2493; or *Sandals Montego Bay Resort*, Tel. 952–5510. The boat to the sub leaves from Sandals' dock and from Pier One. The excursion over the reefs is about an hour and costs about US $35.

TENNIS: There are public courts downtown at Walter Fletcher Beach; otherwise, the courts available to cruise passengers are located at hotels. Most hotels in Jamaica do not charge their guests for the use of courts and give hotel guests preference over visitors, who must pay a fee. You should make arrangements in advance, particularly in high season.

Half Moon Club (Rose Hall area; Tel. 953–2211) has one of the finest facilities in the Caribbean with 13 courts, a fully equipped pro shop, and a resident pro. You must write in advance or call for court time; prices vary by season for nonguests. The hotel also has four squash courts; rental equipment is available. *Seawind Beach Resort* (Tel. 952–4874) is within walking distance of the pier and has three courts. The hotel is a large complex; you might have to wait for a court.

WINDSURFING: *MoBay Windsurfing* (Doctor's Cave Beach; Tel. 952–5505) and *Whaleback Ocean Skills* (Cornwall Beach; Tel. 952–2578) are two shops convenient to downtown, but you will find the sport at all beachfront resorts on the north coast. Cost: about US $18 per hour.

INTRODUCTION TO OCHO RIOS

B y design and a great deal of help from nature, *Ochi*, as Ocho Rios is called locally, is a town created for Jamaican tourists as much as foreign ones. Situated on one of the widest, prettiest beaches on the north coast, Ocho Rios, a former fishing village, is said to take its name, meaning "eight rivers" in Spanish, from an English corruption of the town's Spanish name, Las Chorreras, "the waterfalls." There are waterfalls in town near the pier, and Dunn's River Falls, a dramatic cascade of 600 feet, is only a few miles away.

Ocho Rios is centrally located on the north coast within easy reach of three completely different faces of Jamaica, which is one reason for its popularity as a cruise port. In a radius of 20 miles, the beach-trimmed shore is punctuated by tiny fishing villages between major resorts while the interior behind the coast is dotted with tourist-free small towns and hillside hamlets where Jamaicans earn a simple living from the land.

Separating the tourist coast of the north and the Jamaican's Jamaica of the south are the awesome Blue Mountains where the famous coffee grows and where the wild forests are home to hundreds of exotic birds and butterflies, tropical plants, and flowers—many unique to Jamaica. The main highway over the towering mountains leads to Kingston, the capital and heart of the country's business, government, and cultural life.

Ocho Rios's location at the center of many varied attractions enables it to offer so many choices, you may have difficulty deciding which to select. For water sports enthusiasts, there is boating, fishing, waterskiing, windsurfing, scuba, and snorkeling—all available at the public beach next to the pier from concessioners licensed by the Jamaica Tourist Board. For shoppers, there are craft markets; boutiques with locally made clothing, and other products; duty-free shops; and supermarkets for Jamaican spices, coffee, and other local goods.

For serious explorers, Ocho Rios's attractions stretch from Port Maria on the east to Discovery Bay on the west. Hidden in the hills behind the coast are exquisite gardens, bird sanctuaries, and working plantations of citrus, bananas, mangos, and a host of other tropical fruits. The lush landscape and its natural beauty are the features that appeal most to visitors and easily convince them that Ocho Rios deserves its title as the Garden of Jamaica.

 **PORT PROFILE: OCHO RIOS**

EMBARKATION: The cruise ship dock and Reynolds Pier (both used by cruise ships) are located on the western side of the town's public beach, anchored at the east end by the Renaissance Jamaica Grande Resort. Some ships pull dockside; others tender. No special identification is required; passengers may go to and come from their ships freely. A Jamaican Tourist Board representative is on the pier to assist visitors. There is a bank on the pier for cruise passengers.

Upon exiting the small terminal building, you will find fleets of taxis and tour buses awaiting cruise passengers. Those who are not on an organized tour will be bombarded by taxi drivers who want to be their guide

for a tour. Prices are supposed to be set by the taxi association, but do not hesitate to bargain. If you do not want a taxi or tour, just smile, say "No, thank you," and keep walking. Public telephones, shops, restaurants, and the Jamaica Tourist Board office are in the Ocean Village Shopping Center on Main Street, an easy half-mile walk east of the pier. Adjacent to the center is the Ocho Rios Crafts Market.

LOCAL TRANSPORTATION: *Taxis:* JUTA (Jamaica Union of Travellers Association) is the government-licensed and -approved fleet which sets and publishes rates that most companies follow. Remember, in Jamaica you hire the taxi and can share the costs with up to three other people. A taxi from the pier or Main Street to one of the nearby posh hotels, such as Jamaica Inn or Sans Souci, is about US $6 one-way.

Buses: There are no public buses from the piers. Jamaica has an intra-city bus service between Ocho Rios and Montego Bay, but it is seldom used by tourists. Given the limited time most ships are in port, you are better advised to hire a taxi, especially if you have others with whom to share the cost.

BIKES/MOPEDS/MOTORBIKES: You will need to walk or take a taxi from the pier to the place in town where you rent motorbikes and scooters. *Motor Trails* (Carib Arcade, Main Street; Tel. 974–5058) has Honda CM200 motorcycles for $38 a day, unlimited mileage, and Honda A80 scooters for $33 a day, unlimited mileage. A credit card or deposit of US $200 is required; American Express, Visa, and MasterCard are accepted. It is imperative that you be an experienced driver. Behind the wheel of a car, Jamaican drivers are a wacky bunch and usurp the entire road—blind curves and all—for themselves!

CAR RENTALS: There are two problems with renting a car in Jamaica. Jamaicans pay extremely high import duties on cars and parts, and thus, car rentals are expensive. As an example, *Island Car Rental* charges US $65 for a subcompact with standard shift; US $71 for an automatic; and US $77 with air-conditioning; rates include unlimited mileage and compulsory insurance. Second, in high season there are often not enough cars to meet the demands of hotel guests; hence, day visitors may find no cars available.

Car rental firms in Ocho Rios have pickup service at the port if you have made reservations in advance, but do not be surprised if your car is not on hand for your arrival. If not, go directly to the rental office, as you could waste a great deal of time waiting for your car to show up. Avis, Main Street, Tel. 974–2057; Budget, Evelyn Street, Tel. 974–2178; Hertz, Main Street, Tel. 974–2334; National, Carib Arcade, Shop No. 6, Tel. 974–2266.

EMERGENCY NUMBERS:

Medical Service—Tourist Board Courtesy Unit, Tel. 974–2570;

Police Dept., Dial 119;

Ambulance, Dial 110

SERVICE CLUBS: The Renaissance Jamaica Grande is the venue for *Rotary* on Wed., 5:30 P.M.; *Kiwanis* on Thurs., 6:30 P.M.; and *Lions* on the first and third Tues., 6 P.M.

INFORMATION: Jamaica Tourist Board's office (Tel. 974–2570; 974–2582) is conveniently located in the Ocean Village Shopping Center. A staff member is on hand to assist visitors, and brochures on local attractions are available.

AUTHOR'S FAVORITE ATTRACTIONS

PROSPECT PLANTATION OR DUNN'S RIVER FALLS

HARMONY HALL ART GALLERY

MEET THE PEOPLE

NOEL COWARD'S *Firefly*

HORSEBACK RIDING: CHUKKA COVE

OCHO RIOS SHORE EXCURSIONS

The following tours are those most frequently offered by cruise ships and local travel agencies. They can also be arranged with a taxi driver/guide. Descriptions of the attractions are given later in the section. Tour length and prices vary from one tour company to the other; those here are examples only.

Ocho Rios Highlights Tour: Four-and-a-half hours, US $35. Tour combines the area's main mountain and garden attractions: Fern Gully; Shaw Park Gardens or Coyaba River Gardens; and Dunn's River Falls, Jamaica's most famous natural attraction where you can climb a waterfall and enjoy lunch and a superb look at Jamaica's lush flora. A three-hour version, US $30, is sometimes available. Since it's the single most popular tour in Jamaica, you will do your visiting in a crowd. Bathing suit and sneakers are a must.

Prospect Park Plantation Tour: Three-and-a-half hours, US $20 to $27. Journey by jitney (or horseback) through citrus groves and forests on a guided tour of a thousand-acre working estate. An ideal tour to get the "feel" of Jamaica in the short time. (See description later in this chapter.) When combined with Dunn's River Falls, cost is $44.

Nautilus Submersibles: See description later in this chapter.

Heliotours (120 Main St., Ocho Rios; Tel. 974–2265). Flight-seeing by helicopter in the Ocho Rios vicinity: $50 for 15 minutes; $95 for 30 minutes; $190 for 60 minutes.

Rafting on the Rio Grande: full day, $65 with lunch; $48 without lunch. See Port Antonio section for description.

Scuba Diving: Four hours, US $40 one tank; $55 two tanks. Divers must have certification cards. You can reduce the cost of rentals by bringing your own mask, fins, and snorkel. Trips usually depart at 9 A.M. for four hours and 2 P.M. for two hours.

Art, Literary Gems, and Nature: Three to four hours. Several lesser-known attractions east of town make a interesting tour for those on their own. *Harmony Hall,* an art gallery in a pretty colonial manor house near Ocho Rios; *Firefly,* Noel Coward's modest hilltop retreat; and Crystal Springs, a pretty garden with picnic areas are among those included.

Custom-Built Tours: For excursions focusing on nature, birds and gardens, art, or architecture, *The Touring Society of Jamaica,* based near Ocho Rios (Boscobel Post Office, St. Mary; Tel/fax: 809–975–7158), specializes in custom-made programs that take in places standard tour companies never visit. Prices are based on the number of people and itinerary. Contact Lyndalee Burke in advance of your cruise to plan arrangements.

OCHO RIOS ON YOUR OWN

Be prepared! Cruise ship arrivals turn this town into a beehive of excitement. Like many Caribbean ports, Ocho Rios has a street-fair atmosphere when cruise ships are in port. Everyone in Ocho Rios—or so it seems—will be on hand at the dock and along the main road to welcome you and try to persuade you not to leave town without taking their tour or buying their necklace, doll, hat, or the hundred other souvenirs they want to sell you.

Taxi drivers, minibus tour operators, higglers, and craft peddlers all jockey for the best positions to get your attention. Just smile and keep walking. If you can enter into the spirit of the affair, you can have fun, try your hand at bargaining, take some great pictures, and come away with attractive souvenirs at cheap prices. Some visitors find this exuberant salesmanship intimidating and others say it's simply irritating, but if you deal with such encounters as sport, you will quickly get the knack of enjoying Ocho Rios.

A note of warning: Ocho Rios has worked hard in the past several years to clean up its act. The great majority of entrepreneurs are warm, friendly, and trusting people, but like ports anywhere in the world, there are hustlers among them not to be trusted, and definitely NOT to be hired as guides. **DO NOT** go off by yourself in a rented car or on foot with anyone wanting to "show you a special place." They are hustlers posing as guides and could leave you stranded and cashless or worse. Licensed guides and taxis are just that—licensed. Authorized drivers/guides wait at the pier, dressed in uniforms with the company logo clearly visible on their shirts. Anywhere else, you should ask to see their credentials. If you have any doubt about a guide, you need only ask him to step into the Tourist Board Office with you. Or, if you feel you are being harassed, don't hesitate to ask a policeman for assistance.

The Tourist Board maintains a "Courtesy Corps" of men and women especially trained to help tourists; they have the powers of arrest, if that should be necessary. You can recognize them by their uniforms: black trousers, green shirts, and yellow lanyards—the colors of Jamaica's flag.

MEET THE PEOPLE For a close-up look at the lifestyles and culture of Jamaica, the Tourist Board has a Meet-the-People program through which visitors can spend time with a Jamaican host with whom they may share a common interest. You can ask to participate at the Tourist Board's Ocho Rios office, Ocean Village; however, to ensure someone is available with your particular interest, contact the U.S. office of the Jamaica Tourist Board nearest you in advance.

A WALK AROUND OCHO RIOS

Downtown Ocho Rios, except as a place for browsing through shops and craft stalls or sampling local restaurants, does not merit a walkabout. Your time can be better spent enjoying the fine town beach and water sports or on excursions to interesting attractions in outlying areas. The heart of town is one block south of the waterfront along Main Street, the principal thoroughfare. If you turn east (with the traffic) on Main Street, a five-minute walk will bring you to the Ocean Village Shopping Center and Crafts Market, the shopping area closest to the pier. A walkway at the village also leads to the public beach. Five minutes more brings you to the Renaissance Jamaica Grande Resort, where there are shops, restaurants, and sports facilities—all can be seen in an hour.

Nautilus Submersibles (42 Fort St., Montego Bay; Tel. 979–0102; Fax 979–0101) was scheduled to begin a brand-new attraction for the Ocho Rios area in October. *Natulius 1000,* a recreational submarine that can dive to 1,000 feet and holds six passengers, will offer dives six times daily in the Ocho Rios Marine Park. Passengers are shuttled from the cruise pier to the dive site by a fast boat and, once there, transferred to the mother vessel. Through its huge windows, passengers view the underwater life while divers, who are connected to the sub via underwater communications system, give commentary.

The underwater trip lasts seventy minutes and costs $165 per person. Prior to Jamaica, the *N-1000* served for two years as the highly publicized "Loch Ness Submarine" in Scotland. In April 1997, the company plans to introduce the *Nautilus 250,* with a maximum depth of 250 feet; it seats fifty-two passengers and will offer tours ten times daily for $65 per person.

WEST OF OCHO RIOS

FERN GULLY Highway A-3 (a road perpendicular to A-1, the main coastal highway) is the main artery south of town. It winds through an old riverbed bordered by hundreds of species of fern. The lacy branches of the giant ferns and lush vegetation form a natural canopy over the highway, cooling and refreshing the air. The gully is also the first 3 miles of the road to Kingston, the capital of Jamaica.

SHAW PARK GARDENS Watch for the turnoff to Shaw Park Botanical Gardens and Bird Sanctuary where you will need at least an hour to tour the pretty grounds and enjoy the spectacular view of Ocho Rios. The variety of indigenous flowers, trees, shrubs, and rushing streams and waterfalls makes this a popular photo stop as well. Hours: 9 A.M. to 5 P.M. Admission: US $2. Refreshments are available. Tel. 974–8888.

COYABA RIVER GARDEN AND MUSEUM A garden 1 mile from Ocho Rios, at 420 feet, is named for the Arawak word meaning "paradise." The museum displays pre-Columbian artifacts and exhibits covering the island's history. There are walkways for strolling through the gardens to enjoy natural waterfalls; a gift shop featuring local products; and an art gallery of good-quality paintings, prints, and sculptures. Admission: US $4 including tour and welcome drink. Hours: daily 8:30 A.M. to 5 P.M. Tel. 974–6235.

DUNN'S RIVER FALLS The magnificent waterfall gushes from lush, wooded limestone cliffs along the inland ridge and cascades 600 feet over a series of natural stone steps to the sea. Surefooted tourists climb the rocks—in bathing suits—fighting the rushing water like salmon beating upstream. You can climb with or without an official guide. We strongly recommend a guide. The rocks are very slick and the water torrents powerful enough to knock you off balance. Daily tours to the falls are available from all of Jamaica's main towns, including Kingston. Hence, the falls are frequently crowded with visitors, not only from cruise ships but hotels as well. The later in the day you go, the less crowded the area is likely to be. Hours: Daily 9 A.M.–5 P.M. Admission: US $6 adults; $3 children.

The prettiest part of the falls, known as *Laughing Waters,* is private property where some scenes from the James Bond movies *Dr. No* and *Live and Let Die* and, more recently, the television series "Going to Extremes" were shot.

DISCOVERY BAY West of Dunn's River Falls are three small villages which had big moments in Jamaica's history. Until excavations at St. Ann's Bay (1 mile west of the falls) in the 1980s raised doubts, Discovery Bay (15 miles west) was traditionally marked as the site where Christopher Columbus first sighted Jamaica in 1494. The event is commemorated in a seaside monument and memorial park, built by Kaiser Aluminum, the principal company that once mined Jamaica's bauxite. The park has a sugar refining display—a reminder of Jamaica's plantation economy for most of its colonial history.

On Columbus's fourth voyage in 1503 two of his ships were damaged beyond repair and were beached on Jamaica's north shore. Columbus spent a year on the island awaiting rescue—thus giving Jamaica the unique status as the only place in the New World where the great explorer lived.

NEW SEVILLE After Columbus's death in 1506, his son Diego came to the New World as governor of the Indies and from Santo Domingo sent Juan de Esquivel, a former lieutenant of Columbus's, to Jamaica to establish a colony. Under him the town of *Sevilla la Nueva,* or New Seville, was laid out in 1509. It served as the capital of the Jamaica colony until 1534 when it was abandoned for the new capital of St. Jago de la Vega (present-day Spanish Town) on the south coast. Excavations near the village of *St. Ann's Bay* uncovered the remains of a settlement and church dating from the fifteenth and sixteenth centuries; scholars have identified it as New Seville. Although silt from the sea and adjacent river has altered the shoreline in the intervening five centuries, authorities established the authenticity of the site from artifacts found in the excavations.

SEVILLE GREAT HOUSE About a mile from the site on a hillside is Seville Great House, a nineteenth-century plantation house; nearby, an Arawak site has also been excavated. It is but one of more than 200 Arawak sites identified in Jamaica. History has recorded that Diego Columbus was the first in a long list of European explorers who succeeded in annihilating the Arawaks within 50 years of Columbus's arrival. Little remains to help scholars reconstruct native life at the time the Europeans arrived or to understand the co-mingling of the two cultures.

HIGH HOPE ESTATE High on a hillside above St. Ann's Bay, one of the north coast's loveliest settings is yours to enjoy for the day, or to rent, if you can afford it, for a longer, luxurious stay. Although the antique-filled, seven-bedroom villa was built only in 1961, its classic Mediterranean style, spacious rooms, airy verandas, gracious furnishings, and magnificent setting make it seem older, belonging to another era.

Set in beautiful gardens under enormous shady trees, High Hope was the home of the somewhat eccentric Kitty Spence, the granddaughter of William Jennings Bryan and the daughter of America's first woman ambassador (to Denmark). An international bon vivant and hostess, Kitty had as many husbands as Anne Palmer of Rose Hall fame. One was Robert Lehman of Wall Street riches, and the last, Derrick Spence, was heir to the British alum-mining monopoly—which explains the king's ransom in exquisite marble, wood, and antiques filling the house and the impressive list of celebrities and luminaries filling the guestbook.

When the Spences were not entertaining the likes of Ian Fleming, Noel Coward, and Charlie Chaplin, Derrick Spence was indulging his interest in horticulture, cultivating a great variety of tropical flowers and fruit trees and over 500 varieties of hibiscus, almost half of which fill the gardens today. From the swimming pool, the gardens flow to the edge of the wooded hillside, from where there are expansive views to the coast. The treetops are filled with a wide variety of birds, but the special treat is the doctor bird and Jamaica's national bird, a beautiful long-tailed hummingbird, abundant in the gardens.

Recognizing a good thing when he saw it, Dennis Rappaport, who escaped from a California fast track to become a Jamaica habitué, fell upon High Hope in the 1980s, long after the Spences had passed from the scene. He turned the villa into a bed-and-breakfast inn, retaining enough of the Spences' echo to give it an air of nostalgia; began a commercial venture to produce exotic flora and fruit—not to mention mushrooms; and developed a tour for travelers who want a respite from the commercial north coast and are in search of the "real" Jamaica. For information, Tel. 800–925–5300; 809–972–2277.

EAST OF OCHO RIOS

East from town, Main Street becomes Highway A-3 and passes some of the area's best resorts—*Jamaica Inn,* or *Sans Souci Lido*—in ravishingly beautiful settings. If your ship is in port on a Sunday and you are more in the mood for elegance than exploration, you should treat yourself to the luncheon buffet—complete with white-gloved waiters—on the terrace of Jamaica Inn overlooking the pretty gardens and beach, one of the most romantic settings in the Caribbean. But then, Jamaica has many settings equally as romantic and beautiful. You need several return visits to see them all.

PROSPECT PLANTATION Near the White River, a clearly marked road leads inland 1 mile to a working plantation and wooded estate covering 1,000 acres. Here you will see a great variety of tropical trees, shrubs, and flora typical of Jamaica and the Caribbean, and—unlike so many other locations—species here are labeled. The guides, too, are knowledgeable and make tours interesting and enjoyable, stopping along the way for scenic views of the coast, a lookout over the heavily forested ravine through which the White River flows, and a lane of trees planted by such famous visitors as Winston Churchill, Noel Coward, and Charlie Chaplin. The tour in a jitney bus leaves the tour center at 10:30 A.M., 2 P.M., and 3:30 P.M. weekdays; Sunday, 11 A.M., 1:30 P.M., and 3 P.M. Cost: US $12 adults; children 12 and under free; price includes drink and fruit sample. There is also miniature golf and horseback riding as well as a bar and shop for locally made products.

BRIMMER HALL Approximately 10 miles farther east is a similar working plantation, the two-century-old Brimmer Hall Estate, which also offers guided tours. The tour in a tractor-drawn jitney leaves the Great House three times a day at 11 A.M., 1:30 P.M., and 3:30 P.M. daily. Cost: US $15. There are a swimming pool, bar, and shops for locally made products.

HARMONY HALL Beyond White River (4 miles east of Ocho Rios) Harmony Hall is a handsomely restored nineteenth-century great house of a small pimento plantation which now houses a fine art gallery (Tel. 975–4222) and garden restaurant (Tel. 975–4478). The gallery specializes in top Jamaican art and sculpture, quality crafts, antiques, and old prints. All works on display are for sale. The 1886 Victorian structure has its original stonework; its new gingerbread trim and balustrade were designed by a batik artist and produced on the property by local craftsmen. The art gallery has a representative collection of contemporary artists, including Jamaican Primitives or Intuitives, as they are called, and other young artists whom the gallery owner, Annabella Proudlock, herself an artist, encourages through frequent expositions year-round. Harmony Hall is particularly valuable for those who have not visited Kingston where the National Museum of Art and major galleries are located.

The gallery has a collection of prints and gifts mounted with miniature copies of prints by English artist Jonathan Routh from his popular book, *Jamaican Holiday: The Secret Life of Queen Victoria.* There are also prints by Australian artist Colin Garland, who has lived in Jamaica for more than 30 years and teaches in the Ocho Rios area. Garland's paintings have been so deeply influenced by his Jamaican environment that he is looked upon as a local artist and included among the Jamaican artists in the National Collection.

Farther east, Rio Nuevo is the spot where the British finalized their claim to Jamaica by routing the last of the Spanish forces from a stockade at the river's mouth. A small monument marks the battle site.

GOLDENEYE At the next town, Oracabessa, a small lane leads to the beach and to Goldeneye Estate, the haunt of Ian Fleming, the author of 13 James Bond novels. Fleming spent winters here from 1946 until his death in 1964, often keeping company with his friend Noel Coward, whose home is farther east. The estate is now privately owned by Jamaica's most successful music promoter, Christopher Blackwell, who is credited with helping to launch reggae superstar Bob Marley and others. It will now anchor a 70-acre beach resort community with townhomes, beach cottages, two hotels, and the renovated village of Oracabessa as the centerpiece. Restoration of historic buildings is under way and new ones are being built in the same style to retain the ambience of a Jamaican seaport of bygone days.

FIREFLY Farther east, a small sign directs you to turn south off Highway A-3 and up a winding hillside road, past modest homes, through lush vegetation to a lane lined with towering hardwood trees. At the end on a hillside overlooking Port Maria is *Firefly,* the cottage and refuge of playwright Noel Coward. The modest bachelor pad was donated to the country by his estate after his death in 1973. First renovated by the Jamaica National Trust and opened as a museum in 1985, it was leased in 1993 by Christopher Blackwell, who made extensive renovations, reopening it as a museum evoking its glamorous heyday of the 1950s, when the songwriter and wit entertained his friends—all the most famous stars and celebrities of his day.

Coward is buried, as he had requested, in the far northwest corner of the garden beneath a simple marble slab, protected by a white wrought-iron gazebo. The site was his favorite evening roost to watch the sunset and sip his brandy and ginger. The view from here is one of the finest panoramas in the tropics. Also on the property is a small limestone building, said to have been the perch of the seventeenth-century pirate Henry Morgan, the first to discover the site—apparently as an ideal lookout for preying on Spanish galleons. That's before he became governor of Jamaica and was knighted! Firefly is used for weddings and special events to augment the museum's income, but this is Blackwell's ode to Jamaica—a labor of love and some nostalgia: Blackwell's uncle had sold the land to Coward for Firefly; his mother was a long-time friend of the playwright. Admission: US $5.

CRYSTAL SPRINGS About 2 miles beyond Buff Bay en route to Port Antonio, a small road leads inland to Crystal Springs, a rustic park on 156 acres of woods with streams, a bird sanctuary, and natural beauty. There are also manmade attractions such as a swimming pool, orchid garden, and picnic facilities. You can go on your own or join an excursion.

East of Ocho Rios is the beautiful small town of Port Antonio. Even if you have a full day to explore the route east of Ocho Rios, you will not have time to see Port Antonio unless you eliminate most of your sight-seeing en route, which we would not recommend. Occasionally, Port Antonio is port of call.

 **RESTAURANTS**

Parkway (off Main Street; Tel. 974–2667) has fast service and generous portions of good, simple local fare and some American selections. The Jamaican lunches—fish, stewed beef, curried goat, conch—are one of the town's best values. Inexpensive.

Double V (Main Street, off Pineapple Place) is an open-air restaurant and bar, popular for jerk. Of late, however, the music has been so loud, it's hard to enjoy your meal, and the owner arrogantly ignores any request to turn it down. Inexpensive.

The Ruins (Da Costa Drive; Tel. 974–2442) serves Chinese dishes, some with a Jamaican flavor, in a romantic outdoor setting amid tropical gardens and a natural waterfall. Moderate.

Almond Tree (Hibiscus Lodge, Main Street; Tel. 974–2813) has good local and continental selections, particularly seafood and soups, in a delightful setting of several terraces that spill down the cliffside overlooking the sea. The daily lunch specials are a good value. The smoked marlin is fabulous. Moderate.

 **SPORTS**

BEACHES: Within sight of the cruise ship dock upon arrival in Ocho Rios is the public beach, one grand strand of white sand curving from Turtle Beach Towers Apartments to the Renaissance Jamaica Grande. It is complete with water sports facilities, refreshment stands, and hordes of independent vendors eager to sell you anything from wood carvings to hair-braiding. There is also a nice beach below Dunn's River Falls west of town.

BOATING: *Heave-Ho* (11A Pineapple Place; Tel. 974–5367) has large catamarans for charter for 10 or more people to go sailing and snorkeling, with drinks and barbecue lunch. Other cruises can be arranged through *Watersports Enterprise* (Renaissance Jamaica Grande). Sunfish and day cruises are available from *Sea Jamaica Ltd.* (Shaw Park Beach Hotel; Tel. 974–2552). Rates are available upon request for nonguests.

DEEP-SEA FISHING: Available at *Watersports Enterprise;* (Tel. 974–2151); and *Sea and Dive Jamaica Ltd.* (Shaw Park Beach Hotel; Tel. 974–2552). Rates for boats with crew are US $350 to $420 per half day, including bait and tackle for marlin and other deep-water game fish.

GOLF: In Ocho Rios, *Upton Golf Club* (6,600 yards; Tel. 974–2528), which belongs to the all-inclusive chain, Sandals, is an 18-hole course a few miles east of town. Greens fees: US $25; carts: $20 to $30 depending on the season. At Runaway Bay, the course belonging to *Breezes Jamaica* charges $50 for 18 holes. Phone in advance for starting times, especially during the peak season of December to April.

HORSEBACK RIDING: *Chukka Cove Farm Equestrian Center* (St. Ann's Bay, P.O. Box 160, Ocho Rios; Tel. 972–2506) is a full-scale operation with facilities for serious and recreational riders. The center offers beach rides as well as mountain trekking; rates are US $30 for one hour or so; three- to six-hour treks are US $70 to $110. The farm also stages shows and tournaments throughout the year. *Prospect Plantation Stable*, two miles east of Ocho Rios, offers one- and two-hour treks through a working plantation. To reserve, Tel. 974–2058 or contact *Watersports Enterprise* (Renaissance Jamaica Grande).

POLO: Regular polo matches are played Thursdays at *Chukka Cove* (St. Ann's Bay) and Saturday at *Drax Hall Polo Field* (five miles west of Ocho Rios). Chukka Cove offers lessons at various times of the year, but to play in a match a visitor would need to phone (Tel. 972–2506) or write ahead (P.O. Box 160, Ocho Rios) and include information on his credentials.

SCUBA DIVING: Good shallow reefs, tunnels, archways, and drop-offs close to shore make scuba diving interesting in Ocho Rios. Resort courses are available for beginners; boat dive trips require that participants have certification cards. *Resort Divers* (Island Plaza, second floor, Tel. 974–5338) is a PADI operator headquartered in Ocho Rios. An introductory course is US $60; one-tank dive, US $30; two-tank, $55, including equipment. Other water sports operators are found at the Renaissance Jamaica Grande Hotel and *Sea and Dive Jamaica Ltd.* (Shaw Park Beach Hotel; Tel. 974–2552). One-tank dive trips cost about US $35 including equipment; snorkeling is US $15.

TENNIS: Courts within walking distance of the pier are at the Renassiance Jamaica Grande, which has four courts. Nonguest fees are $8 per hour; use of courts is subject to availability, and since it is a large hotel, the likelihood of finding a free court is not in your favor.

WINDSURFING AND OTHER SPORTS: *Watersports Enterprise* at the Jamaica Grande can arrange almost any activity you need. Windsurfing costs US $20 per hour; waterskiing, US $25 per half hour.

PORT ANTONIO

In the extravagantly beautiful tropical setting of this old port, it is easy to believe that if there is an Eden on this earth, you have found it. You will not be the first to have made this discovery, and you will be in very good company. Yet, despite the steady flock of admirers—all eager to help her—Port Antonio always seems to be on the verge of a new day that never comes.

Port Antonio is the place where Jamaica's tourism began. In 1871 a Yankee skipper by the name of Lorenzo Dow Baker sailed out of Port Antonio with a cargo of bananas—introduced by the Spaniards three centuries earlier. When he sold them in Boston, he made such a killing, he returned to Jamaica, bought land, planted bananas, and began shipping the fruit to markets in the United States and Europe. From that enterprise grew the United Fruit Company whose name has been synonymous with bananas—not to mention banana republics—for most of this century.

But Baker did not deal in bananas only. The ships that took the bananas north brought tourists south. They stayed at Baker's inn, the Titchfield Hotel, described in an 1898 guidebook as a "novel hotel admirably adapted to a hot climate."

MITCHELL'S FOLLY The next Yank to fall under Port Antonio's spell was quite eccentric. Alfred Mitchell, a wealthy mining engineer, built a 60-room palace for his child bride, a Tiffany heiress. As the story goes, the palatial mansion was painted white, white flowers filled the gardens, white birds flitted about the grounds, white horses filled the stables, and white monkeys played on an islet at the shore. But his wife refused to live in the fabled retreat, and it became—you guessed it—a white elephant.

In building the mansion, salt water had been used to mix the mortar, and as the salt ate away at the stone, the mansion crumbled. It became known as Mitchell's Folly, although Mitchell lived here until he died in 1912. Today, it is a melancholy ruin that looks like the ideal set for a Greek tragedy.

FLYNN ESTATE Over the years many others who came to Port Antonio were intoxicated by her beauty, but none as much as matinee idol Errol Flynn. Some say Jamaica was his only lasting love affair. Flynn happened onto Port Antonio in the late 1940s while cruising the Caribbean on his yacht, *Zacca*. A sudden storm forced him to change course and head for the nearest shelter. When he saw the twin-harbored port, he apparently was so taken with it, he bought Navy Island, an islet at the entrance to the harbor, the Titchfield Hotel, and 2,000 acres of a coconut plantation and cattle ranch, and set out to create his Eden. But the famous actor died before he could realize the dream house and the other projects he had in mind. His widow, Patrice Wymore, still lives on the estate, which is now a working plantation.

RAFTING ON THE RIO GRANDE Flynn left another legacy that will never die. Rafting on the Rio Grande had been a Port Antonio pastime since 1911 when Simon Grant, a United Fruit Company representative, got the idea after watching bananas being towed by raft downstream to the docks for loading onto ships. But it was Flynn who popularized rafting by launching the first rafters' race.

Today, the excursion on the Rio Grande is Port Antonio's number one tourist attraction. The trip starts about eight miles upstream at Berrydale, where passengers board a 30-foot-long bamboo raft that seats two. With the Blue Mountains towering in the background, a skilled and experienced helmsman guides the raft at a leisurely pace for two to three hours down the Rio Grande while passengers enjoy the river's tropical setting. They can also stop for a swim.

Along the way, you see cattle grazing, children playing, mothers laundering, birds darting about, and banana groves and wild orchids growing in profusion.

The serenity makes it easy for anyone to fall in love with Jamaica all over again. Cost: $40 for two people for two-and-a-half hours; Tel. 993–2778. At the landing at the river's mouth west of Port Antonio, there is a pretty indoor/outdoor restaurant and tourist facility designed and operated by Earl Levy, the owner/architect of the elegant Trident Resort and Villas, one of Jamaica's leading resorts.

NONSUCH CAVES And there's more. Another Yankee saw an ad in the *Wall Street Journal* for a 185-acre estate for sale 6 miles east of Port Antonio. He bought it—the Seven Hills of Athenry Plantation along with the Nonsuch Caves. Today, lighting and walkways in the caves make it possible for visitors to view the underground world of stalactites and stalagmites. The plantation is covered with coconut and pimento trees. Pretty footpaths through the gardens lead to a hillside pavilion that offers a grand view of the densely forested mountains in the background and Port Antonio, the coast, and the sea ahead. There is a gift shop. A guided tour costs about US $5; Tel. 993–3740.

BLUE LAGOON Six miles east of Port Antonio is the Blue Lagoon, which many Jamaica devotees call the most beautiful spot on the island. Well, maybe. Local folks claim the Blue Lagoon is bottomless; others say it's been measured to be 185 feet deep. It is fed by freshwater springs, one of which has the power to increase virility, according to local lore. After a long controversy over conservation, Blue Lagoon reopened in May 1995; it has a restaurant and organized water sports. The US $5 admission is deducted from the meal check when you dine at the restaurant. At San San Bay next to Blue Lagoon is Princess Island, a honeymoon gift of Prince Sadruddin Khan to Nina von Thyssen. And down the road another millionaire built Dragon Bay, a resort.

THE CASTLE But the most curious story of all is about the Castle, situated on a rocky promontory next to the *Trident Hotel*. In 1979 a German baroness, Elizabeth Siglindy Stephan von Stephanie, began building an enormous structure complete with turrets that might have a duplicate on the Rhine. Then, as abruptly as construction had begun, it stopped, and the baroness vanished. The owner of the *Trident Hotel* completed the structure as a private mansion for use in conjunction with the hotel. Ah, but the story does not end. In 1988, the baroness returned and built the *Jamaica Palace,* a hotel directly across the bay from the Castle. Less imposing, perhaps, but no less grand, the hotel is furnished with antiques, crystal chandeliers, and splendid oriental carpets. Among its many bizarre features are round beds with navy blue satin bedspreads and a swimming pool in the shape of Jamaica, which has a full view of the Castle.

TOURING PORT ANTONIO

The town of Port Antonio is very small and can be seen in a few minutes' walk. The most interesting sights are out of town and too far away for walking. The easiest way to see the area is on a tour that begins with a harbor cruise on a glass-bottom boat from Huntress Marina (16 West Street); followed by a bus ride to Athenry and a visit to the Nonsuch Caves; a pub-style lunch at the garden pavilion to enjoy the grand view of Port Antonio; a stop at San San Beach for a swim; and last, a visit to Somerset Falls. A guided tour can be arranged through the Jamaica Tourist Board office in Port Antonio (Tel. 993–3051).

BIKING TOURS: *Blue Mountain Bicycle Tour* (Tel. 993–2242), a small company located near the Jamaica Tourist Board, offers biking in the mountains behind Port Antonio for US $80, which includes transportation, lunch, and a guide.

KINGSTON

Jamaica's capital, a city of over 800,000 people, is the hemisphere's largest English-speaking city south of Miami. It is the commercial, political, administrative, and cultural center of Jamaica but is largely ignored by tourists. The much-maligned capital is neither the dangerous den nor the ugly duckling publicity has made it. Indeed, the city enjoys a rather spectacular setting by the sea on the world's seventh-largest natural harbor with the lofty Blue Mountains in the background.

The capital is the headquarters of Jamaica's theater, music, dance, and art, but the opportunity to enjoy the best talent is a matter of timing. *The National Pantomime Theatre* performs January to March; *the Jamaica Folk Singers,* March to April; *the University Dance Society,* May; and *the National Dance Theatre,* July to August. Many also have "mini-sessions" during the Christmas and New Year period.

Plays written by Jamaicans are presented year-round at the Ward Theatre, one of the oldest theaters in the Western Hemisphere; at the University of the West Indies' Creative Arts Centre; and at other playhouses in Kingston. The Cultural Training Center near the Pegasus Hotel in New Kingston has a year-round schedule of music, dance, and art exhibits and other cultural activities.

NATIONAL GALLERY OF ART The gallery's collection represents Jamaica's most important native artists from the nineteenth century to the present as well as foreign artists who have worked here. One room is devoted entirely to the works of the late Kapo, Jamaica's leading primitive artist, known particularly for his sculpture. One of the museum's most outstanding collections is of works by Edna Manley, the wife of the first prime minister and the mother of Michael Manley. Her sculpture "Negro Awakened" is considered one of the most significant works in the body of Caribbean art.

CONVENTION CENTRE Next door is the Jamaica Convention Centre, built entirely with Jamaican design and materials and itself something of a work of art, with exquisite interiors of fine Jamaican wood artfully deployed throughout.

INSTITUTE OF JAMAICA Founded in 1879 and similar in scope to the Smithsonian Institution, the Institute of Jamaica is an umbrella organization with wide-ranging responsibilities for the Jamaica National Trust Commission, which has identified hundreds of old buildings, churches, houses, and other structures for preservation and oversees archaeological excavations. The Institute's West Indian Reference Library chronicles Jamaican and Caribbean political, social, and economic developments and maintains the world's largest collection of books, articles, and prints on the West Indies. It also maintains the Natural History Museum, which collects and studies the flora and fauna of Jamaica including hundreds of species unique to the Caribbean. It also publishes *Jamaica Journal,* a quarterly on the culture of Jamaica and the Caribbean.

DEVON HOUSE With the opening of the new National Gallery in 1984, Devon House, a beautifully restored nineteenth-century mansion of Jamaica's first black millionaire, was made into a museum and a showplace for Jamaican crafts. Things Jamaican, a quasi-governmental project to upgrade and promote local crafts, and others have shops here. The coach house of the Devon estate was converted into an attractive restaurant, the Grogge Shoppe, serving light lunches and Jamaican dishes; other buildings house shops for Jamaican products, a bakery, a smoke shop, an ice-cream parlor, and displays of musical instruments.

PORT ROYAL Jamaica's past is as well represented as its creative present at two important sites within easy reach of the capital. Port Royal, on a spit of land west of Kingston airport, was Jamaica's infamous pirates' port in the seventeenth century. It was destroyed in 1692 when an earthquake caused 90 percent of the town and its legendary treasures to sink into the sea. Although several excavations were attempted in the last century, the first organized work was conducted by the National Geographic Society, the Smithsonian, and the Institute of Jamaica in 1959, and again in 1968 by the National Trust. More recently, after several years' restoration work, Port Royal has been made into a park and museum. Another ambitious project calls for excavating Port Royal's underwater ruins.

SPANISH TOWN Located 12 miles west of Kingston is the town founded in 1523 by Diego Columbus as *Villa de la Vega;* it was renamed *St. Jago de la Vega* when it became the capital in 1534. The town was destroyed by the English after they seized Jamaica in 1655. They built their own town on the same site but continued to call it *Spanish Town.* Today, the cathedral on the site of the previous Spanish one is the oldest Anglican church in the New World. Tombstones on the church floor date from the seventeenth century. Government buildings on the town square and a few private houses on the adjacent side streets date from the eighteenth and nineteenth centuries. Recently, the Spanish Town Historic Foundation launched an effort to get private individuals and investors to restore historic homes and buildings and to preserve the town's historic character and make it a "living" museum.

BLUE MOUNTAIN NATIONAL PARK The main highway between Ocho Rios and Kingston is a scenic drive of 54 miles over the mountains. A narrow, winding, and even more scenic road passes through the heart of the Blue Mountains between Newcastle and Buff Bay. The 193,000-acre Blue Mountains/John Crow Forest National Park, located in these rugged mountains, contains some of the most diverse tropical rain forests in the world. Its peaks and valleys are home to seven distinct forest communities and to the endemic swallowtail butterfly, the world's second largest butterfly. Old logging roads and trails provide nature lovers with some of the most beautiful and interesting hiking in the Caribbean. A night hike during full moon up Blue Mountain's peak, arriving at over 7,500 feet in time for the sunrise, is one of the great outdoor experiences of all times.

The Cayman Islands

GRAND CAYMAN, CAYMAN BRAC, LITTLE CAYMAN

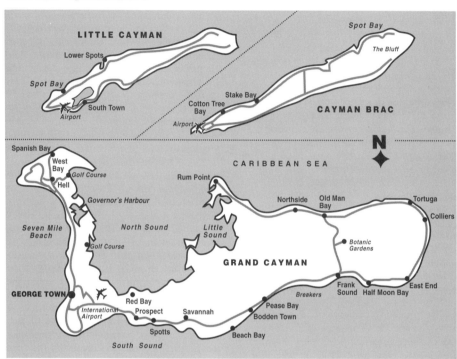

AT A GLANCE

Antiquities	★
Art and Artists	★★
Beaches	★★★★★
Colonial Buildings	★★
Cuisine	★★
Culture	★
Dining/Restaurants	★★★
Entertainment	★
History	★
Museums	★
Nature	★★★★★
Nightlife	★
Scenery	★★
Shopping	★
Sight-seeing	★★
Sports	★★★★★
Transportation	★★

CHAPTER CONTENTS

THE DIVER'S MT. EVEREST

The history of the British Crown Colony of the Cayman Islands might be called the tale of the turtles and the pirates. The Cayman Islands were discovered by Columbus in 1503 on his fourth voyage when a chance wind blew the great explorer's ship off course and thrust it onto "two very small islands full of tortoises," which led Columbus to dub them "Las Tortugas." On later maps, the islands were shown as *Caimanas,* a Carib Indian name for the marine crocodile. Sir Francis Drake also called them *Caymanas* when he arrived to claim them for Britain in 1586. That's when the pirates came too.

At the close of the sixteenth century and for the next one hundred years, the Cayman Islands became a favorite hiding place for Blackbeard, Henry Morgan, Neal Walker, and other pirates (including the infamous women, Anne Bonny and Mary Read), buccaneers, privateers, and the whole corps of sea captains and adventurers who preyed on Spanish galleons laden with treasures from Mexico and the Spanish Main.

(When one was a dashing corsair like Drake and had the blessing of the Crown, he went down in history as a swashbuckler or privateer, but if he had a reputation like Edward Teach, better known as Blackbeard, history more accurately called him a pirate—the most notorious scoundrel of his day.)

Whether because of the pirates or the turtles, little effort was made to colonize the islands, and as late as the early nineteenth century fewer than 1,500 people lived here. In 1863, as part of the territory under the British governor of Jamaica, the Cayman Islands became a Crown Colony. But it did not become a separate entity until a century later, when Jamaica got its independence in 1962.

Situated 480 miles south of Miami and about 200 miles from Cuba and Jamaica, the Caymans are made up of three islands: the 22-mile island of Grand Cayman with the capital and major port of call, George Town; Cayman Brac, 12 square miles of untamed tropics 86 miles to the northeast of the capital; and Little Cayman, the smallest of the trio, 5 miles from the western end of Cayman Brac.

Today's residents have taken both the turtles and the pirates to heart. A turtle dressed as a pirate has become the emblem of the islands' airline, Cayman Airways. Sea turtles, which are on the endangered species list, are bred at the world's first sea turtle farm at the rate of 50,000 a year. Local menus feature turtle steak and turtle soup. The pirates turn up once a year to reclaim their lair during Pirates Week, the Caymans' Carnival, usually held in late October.

Cynics might also note that the turtle-paced islands are still an ideal place to stash away a treasure or two. As a tax-free haven and offshore banking center, they are favored especially by the fast-track world of international finance. Thanks to their commerce, the Cayman Islands have the best communications, the lowest unemployment, and the highest standard of living in the Caribbean.

Yet of all the Caymans' assets the most appealing and enduring is the gift of nature—magnificent beaches and spectacular coral gardens and marine life, often less than 100 yards from shore and in water so clear visibility of 200 feet is not unusual. As a further incentive to divers, there are 350 shipwrecks recorded in these waters—apparently, not all of the pirates made it in and out of the tricky waters of their hideaway. Then, too, not all the wrecks were accidents. Some, it is said, were lured onto the reefs by islanders who plundered the wrecks as a means of livelihood.

In addition to their banks and beaches, the Cayman Islands claim to be the bonefishing capital of the world (though Andros in the Bahamas would give them an argument). Grand Cayman has two 18-hole golf courses, one of which is unusual and features the "short" ball developed by golfing great Jack Nicklaus. And June is sportfishing's million-dollar month, when fabulous prizes are awarded to those who break local records.

FAST FACTS

 POPULATION: The Cayman Islands were settled by deserters from Oliver Cromwell's army, shipwrecked sailors, pirates, and freed slaves. To this day the racial and ethnic mix of the original settlers is reflected in the 33,600 people who inhabit the three islands, 90 percent of whom live on Grand Cayman. Intermarriage has made the Cayman Islands one of the most well-integrated societies in the Western Hemisphere.

 **MAIN TOWN:** George Town

GOVERNMENT: Great Britain got Jamaica and the Cayman Islands from Spain in the Treaty of Madrid in 1670. The Caymans were a dependency of Jamaica until 1961. The following year, after the failure of the short-lived West Indies Federation,Jamaica became independent, but the Caymans chose to remain a British Crown Colony, self-governing in all internal affairs but administered by a governor appointed by Great Britain.

CLIMATE: The western Caribbean is noted for calm balmy weather. Temperatures average 75°F in January and 82°F in summer, and there are many more sunny days than elsewhere in the area. Short tropical rains often catch you by surprise, particularly in the fall and spring, but they rarely last more than a few minutes.

CLOTHING: Tropic-casual is right in style here. Lightweight suits are appropriate for those transacting business. A sweater may be needed on cloudy days in the winter.

CURRENCY: The Cayman Island dollar, called the "CI" locally, is tied to the U.S. dollar at a set rate of CI $1.25 to US $1. One hundred U.S. dollars equals 80 CI dollars, when you exchange cash, and equals 82 CI dollars for checks. Travelers checks and credit cards are widely accepted.

CUSTOMS REGULATIONS: Cruise passengers are admitted without formalities. However, it is always wise to carry a passport, birth certificate, driver's license, or voter's registration card for identification when you travel outside the United States. If you depart the Caymans by air you will need proof of citizenship. The departure tax is US $10.

ELECTRICITY: 110 volts, 60 cycles as in U.S.

LANGUAGE: English, but with a lilt all its own, a delightful mixture of West Indian and Scottish brogue.

POSTAL SERVICE: Air mail to the United States takes four to ten days for delivery. In George Town, post offices are located at the end of Cardinal Avenue two blocks from the pier and in the West Shore Plaza on West Bay Road (Seven Mile Beach); both are open 8:30 A.M. to 3:30 P.M., Monday through Friday.

PUBLIC HOLIDAYS: January 1, New Year's Day; Agricultural Show; Ash Wednesday; Good Friday; Easter Monday; May 19,Discovery Day; mid-June, Queen's Birthday; July 7, Constitution Day; November 10, Remembrance Day; December 25, Christmas Day; December 26, Boxing Day.

TELEPHONE AREA CODE: 345. When calling from the United States, add "94" in front of the five-digit local number:1–345–94 + local number. Special direct phones to call the United States are available at the dock and other selected locations where cruise passengers disembark.

VACCINATION REQUIREMENT: None.

AIRLINES: Cayman Airways, the national carrier, has daily flights to Grand Cayman from Miami and offers daily connections from Grand Cayman to Cayman Brac and Little Cayman. It also operates flights from Houston, Orlando, Tampa, and Atlanta to Grand Cayman. Others flying to Grand Cayman are American Airlines, Northwest, United Airlines, and USAir.

INFORMATION:
In the United States, Cayman Island Tourist Offices:

Chicago: 9525 W. Bryn Mawr, No. 160; Rosemont, IL 60018; 708–678–6446; fax 708–678–6675.

Houston: Two Memorial City Plaza, 820 Gessner, Suite 170; TX77024; 713–461–1317; fax 713–461–7409.

Los Angeles: 3440 Wilshire Blvd., No. 1202; CA 90010; 213–738–1968; fax 213–738–1829.

Miami: 6100 Blue Lagoon Dr., No. 150; FL 33126; 305–266–2300; fax 305–267–2932.

New York: 420 Lexington Ave., No. 2733; NY 10170; 212–682–5582; fax 212–986–5123.

In Canada:

Earl B. Smith, Travel Marketing Consultants, 234 Eglinton Ave. East, No. 306; Toronto, Ontario, Canada M4P 1K5; Tel. 416–485–1550; fax 416–485–7578.

In Grand Cayman:

Harbour Centre, 4th Floor; P.O. Box 67, George Town, Grand Cayman, British West Indies; Tel. 345–949–0623; fax 345–949–4053.

Cayman Islands National Trust,
Eastern Avenue; Tel. 345–949–0121;
fax 345–947–7873.

BUDGET PLANNING

That there are no taxes in the Cayman Islands would at first seem to be a blessing. However, there is, as we all know, "no free lunch" either, and the government supports itself with a steep customs duty on everything brought into the islands. The duties run from 15 to 20 percent on the cost of all imports including shipping charges to bring goods into the islands. As always, these prices are passed on to the consumer, making just about everything you buy, with the exception of a limited number of local products and duty-free items, expensive. You should always review the prices of taxis, restaurants, and anything else you buy to avoid any unwelcome surprises.

Fortunately, your feet can get you around George Town easily enough. If you are taking a taxi any distance, consider sharing with some fellow passengers. A moped for about US $25 a day, with an additional charge of $5 for insurance and driver's permit, and bikes for $10 to $15; or a car rental for US $42 and up a day, with $5 fee for driver's permit for visitors, easily given upon representation of valid U.S. driver's license—shared with friends this will supply you with modest, convenient means of transportation.

If you are watching your budget, public buses operate frequently along West Bay Road to all the beaches and can be picked up at bus stop signs en route. The fare is CI $2.50.

PORT PROFILE: GRAND CAYMAN

LOCATION/EMBARKATION: George Town, the Caymans' capital and port of call, is located on the west side of Grand Cayman. It is perhaps not what you would expect of a Caribbean port. Downtown George Town, which stretches east directly behind the harbor, looks more like a metropolitan banking and financial center than the capital of a Caribbean island. That's not surprising when you learn that 563 banks from over 60 countries,1,001 entities registered or licensed as mutual funds, and 33,792 other companies are doing business here. The Cayman Islands is now the fifth largest international financial center overall. Little wonder it is called the "Switzerland of the Caribbean."

Cruise ships anchor just outside the harbor and tender passengers to a dock at the center of town. You can hardly get lost as the center of town is only three blocks wide and three blocks deep, clean and neat, filled primarily with shoppers and business people.

Occasionally when the sea is rough cruise ships dock on the south end of the island at Spotts Landing, about six miles from George Town. There is a welcome/information center here, and taxis are on hand to take passengers to the town center or on tour.

FACILITIES: While George Town may not have the "feel"of a typical tropical port, this center of international finance demands and gets the most efficient transportation,communications, and technical facilities available in the Caribbean. As soon as you get off your tender there is a special phone available for making calls to the United States, and you can charge the call to a credit card number. Public phones, which almost always work in George Town for local calls, are available, but you will need Caymanian coins to use them. A tourist office is also located at the end of the dock.

Walk straight ahead across Church Street down Cardinal Avenue and you will find most of the shopping and a half dozen banks where you can change money. (U.S. dollars are acceptable everywhere; you need Cayman coins only for local phone calls.) If you don't plan to leave George Town by taxi or tour, everything you need in port is within a few hundred yards of the town dock. Your ability to come and go between ship and shore is restricted only by the tender schedule.

LOCAL TRANSPORTATION: Taxis are available at the dock whenever there is a ship in port. There are taxi stands in town and at the Holiday Inn at Seven Mile Beach on West Bay Road. The drivers speak English, although their lilting accent and their tendency to speak softly take some getting used to. There are no meters, and the rates tend to be high by U.S. standards. Be sure to negotiate the rate before you get in the taxi and be sure,also, that you and your driver understand whether the amount is Cayman Islands or United States dollars. As an example, the fare from the dock to a hotel on Seven Mile Beach costs about US $12 for up to four people, or US $3 to $4 for a seat in a taxi van.

BUSES: Vans with red and white license plates serve as buses along West Bay Road to Seven Mile Beach and cost CI $1, but they do not have a set schedule. You might find it more efficient, when your time is limited, to take a taxi or, if you are planning to tour the island, to rent a car.

CAR RENTAL: Driving is on the **LEFT.** Several car rental companies on Grand Cayman offer excellent service. For a car, expect to pay about CI $37.50 a day and up, with unlimited mileage (without insurance); for gas, about CI $1.80 per gallon.You will also need a valid driver's license from home and a visitor's driving permit, which costs US $5 and is obtained at the time you sign out the car.

Due to the heavy demand during the peak winter season, rental cars are often not available. You would be wise to make reservations in advance from home before departing on your cruise. Most car rental companies have toll-free 800 numbers. Car rental companies will deliver cars anywhere on the island including the town dock. Ace-Hertz (Industrial Park), Tel. 949–2280, 800– 654–3131; Andy's Rent a Car (Seven Mile Beach), Tel. 949–8111, fax 949–8385; Budget Rent a Car, Tel. 949–5605, 800–527–0700; Cico Avis (near airport), Tel. 949–2468, 800–331–1212, fax 949–7127; Coconut Car Rentals (Crew Road), Tel. 949–4037, 800–262–6687.

MOPEDS/BIKES: Scooters and mopeds are a good way to get around George Town and out to the beaches; for longer distances around the island, a car is more practical. Scooters and mopeds are available from *Soto Scooters* (Tel. 949–4652) and *Cayman Cycle Rentals* (Tel. 947–4021) and can be reached quickly by taxi.

Cayman Cycle Rentals offer free pickup service. Prices range from CI $10 for a one-person bike, to CI $18–20 fora moped, to CI $27 motorcycle.

FERRIES: Regular ferry service departs several times daily across North Sound from the Hyatt Resort dock to Rum Point, where Hyatt has developed a facility that includes water sports and a restaurant. The ferry holds up to 120 people and takes 30 minutes to cross. Tickets can be purchased from *Red Sail Sports* (Tel. 949–9098) at the Hyatt. The ferry operates in each direction about every two hours throughout the day. Round-trip fare is US $15 per person; children under 12 ride free. NCL and RCCL use the ferry service for some of their shore excursions.

AUTHOR'S FAVORITE ATTRACTIONS

SWIMMING WITH STINGRAY
SNORKELING/DIVING
TURTLE FARM
RUM POINT BEACH DAY
DEEP-SEA FISHING OR GOLF

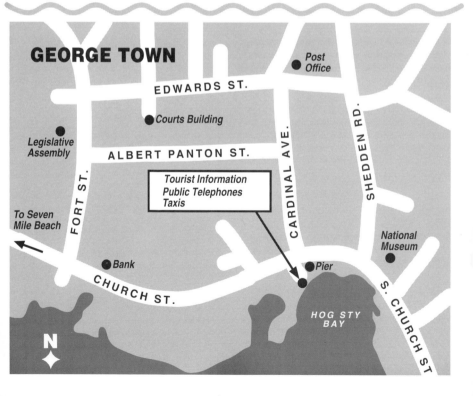

SHORE EXCURSIONS

If you prefer an easy walk with a little shopping, you can stroll about the center of George Town in only a few blocks. The national museum's gift shop, only a few feet from the dock, has an excellent brochure for a self-guided walk of historic George Town. On the other hand, to really see Grand Cayman and get the feel of the Caymans you will need to get out of town to see the island and its fabulous beaches; get out on the sea to enjoy its lovely waters; or get under the sea to enjoy nature's spectacular show. Whichever you choose, you will need transportation.

You can easily negotiate with a taxi driver for a tour of Grand Cayman along West Bay Road to the Turtle Farm, or a spin around the island to East End. However, unless you are sharing the cost with friends that could be expensive. Expect to pay for a half-day excursion US $75 or more.

There are several tours available that will give you a good look at Grand Cayman's shore-side attractions. Among the agencies providing sight-seeing are *EVCO Tours* (Tel. 949–2118); *Majestic Tours* (Tel. 949–7773); *Rudy's Travellers Transport* (Tel. 949–3208); and *Tropicana Tours* (Tel. 949–0944).

The first three of the following tours are those most frequently available on cruise ships. The other options are offered by some lines; if your line does not offer them you will need to make arrangements in advance through your travel agent or on your own. Recently, I found a great discrepancy between prices available from local tour companies and sports operators and those being offered by some cruise ships--some tours sold on ships are as much as 40 percent higher. Prices are U.S. dollar sunless specified otherwise.

George Town/West Bay: Two-and-a-half hours, US $23–28. The tour briefly visits downtown George Town's shopping district and continues along Seven Mile Beach to West Bay with a stop at Turtle Farm and "Hell" to send postcards. You can be dropped off at the beach or returned to town for shopping. A longer version adds lunch at the beach and time for a swim, $36 or $18 without sight-seeing.

Atlantis Submarine Reef Trip: Two hours, $69 by day or night for adults, $34.50 for children 4 to 12 years. (Tel. 949–7700). For a close look at Grand Cayman's famous reefs, cruise 150 feet below the surface in a 46-passenger, 50-foot-long submarine. (See diving section at the end of this chapter.)

Atlantis Research Submersibles: Two hours, $299 per person. (Tel. 949–8296). For a once-in-a-lifetime experience, you can dive in a submarine, down to 800 feet depth, to view reefs and underwater life never seen even by the many divers who come to Grand Cayman. Only two passengers per dive. (See diving section for details.)

Tour of Grand Cayman: Five to six hours, $50. The tour covers the whole of the island as described in the section "Driving Tour of Grand Cayman." The excursion is more rewarding by car as it enables you to set your own pace, stopping for a swim, photo, picnic, or scenic view as you like.

Stingray City/Island Tour: Three hours, $25. ($39 as cruise ship shore excursion.) For the thrill of a lifetime, try swimming and snorkeling with a dozen or so stingrays. (See later in this chapter for a description.) The boat departs from the northwest side of North Sound, a dock near the Hyatt Hotel, or other locations. In addition to snorkel excursions there are glass-bottom boat trips combined with an island tour, $37; and one-tank dives for certified divers, $45.

Seaworld Explorer Semi-Submarine: One hour, $29. ($34 as cruise ship shore excursion). Float in a semisubmersible with large glass windows at 5 feet below the surface of water to see the reefs, fish, and shipwrecks near the cruise ship pier.

Golf: Brittania Golf Course, part of the Hyatt complex, or The Links, the newest course. (See sports section for fees.)

Flight-seeing: Seabourne Flightseeing Adventures (Tel. 949–6029) offers tours in small planes, departing from the international airport from December through June. Cayman Helicopters (Tel. 949–4400) also arranges tours. Prices are based on flight duration and number of passengers.

GRAND CAYMAN ON YOUR OWN

George Town's epithet "The Switzerland of the Caribbean" refers not only to its major position as a financial center for offshore banking and insurance but to a certain Swiss-like efficiency, cleanliness, and businesslike attitude. Although the best of Grand Cayman is out of town, you might want to take a walk in the immediate area before you leave the dock.

CAYMAN ISLANDS NATIONAL MUSEUM This museum opened in 1990 in the Old Courts Building, which dates from the 1830s and was restored through a grant from the United Nations, which also provided museum experts. The courthouse/jail has served as a public library, bank, church, and local social center. A good example of Cayman-type architecture, the building won an American Express Preservation Award. Although it is an important tourist attraction, the air-conditioned museum was created mainly to give the local population a place to preserve its natural and cultural history.

Exhibits, some with dioramas, highlight the islands' important events. The ground floor is devoted to exhibits on the Caymans' natural historical and marine life; the second floor has historical and cultural displays. Hours: Tues.–Fri., 8:30 A.M. to 4:30 P.M.; Sat., 10 A.M. to 5 P.M.; Sun., 1 to 5 P.M. Admission: $5 adults; $2.50 children. The section holding the gift shop was once a jail. The shop is open daily except Sunday from 9 A.M. to 5 P.M. There is a snack bar with local food.

DRIVING TOUR OF GRAND CAYMAN

Driving is on the LEFT.

Although Grand Cayman is only 22 miles long and about 8 miles wide, you will need to leave yourself plenty of time if you plan to tour the entire island. Unlike many Caribbean ports of call where the road goes around the island, Grand Cayman does not have a loop road encircling it. Rather, the island is shaped something like a boomerang; hence the roads go either to the west side or the east side of the island. You will need to backtrack from any extended drive in either direction in order to return to town and your ship.

From your starting point at George Town with a good map in hand (available at the Tourist Office and in bookstores) you have two choices. First, you can follow North Church Road to West Bay Road, the island's main north-south artery along Seven Mile Beach. This plan takes you into the West Bay section, a peninsula that borders the North Sound and contains the vast number of the island's hotels and condo developments, the Turtle Farm, most restaurants, the island's best beaches, water sports and fishing centers, tennis courts, and golf courses. All the roads in West Bay feed back to West Bay Road, which leads directly into George Town and the harbor. Permitting a reasonable amount of sightseeing time, you can tour West Bay in two hours.

As a second option, you can head south on South Church Road, which leads out of town into rural Grand Cayman to Bodden Town and East End. Eventually, the drive will take you to Rum Point on the northwestern most tip. This tour requires three to four hours, or longer if you stop along the way to enjoy the sights, picnic, and swim.

To make both the west side and east side drives, you need a minimum of six hours going even at a fast clip. Remember, with each tour you will have to double back to George Town, so plan to turn back when you have used up half of your allotted time.

Also, stick to the main coast road. It adds a few more miles to your trip, but the route is far more scenic, easier to follow,and will bring you directly back to the harbor without any turnoffs. There are shortcuts through the middle of town to or from the harbor, but do not use them if you are unfamiliar with George Town. Traffic is heavy, and you could get lost quickly on the twisting roads, particularly when you are concentrating on staying LEFT while at the same time trying to follow a map.

TO THE WEST END

For the western drive, head north from the harbor toward West Bay and along the famed Seven Mile Beach. For the next few miles you will be traveling straight north with the beach on the left (west), past the hotels and luxury condominiums that line both sides of the road.

GOLF CLUB and GOVERNMENT HOUSE Some points of interest to note are the Holiday Inn (location of the water sports recreational center along Seven Mile Beach); the Brittania Golf Club (which features the Jack Nicklaus short-ball course and is adjacent to the Hyatt Regency); the public beach (just beyond the Holiday Inn); and Government House, the residence of the governor, also near the public beach.

TURTLE FARM After about five-and-a-half miles, you will come to a fork in the road; the road on the left takes you directly to the Turtle Farm. Here at the world's first sea turtle farm, which is also a research station, you will be able to observe turtles in their breeding ponds at various stages of development, and you can even pick up one from the water for a photograph. Some grow as long as 4 feet and weigh up to 600 pounds. The farm breeds turtles—at the rate of about 50,000 per year—under contract to restock the waters of countries around the world as well as for commercial purposes. There is a museum and gift shop. However, we must warn you, tortoise shell is not allowed into the United States as these animals are still on the endangered species list. For information: Cayman Turtle Farm, Box 645, West Bay, Grand Cayman; Tel. 949–3892. It is open seven days a week from 9 A.M. to 5 P.M. Entrance is US $6 adults, $3 children.

HELL You can take a detour to Hell. By following the right fork, the road will take you away from the tourist areas and into the residential sections of West Bay. Follow the signs to Hell, which was given its name because of the area's dramatic and ominous coral and limestone formations known as ironshore, a dominant feature of part of the Cayman shore. "Hell" postmarks on your postcards—and, of course, Hell T-shirts—are the main industries here. This unusual attraction was given its name in the 1930s and its post office in 1962. In 1986, Hell got a facelift that added a boardwalk with better access for viewing the rocks, as well as craft shops, plants, and a new post office.

BARKERS The West Bay Road to the northwest end of West Bay will bring you to Barkers, a district named for the reef it fronts. Here you will be able to watch a Caymanian fishing harbor at work. The eastern end of Barkers extends into North Sound, a huge estuary popular for birding, snorkeling, and diving. Parts are protected by the Cayman National Land and Marine Park. Approximately half of the 180 bird species recorded in the Caymans, which are located on migratory routes, have been spotted in the Barkers vicinity.

NORTH SOUND/STINGRAY CITY Across the mouth of North Sound is a barrier reef; just inside is one of the Caribbean's most unusual sites, dubbed Stingray City. In only 12 feet of water, divers can touch, feed, and photograph a dozen or more friendly Southern Atlantic stingray. These creatures look prehistoric and frightening, but they are actually very gentle, with skin as soft as velvet.

To THE EAST END

For the second option to the south and eastern parts of the island, South Church Street will take you along the manicured residential areas of the South Sound, around the town, and along South Sound Road, which borders the sea on one side and edges mangroves and pools on the other—all popular locations for birdwatching. The Caymans, because of their location on the migratory routes between North, Central, and South America, are visited by a large number of bird species in fall and spring; there are, in addition, endemic species. The road turns inland for a short distance before reaching the village of Savannah.

PEDRO'S CASTLE In 1992, the Cayman Islands Government bought the historic 7.65-acre Pedro Castle to restore as a National landmark and develop as a tourist attraction under the supervision of the Cayman Islands National Trust. Built in 1780 by William Eden as a private residence called St. James Castle, the ruins are the oldest standing structure in the Cayman Islands and are constructed from coral rocks common in that area. The most important recorded event here was a meeting on December 5, 1831, establishing the country's first elected legislature.

Along with its historical significance, the castle has one of the most scenic and tranquil locations on Grand Cayman's rugged south coast. It lies on Pedro Bluff, a limestone ridge that rises 20 feet from the sea and supports a variety of native flowering plants and shrubs, including the silver thatch palm, a plant that has had an important role in the islands' crafts and heritage. Comprehensive research on the site's history, restoration of the structure, and landscaping are part of the Trust's plans to make the site a national park equipped with a variety of facilities. The Trust, established in 1987, is charged with protecting the islands' historical, natural, and maritime heritage.

BODDEN TOWN After Savannah the main road turns back out again to the small village of Bodden Town, once the capital of Grand Cayman. Here, you will have a look at a different Caymanian life-style—one that depends on the sea and land for survival. There are caves here that legend says were once pirate hideouts.

After another 6 miles, you will see a lighthouse on the right. Use this as a checkpoint to find the Frank Sound Road just beyond to the left. If your time is limited, you can use this cross-island highway to drive from the south coast to the northside of the island and trim about an hour off your trip. It passes the entrance to the Botanical Park.

QUEEN ELIZABETH BOTANICAL PARK Since 1991, the National Trust of the Cayman Islands has been developing this nature park to preserve the islands' natural environment and wildlife, provide a place for local people to enjoy their natural heritage, and create an attraction for eco-tourists. The park, situated on a 60-acre tract of woodland, was donated to the government by a private owner. As much as 80 percent of the park land is being preserved as native woodlands with sign-posted walkways and interpretive displays. A nature walk bordering the heart of the area was completed in 1993, and the park was officially opened the following year by Queen Elizabeth, for whom it is named.

Some areas are to be developed as display gardens to showcase vegetation native to the Cayman Islands. An estimated 40 percent of the plants endemic to the Caymans are found in this area, and more species of native flora are being added. The largest gardens and main tourist attraction will be the "Heritage Garden," a historically oriented display of the plants raised by the local population over the years and their uses.

The area is a habitat for the Caymans' two subspecies of Cuban parrots and Grand Cayman's endemic blue iguana, an endangered species estimated to number less than 50 in the wild. The park has a captive breeding program underway for the iguana. A visitor's center and gift shop are being completed. Admission: $3.12 adults; $1 children.

EAST END If you continue straight ahead along the coast instead of turning into Frank Sound Road, you will soon come to East End, which is the name for both the area and one of the most historically authentic Caymanian villages, where you can have a look at Grand Cayman's past. The shipwreck lying at the fringe of the reef is the remains of the *Ridgefields,* a U.S. cargo vessel that went aground during the Bay of Pigs operation—a reminder that the Caymans are located only 200 miles south of Cuba.

As you round the eastern end of the island, you pass Morritt's Tortuga Club, one of Grand Cayman's oldest resorts. Just beyond the club, where the road bends west onto the Queen'sHighway, there are short trails to the seaside cliffs on the north side and others into the bush on the south. Several rare species of bird are found only here.

OLD MAN BAY Continuing west along the north road about 5 miles, you will come to Old Man Bay and the northern terminus of Frank Sound Road, the north-south artery connecting the north and south shores of the eastern peninsula. Your fastest way back to George Town, if you are short on time, is to turn left (south) and go back to South Sound Road, which will take you into George Town.

RUM POINT If your time permits, you can continue straight ahead to Rum Point overlooking North Sound. This area has one of the island's nicest stretches of sand, second only to Seven Mile Beach, and in the winter it is the site of the island's most spectacular sunsets. "Stingray City" is just off the coast. In late 1995, Hyatt Regency Grand Cayman opened a rustic-style restaurant, the Rum Point Club (Tel. 947–9203), designed in bright Caribbean colors with high ceilings and exposed beams and a sheltered veranda, and specializing in seafood and Caribbean specialties. Red Sail Sports, Hyatt's water sports operator, has a complete water sports facility on the beach and is open daily. A 400-foot dock accommodates the ferry that runs across North Sound between the Hyatt and Rum Point. Ferry reservations: 949–9098; $15 round-trip.

To return to George Town from here, you must retrace your route to the Frank Sound Road and turn right (south). At South Sound Road turn right (west) again. Along the way you will come to two forks in the road en route to town. Again, if you hug the coast, always taking the left road at these forks, you will minimize the risk of getting lost on your way back into town.

SHOPPING

Grand Cayman is not known as a major shopping island. Heavy import duties make most items rather expensive, but duty-free shopping on a limited number of items offers good buys. Recently, the Cayman Islands Chamber of Commerce and Better Business Bureau have been working with the Department of Tourism to offer quality guarantees for customers at the Chamber's member stores.

The quality of native art and handcrafts is good, but the supply is limited. The prosperity of the Caymans is reflected ina general appetite for imported high-tech consumer goods. Not surprisingly, Caymanian youth gravitate toward high-paying, skilled jobs and unfortunately show little interest in learning the traditional crafts and artistic skills of the islands. The best of Cayman's artisans are not being replaced, and native art and handcrafts have suffered severely as a result.

A word of caution. Those highly polished turtle shells and other turtle products for sale in Grand Cayman CANNOT be imported into the United States. Such products, even when produced on a commercial farm, are prohibited because the sea turtle is on the endangered species list. U.S. Customs will confiscate these items upon your return, and you may be subject to a fine.

ANTIQUES: *Artifacts* (Harbour Drive) has prints, maps, coins, silver, and other interesting pieces mainly from England. The most popular antiques are authentic gold and silver coins set into jewelry by local craftsmen.

ART AND ARTISTS: Several shops, all within walking distance of the harbor, are worth visiting in George Town. *Pure Art Gallery* (South Church Road) is an art lover's dream. If you had to select only one place on the island to shop, this would be the best choice. Even if you do not plan to buy, you will enjoy a visit to see the array. The gallery is set in a charming old Cayman cottage where every nook and cranny is filled with art, the usual crafts, herbs, and spices. Most of the items are locally made or come from other Caribbean islands; all reflect high quality and creativity. Among the crafts are the popular birdhouses by Charlie Ebanks. The gallery has a second outlet at the Hyatt Regency Hotel.

Cayman Fine Art & Framing Centre (West Shore Center, West Bay Road) stocks local and foreign artists who spend time in the Caymans, and *Heritage Craft* (Shedden Road, Merrin's Market, second floor) carries native crafts and souvenirs.

The Amazing China Turtle (at the waterfront) has a variety of native handcrafts, souvenirs, and fine linens.

Traditional Caymanian baskets and other woven items are a particularly good buy. Made from thatched palm fibers of a particularly strong species that grows in the Caymans, these baskets are tough and durable.

CHINA/CRYSTAL: Several duty-free shops are within an easy walk of the harbor. English crystal and china are specialties. The prices are good and the selection wide. *Kirk Freeport Center* (Albert Panton Street, north of the harbor) and *Waterfold/Wedgwood Gallery* (Cardinal Avenue) have the best selections of duty-free china and crystal. *Duty Free Stores* (at the harborside Anchorage Center) has excellent selections of perfumes and designer items such as watches.

CLOTHING: Generally most clothing items are imported from the United States, and the selection is limited. Resortwear is plentiful, but at resort prices. One of the most attractive shops is *Shellections* (Hog Sty Bay Tourist Landing), which is a vision in pastels and flowers with hand-painted resortwear for the whole family. There are dresses, summer garden party hats, painted shirts and dresses, jewelry, and jewelry boxes. *Java Wraps* (Westshore Center) has attractive batik shirts, tropical skirts, and dresses, but prices here are higher than on other Caribbean islands.

JEWELRY: You will see black coral jewelry advertised everywhere, but the Cayman Islands prohibited its harvest in 1986 when it established its marine reserves. The coral you see is mostly from Central America. Those who care about the environment will have trouble understanding the logic in the Caymans' protecting their own coral but allowing that from other countries to be sold in local stores. If you buy it, you only encourage the practice.

And if you can afford them, *Smiths of Cayman* (Fort Street; Tel. 949–7877) has Spanish pieces of eight from the Treasure Fleet of 1715 made into jewelry and an exhibit of other artifacts discovered only in 1985. Hours are 10 A.M. to 5 P.M.; phone for an appointment.

Some of the most attractive ancient coin jewelry is found at *Venture Gallery* (West Shore Center); a certificate of authenticity accompanies all purchases. The store also makes delightful gold charms of marine life, such as stingray, scuba divers, and dolphins; they are sold by weight and are reasonably priced. And for fun, you can strike your own coin on an authentic old press for as little as $5 at *The Pirates Mint* (Soto Freeport Building).

LIQUOR: With nearly $28 per gallon duty on alcohol coming into the Cayman Islands, liquor is no bargain for local residents. However, cruise passengers can buy duty-free liquor in bond at *Tortuga Rum* (South Church Street) near the pier and at the airport. There

is no locally made rum or other spirits as in many Caribbean islands. But for a great treat, Tortuga Rum Cake is baked daily using a century-old recipe, and it's vacuum packed.

DINING AND RESTAURANTS

In the last few years the range and quality of restaurants on Grand Cayman has widened considerably. The bad news about dining in Grand Cayman is that it tends to be expensive. Again, the need to import most ingredients, high labor costs, and a steep duty on imported items keep the prices high. Expect to pay $50 or more per person with wine in an expensive restaurant.

Native Caymanian cooking emphasizes seafood. Fish served in Grand Cayman's top restaurants is usually ocean-fresh and prepared well. Turtle steak is a national delicacy which, if properly prepared, can be good. Turtle has a taste best described as a cross between chicken and veal. However, the supply of turtle meat is limited, and it can be hard to find in local restaurants.

Billy's Place (North Church St., Tel. 949–0470). Don't be put off by the nondescript decor; the food is good—Caribbean in flavor with Jamaican jerk dishes and Indian curries, and reggae and calypso to go with it. Billy alone is worth the visit if you want to catch some local color and lore. Moderate.

Cayman Arms (at the harbor, second floor; Tel.949–2661) has a British pub atmosphere, but with good native cooking along with typical pub food. It is a good lunch spot and one of the best bars in George Town for mixed tropical drinks. It's a convenient place to try a potent planter's punch, as you are only 50 feet from the tender to take you back to the ship! Moderate.

Chef Tell's Grand Old House (South Church Street; Tel. 949–2020) was the first of Grand Cayman's elegant restaurants. It is located in a turn-of-the-century plantation house and serves seafood and continental cuisine with a distinct West Indian touch. Expensive.

Crow's Nest (South Sound; Tel. 949–6216) is the Caymanian version of a roadside diner; it is local and on the beach, but it has surprisingly good food; a good place to try the native cuisine as the Caymanians serve it. Inexpensive.

Hog Sty Bay Café (North Church Street; Tel. 949–6163). It's close to the harbor and it's fun, as popular with residents as with visitors. Cayman and Caribbean specialists in a colorful atmosphere. Moderately expensive.

The Wharf (Seven Mile Beach; Tel. 949–2231), with its pretty setting of white-washed gazebos stepping down to the water's edge, is one of the island's most popular restaurants. The menu offers an interesting variety of creative fish and meat dishes. Moderately expensive.

White Hall Bay (North Church St.; Tel. 949–8670) serves local cuisine in a renovated Caymanian-style cottage in a romantic setting overlooking the sea. Its menu includes turtle stew and turtle steak. Moderate.

In West Bay, *The Cracked Conch, Liberty's,* and *Island Taste* serve moderately priced Caymanian specialties.

SPORTS

BEACH/SWIMMING: There is but one beach on Grand Cayman worthy of your time. Seven Mile Beach runs north of George Town for—yes, 7 miles. It is one of the best anywhere in the Caribbean. The crest of white powdery sand edged by tall Australian pines slopes gently into a waveless turquoise sea. There are other beaches on Grand Cayman, but for cruise passengers with a limited amount of time, we recommend Seven Mile, a ten-minute taxi ride from the harbor.

For active water sports, head for the *Holiday Inn* water sports center or Red Sail Sports at the Hyatt Regency. Both rent every imaginable type of equipment. On the other hand, if you prefer a quiet spot of sand with little to do but swim and sun, have the driver take you farther down the road to the public beach. Don't worry about the crowds. Few local people go to the beach in the Caymans—so the public beach is quite private. Walk south and find your spot. When you are ready to return to George Town and the ship, walk to the Holiday Inn, where you can pick up a taxi. On the south end of Seven Mile Beach, on a nice stretch of the coast north of the Radisson Beach Hotel, *Jekayl Beach Party* is designed for cruise passengers and other day visitors and offers water sports, lounge chairs ($3), and a bar and grill.

BOATING: You have the choice of several small sailing craft from Sunfish to Hobie cats, or a 60-foot catamaran with crew available for charter. *Aqua Delights* (Holiday Inn; Tel. 947–4444, ext. 686) can take care of your needs. Day sailors and Hobie cats rent for $28 an hour. *Ocean Safari* (Tel. 345–947–2557) has half-day cruises for $35. *Ron Ebanks Sound Experience* (Charter Boat Headquarters, Coconut Place, West Bay Road; Tel. 947–4340) offers a daily guided snorkeling excursion to Stingray City for $30 including lunch. It departs at 9 A.M. and returns at 4 P.M. Their rates are considerably lower than prices of similar packages sold on cruise ships. The company frequently handles reser-

vations from cruise passengers who reserve in advance.

DEEP-SEA FISHING: You cannot find a more perfect spot than the Cayman Islands for deep-sea fishing. It's a passion here, and just about every type of boat is available. The waters are noted for marlin, blue- and yellow-tail tuna, wahoo, dolphin, and barracuda.

All equipment is available for rental, from smaller boats to fully–equipped charters for deep-sea fishing. The latter range from $350–600 for four to eight people for a half day; and $475–1,000 for four to eight or ten people for a full day, depending on the boat. A list of charter boat operators is available in the Tourism Department's booklet, *Cayman Islands Rates and Facts,* updated seasonally. Charter Boat Headquarters (Tel. 947–4340; fax 947–5531) will also put together shared and split charters.

GOLF: Grand Cayman has two golf courses. The first of its kind, Britannia Golf Club, is part of the Hyatt Regency and was designed by Jack Nicklaus as a regulation 9-hole course overlapped by a special short-ball 18-hole course, now known as Cayman Golf. The course is located about a 10-minute taxi ride from the harbor. All equipment is available. The 18-hole Cayman course is available for play from 8 to 11 A.M. and costs US $30. The regulation 9-hole course is open from noon to sunset and costs US $35, and when played as 18 holes, US $50. Reservations are necessary and can be made through Hyatt Hotels' U.S. reservations or by contacting the Britannia (Tel. 949–7440). As a cruise ship shore excursion, $90.

The Links is a new 18-hole championship course in the West End at Safehaven, a 280-acre resort and residential development. The course (par 71, 6,519 yards) was designed by Roy Case to suggest the old Scottish coastal courses; each tee has five separate tee placements to accommodate players of varying skills. The clubhouse has a restaurant/bar, pro shop, and changing facilities. Greens fees: US $80 per person, including the cart, which is mandatory. Club rental: US $15–35. Tee-off times begin at 7:30 A.M. and play runs through dusk.

SCUBA DIVING/SNORKELING: The Cayman Islands, which *Skin Diver* magazine has called "The Mount Everest of Diving," are considered by many scuba divers to have the best waters in the Caribbean for diving and snorkeling. If you are a certified diver (and can prove it with current PADI, AUI, or YMCA "C" card) you should certainly put diving the Caymans at the top of your priority list.

Although there are dives to be made from shore and even shipwrecks right at George Town harbor, the particularly interesting features of Cayman diving are gigantic corals, canyons, and walls in areas that one must take a boat to reach. In some places there are freestanding coral heads up to 30 feet or more in height and many caves to explore. The Cayman Islands' coast and waters are protected by a Marine Park created in 1986 and have 206 permanent mooring positions off the three islands.

One of the most popular snorkeling and dive sites is just south of George Town harbor near Eden Rocks. It is a complex system of underwater tunnels connecting coral heads in 40 feet of water and rising to within 5 feet of the surface. Fish life, too, is abundant with schools of yellow-tail snapper, blue tangs, and an occasional moray eel and stingray. North of George Town are fine shallow reefs and good drop-offs; and at East End and along the south shore to South West Point, the highlight is shallow elkhorn coral reefs that crown labyrinths of limestone caves and grottos housing grouper and giant blue parrotfish.

Because Grand Cayman's North Sound is, in effect, a marine estuary, fish life is abundant. The 20 miles or so of North Wall, off Rum Point, offers great wall diving, with craggy fissures and cuts predominating in certain areas. Circular chimneys that drop 30 to 50 feet and then open out into the ocean are commonplace. However, do not have your heart set on going to one particular place or you could be disappointed. Dive operators choose the dive sites, and they base their choices on the weather and currents, and the level of experience of the participants.

The Cayman Islands' Department of Tourism's annual publication *Rates and Facts* has a map and list of the Caymans' three dozen or more dive operators with their addresses, phone numbers, services, equipment, prices, and other pertinent information. The booklet is updated seasonally. Prices here are very competitive and about the lowest in the Caribbean.

Most cruise ships calling at Grand Cayman offer dive packages, but they are often more than double the price than when you make arrangements directly with local operators. We recommend you call or write from home for a reservation before leaving on your cruise, particularly during the winter season. When you arrive you will have to get yourself to the dive operator by taxi. Timing is very important as most dive trips depart at 9 A.M.

Bob Soto's Diving (Tel. 949–2022; 800–BOB–SOTO), which has been in business for almost four decades and is owned by Ron Kipp, is the best-known dive company. It has the largest operation, catering to many cruise ships, plus one of the most efficient fleets of dive boats. The firm has several locations on Grand Cayman and an 800 number for advance reservations. The location closest to the harbor is less than a half-mile west of town. A one-tank dive is US $40, and a two-tank dive is US $60. A snorkeling trip for

those accompanying divers is US $20. Similar cruise ship shore excursions cost $74 for dive; $40 for snorkeling.

Other excellent dive operators include *Don Foster's Dive Grand Cayman* (Tel. 949–5679; 800–83–DIVER) and *Quabbin Dives* (Tel. 949–5597; 800–238–6712). *Ocean Photo Centre* (Radisson Resort, Seven Mile Beach) is a full-service underwater photography shop and offers instruction as well as rental equipment.

Stingray City is just inside the barrier reef that protects North Sound and is one of the most unusual sites in the Caribbean. Here, in water never more than 12 feet deep, divers and snorkelers can see, touch, and photograph a group of friendly stingrays inhabiting the area. This unusual fish, which has eyes on top of its body, has a wingspan of up to 5 feet and looks like a ship from outer space as it glides gracefully through the water. When purchased directly from a local operator, the going rate for a snorkeling excursion to Stingray City, as the site has been dubbed, is $25 ($49 as a cruise ship excursion) and $45–60 for a dive ($74 as a cruise ship excursion). *Ron Ebanks Sound Experience's* package, the best deal, is described earlier in the "Boating" section.

WINDSURFING/KAYAKING: The calm waters along Seven Mile Beach are a good place to learn to windsurf; most resorts have equipment. For greater challenge, the northeast coast is one of the main windsurfing locations. *Sailboards Caribbean* (Plantana Condominiums, West End; Tel./fax 949–1068) has rentals ($25 per hour) and an hour's introductory lesson ($60). It also has kayaks for rent for $20 per hour. Kayaks at Don Foster's Watersports (Seven Mile Beach; Tel. 949–7181) cost $15 per hour.

UNUSUAL DIVE OPPORTUNITIES FOR NONDIVERS

For those who are not divers, Grand Cayman offers two extraordinary opportunities to see the underwater world. The *Atlantis* is a submarine designed specifically for recreational undersea travel; it can dive to a depth of 150 feet. The 50-foot-long ship holds 46 people and a two-member crew and has one extra-large window in front and eight large view ports along the sides, from which passengers can see nature's display. The ship makes day and night dives along the famous Cayman Wall where divers normally swim at 40 to 90 feet. The ship is air-conditioned and all its systems are duplicated to ensure safety. A surface vessel travels with the submarine and is inconstant contact by underwater telephone or VHF radio.

Passengers go by motor launch, which leaves about every hour from 9 A.M. throughout the day from George Town harbor for a 10-minute ride to the *Atlantis* boarding point. The dive itself is about one hour along the wall to a depth of 90–150 feet and is accompanied by a guide who gives a running commentary on the various fish and coral. The cost for adults is US $69 for day and night dives, and for children ages 4 to 12, $35. Those three years old and under are not admitted. You should buy this as a ship's shore excursion as the price is the same when bought directly.

The Atlantis Research Submersibles offer an even more unusual experience. A submersible is a 20-foot-long, 5.5-ton observation craft that can dive to 800 feet. In addition to the pilot, it accommodates two passengers who have a 36-inch front viewport from which to see. The vessel is equipped with five 500-watt lights to illuminate the underwater setting.

The dive is made along the Cayman Wall, which starts at about 80 feet and drops to 550 feet, where it slopes at an 80-degree angle for several miles to the Cayman Trench, which plunges 6,000 feet. In addition to the thrill of the trip, passengers have the rare opportunity to see the changing character of the wall and the various strata of sea life as the craft drops deeper and deeper in the sea. During the trip, which lasts about one hour, the pilot provides a running commentary.

Passengers go by motorboat in about 30 minutes from the dock in George Town to the submersible; they are given a 15-minute audiovisual presentation and pre-dive briefing on the operation of the emergency contingency systems. The cost is $299 per person. For photographing, you are advised to use high-speed film (ASA400) and normal lenses. The craft makes five dives per day, Mon.—Sat. The dive is sold on most cruise ships, but in high season you might want to make reservations in advance: (345) 949–7700 or write P.O. Box 1043, Grand Cayman Island, B.W.I. Couples have gotten married in the craft at 800 ft. below sea level.

ENTERTAINMENT / NIGHTLIFE

Cruise ships seldom remain in port in the evening, but if yours does you will find clubs with live entertainment, a comedy club, discos, and even a karaoke bar. The island's famous band, The Barefoot Man, plays everything from calypso to pop at the *Holiday Inn* from Wednesday to Saturday (Tel. 947–4444). The *Harquail Theatre* (West Bay Road) is used to stage plays and musicals.

FESTIVALS AND CELEBRATIONS

High on the list of unique entertainment in Grand Cayman is the annual Pirates Week Festival in late October. In celebration of its history as a pirate lair the whole island is transformed into a pirate encampment complete with a mock invasion of George Town, parades, pageants, parties, and the crowning of a pirate queen. If you happen to land here during Pirates Week, be ready to be swept up into the fun and frolic. The Batabano Festival in early April is the more traditional Carnival.

Anglers who arrive in Grand Cayman during June have a chance to take home cash and other prizes during the Million Dollar Month Fishing Tournament. All you have to do is catch an Atlantic blue marlin weighing in excess of 584 pounds, the local record. There are also lesser prizes for lighter fish.

For the less energetic, May brings the annual flower show and a chance to see the Caymans' spectacular varieties.

The Mexican Caribbean

COZUMEL, PLAYA DEL CARMEN/CANCÚN

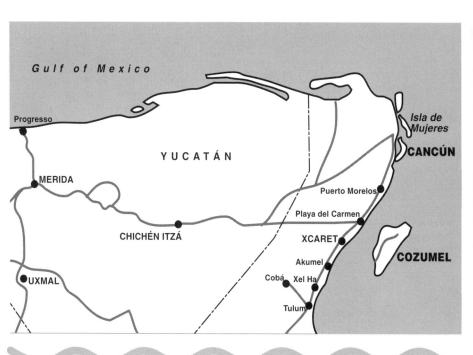

Gulf of Mexico

Progresso

Isla de Mujeres

YUCATÁN

CANCÚN

MERIDA

Puerto Morelos

Playa del Carmen

CHICHÉN ITZÁ

XCARET

COZUMEL

Akumel

UXMAL

Cobá   Xel Ha

Tulum

AT A GLANCE

Antiquities	★★★★★
Archaeology	★★★★★
Art and Artists	★★
Beaches	★★★★★
Crafts	★★★★★
Cuisine	★★★
Dining/Restaurants	★★★
Entertainment	★★★
History	★★★★★
Museums	★★
Nightlife	★★★★
Scenery	★★
Shopping	★★★★
Sight-seeing	★★★★
Sports	★★★★★
Transportation	★★

CHAPTER CONTENTS

WHERE THE PAST MEETS THE PRESENT

The Mexican Caribbean is one of the oldest, most historic regions of Mexico and one of its newest, most popular vacation resorts. It is best known by the names of two recently developed islands, Cancún and Cozumel, famous for their lovely beaches and magnificent water rich in coral gardens and marine life.

Both islands are located on the tip of the Yucatán Peninsula at the easternmost extreme of Mexico where the Caribbean Sea meets the waters of the Gulf of Mexico. Cancún is connected to the mainland by roads and bridges and seems more like an extension of the mainland than an island. Cozumel is located about 10 miles off the coast, directly east of the port of Playa del Carmen, about 40 miles south of Cancún.

Cancún bills itself as the first resort of the computer age. The site was nothing more than a sandbar in 1973 when it was selected by computer analysis as the best place to start Mexico's long-range development of its coast. Today, it is an international playground with glamorous resorts and restaurants, golf, tennis, and a full complement of water sports.

Cozumel, too, has come into her own as a resort in the last two decades with an array of hotels, restaurants, and sporting activity, but the island was put on the tourist map even earlier by scuba divers. It has been a prime location for diving for over 30 years. Today, it is as popular with shoppers as with divers. Yet for all their up-to-the-minute fun and facilities, both resorts are part of a land whose history stretches back over a thousand years before the arrival of Columbus.

BEFORE COLUMBUS AND CORTÉS

Long before the discovery of America by Columbus and the conquest of Mexico by Cortés, there were civilizations throughout the Americas—the Inca, the Aztec, the Maya—which reached great heights of culture and achievement. One of them, the Maya, dominated the region of the Yucatán from about the first to the twelfth century A.D. Today the remnants of their civilization are among Mexico's most important antiquities.

At its height the Mayan domain comprised an area extending roughly 550 miles north to south and 350 miles east to west. This included the present states of Yucatán, Campeche, and Quintana Roo in Mexico, as well as Belize and Guatemala. By the time the Spaniards conquered Mexico in the early sixteenth century, the Mayan culture had already declined and many of the towns had been abandoned. Why this happened is one of the many mysteries about the Mayas confronting archaeologists.

Indeed, Mayas are almost synonymous with mystery. They stepped into history, seemingly from nowhere, spawned a civilization that lasted 1,500 years, and disappeared almost as suddenly as they came. Archaeological evidence shows the Mayas established large cities with as many as 50,000 inhabitants, constructed stone pyramids 17 stories high and palaces of a hundred rooms or more, chiseled massive sculpture, and painted detailed murals and friezes that can still be seen on their magnificent temples and pyramids throughout the Yucatán.

The Mayas had a complex written language, charted the revolution of the sun and the planets in their observatories, calculated great mathematical sums, developed a calendar more accurate than the one we use today, practiced brain surgery, composed music, and wrote books (destroyed by zealous Spanish priests). And what makes the Mayas all the more remarkable is that they gained these achievements without benefit of the wheel, the plow, and other aids usually associated with an advanced civilization.

Archaeologists estimate that less than ten percent of the Mayan cities have been found. The best known of the archaeology sites today are *Chichén Itzá*, about 70 miles from Mérida, the capital of the Yucatán near the northwest coast; *Uxmal*, 35 miles south of Mérida; and *Tulum* and *Cobá* about 35 miles from Playa del Carmen on the east coast.

The combination of superb sports and modern facilities, Mexican crafts, cuisine, and proximity to some of the most important archaeological sites in the Western Hemisphere have made the Mexican Caribbean resorts popular as ports of call.

FAST FACTS

MAIN TOWNS: Cancún, 350,000; Playa del Carmen, 20,000; San Miguel (Cozumel), 60,000.

CLIMATE: Consistently warm, around 80°F year-round and dry.

CLOTHING: Casual and comfortable summer sportswear for day and only a little less casual for evening.

CURRENCY: The unit of currency is the Mexican peso, written with a "$" dollar sign. In January 1993, the government introduced a new peso, dropping the last three zeros on the old peso. The new peso is represented by "N $" to distinguish it from the old peso. Now, US $1 equals N $7.6 instead of 76,000 pesos. Banks are open Monday through Friday, 9 A.M. to 1:30 P.M.

Because of the continuing fluctuation in the peso, we have included very few prices in this chapter. Those that are included are provided for readers' planning purposes. None of them are likely to be precisely accurate at the time of your visit, but we hope they are close enough to be useful.

 CUSTOMS REGULATIONS: If you disembark in Mexico to return to the United States by plane there is a departure tax of $12.

 ELECTRICITY: A.C. 60, 110 volts.

 ENTRY FORMALITIES: Normally, visitors need tourist cards to enter Mexico. These formalities are handled by the cruise lines. However, you should have your passport with you for identification, and you will need a driver's license and a major credit card to rent a car.

 LANGUAGE: Spanish. English spoken at hotels and most, but not all, shops.

 POSTAL SERVICE: The post office in Cozumel is located at the corner of Calle 7 Sur and Avenida Rafael Melgar (known as the Malecon).

 TELEPHONE AREA CODE: Mexico—52; Cancún——984; Cozumel—987. From the U.S. dial 011–52+ 98 and the local, six-digit number for Cancún, or 987 and the local, five-digit number for Cozumel.

 TIME: Cancún, Playa del Carmen, and Cozumel lie in the Central Standard Time Zone, one hour behind Eastern Standard Time.

 VACCINATION REQUIREMENTS: None.

 AIRLINES: *From the United States:* American, Continental, Mexicana, Northwest, and United. *Between Cozumel/Cancún/Mérida:* Aerocaribe/ Aerocozumel, Mexicana Inter, and Taesa.

INFORMATION:
In the United States:
Mexican Government Tourism Offices:

New York: 405 Park Ave., No. 1401; NY 10022; 212–755–7261; fax 212–753–2874; 800–44–MEXICO/800–CANCUN8 (for brochures).

Chicago: 70 East Lake St., No. 1413; IL 60601; 312–606–9015; fax 312–606–9012.

Houston: 5075 Westheimer Blvd., No. 975 West; TX 77056; 713–629–1611; fax 713–629–1837.

Los Angeles: 10100 Santa Monica Blvd., No. 224; CA 90067; 310–203–8191; fax 310–203–8316.

Washington, D.C.: 1911 Pennsylvania Avenue; DC 20006; 202–728–1750; fax 202–728–1758.

In Canada, Mexican Government Tourism Offices:
Montreal: 1 Place Villa Marie No. 1526, Que., H3B 2B5; 514–871–1052; fax 14–871–3825.

Toronto: 2 Bloor St. West, Suite 1801, Ontario, M4W 3E2; 416–925–0704; fax 416–925–6061.

 # BUDGET PLANNING

Mexico is one of today's best travel bargains, but you may not see the benefit as a cruise passenger because the Mexican Caribbean is a tourist resort area where prices tend to be higher than in the interior of the country.

If you are on a budget, stay away from fancy bars and restaurants, particularly in resort hotels. You will do best eating at places that specialize in Mexican fare, drinking local Mexican drinks, and dealing directly with tour companies and dive operators. You do have the alternative of good public transportation in Cancún, particularly if you speak Spanish.

 # AUTHOR'S FAVORITE ATTRACTIONS

SCUBA DIVING—COZUMEL
CHICHÉN ITZÁ AIR TOUR FROM COZUMEL
BUS TOUR FROM PLAYA DEL CARMEN
A DAY AT XCARET

SHORE EXCURSIONS

Generalizations about shore excursions for Cozumel, Cancún, and Playa del Carmen are difficult because there is little consistency in cruise ship arrivals and departures or the ports they use or the price. Some ships arrive early in the morning and leave in the afternoon about sunset; others arrive in Cozumel in the evening and remain through all or most of the next day while passengers make their excursions to the mainland by ferry, plane, or hydrofoil. A few call at Cozumel only or Playa del Carmen only, while even fewer make stops at both Playa del Carmen and Cozumel or dock directly at Cancún.

As for prices, to take only one example, the Tulum / Xel-Ha tour varies from an overpriced US $65 for a three-hour excursion from Playa del Carmen, to a moderate $55 to $68 for five to six hours from Cozumel, to a low price $39 for seven hours from Cancún—all for the same tour.

Adding to the confusion in terms of planning your day in port is the listing in some brochures of Cozumel and Playa del Carmen as though they were one port. Playa del Carmen is on the mainland about 10 miles directly west of Cozumel island and 40 miles south of Cancún. More often than not when a ship's itinerary is shown as Cozumel/Playa del Carmen, the ship stops in Cozumel only. To reach the mainland, you must go and return via a 45-minute ferry ride from Cozumel to Playa del Carmen for the excursion to Tulum. Or, on your own, you can take a 15-minute plane ride from Cozumel Airport to Cancún or a 35-minute plane ride to Chichén Itzá. There are "fast" or "express" ferries—i.e., hydrofoils—between Cozumel and Playa del Carmen, which depart about every one to two hours during the day from the main pier in town and take 30 minutes. However, these are often under contract to cruise lines at certain times of the day and cannot always be depended upon as transportation for independent travelers.

Out of the two dozen or so cruise ships on regular Western Caribbean cruises, the majority's itineraries now read Playa del Carmen/Cozumel. That means the ship anchors at Playa del Carmen long enough for passengers to disembark for their excursions and then the ship continues to Cozumel. Passengers return to their waiting ships in Cozumel by ferry.

You should study the cruise line's brochure carefully, and if you are interested in visiting a locale such as Chichén Itzá, ask your travel agent to obtain advance information on shore excursions offered on your

cruise. Some cruise lines offer a Chichén Itzá excursion; otherwise you must make your own arrangements, and knowing which port or ports your ship visits is essential to your planning. Another caution when making independent arrangements: Some excursions do not operate daily except in high season from mid-December to mid-April.

The following tours are described elsewhere in this chapter. The order of priority is based on my experience, but you should be guided by your personal interest in making a selection. When shore excursions run longer than four hours, a box lunch will be provided by your ship.

Note to Photographers: At all archaeological sites, a charge of US $10 is levied by the Mexican government for video cameras.

COZUMEL

Chichén Itzá Air Tour: Five to six hours, $140. Arrangements can be made through *Fiesta Cozumel Holidays* (P.O. Box 125, Cozumel; Tel. 011–52–987–0433). When this trip is sold as a shore excursion aboard ship, the cost is likely to be $190 per person.

Robinson Crusoe Boat Excursion: full day, $44. The boat sails along the leeward coast to a secluded cove for swimming, snorkeling over the reefs, and a seafood lunch. The trip is usually sold aboard ship as a half-day excursion without lunch, $39; or party cruise on a boat for 200 people, which is not recommended unless you want this kind of atmosphere, $35.

Cozumel Diving: $40 for one-tank dive; $50, two-tank dive. The best dive sites are an hour from Cozumel; boats depart between 9 A.M. and 10 A.M. See sports section for details. As a cruise ship shore excursion, a half-day dive trip will cost $69–79; for snorkeling, $25–49, depending on the ship.

Subsea Excursion: Two hours, $35. The *Mermaid,* a semi-submarine seating 48 people, floats over the coral gardens around Cozumel, enabling passengers to view the colorful marine life and other points of interest.

Fiesta Evening: $30. A nightclub show at a hotel features mariachi bands and Mexican dancers. As a cruise ship excursion, the cost ranges from $33–39 adults, depending on the ship.

Island Tour: Three-and-a-half hours, $31. Tour the island by bus, visit Mayan ruins, stop for a swim at a coral beach on the windward side, visit National Marine Park at Chankanaab Lagoon, and shop in San Miguel. As a cruise ship excursion, the cost ranges from $36–39 adults, depending on the ship.

PLAYA DEL CARMEN

Tulum and Xel Ha Lagoon: Three hours, $40–44; or 5 to 6 hours, $55 to $72 when return is by ferry to Cozumel to rejoin ship. The tour includes a visit to the archaeological site of Tulum and a swim and refreshments at the lagoon. Take your snorkel gear and towel. Instead of Xel Ha, some tours stop at Xcaret, a nature reserve and recreational park a few miles south of Playa del Carmen. The cost will be higher in this case.

Snorkeling Excursion: Three hours, $30. Snorkeling at Akumal Bay and Yalku, a spring-fed saltwater lagoon; lunch is included.

Chichén Itzá Tour: Nine hours, $98. All-day trip by air-conditioned motorcoach to the Yucatán's most important antiquity site.

Sian Ka'an: Full day, US $115, including bus transportation, breakfast, and lunch. The largest nature preserve in Mexico, made up of tropical forest, wetland and mangroves, and coastal and marine environments, stretches a hundred miles south of Tulum. It was declared a Biosphere Reserve in 1986 and part of UNESCO's World Heritage List. (See description later in chapter.)

Cancún City and Shopping Tour: Three to Four hours, $25. Tour of Cancún City and the Hotel Zone with stops at the town market or shopping plazas. Rather than an organized tour, some cruise ships provide a shuttle from port to Cancún for $15; other ships offer a five-hour trip for $38, including a box lunch.

Golf: To be arranged on your own. (See Sports later in this chapter.)

CANCÚN

Chichén Itzá Tour: full day, $55. The all-day excursion is by air-conditioned motorcoach to the archaeological site, 125 miles west of Cancún. It is available from Cancún Holidays (Plaza Quetzal, Box 558, Cancún; Tel. 30161). As a cruise line excursion, the trip costs $78.

Isla Mujeres Day Excursion: full day, $35; as cruise line excursion, $68. A day sail to the Island of Women, 4 miles north of Cancún, includes snorkeling at Garrafon Reef, a marine shelter, and a seafood lunch at the beach. It leaves at 10 A.M. and returns at 4 P.M. daily. An advantage of the cruise ship excursion is that it brings you back directly to your ship.

Jeep Adventure: full day, $90. Excursion departs Continental Villas Plaza at 8 A.M. and returns at 5 P.M. It visits the corridor south of Cancún with a stop at the Crocodile Farm and zoo, a jungle tour on hidden trails,

snorkeling at Yal-ku, swimming at a beach and lagoon, horseback riding, and a buffet lunch. For information: Tel. 83–10–60.

Golf: Pok Ta Pok Golf Club, designed by Robert Trent Jones, in the heart of the Hotel Zone. The club has a restaurant, a pro shop, showers, a swimming pool, and tennis courts. Open 6 A.M. to 6 P.M. Tel. 83–08–71.

PORT PROFILE: COZUMEL

EMBARKATION/LOCATION: Some cruise ships anchor in front of San Miguel, the island's only town, and tender passengers directly to the ferry dock at the center of town. Others dock at the International Pier about 2 miles south of San Miguel. No special identity or security measures are required. Passengers are allowed to go to and come from their ships freely. There are ample taxis going constantly between the port and town. Be sure to set the price with the driver before you get in his car. The current price is US $4 for the car for up to four passengers.

Cozumel is an easy place to be on your own. You can walk the entire length of the Malecon, the main street fronting the sea, in 30 minutes, but you will probably need two hours as you are likely to stop in shops along the way. Shopping is the town's main attraction. For those interested in diving, the main dive operators are located at the south end of town on the Malecon.

LOCAL TRANSPORTATION: Taxis provide local transportation and can be found easily on the Malecon. From the International Pier to the town center costs N $30 or about US $5. Always ask the price in advance, and if you think it is too high do not hesitate to bargain. This is particularly true when you hire a taxi for a few hours to tour around the island. The price could range from $30 to $50, depending on your ability to bargain and the driver's eagerness for your business.

CAR RENTAL: Avis, Budget, Hertz, and several local car rental agencies are located on the Malecon or its side streets. Cars and jeeps range from $35 to $50 for day rate, 8 A.M. to 8 P.M. You will not need a car unless you want to tour the island on your own.

MOTORSCOOTERS: Motorscooters or mopeds rent for about $20–25 per day at several locations on the Malecon and Avenida 5 Sur, one street east of the waterfront, and on several side streets in between. They are the most popular means of transportation as the island is very flat and distances are not great. *Rentadora Cozumel* (Hotel Flores, 10A, Avenida Sur No. 172,

Cozumel; Tel. 21120; 21429) rents mopeds for $25; bikes, $5; and Volkswagen cars, $45. It is open from 8 A.M. to 8 P.M.

FERRY SERVICE: Regular ferries and the Water Jet Mexico depart every hour or two from the dock in San Miguel for Playa del Carmen. Cost: N $25 (US $3.25) one way.

AIR TRANSPORTATION: The airport is located 1 mile north of San Miguel. Flights to Cancún Airport (12 miles south of Cancún) leave about every two hours during the day. There are also flights directly to Chichén Itzá and Mérida. Inquire from Aerocozumel (Tel. 20877/23456) or Mexicana (Tel. 20133/22945), which have offices in San Miguel on the Malecon.

COZUMEL

The island of Cozumel was the first place in Mexico discovered by Cortés, the Spanish conqueror, who used it as a staging area for his first expedition to the mainland in 1518.

The island, 30 miles long and 10 miles wide, was also the first of the Yucatán's islands to be discovered by scuba divers who came—as early as the 1950s—to enjoy the world's second largest underwater reef. In the intervening years the divers were joined by deep-sea fishermen, boating enthusiasts, and beachcombers trying to keep one pace ahead of the crowd. But by the 1980s, with an international airport, a host of new hotels, and up to a dozen cruise ships making regular calls, the crowds had come too.

In antiquity, according to local legend, Cozumel was something of a Garden of Eden from which the gods departed to populate the rest of the mainland. Even up to the time of the Spaniards it was considered a sacred place. Remnants of temples and artifacts used in religious rites have been found throughout the island.

In the days of the Spanish Main, the coves and inlets of Cozumel became favorite hideouts for pirates, including the infamous Henry Morgan and Jean Lafitte, who preyed on Spanish treasure ships as they passed en route from Spain's gold- and silver-rich colonies in South America to the mother country.

It seems, however, many pirates' ships never made it home safely; there are dozens of old wrecks in these waters, and more are being found all the time. Today, they are part of the rich treasures for divers to explore in Cozumel's underwater wonder world. It is not unusu-al for them to find real treasures as well.

In the waters surrounding Cozumel, over two dozen reefs have been named and charted for diving. The south shore of the island alone has a dozen dive sites. The best known is *Palancar Reef,* which lies about a mile off the south shore and stretches for a distance of 3 miles. Here visibility ranges from 150 to 200 feet; the reef is considered by experts to be one of the most spectacular in the Caribbean for its coral formation.

In the early 1970s—and none too soon—the government introduced strict laws to halt the destruction and exploitation of the reefs. The protected waters lie from the International Pier south for 20 miles to Punta Celeraín on the south coast. More recently, Chankanaab Lagoon National Park, a marine park on the coast about 5 miles south of San Miguel, was created. It has nature trails.

Diving and the marine life are only part of Cozumel's diversions. Birdwatchers and naturalists have almost as much to enjoy on land as divers do in the sea. Only about a third of Cozumel is inhabited; the rest of the island has a wild, natural landscape barely touched by development. Cozumel's plants and trees are unusual, even for the Caribbean, and scampering about the undergrowth are lots of weird little creatures, including a 3-foot-long iguana that looks like a miniature dinosaur.

It is easy to explore the island by car or jeep; there is a coastal road around about two-thirds of it. At the excellent museum in town you can learn about the island's natural environment and diversity. A visit is highly recommended as it will help you plan your sightseeing. There is also an Archaeological Park that can give you a brief look at Mexico's pre-Colombian civilizations and Cozumel's flora.

San Miguel, the island's port and only town, was a sleepy little village with a World War II airstrip when tourism began three decades ago. Over the years it grew and prospered, but it did not really take shape until the early 1980s with its growth as a cruise port.

The most recent development and beautification program came after Hurricane Gilbert in 1988. The island folks pulled together and in record time restored the damage, making the town look better than ever. The main plaza is closed to traffic and designed as a pedestrian mall with shops and handcraft markets. The wide, flower-bedecked street along the waterfront, Avenida Rafael Melgar, is better known as the Malecon. Here you will find the museum, dive shops, jewelry shops, clothing boutiques, pretty open-air restaurants overlooking the sea, lively bars with mariachi music, and more souvenir and T-shirt shops than you would ever want to see.

San Miguel is laid out in a grid with streets, or *calles,*

running from the Plaza *norte,* or north, having even numbers and those running from the Plaza *sur,* or south, having odd numbers. From the waterfront, the streets that are east-west are called *avenida* (avenue) and run for sixteen blocks. These are numbered in increments of five and carry the suffix *norte* or *sur,* e.g., Avenida 5 Sur, Avenida 10 Sur, Avenida 15 Sur, etc., indicating the avenue is north or south of Avenida Benito Juarez and the Plaza.

The most fashionable stores are on the Malecon. Since these stores pay a premium for their location, their prices are sometimes higher than the stores on streets farther inland from the waterfront.

MUSEUM OF COZUMEL: *Museo de la Isla de Cozumel* (Malecon at Calle 6; Tel. 21545), which opened in 1987, is a wonderful museum and the best place to start your acquaintance with the island of Cozumel. Comprehensive exhibits utilize relief maps and dioramas to describe the natural environment, including its history of land and sea formations and wildlife; others depict the history of the Maya and the arrival of the Spaniards. In the center of the building is a table map that lights up when you press the name of a particular location so you can easily and quickly find places you might want to visit. The museum is situated in a lovely old colonial-style house. On the second floor is a book and gift shop and a veranda with an attractive restaurant overlooking the Caribbean Sea.

ARCHAEOLOGICAL PARK: One of the island's newest attractions is a small park with a walk-through tour of the archaeological history of Mexico, region by region, each with a representative piece of sculpture, stela, column, or something typical of the civilization represented. There are some markers identifying typical trees and several palapas, or thatched huts, where craftspeople demonstrate typical daily activities such as weaving. Entrance fee: N $10; English-speaking guides are available.

SAN GERVASIO: For those not visiting Mayan antiquities on the mainland, San Gervasio is an interesting site, easily reached from the Cross Island Road, with ruins dating from A.D. 300 to 1500. Usually, there is an English-speaking guide at the site.

 **SHOPPING**

For many passengers, Cozumel's top attraction will be shopping. Mexico has wonderful crafts, and they are so inexpensive you could easily do all your Christmas, birthday, and anniversary shopping and pay for your cruise with the savings!

The best buys are colorful papier-mâché decorations, dolls, birds, and animals; Christmas tree decorations; brightly colored straw place mats; hammocks; leather handbags and sandals; cotton dresses, skirts and blouses for women and shirts for men; silver plates, pitchers, and dishes; silver jewelry (fine-quality work is not cheap, however); copper plates and cooking utensils; clay and ceramic dishes; toys; handwoven tapestries; colorful paintings on bark; and more.

Larger stores tend to carry some of all these crafts. Quality and workmanship vary a great deal, so look around before you buy and don't hesitate to bargain. Cozumel is a free port, but I have not found the usual duty-free items such as perfume to be particularly good buys. You'll probably do as well on board your ship. Many stores are open from 9 A.M. to 9 P.M. Using cash rather than credit cards can sometimes get you up to a 20 percent discount.

ART AND ARTISTS: *Cozucove Galeria* (Avenida 10 and Adolfo Sosado; Tel. 20958) features local artists. *Gallery del Sol* (Avenida Rafael Melgar 27, at the north end of the Malecon; Tel. 20170) is the gallery in the complex of *Los Cinco Soles,* the well-established crafts store of Sharon Welch de Morales, an American transplant, and her husband, Francisco. It has local artists and foreign artists living in Cozumel. The gallery is set in a restored colonial house and offers early evening lectures on the area's archaeology and cultural history. A small admission fee includes a welcome drink. The gallery is open daily except Sunday. You enter through a courtyard cafe, *Pancho's Backyard.*

Studio One (30 Avenida, Sur #681, Cozumel, Quintana Roo 77600; Tel. 20691) is the gallery of artist Gordon Gilcrest and his wife Jennifer, another gringo transplant. Gilcrest's forte is sketches inspired by Maya and other pre-Columbian antiquity sites and motifs but with an artist's eye and talent that makes them more than reproductions. You can meet the artists by calling for an appointment or attending one of their illustrated talks on the art and culture of early Mexico.

CLOTHING: On the Malecon, *Bye-Bye,* the Benetton of Mexico, has cotton sportswear with prices 30 percent lower than those elsewhere in the Caribbean. Miro (on the Malecon south of the Plaza) features distinctive sportswear with stylized toucan in bright primary colors.

There are so many souvenir and T-shirt shops, it's hard to distinguish any; they stock similar merchandise. Look before you buy. The streets behind the Malecon and east of the Plaza are better places to look for typical, inexpensive Mexican cotton dresses with appliqué, and kaftans. *Unicornio* (5A Avenida Sur No. 2) has a vast array at reasonable prices. The store also stocks a variety of crafts. *Cuernavaca* (5A Avenida Sur and 1A Calle Sur) has handsome batik T-shirts with Mayan characters and unusual papier-mâché masques.

CRAFTS: *Bazaar del Angel* (on the Malecon) has a large selection of Mexican crafts and clothing. *Mi Mexico* (at the International Pier) stocks an array of Mexican crafts, toys, resort clothes, and accessories. Take a look to see what's available, but wait until you get to town to buy.

Los Cinco Soles (Avenida Rafael Melgar 27, north end of the Malecon) is Cozumel's best craft store with quality products generally a cut above the others. My advice is to walk as far as this store before you buy anything. You will have passed many similar shops and gotten an idea of price. Los Cinco Soles, set in a series of colonial-style houses, also features a large collection of silver jewelry and clothing by Mexican designers. *Mayabella* is a separate boutique highlighting the work of a Yucatàn crafts cooperative under whose initiative and guidance approximately 1,000 artisans in Mayan communities throughout the Yucatán have revitalized the region's art heritage. Mayabella, headquartered in Mérida, has a staff of 30 top designers who create hand-painted decorative accessories in seven categories, including whimsical items and children's toys.

La Concha (Commercial Center, half a block from the main square) carries crafts from villages all over Mexico. The *Museo de Arte Mexicano* (on the Malecon) is not a museum, but it does have a large variety of crafts from various parts of Mexico. Some Mexican leather work is excellent; too much of it is junk. There are several tiny shops facing the Plaza. El Sombrero (Avenida Rafael Melgar 29), a long-established store, has a large selection of wallets, belts, boots, bags, attachè cases—and not a bargain in the lot.

GIFTS AND JEWELRY: *Casablanca* (Avenida Rafael Melgar 33) is as much a gallery as a store and has the finest jewelry, gifts, and art objects in Cozumel. But it's very expensive. If you are interested in seeing the high quality of design and workmanship that Mexican craftsmen can attain, you should visit the store to see the displays.

HOUSEHOLD ACCESSORIES: *Talavera* (5A Avenida Sur No. 349) has the finest, most extensive collection of Mexican ceramics in Cozumel. The pottery comes from Pueblo, Jalisco, Guadalajara, and the other main centers throughout Mexico. The selections range from small individual pieces to full sets of dinnerware, and it's all fabulous. The store also has a good collection of papier mâché fruits and vegetables that are inexpensive, fun souvenirs and can be used to make attractive table centerpieces. *Manuel Azueta* (Avenida 5 and Calle 4 Norte) has hammocks made to order. *Los*

Cinco Soles (Avenida Rafael Melgar 27, north end of the Malecon) has some of all of it—household gifts, clothes, accessories, leather, jewelry (including reproductions of ancient pieces in museums), silver, and more. One of the stores in its complex, *Mi Casa,* sells furniture and other household items.

LIQUOR: Mexico produces some excellent spirits. *Kahlua,* a delicious Mexican liqueur made from coffee; *Tequila,* the distillation of the agave plant and the basic ingredient of the margarita, Mexico's potent answer to a daiquiri. These and other spirits are available at liquor stores on the Plaza and the first and second streets east of the waterfront.

DINING AND RESTAURANTS

Costa Brava (about a half-mile from the Malecon on the south side of town by the sea; no phone). Patronized by local people, it is the best restaurant for Mexican food and seafood for the price that I've found on the island. Most selections cost from $3 to $7, except for king crab and lobster, which are $18 to $22. The margaritas are fabulous.

Carlos 'n Charles (Melgar 11, Tel. 20191) is a branch of the famous chain in Mexico City. It has music from 5 P.M. to midnight.

La Laguna (Chankanaab National Park) serves a light lunch with a view of the Caribbean and mariachi music. Moderate.

La Mission (two blocks east of the Plaza on Benito Juarez at 10 Avenue). An outdoor/indoor restaurant specializing in seafood. Moderate.

Morgan's (on the Plaza) is a twist for a restaurant named Morgan (the pirate Henry Morgan, that is) with buccaneer decor; it's situated in a building that once held the Customs House! The specialty is lobster; and there are Mexican selections too. Moderate.

Pancho's Backyard (Los Cinco Soles, Avenida Rafael Melgar 27; Tel. 22142) is an attractive courtyard cafe serving light Mexican specialties. Moderate.

Palmeras (on the Malecon, across from the ferry dock) may never win a Michelin star, but it's a classic of a Mexican restaurant catering to tourists, with lively music, generous drinks, and lots of food. Moderately expensive.

Sportspage (Avenue 5, Norte 2; Tel. 21199). A restaurant/bar with television screens for viewing satellite-delivered U.S. and other sporting events. The decor is made up of pendants and polo shirts of every college and major league team one might imagine, and the food is sort of Tex-Mex. Prices are moderate. And there's a *Hard Rock Cafe* (on the Malecon) that's open until 1 A.M., *Pizza Hut,* and *Kentucky Fried Chicken.*

 **NIGHTLIFE**

Cozumel's nightlife centers around hotels and a few of the discos in town. As in towns all over Mexico, restaurants frequently have musical entertainment—guitars, mariachis, or the like. Some ships bring local folkdancers and mariachis on board ship to perform.

If your ship remains in port for the evening, one of the shore excursions sold on the ship will probably be a nightclub show with flamenco dancers and mariachis at one of the hotels. If not, check the *Fiesta Americana Sol Caribe Hotel* (near the International Pier), which usually has the best show in town.

The Mexican Folkloric Ballet performs at the *Cabanas del Caribe Hotel* on Thursdays at 7:30 P.M. and at the *Mayan Plaza Hotel* on Saturdays at 7 P.M.

For the disco scene, make your way to *Neptuno's* on the Malecon at the south end of town or *Scaramouche,* a short walk south of the ferry dock in town. There's even a karaoke, *Laser Karaoke,* about a mile south of town.

 **SPORTS**

BEACHES/SWIMMING: Cozumel's water is so spectacular you may want to do nothing more than spend a day on the beach. The nearest one is *Sol Caribe Beach,* next to the International Pier. Better beaches, about 5 miles from the pier, are *San Francisco Beach* and *Palancar Beach* on the south shore. *Passion Island,* offshore, north of San Miguel, is a popular destination for day boat trips. Almost all hotels, except those in the center of town, are on the water.

DEEP-SEA FISHING: Cozumel is one of the prime game fishing areas of the Caribbean, particularly noted for sailfish, blue marlin, white marlin, tuna, dolphin, wahoo, shark, and barracuda, as well as bonefish in quiet lagoons and hidden bays. Boat charters can be arranged through *Fiesta Cozumel Holidays* (Box 125, Cozumel; Tel. 011–52–987–0433) or local boat operators and range from $200 for a half day and to $800 or more for a full day, depending on the time of the year.

SNORKELING AND SCUBA: When you have come to one of the world's prime scuba diving locations, if you are a certified diver, you will certainly want to include a

dive here. The island is surrounded by two dozen or more reefs; those off the south shore offer the best diving. Cozumel has both reefs close to shore and drop-offs farther out at sea.

There is diving from the beach at several locations within walking distance of the International Pier. *Paraiso Reef North* is about 200 yards off Sol Caribe Beach in depths of 30 to 50 feet, with visibility up to 100 feet. *La Ceiba Reef* and *Plane Wreck* in front of La Ceiba Hotel, next to the pier, have an underwater trail designed by marine ecologist George Lewbel. The trail was created by Pancho Morales, former owner of La Ceiba Hotel and current proprietor of Los Cinco Soles. It starts at the plane, sunk for the filming of a movie, and continues along the reef for 120 yards with signs explaining various types of corals and sponges. Diving depths are 30 to 50 feet. The location is popular for cruise ship dive excursions. *Paraiso Reef South* is a continuation of the same reef and is rich in fish life. It is particularly popular for night dives.

Continuing south, the next group of reefs are in the *Chankanaab Lagoon* area. Close to shore are huge coral heads and along the shoreline are caves that go back under the shore. These can be reached from the beach; the area can be enjoyed by snorkelers as well. The reef is farther out and is reached by a boat.

Between Punta Tormentos and Punta Tunich, just before San Francisco Beach, is *Tormentos Reef*, popular with photographers for its coral heads, seafans, and abundant fish. *Yocab Reef*, at a depth of about 30 feet, is a good location for beginning divers. *San Francisco Reef*, situated about a half-mile directly in front of San Francisco Bay, is popular because of its abundant fish.

Palancar Reef, the best known, lies about a mile off the south shore and stretches for 3 miles with visibility up to 200 feet. The variety of formations is the attraction. Here the wall is sloping, rather than a sharp drop-off, and starts about 50 feet down. It is a maze of canyons, tunnels, and caves. The south end has enormous coral pinnacles spiraling up to 60 feet or more. *Maracaibo Reef* off the southwestern tip of the island is the most challenging for experienced divers.

If a scuba or snorkeling package is not available on your cruise ship, you will find a dozen dive operators on the main street at the east end of the town. You should contact them in advance or plan to get to them early; most morning dive trips leave by 9 or 9:30 A.M. You must show a certification card before going out on a boat or renting tanks. Each offers regularly scheduled half- and full-day dive packages, and prices are very competitive. Cozumel is one of the least expensive places in the Caribbean to enjoy diving.

As an example, *Dive Paradise* (P.O. Box 222; Cozumel, Q.R., Mexico 77600; 601 Rafael Melgar Ave.

Tel. 21007, which is a PADI, NAUI, and SSI training facility, operates a fleet of dive boats with daily excursions for up to 6 or 12 people. The shop, owned by American-born Rene "Apple" Applegate, is open daily from 8 A.M. to 9 P.M. Boats depart at about 9:15 A.M. and return between 2:30 and 5 P.M., depending on their destinations. The cost is $49 for a two-tank trip but the operator has a very wide range of dives, depending on your level of experience–from novices to very experienced divers and trainers. You can contact Dive Paradise directly or through *Tropical Adventures* of Seattle (800–247–DIVE), or try *International Scuba* of Pasadena, Texas (800–284–3483), U.S. dive specialists who can make your arrangements in Cozumel as well as most other locations in the Caribbean.

A typical day consists of two dives on different reefs and lunch on a beach. The first dive is usually about 60 to 80 feet, or more depending on your level of experience; and the second shallower dive is about 40 feet. The exact location of the dives is determined by the dive-master on each boat, depending on weather conditions, currents, and the like.

Among other Cozumel operators are *Aqua Safari* (Avenida Rafael Melgar 40 Sur; Tel. 20101); *Caribbean Divers* (38B Avenida Melgar, P.O. Box 191, Cozumel; Tel. 21145); *Dive Cozumel* (241 Avenida Melgar, P.O. Box 165, Cozumel; Tel. 20280); and *Dive House* (Main Square; Tel. 23068).

Servicios de Seguridad Sub-Aquatica (Calle 5 Sur – 21b; Tel. 22387; VHF 16 and 21) is a professionally operated recompression center. It is open from 8 A.M. to 8 P.M. and can be reached at other times by radio. The Cozumel Association of Dive Operators has more than 30 members and must adhere to certain training and safety regulations.

TENNIS: *Stouffers Presidente Hotel*, about 1 mile south of the International Pier, has three courts, and there are courts at the *Fiesta Americana Sol Caribe, Cozumel Caribe,* and *Plaza Azul* hotels. You should contact the hotels in advance to request permission to play.

WINDSURFING: Available at beach-side hotels for about $20.

PLAYA DEL CARMEN (CANCÚN)

P laya del Carmen, 40 miles south of Cancún, has grown in the past decade from a tiny village to a town of about 20,000 people; because of its location, the town has become the gateway to the Yucatán for cruise ships. It is 10 miles directly west of Cozumel and about equidistant between Cancún on the north and Tulum, an important Mayan temple complex, on the south shore. Either is about a 45-minute drive from the dock.

A word of caution: Some cruise line brochures leave the impression Cozumel/Playa del Carmen is one locale. They are not. Some ships stop only in Cozumel. You must take a 45-minute ferry ride to Playa del Carmen or a 15-minute flight to Cancún to reach the mainland. Other ships stop in Playa del Carmen only long enough to disembark passengers taking the ship's shore excursions and continue on to Cozumel. Those who want to be on their own will find ample services in Playa del Carmen for tours, car rental, and taxis. In addition, there are public buses from Playa del Carmen to Cancún. Hotels directly on the beach are only a few steps from the dock.

As soon as you walk off the pier, you will see signs for these services, and there will probably be someone standing by waiting to sell you one of the tours listed on a large board next to the kiosks that sell tickets for the ferries between Playa del Carmen and Cozumel. You should try to time your return to your ship via ferry either before or after the rush of passengers returning from shore excursions. These groups get priority and individuals often have to fight their way on.

The region has a great deal of interesting sight-seeing. If your ship offers an excursion to Chichén Itzá and you have any interest in history and archaeology you should put this tour at the top of your priority list. If you do rent a car, there are also several important sites of antiquity within a short drive from the pier. Be sure to have a full tank of gas before starting out: gas stations on the highways are few and far between.

NORTH OF PLAYA DEL CARMEN

The main highway (No. 307) between Playa del Carmen and Cancún is an excellent two-lane road that runs as straight as an arrow about a mile or so inland from the sea until just south of Cancún, where it become a four-lane parkway. The stretch from Playa del Carmen is gradually being developed with small towns, resorts, and attractions, but to reach most of them you need to turn off the main road and head toward the sea. (Mileages indicated are measured from Playa del Carmen.)

PUNTA BETE (11 miles) is about a 3-mile drive over a dirt road through jungle and banana trees to a rustic, palm-fringed 3 miles of white sand beach, popular for swimming and snorkeling. *La Posada del Capitán*

Lafitte (Tel. 23–04–85) is a modest, attractive beachside resort with a pool, showers, and a restaurant overlooking miles of beautiful, reef-protected white sand; snorkeling on the reef is available. Another 2 miles north (at kilometer 51) is the turn off to a new resort, Maroma, where small groups of four or six people are welcome to have lunch and swim. It's ideal for those who want to get away from the crowds. Call or fax in advance.

PUERTO MORELOS (22 miles) is the oldest port in Mexico. A quiet fishing village with inexpensive beachfront restaurants where you can enjoy the day's catch, it has been bypassed by developers, at least for now. Just beyond the village is the 150-acre *Dr. Alfredo Barrera Marin Botanical Garden,* which features flora of the Yucatàn region. It has a small archaeological site and nature trails through thick dry forest. The park is maintained by the Quintana Roo State Research Center. Entrance fee is N $12. There is a gasoline station at the turnoff for Puerto Morelos village.

CROCOCÚN AND PALANCAR AQUARIUM (24 miles) Crococún, a crocodile farm, has several species of crocodiles ranging in age from 1 to 25 years. There are also spider monkeys, Mexican raccoons, and other species native to the Yucatán. The entrance fee is N $12; a guide is available for an extra tip. Next door is the *Palancar Aquarium,* named for the reef that lies off the coast of Cozumel. The aquarium has exhibits on all aspect of the region's marine environment.

CANCÚN

Cancún came out of a computer. Well, almost.

In the late 1960s when the Mexican government set out to develop the country's coastal regions for tourism, researchers fed a pile of data about climate, water, land, history, and the like into their computers to find the most ideal area in which to begin. All the positive signs pointed to a 14-mile sliver of land off the Yucatàn northeastern coast on the Caribbean Sea, known as Cancún.

Most people's response was "Can–who?" And understandably. Cancún was not much more than a sandbar, and the eastern zone of the Yucatàn was an uninhabited jungle. There were no roads, no water, no electricity, and only about 120 people living there.

Today, Cancún has more than 100 hotels in all categories, with such well-known names as Sheraton and Ritz Carlton. There are over 200 restaurants, large shopping centers, native markets, two 18-hole golf courses, a convention center, a wide range of sports and entertainment facilities, and a town of about 300,000 people.

A hotel/resort zone was created on the island of Cancún, and the commercial district was placed on the mainland. The hotel area's strict zoning prohibits garish signs and buildings over nine stories. There is frequent bus transportation between the island and town; the international airport is 12 miles away.

The island of Cancún has the shape of the number 7 connected at both ends to the mainland by bridges. The long side of the island faces the Caribbean on the east and the Nichupte Lagoon on the west. Most resorts are located along the beach on the road heading north to Punta Cancún.

Cancún's flat terrain, which might surprise those who have traveled elsewhere in Mexico, and the Yucatán jungle bear no resemblance whatever to the tropical lushness of Jamaica or the Eastern Caribbean. On the contrary, the jungle is thick, low brush—miles and miles of it.

THE BEACHES What Cancún lacks in verdant tropical splendor is more than made up for in its beaches and water. Cancún has the most beautiful beaches this writer has ever seen anywhere in the world (and I've seen a lot of beach!). What makes them so spectacular is both the color and the quality of the sand and water. The powderfine, blinding white sand looks as though it would scorch your feet, but it is actually cool to the touch. That the sand, which is coral and limestone in origin, is very porous accounts for this unusual characteristic, and was one of the determining factors in the computer's selection of Cancún. The intense, deep blue-green color of the water is marvel enough, but when you step into it, you will discover it has an unusual silken quality.

That's the good news. The bad news is that some parts of the coast have a strong undertow. Warning signs are posted, but many tourists do not take them seriously. Never go far from shore and never swim where someone on shore cannot see you. The water of the lagoon and the north shore of Cancún island are considered the safest places. Hotels have swimming pools.

HOTEL ZONE Hotels—many of which are fabulous architectural creations—line the beach for 14 miles, from Club Med and the huge Caesar Park Resort on the south to the Fiesta Americana and El Presidente Inter-Continental on the north. Most of the hotels tend to be self-contained resorts with their own sports and entertainment, which is helpful for cruise passengers with limited time because they can select one and stay. But if you want to check out the scene at another hotel, it takes more effort than a simple stroll down the beach. A paved pedestrian walkway, the *ciclopista*, winds through the northern part of the Hotel Zone and is a pleasant walk for those who want to have a look at some of Cancún's beautiful hotels.

SPORTS AND ATTRACTIONS In addition to the water sports facilities at hotels, the Hotel Zone has many water sports centers where you can find equipment for snorkeling, scuba diving, and fishing. Most major resorts have tennis courts. Windsurfing is best at Bahía de Mujeres.

Pok-ta-Pok Golf Course is on a series of islands in the lagoon, connected by road to the Cancún Hotel Zone. The course is open from 6 A.M. to 6 P.M. The cost is US $50 for 18 holes; carts, $30; clubs, $15; and caddy, $9 per person. A second golf course is part of the Caesar Park complex.

Rancho Lona Bonita (Km. 49 near Puerto Morelos; Tel. 84–08–61) offers horseback riding along the beach or jungle trekking. Guided tours are scheduled from 7:30 A.M. to 1 P.M. and 1:30 to 6:30 P.M.

Subsea Explorer, a semi-submersible, offers a combination tour and snorkeling for $50; $15 discount coupons are widely distributed locally. Contact *Marina Aqua Ray* (Kulkulcán, Km. 10.5; Tel. 83–30– 07).

When you come into Cancún from Playa del Carmen, as most cruise passengers do, you arrive at the south end of the island where *Club Med* (Tel. 85–23–00) is located. The resort has a day pass for US $35, which includes lunch, a guided tour (at 10 A.M. and 4 P.M.), and use of the beach, tennis courts, pool, and water sports.

RUINS DEL REY Farther north, beyond the Holiday Inn, Dolphin Beach is a beautiful stretch of open beach. Hard as it may be to imagine, all of Cancún looked like this only two decades ago. On the lagoon side of the road is a Mayan archaeological site, *Ruins del Rey,* uncovered only less than a decade ago. About midway along the Hotel Zone is the Cancún Sheraton, whose central building is designed in the form of a Mayan pyramid; it fronts a magnificent beach.

YAMIL LU´UM The *Sheraton* obliges you with its own Mayan ruin, Yamil Lu´um, a small temple complex on a mound next to the hotel. One of the temples contained an impression of a Mayan footprint, which is now exhibited in the Cancún Archaeological Museum. The *Melia Cancún,* topped with a glass pyramid, has one of the most dramatic lobbies of the hotel group.

CONVENTION CENTER At the north end of the island at Punta Cancún is the Convention Center, within easy walking distance of many hotels and several of the largest shopping plazas. The center was the venue for the first economic summit, attended by President Reagan in 1981; the Miss Universe Contest in 1988; and many other major events. The center's showpiece is a tower that rivals Paris's Eiffel Tower in height, with a revolving restaurant at the top. The center is also the home of the Museum of Anthropology and History of Cancún.

SHOPPING Among the largest shopping malls are *Plaza Caracol* and *La Fiesta* at Punta Cancún and *Plaza Kukulcán* about midpoint in the Hotel Zone. Incidentally, all of Quintana Roo—the easternmost province of Mexico, in which Cancún and Cozumel are located—is a duty-free zone. Generally, business hours are 10 A.M. to 1 P.M. and 4 to 8 P.M. Not all stores close for the siesta, nor do downtown markets.

CANCÚN CITY From Punta Cancún to Cancún City, the commercial center on the mainland, is 6 miles. Cancún City is a completely new town that is gradually acquiring character. There are wide, tree-lined streets and parks and an outdoor market with typical Mexican crafts of cheaper quality and price than those found in the large shopping plazas.

FONATUR The government agency that developed Cancún, Fonatur, has a tourist information office on the corner of Avenida Nader and Calle Cobá (Tel. 84–32–04; 84–38–94; 84–14–26). Recently, it added a toll-free number, 800-CANCUN8, which can be dialed from the U.S.

RESTAURANTS Cancún has more than 200 restaurants and new ones are opening daily. Some restaurants convenient to the Hotel Zone are *Captain's Cove* (across from the Mayaland Hotel) and *Lorenzillo's* (Hotel Zone, Km. 10.5), with romantic settings overlooking the lagoon. Both serve seafood and are moderately expensive.

Carlos & Charlie's (overlooking the marina) is a moderately priced member of a famous Mexico City chain specializing in seafood; and *Grimond* (next to Casa Maya) is a posh and expensive French restaurant in the beautiful setting of a large Spanish colonial-style house that formerly belonged to the mayor.

For specialties of the Yucatán, *Los Almendros* (across from the bullfight ring; Tel. 84–08–07) is open from noon to 11 P.M. And if you hunger for a Big Mac, McDonald's has four locations; or for yogurt, there's an I Can't Believe It's Yogurt in the Plaza Caracol; or for pizza, there seems to be a pizzeria on every corner.

Entertainment Cancún is famous for its nightlife and has the variety to suit most everyone. Unfortunately, most cruise ships leave by sunset and Cancún's nightlife doesn't even begin to flicker until after 10 P.M. If you are here in the evening, however, you can learn what is happening from one of the free local publications, *Cancún Tips* or *Caribbean News*. Nightly except Sunday, *Fiesta Mexicana* at the Hyatt Regency Cancún (Tel. 83–12–34) features a dinner buffet and a folkloric ballet

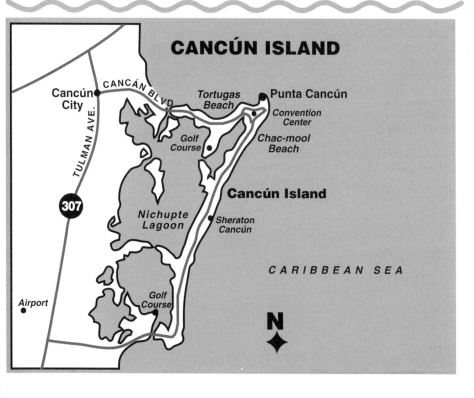

show followed by live music and mariachis; and *Continental Villas Plaza* (Tel. 85–14–44) offers a similar evening with the *Ballet Folklorico Nacional.*

There are *Planet Hollywood,* the *All-Star Cafe, Hard Rock Cafe,* and *Coconuts Comedy Club* (Flamingo Plaza) and rock, jazz, salsa, and reggae bars galore. A popular nighttime activity is lobby bar hopping. The lobbies are often architectural masterpieces, and many feature live musical entertainment from classical guitar to jazz. But Cancún is also known for its discos, which do not open until 10 P.M. and don't really get going until midnight or later.

Bullfights are staged at the stadium, *Plaza de Toros Cancún* (Avenida Banampak, Lote 1; Tel. 84–56–29) on Wednesdays at 3:30. The cost is US $36 for adults; children under 12 are admitted free.

TRANSPORTATION Taxis are available at all Cancún hotels, and there is frequent bus service between the Cancún resorts and Cancún City. There are car rental offices at major hotels, in the plaza of the Convention Center, and in Cancún City. Budget Rent a Car (Alquiladora Montejo S.A., Avenida Tulum 214; Tel. 84–69–55) has American, European, and Japanese models that cost from US $60 to $80 per day, depending on the model. Generally, car rentals in Cancún are overpriced—about double the prices in the U.S. or even those in Cozumel—but none are as much of a ripoff as National Car Rental. On a recent trip, I found that a four-cylinder Volkswagon cost $148 with a $1,000 deductible on the insurance. It is important to compare the terms as well as prices of rentals. Avis (Airport; Tel. 86–02–22) has the most favorable local rates among the international companies; the insurance has no deductible.

If you plan to spend the day exploring on your own, you should either rent a car or moped or hire a taxi with a driver because distances are too great for walking. Bus stops, marked *parada,* are conveniently located throughout the Hotel Zone and in the downtown area; the fare is N $2. "Turicun" buses are air-conditioned and more plush; they cost N $3.

Useful Numbers

> *Tourism Office: Tel. 84–80–73*
>
> *Police: Tel. 84–19–13*
>
> *American Hospital: Tel. 84–61–33*
>
> *Aerocozumel: Tel. 84-20-00*

ISLA MUJERES

Four miles off the north coast of Cancún is Isla Mujeres, the Island of Women, so named by the Spaniards be-

cause of the large number of erotic terra-cotta female idols they found when they landed there in 1517. A Mayan temple, believed to have been dedicated to the goddess of childbirth and weaving, suggests it was a sanctuary.

Today, the 5-mile-long island, where life is even more carefree and casual than on Cancún, is noted for its scuba and snorkeling and good seafood restaurants. Like Cancún, Isla Mujeres has been transformed and now has a population of 15,000. The island is a duty-free port, too.

Day trips to Isla Mujeres depart from the marina next to El Presidente Inter-Continental at 10:30 A.M. and return at 4 P.M. A similar excursion leaves from the Playa Linda dock at 9:30 A.M. The price (about $30) includes snorkeling on El Garrafon Reef and a seafood lunch. Fast water taxis make the trip to Isla Mujeres from Puerto Juarez or Punta Sam in about 20 minutes. Cost is N $80 for the boat. Ferries leave frequently throughout the day for N $4.50.

CONTOY ISLAND

Approximately 15 miles north of Cancún is Contoy Island, a national bird sanctuary and nature preserve scalloped with pretty beaches. Only 2 miles long and less than half a mile wide, Contoy is the Cancún of two decades ago. The island is home to about a hundred species of birds, including frigatebirds, pelicans, cormorants, flamingo, and several species of heron.

Until recently, the island had been closed to the public due to careless use; it has now been reopened but under more controlled conditions. The boat trip to Contoy with a stop for snorkeling en route takes two hours. Normally day excursions depart daily.

 ## SOUTH OF PLAYA DEL CARMEN

An excellent road, Highway 307, runs directly south from Playa del Carmen to the Belize border about 150 miles away. Along the way are several places that you may find more rewarding to visit than Cancún. The choice depends upon your personal interests. In addition to organized tours available on board ship and car rentals and taxis that can be arranged in port, there are public buses from Playa del Carmen to the Tulum turnoff, from where you will need to walk a few hundred yards to the temple complex. If you rent a car or hire a taxi, you can combine a dive or snorkel at Xcaret or Akumal with sight-seeing at Tulum.

Highway 307 runs slightly inland and because the land is so flat, you cannot see the sea from the road.

Instead you drive through low, thick brush which is, frankly, boring from a scenic point of view. (Mileage is indicated from Playa del Carmen.)

XCARET (pronounced *ish*-ca-ret) (4 miles) is a privately owned, 180-acre park with nature trails, walkways, a beach, recently excavated Mayan ruins, a lagoon, and underwater tunnels that snorkelers and divers can explore. Xcaret, which means "small cove," is said to have been an important Mayan ceremonial center and port where Maya from all over the peninsula came to purify their bodies and souls in the sacred baths of the *cenotes* or sinkholes. Two huge *cenotes* where you can snorkel have water so clear you hardly need a mask.

The resort offers a three-hour dive course and horseback riding, and there are two restaurants, a bar, lockers, and thatched umbrellas and chairs for refuge from the bright sun. Entrance fee is a steep US $17, but worth it if you plan to spend the day here. A packaged tour from Cancún costs US $45, including the entrance fee. Some cruise ship excursions combine Tulum with Xcaret. Hourly bus service between Xcaret and Cancún runs daily except Sunday.

The large entrance hall at Xcaret has very well-made table displays of the most famous Mayan antiquity sites in Mexico, including Chichén Itzá, Uxmal, and Palenque.

PUERTO AVENTURAS (16 miles) is said to be the largest privately financed resort development yet undertaken in Mexico. The 766-acre development has a large marina and yacht club, a beach club, a tennis club, a PADI dive center, a gym, two hotels and ten condominium buildings, residential homes, nine restaurants, five snack bars, six bars, a golf course, a shopping complex, a disco, a bird sanctuary, a dolphin aquarium, the CEDAM Nautical Museum, and an archaeological site. It has been designed to retain 65 percent of the area as green space in a natural, park-like setting. If you want to spend the day here and play golf, you should make the arrangements in advance, but you will most likely have to listen to a real estate sales pitch somewhere along the way.

AKUMAL (23 miles) The Bay of Akumal is sheltered by one of the longest coral reefs in the Western Hemisphere; visibility is 150 to 200 feet. Of course, the big attraction here is snorkeling and diving, as well as fishing. There is a Spanish galleon wreck just off the coast, which adds interest for divers.

Hotel Club Akumal Caribe, begun two decades ago as a private club, is open to all and welcomes day visitors. It began as a rustic hideaway about as off-the-beaten-track as you can get, but the rest of the world has now discovered it and a new resort has been added. It's still easy to spend a few hours, or even days, here enjoy-

ing the beach and the transparent waters. Scuba and snorkeling gear is available for rent. Snorkeling packages sold on cruise ships often use this location.

DIVING AND FISHING Adjacent to the hotel is a dive operation, *Excursiones Akumal* (Postal 984, Cancún, Quintana Roo, Mexico; Tel. 41945) operated by a transplanted American, Dick Blanchard. It has a full range of services, dive boats, PADI-certified instructors, and 60 tanks. It offers two dives daily, at 9:30 A.M. and 2:30 P.M. for up to eight divers per dive-master. The shop also offers an hour's excursion on a glass-bottom boat and a Robinson Crusoe excursion to a nearby secluded beach with lunch and snorkeling. The latter must have a minimum of six people and be booked in advance. A fishing excursion, for a two-hour minimum, takes a maximum of four persons.

YALKU A small lagoon about a mile from Akumal, Yalku, is full of fish so tame you can have them eating out of your hands. Your tour guide will tell you to bring some bread along so you can watch the fish swarm in to feed. It's great for picture-taking.

XEL HA (32 miles) Farther south is Xel Ha, another lovely lagoon with water so clear one does not need a mask to see the fish. It is also a popular swimming spot. Cruise ship shore excursions to Tulum often stop here for passengers to have a swim; some include a picnic lunch. About a mile away, there are Mayan ruins with murals of birds and jaguar, and a *cenote,* which attracts wildlife. Recently a group of visitors reported seeing a jaguar. There is a small entrance fee.

TULUM

The walled city of Tulum, about 36 miles (less than an hour's drive) from Playa del Carmen, is perched on a cliff overlooking the Caribbean. It is the only known walled city built by the Maya on the coast. Tulum and other towns of the Yucatán were once connected by an elaborate road system that is still visible in some sections.

In 1518 a Spanish expedition exploring the Yucatán coast prior to Cortés's conquest of Mexico sighted Tulum; one of its members later wrote, "We saw in the distance a town so large the city of Seville could not be better or larger."

Tulum was one of many coastal towns and temple sites that continued for some time after the Spanish conquest, but for how long we do not know. By the mid-nineteenth century when Tulum was "re-discovered," most of the former Mayan sites were buried under the growth of the Yucatán jungle—and still are.

When compared to Chichén Itzá or Uxmal, the ruins of Tulum are not grand, but they are interesting. The site dates from about A.D. 700 to 1000, the Post-classic period after the Mayan civilization had reached its peak, and shows the influence of the Toltecs who conquered the Yucatán in the tenth century A.D.

Originally named Zama, "the dawn," because it faced east to the sea, Tulum sits dramatically on cliffs 40 feet above the Caribbean and was protected by the reefs from invasion by way of the sea. The other three sides had walls more than 6 feet thick and varying in height from 4 to 19 feet. There were five entrances; today's entrance is on the west.

The site is dominated by *El Castillo,* the castle, the name the Spaniards always gave to the central grand structure of a temple complex. The view of the sea from the top of the castle is lovely. After passing through the entrance and walking directly east, you will see a group of buildings—the *Temple of the Frescos* on the south and the *Great Palace* on the north. Directly in front is the Castle, approached by a long series of steps. The first level was the dance platform for religious observances.

The *Temple of the Frescos* is the best preserved and most interesting structure at the site because it still has remnants of the murals that once covered the walls of all the buildings in the complex.

On the east side of the Castle is the *Temple of the Descending God,* so called because in the band of decoration over the doorway the figure of the god is pointed toward the ground. The symbol appears in the Castle ornamentation and elsewhere and is said to represent the bee god of the Mayans. The cultivation of bees was important to the ancient Mexicans, as honey served as their sweetener; they had no sugar.

On the west side of the Castle is the *Temple of the Initial Series,* which takes its name from the method by which Mayan dates were calculated.

The archaeological site is open from 8 A.M. to 5 P.M. daily. If you speak Spanish the guard at the site can act as your guide; you will need to tip him. Booklets are available for purchase at the site as well. When you visit on a cruise ship excursion, an English-speaking guide is provided.

SIAN KA'AN

A vast region covering 2,026 square miles (or 1.3 million acres) and stretching a hundred miles south of Tulum down the Caribbean coast was declared a Biosphere Reserve in 1986 and added to UNESCO's World Heritage List. The largest nature preserve in Mexico, it is made up of one-third tropical forest, one-third wetland and mangroves, and one-third coastal and marine environments. It is inhabited by jaguar, margay, cougar, puma, lynx, ocelot, monkey, manatee,

tapir, and white-tailed deer, as well as 340 species of birds; it is also rich in flora, with more than 1,200 plant species. Part of the reserve is the barrier reef fronting the Yucatan which forms part of the world's second longest reef, stretching south to Honduras. Scattered throughout the reef are cays, or islets, that provide nesting grounds for thousands of water birds, including such rare species as the jabiru stork and roseate spoonbill, and four species of endangered sea turtles.

The reserve consists of three parts where environmental conservation and sustainable development are working together: a Buffer Zone where fishing, tourism activity, and agriculture is permitted under certain guidelines; a Gathering Zone, reserved strictly for local people to hunt, fish, gather food, and build; and a Core Zone, accounting for 80 percent of the area, where only scientific research is allowed. The region is dotted with archaeological sites, some of which are 20,000 years old. The area can be visited with advance arrangements through the *Friends of Sian Ka'an Association* (Plaza America, Coba No. 5, 3rd Floor, No. 48–50, Cancún; Tel. 84–95–83), which is a private, nonprofit conservation organization promoting national and international support for the reserve and managing certain projects under the authority of SEDUE (Secretary of Urban Development and Ecology).

The Association offers an all-day tour escorted by a naturalist guide, with bird-watching and snorkeling in a *cenote.* Cost is US $115 including bus transportation, breakfast and lunch, and contribution to the reserve's upkeep. The tour is limited to seven people. During the winter season you need to make reservations at least one month in advance; during the off-season, reservations should be made two to three weeks ahead of time. With advance arrangements, the Association's tour bus will pick up cruise passengers at the ferry dock in Playa del Carmen about 8:30 A.M. and return about 4 P.M. The tour includes a three-hour boat ride through the coastal lagoons and lunch at *Anna y José,* a rustic seaside inn.

COBÁ

The archaeological site of Cobá is 25 miles inland from Tulum. (It can also be reached by another road west of Playa del Carmen.) More extensive than Chichén Itzá, Cobá covers 10 square miles with an estimated 6,500 structures. The area is dominated by a building known as the Church which stands ten stories high. Two miles away is *Nohoch Mul,* the largest pyramid found in the Yucatán, rising 120 steps to the top at an incline that is almost perpendicular.

Little of the huge site has been excavated, and scholars do not yet know its origin, except to establish that it is older than Tulum. Recent excavations have led archaeologists to question whether Cobá belonged to a civilization even earlier than the Maya. Since some parts of Cobá date from the Classic period (after A.D. 600), it is assumed that the Maya inhabited the site. However, pre-Classical remnants have been found, indicating that the area was occupied prior to the period of the Maya. Someday, when more excavations have been completed and further information is available, Cobá will likely be as important an archaeological site for visitors to the Yucatán as Chichén Itzá.

There is a *Villa Arquelogica,* one of several villages operated by Club Med at archaeological sites in Mexico. It has a swimming pool, dining room, bar, and tennis court.

WEST OF PLAYA DEL CARMEN

To visit Chichén Itzá you should take the shore excursion by air or motorcoach, as the case may be, if offered by your cruise line. If not, and your cruise ship remains in port long enough to make the trip, ask your travel agent to book your arrangements in advance, as there will probably not be enough time upon arrival in port to do so. Excursions leave early in order to maximize visitors' time at the site.

There are several alternatives. First, some ships remain in Cozumel overnight or until late in the day, enabling passengers to make the full-day excursion to Chichén Itzá by air. (See the section on Shore Excursions earlier in this chapter). Second, when a cruise ship visits both Cozumel and Cancún/Playa del Carmen it may be possible to leave the ship in one port and rejoin it in another on the same day.

Highway 180 leads to Chichén Itzá and Mérida from either Cancún or Playa del Carmen; the drive takes about 2.5 hours. The drive from Mérida to Chichén Itzá is 70 miles or 1.5 hours; from Mérida to Uxmal is 35 miles (about an hour). Flights from Cozumel to Cancún take 20 minutes and operate about every two hours throughout the day. There are also flights from Cozumel and Cancún to Chichén Itzá and Mérida. Excursions from Cozumel by air fly directly to Chichén Itzá. Occasionally, a cruise ship will call at Progreso, the port for Mérida.

CHICHÉN ITZÁ

The most important site of antiquity in the Yucatán, Chichén Itzá (pronounced Che-cha-*neat*-za), is 125 miles west of Cancún and Playa del Carmen on Highway 180, the road to Mérida. The city was originally founded in A.D. 432 but abandoned in 608. It was settled again in 960 and prospered until about 1200.

Today, the site covers an area of about 6 square miles. One part has the great pyramids and temples of the Maya; another was built by their successors, the Toltec, who invaded the Yucatán in the tenth century. The Toltec, a fierce tribe from Tula in Central Mexico, brought with them their belief in Kukulcan, the man-god represented as the plumed serpent, and introduced the practice of human sacrifice to the Mayas.

EL CASTILLO The first major excavations were undertaken by Carnegie Tech over a period of 20 years. The site is dominated by *El Castillo,* a giant pyramid 18 stories high. An interior tunnel leads into a tiny throne room where you see a red jaguar shaped into a bench and set with jade eyes and turquoise mosaics. It is thought to be a throne. Jade is not native to the Yucatán, so its use here is one more question in the Mayan puzzle.

The Castle is a calendar in three dimensions. On each of the four sides, 91 steps lead to the top; these, along with the upper platform, correspond to the 365 days of the year. On each side of the stairways there are nine terraces representing the two seasons; combined, they correspond to the 18 months of the Mayan year. The steps are about six inches wide and rise at least a foot each; the climb is steep, but worthwhile. From the top the Yucatán jungle stretches as far as the eye can see.

At the equinoxes on March 22 and September 23, the light and shadow on the steps cast a zigzag pattern from the temple on top of the pyramid to the sculptured snake's head at the bottom of the stairs: the pattern looks like the undulating body of a serpent. For the Maya, the sight represented the return of Kukulcan and heralded the change of season.

The building is so perfectly constructed acoustically that you can clap your hands at its base and hear the echo ripple up each step and then project itself to listeners standing hundreds of yards away across the giant open courtyard the temple once dominated.

TEMPLE OF THE WARRIORS The *Temple of the Warriors* has intricate carving and 1,000 columns.

BALL COURT The 650-foot-long Ball Court is another acoustic wonder: a person standing at one end talking in a normal voice can be heard at the far end. The court was the setting for a ritual game known as pok-a-pok, said to resemble basketball or soccer and played with a hard rubber ball about the size of a baseball. The rules dictated that when the ball was put through a high stone hoop at the side of the court the game was over. Only the knee, foot, or elbow (but not the hands) could be used. The games sometimes lasted three or four days, and then the defeated captain was conducted to an adjoining ceremonial platform where he forfeited his head to the victors' swords.

New research has led scholars to believe the opponents in this game were prisoners—perhaps of a rival city-state or tribe who may have been Maya themselves—forced to participate as a final humiliation. The bloodletting at the end of the match was, apparently, a basic element of Mayan life associated with major events such as birth and death. They had mystical meanings we cannot quite fathom, intended to connect the natural and supernatural worlds. (Such scholarly explanations, of course, do not make the knowledge of such pagan brutality any less revolting, but before we condemn the Maya, it is good to remember that Roman gladiators fared little better.)

Another puzzle: no one has discovered what the Maya did with their dead; human bones have been discovered in only a few of the ruins, a fact that alludes to the subject of human sacrifice. Scholars believe that the practice of human sacrifice was introduced into Mayan rites by the Toltecs.

CEREMONIAL WELL A raised ceremonial road leads to the giant ceremonial well measuring 350 feet long, 150 feet wide, and 60 feet deep, with sinister-looking greenish-black water. A sinkhole in limestone known as a *cenote*, it was once the focal point of the Maya's religious rites where, annually, thousands of people gathered to pray to Chaac, the rain-god, who was believed to live in the well and provide water for the crops.

During the ceremony a young maiden clad in precious jewels was fed to the god. These young virgins were trained by the priests to accept their own sacrifice as the high point of the group's religious life. Weighted down with gold and silver ornaments, they quickly drowned, becoming brides of the rain god and ensuring good crops in the coming season. Knowledge of the events has been pieced together from carvings on the sides of the temples and the thousands of silver, gold, jade, and bone relics recovered from the well.

In other ceremonies at the well captives were painted blue and thrown into the water at dawn to appease the angry gods. If by noon they were still swimming, the priests would pull them out and worship them for the rest of their lives in the belief that they had been to the other world and come back.

CHAC MOOL At Chichén Itzá and elsewhere you will frequently see statues of the ceremonial Chac Mool, a partially reclining stone figure that seems almost whimsical until one learns that his belly was used to receive the heart of the sacrifice during the temple rites.

There is an entrance fee to the antiquity site. Temple rubbings are available at local shops, as are books, literature, postcards, Mexican crafts, and souvenirs.

UXMAL

The structures of Uxmal are considered the finest pre-Columbian relics in Mexico. Located 35 miles south of Mérida (about an hour's drive), Uxmal (pronounced oosh-mal), is pure Maya without the Toltec overlay. It is built of yellowish stone rather than the gray material that gives Chichén Itzá such a sober, forbidding appearance. The site dates from about A.D. 600 and was inhabited for about 800 years. As many as 250,000 people lived in a 4.5-square-mile area around the government and religious center, which was filled with magnificent buildings.

PALACE OF GOVERNORS The massive, ornately decorated *Palace of the Governors,* constructed with over 20,000 cut stones, covers five acres. It is built on an elevated terrace that measures 600 feet by 500 feet. The 320-foot facade has lovely filigree of detailed bas-relief, all the more remarkable when you remember that the Mayas did not have metal tools with which to work.

MAGICIAN PYRAMID Another imposing structure is the *Pyramid of the Magician,* also known as the House of the Dwarf, with 118 steep steps leading to the top. According to legend, the pyramid was built on the site of the house of a sorceress who grieved because she had no children. Finally she hatched an egg, and from it came a small child who grew up to be a dwarf. When he was fully grown, she urged him to challenge the Mayan ruler who, in turn, condemned him to death unless he could build a house higher than any other in one night. And, he did.

NUNNERY The *Nunnery,* named by the Spaniards, was not a nunnery, but part of a quadrangle of four temples that surrounded a courtyard. It is noteworthy for its bas-relief carvings and arches. During the sound and light show, presented nightly in Spanish and in English, audiences sit in this area to watch the show.

Recently a group of authorities on Mayan civilization were reported to have found the key to deciphering the gylphs on some of the Mayan temples. If this news is true, it may mean that we can at last begin to unlock the mysteries of the Maya and answer some of the questions that have puzzled us for so long.

Central America

BELIZE, GUATEMALA, HONDURAS, NICARAGUA, COSTA RICA, PANAMA & THE SAN BLAS ISLANDS

CHAPTER CONTENTS

CENTRAL AMERICA

The land that forms a bridge between North and South America is a complex of seven nations— Belize, Guatemala, Honduras, El Salvador, Nicaragua, Costa Rica, and Panama—dissimilar as often as they are alike. Although the land mass stretches across some 2,000 miles from Mexico to Colombia, separating the Caribbean Sea from the Pacific Ocean, the area is actually quite small: the seven countries together are not as large as Texas.

To most of us the countries of Central America seem exotic and distant, but they are, in fact, among our closest neighbors. All except El Salvador have coastlines washed by the Caribbean Sea. Yet with the exception of Panama and the Panama Canal, the cruise world has largely ignored these countries as places to visit.

Topography, tradition, and turmoil can probably share equal blame. A look at the map reveals a spine of high mountains running almost unbroken from Mexico to Panama and reaching over 12,500 feet at its highest peaks. From their cloud and rain-forested slopes the terrain, carved by many rivers, drops to a skirt of lowlands bordering the Caribbean Sea. The Spaniards who arrived on these shores in Columbus's wake found a hot, humid, hostile climate. Little wonder that after they conquered the highlands with their spring-like weather, the Spaniards stayed and built their capitals there. The majority of people who came later did likewise. Hence, the Caribbean coast was never widely populated and was largely ignored, except perhaps by banana growers such as the United Fruit Company, which built some of the towns and ports of the lowlands that exist today.

As for tradition, the countries of Central America, except for Belize and to some extent Honduras, are not usually associated with the Caribbean since their history and culture have been more closely related with the Latin world than with the West Indian one. But then, Cuba, the Dominican Republic, and Puerto Rico are tied to the Spanish-speaking world, yet they are the very soul of the Caribbean. And, too, Mexico had very little relationship to the Caribbean in modern times until the creation of Cancún and the development of Cozumel. Now these destinations are promoted as the "Mexican Caribbean" and have become standard ports of call on Western Caribbean itineraries.

More relevant, perhaps, was the political turmoil that dominated the headlines of the 1980s, particularly regarding El Salvador, Guatemala, and Nicaragua, and kept tourists away from much of the region. Coincidentally, the decade paralleled the burgeoning of Caribbean cruising when there was, as yet, little demand or necessity for cruise lines to break out of their traditional itineraries, which sailed east from Florida to the Bahamas and the Eastern Caribbean.

Now that may be changing. As Caribbean cruising has begun to mature in the 1990s and the number of ships continues to increase, cruise lines are being driven by competition to develop new itineraries. At the same time, the reservoir of repeat passengers, eager to visit new destinations, is growing steadily. No area of the Caribbean would seem better suited to satisfy these needs than Central America.

Although most Central American countries are still held back from any rush of cruise ships by the lack of adequate docking facilities, a developed tourism plant, and other infrastructure requirements, a start has been made by some small cruise lines with small ships offering adventure-type cruises, usually focusing in depth on one or two destinations; even a few cruise lines with larger ships test the waters from time to time. Currently, cruise ships visit Belize, Guatemala, Honduras, Costa Rica (although more frequently stopping at attractions on its Pacific coast than the Caribbean one), and Panama.

No doubt, with a new era of peace and stability, interest in the area will grow as these nations, young in tourism, develop over the next decade and beyond. Meanwhile, anyone who selects a cruise that touches on the region will not be disappointed.

History buffs will find colonial cities, Indian villages, and some of the most important sites of antiquity in the Western Hemisphere; shoppers will be thrilled with the colorful markets filled with excellent and unusual crafts; and outdoor enthusiasts have many new worlds to discover from palm-fringed coasts with porcelain beaches to mighty mountains with rain forests, volcanoes, and wildlife preserves that are the last refuge for some of the exotic animals and birds once abundant in the Western Hemisphere.

Fronting the Caribbean coast from Mexico to Honduras lies the longest barrier reef in the Western Hemisphere, second only to the Great Barrier Reef of Australia. These pristine waters, particularly off the coasts of Belize and Honduras, offer outstanding snorkeling and diving and some of the best fishing in the world. Several cays, or tiny islets, are nesting places for significant numbers of birds, while mainland marshes and river deltas provide habitat for the manatee and other endangered wildlife.

BELIZE

Long before conservation and environmental protection became fashionable causes, this small country earmarked over a third of its territory for preservation. Within these borders lie spectacular Mayan ruins, forests, mountains, rivers, waterfalls, and a great variety of wildlife that includes 500 species of birds, 250 types of orchids, howler monkeys, pumas, ocelots, and the 100,000-acre Cockscomb Basin Wildlife Reserve, the world's only jaguar sanctuary.

Belize also has one of the longest chains of caves in the Western Hemisphere and the world's seventh-highest waterfall; its coast faces the world's second-longest barrier reef, dotted with hundreds of islets encircled by white sand beaches and fantastically clear waters teeming with fish.

Formerly known as British Honduras, Belize is bordered by Mexico on the north and by Guatemala on the west and south. About the size of Massachusetts, it is one of Central America's most stable countries, with an English- and Spanish-speaking multicultural population of 200,000. Belmopan, a small interior town, is the capital, but Belize City on the coast is the center of commerce, transportation, and activity and the departure port for the Mayan Coast cruises of American Canadian Caribbean Lines and Temptress Voyages, among others.

Belize City is something of a hodgepodge, with elevated tin-roofed wooden buildings beside British colonial and modern ones overlaid with a West Indian atmosphere. Its Cathedral of St. John, built in 1812, is the oldest Anglican Church in Central America. Although the town is short on sight-seeing attractions, it makes a good base for reaching some of Belize's most interesting sites.

Belize Zoo: Topping the list is the unusual, if not funky, Belize Zoo 30 miles west of town. Here, amid handprinted, funny, hokey but charming signs you can see more than 100 species of native animals including jaguar, tapir, howler monkeys, toucan, and more. The zoo was created originally by happenstance. Sharon Madola came to Belize in 1982 to care for a group of native animals that were being used in a nature film. But the project ran out of money before it could finish. The fate of the animals was a big concern.

Since Belize did not have a zoo, Sharon asked, why not start one? And she did. Through the schools particularly, she raised interest and awareness, enabling her to get government and private help, and in a decade of hard work she turned the zoo from a noble idea into a Belize institution which everyone loves.

Altun Ha: About 30 miles north of Belize City is the country's most accessible Mayan ruins, where 13 temples and residential structures have been uncovered. Here, a jade head—the largest carved jade object ever found in the Mayan region—was uncovered. It represents the sun god Kinich Ahau, a national symbol of Belize that can be seen on the nation's currency. Altun Ha was a major ceremonial center in the Classic period A.D. 250–900 and a trading center linking the Caribbean coast with Mayan centers in the interior.

Bermudian Landing Baboon Sanctuary: The 18-square-mile reserve, an hour's drive north of Belize City, was established in 1985 to protect the black howler monkey through an unusual voluntary grass-roots conservation program dependent upon the cooperation of landowners and villagers in farming communities bordering the monkey's habitat on the Belize River.

The black howler monkey, known in Belize as the baboon, is an endangered species whose range is now limited to Belize, southern Mexico, and isolated areas of Guatemala. When the Bermudian Landing community learned of the need to preserve the howlers' dwindling habitat and the benefits they could derive from conservation, its members responded by signing pledges to abide by certain guidelines. These include protecting forests along riverbanks, leaving food trees when clearing land, and maintaining corridors of forest around farmed areas. In turn, the landowners have benefited by reducing erosion, preventing silting of the river, and allowing for more rapid replacement of forests. The community derives some revenue from visitors as well.

In addition to the monkeys, hikers on the reserve's forest trails can see iguanas, coati, anteaters, and other exotic animals and some of the nearly 200 bird species observed here. A visitors center and exhibit are supported by the World Wildlife Fund and the Zoological Society of Milwaukee County.

Crooked Tree Wildlife Sanctuary: A 3,000-acre reserve of lagoons and marshes 33 miles northwest of Belize City, this is a bird-watcher's mecca. There are dozens of species to be seen, but the sanctuary is best known for the thousands of jabiru stork, the largest flying bird in the hemisphere, that reside here during the dry season from November to early May.

Mountain Pine Ridge: For hiking, the most accessible area is the 300-square-mile Mountain Pine Ridge west of Belize City, known for its scenic pine forests, streams, caves, and the 1,000-foot Hidden Valley Falls.

Other Mayan Sites: Among other important Mayan ruins in western Belize are the ceremonial center of

Xuantunich and Caracol, the most impressive Mayan site in Belize, accessible by road only in the dry season. West of the town of San Ignacio, just across the Belize/Guatemala border is Tikal, one of the largest, most important Mayan sites in Central America. People often visit it from Belize.

THE CAYS

A short distance offshore is a string of tiny islands along the 185-mile-long barrier reef, the largest in the Western Hemisphere. Development is concentrated on Ambergris Caye, 35 miles to the north of Belize City, and Caye Caulker, 14 miles south of Ambergris Caye; another dozen have one or two hotels. San Pedro, the main town on Ambergris Caye, is usually a stop for small cruise ships where passengers can enjoy fabulous white sand beaches, excellent deep-sea fishing, snorkeling on the shallow water reefs of the Hol Chan Marine Preserve, a 5-mile-square area of shallow water coral gardens at the southern tip of Ambergris. Trips to Mayan sites and jungle retreats on the mainland depart daily from San Pedro.

Other locations along the reef that are often stops for small cruise ships are the Turneffe Islands, 18 miles east of Belize City, a large atoll with abundant fish and large ray; Lighthouse Reef, about 30 miles farther east, where Half Moon Cay is a sanctuary for nesting red-footed boobies and magnificent frigate birds; and Glovers Reef, 30 miles east of the southern coastal town of Dangriga.

American Canadian Caribbean Line ships cruise from Belize to neighboring Guatemala via the barrier reef, stopping at pristine cays for swimming and snorkeling and the coastal villages of Placencia and Punta Gorda in Belize before reaching Livingston in Guatemala, where the ship turns into the Rio Dulce, a jungle river near the Honduras border, and sails upriver to Lake Izabel and enables passengers to visit the Mayan ruins of Quirigua. ACCL's ships, with their shallow drafts and bow ramps, are ideal for these waters, allowing passengers to disembark in remote places where large ships cannot go.

In 1995, Temptress Voyages introduced very innovative cruises along the barrier reef and Belize coast, departing year round from Belize City and visiting many places only accessible by sea. Among the stops are Goff's Caye for swimming, snorkeling, and a beach barbecue; Manatee Lagoon (Gail's Point), which has a large concentration of manatee, and Rendezvous Caye, before sailing to the coast at Sittee River and Hopkins, for a viewing of jungle flora and wildlife. Directly west of both villages is the famous jaguar reserve. The ship

continues to Tabacco Caye, Placencia, Monkey River, Laughingbird Caye, Wild King Caye, and Punta Gorda, the southernmost town in Belize near the Guatemalan border.

FAST FACTS

POPULATION: 200,000, comprised of Creoles (African-European); Garinagus (African-Amerindian); Mestizo (Spanish-Indian), Maya, Europeans and Americans.

GOVERNMENT: A democratically elected parliamentary government and a member of the British Commonwealth.

CLIMATE: Hot and tropical year-round; the dry season from October to May is the most comfortable time.

CLOTHING: Comfortable, casual light clothing for the coastal areas; hiking clothes and shoes for jungle excursions.

CURRENCY: Belize dollar or BZ. US $1 equals BZ $2.

DEPARTURE TAX: US $10 plus US $1.25 for security tax.

ELECTRICITY: 110 volts A.C.

Entry formalities: No visa required for U.S. or Canadian citizens, but you must have a valid U.S. passport.

LANGUAGE: English.

TIME: Central Standard Time.

TELEPHONE AREA CODE: 501.

VACCINATION REQUIREMENT: None.

AIRLINES: American, Continental, TACA.

INFORMATION:

Belize Tourist Board, 421 Seventh Avenue, Suite 1110; New York, NY 10001; Tel. 800–624–0686, 212–563–6011.

In Port: 83 North Front St., P.O. Box 325; Belize City; Tel. 011–501–2–77213; fax 011–501–2–77490.

GUATEMALA

Guatemala is a land of superlatives. It has Central America's highest, most active volcano, the most prodigious Mayan ruins, the largest population, and the largest, most authentic indigenous people that has clung the most tenaciously to its ancient culture and customs.

To many, Guatemala is the most beautiful and most interesting of the Central American seven. Certainly, the magnificent scenery, the Mayan antiquities, the colonial treasures, and the native Indians with their exotic faces, dazzling dress, and colorful markets make the country a photographer's dream.

About the size of Ohio, Guatemala offers an amazing variety of landscapes, from volcanic highlands clad with forests and dotted with lakes, to lowlands covered with coffee, banana, and sugar plantations. From its lofty and rugged mountain peaks at over 12,500 feet, the land is carved by dozens of rivers and falls west/southwest to the Pacific and east to a short coast on the Caribbean and a long border with Belize. To the west and north/northeast is a very long, irregular border with Mexico and to the south and southeast, El Salvador and Honduras.

Guatemala City, the capital, is the gateway to the country's Western highlands, where the majority of the native Indians live. The town is a convenient base for touring the main attractions of the region.

Antigua: The former capital and oldest Spanish colonial city in Guatemala is one of the loveliest in Central America, with churches, houses, and flower-filled plazas dating from the sixteenth and seventeenth centuries. It has been declared a National Monument of the Americas.

Lake Atitlan: Northwest from Antigua, the Pan-American Highway leads to the breathtakingly beautiful landscape of a mile-high lake surrounded by towering volcanoes. Around the shores of the lake are Indian villages whose people are directly descended from the Cakchiquel, Tzutuhil, and Quiché tribes, who peopled the region when the Spaniards arrived in 1524. A road west continues to Quezaltenango, the country's second city and another good base for exploring more remote villages and hiking.

Chichicastenango (north of Lake Atitlan; 90 miles from Guatemala City). Perhaps the most popular market town in all Central America, Chichi, as it is known, is certainly the most photographed for the colorful Quiche Indians who inhabit the area, their crafts, and the town's colonial churches.

THE CARIBBEAN COAST

Guatemala has only a small strip of land fronting the Caribbean where the Rio Dulce empties into the sea. Livingston, an old port that can only be reached by sea, is on the north side of the river; Puerto Barrios and

Santo Tomas de Castilla, the newer port and the usual dock for cruise ship, are on the south.

Puerto Barrios was built as a company town by the United Fruit Company when it put in the railway to ship its bananas to the coast, where they were loaded onto ships destined for the U.S. Laid out in a grid, Puerto Barrios has wide streets and typical Caribbean wood-frame houses, many on stilts. In the 1960s, Santo Tomás de Castilla, a short distance to the southwest, was built to serve as the main port.

Livingston: Located just across the border from Belize, Livingston, with its lush tropical landscape and brightly painted wooden buildings, is a village caught in time. It has no airport and no road to the outside; the only way in is by sea. The gateway to Guatemala at the turn of the century, when it was the principal port for goods transported down the Rio Dulce, it lost its *raison d'etre* when the railroad and Puerto Barrios were built.

For some cruise ships, such as those of the American Canadian Caribbean Line, it is still a port of call and starting point for the journey up the Rio Dulce to Lake Izabal. In addition to small cruise ships that sail up the river, the excursion can be made by *cayucos,* motor-

ized dugout canoes that take groups of tourists on river trips for about US $10 per person.

Livingston's population of 2,000 or so is made up mostly of the Black Carib, known in Central America as Garinagus or by their language, Garifuna. They are descendants of African slaves who escaped or were shipwrecked off the coast of St. Vincent and comingled with the Carib Indians there. In the late eighteenth century after a major revolt against the British who had colonized St. Vincent, most of the Black Carib were shipped off to Roatan, an island off the coast of Honduras. Over time, they migrated to southern Belize, Guatemala, and Nicaragua, intermarrying with shipwrecked sailors of other races and with the indigenous Maya and developing a distinctive culture and language made up of African, Carib Indian, Maya, and European elements. They also speak Spanish and English with a lilt similar to others in the Caribbean.

An interesting side note to history: At the time of the Columbus Quincentennial, the Caribs of Dominica, the last of the Carib tribes populating the Caribbean when Columbus arrived, established contacts with the Garinagus in Central America to try to learn more about their heritage by sharing their cultural traditions. If one compares the traditional crafts of the Caribs of Dominica and those of the Garinagus in Belize, the connection between the two people becomes obvious, particularly in the art of straw-weaving, where the type of weaving, straw, and patterns used are so distinctive.

Rio Dulce Cruises: A boat trip up the Rio Dulce is, as one writer described it, an adventure straight out of *The African Queen.* From Livingston, the river passes through a steep-walled gorge thick with jungle greenery and streaming waterfalls and alive with egrets and other tropical birds. At the base of the gorge the sulphurous water from a hot spring provides a delightful place for a swim.

Upon emerging from the gorge, the river widens into an area known as El Golfete, whose north side borders a 7,200-hectar nature reserve, Biotopo Chocon-Machacas. In addition to the beautiful river landscape, the reserve protects mangroves, tropical flora, and exotic wildlife, particularly the manatees that inhabit the waters. The reserve runs for about 7 miles along the river and has a network of boat routes around the jungle lagoons, enabling passengers to get a close-up look at the wildlife. A nature trail begins at the visitors center.

At the western end of El Golfete is a restored seventeenth-century fortress, *Castillo de San Felipe de Lara,* built at the entrance to Lake Izabel (Lago de Izabel) to keep out marauding pirates, who ruled the seas of the Caribbean at the time, from preying on local villages and the commerce traveling on the river. Apparently, the fortress was only minimally effective, as pirates were able to capture and burn it in 1686. Once the pirate threat was removed from the Caribbean, the fortress was used as a prison.

Lake Izabal, a large body whose freshwaters shelter the manatee, has not been developed for tourism, but some small cruise ships sail around the lake, stopping to visit the fort and take passengers from the village of Rio Dulce (also known as El Relleno) by bus to the region's main antiquity sites.

Carretera al Atlantico, the highway from the capital to the sea is on the south side of the lake. At the Morales/La Ruidosa junction (Carretera al Atlantico Km. 245) the highway west leads to Los Amates, less than a mile from the Maya archaeological site of Quirigua in a lovely park setting. It is famous for the huge, intricately carved stelae that can be seen there. The site is open daily from 7 A.M. to 5 P.M.; there is a small admission fee.

The Morales/La Ruidosa junction north crosses to the village of Rio Dulce, where a road leads to Flores, the gateway to El Peten, a vast lowland forest of which 50 square miles are a national park, with some of the most important antiquities in the Western Hemisphere.

Tikal National Park: In the dense jungle of El Peten in northeast region is Tikal, the crown jewel of Guatemala's Mayan antiquites and the largest, most impressive ruins from the Classic period in the Mayan world. The vast area holds the ruins of approximately 3,000 structures. In the Great Plaza, two awesome temples have been excavated, while the tops of three pyramids tower above the jungle's canopy to heights of more than 145 feet. In addition to the prodigious antiquities the forest is alive with exotic flora and wildlife, including brightly colored parrots that squawk from the tree tops and howler monkeys that swing noisily through the branches.

Flores is about a 45-minute drive away. Several lodges are situated near the site, enabling visitors to remain overnight. Some cruise ships offer excursions that travel by motorcoach in one direction and by plane in the other. Tikal is located near the Belize border and is often visited from there.

FAST FACTS

POPULATION: 8 million.

CLIMATE: Hot and humid on the coast; spring-like weather in the highlands.

CLOTHING: Comfortable, casual light clothing for coastal areas.

CURRENCY: The Guatemalan quetzal (Q) is divided into 100 centavos. US $1=Q 5.80.

DEPARTURE TAX: U.S. $10.

ELECTRICITY: 110 volts A.C.

Entry formalities: Valid U.S. passport; tourist card is issued at airline counter before departure or on arrival in Guatemala for U.S. $5.

LANGUAGE: Spanish; some English in coastal areas.

TIME: Central Standard Time.

TELEPHONE AREA CODE: 502.

VACCINATION REQUIREMENT: None.

INFORMATION:

Guatemala Tourist Commission,
299 Alhambra Circle; Coral Gables, FL 33134;
Tel. 800–742–4529, 305–442–0651.

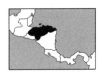

HONDURAS

S tretching east-west between Guatemala and Nicaragua, with El Salvador on the south, Honduras is the second-largest of the Central American seven and boasts a long, beautiful Caribbean coastline backed by tropical jungle-clad mountains that climb to over 7,000 feet. Much of the coast, with its beaches, wetlands, and lagoons full of manatees, howler monkeys, and other wildlife, is protected in coastal and marine parks.

A short distance off the Caribbean coast lie Honduras' best-known attractions—the Bay Islands, idyllic hideaways surrounded by fabulous coral reefs, an extension of the barrier reef off Mexico and Belize. The country's other well-known star is the spectacular Mayan ruins at Copan near the Guatemalan border.

Honduras' interior is comprised mostly of mountains and highland valleys—80 percent of its total 59,160 square miles is made up of terrain ranging from 1,800 feet to almost 9,500 feet above sea level.

Tegucigalpa, the capital, is situated in the central highlands at 3,217 feet in a bowl-shaped valley surrounded by pine-covered mountains and enjoying a springlike climate year-round. The hilly town, with its tile-roofed, pastel houses along cobblestone streets, has retained its colonial atmosphere. The main highway of the region connects Tegucigalpa with San Pedro Sula, the country's principal commercial center, and the coast.

In 1502, on his fourth and final voyage, Christopher Columbus sailed from Jamaica to explore the Central American land mass. He came ashore near Trujillo on Honduras' north coast and named it "Honduras," meaning "depths" in Spanish, for the deep waters there.

The town of Trujillo, founded in 1525 near the site of Columbus's landing, was the first capital of the Spanish colony, but soon the Spanish became more interested in the cooler highlands of the interior. Meanwhile, the British grabbed the coast for its timber and the Bay Islands for their hidden bays and inlets from which British pirates could prey on Spanish ships. It is said that by the early 1600s, Roatan had an estimated 5,000 British pirates. The notorious eighteenth-century pirate Henry Morgan, who later was rewarded by the British crown by making him a governor of Jamaica, was among those who used the islands as a base.

To harvest the mahogany and other hardwoods from the forests, the British brought Jamaicans and other West Indians to Honduras. Today, their descendants largely people the Caribbean coast, along with the mestizos of native Indian and Spanish blood, and the Garinagus, who are a mixture of African and Carib Indians and known in the Eastern Caribbean as the Black Carib.

In the late eighteenth century after a revolt of the Black Carib in St. Vincent, the British rounded up the survivors and shipped them to Roatan. From there, the Garifuna, as they are sometimes called after their language, migrated to the mainland, creating fishing and farming communities along the coast from Belize to Nicaragua and developing their own religion, music, dance, and language, Garifuna, a mix of West African, Arawak, and European speech.

THE BAY ISLANDS

Islas de la Bahía, an archipelago of three main islands—Roatan, Guanaja, and Utila—and many tiny cays, is located about 30 miles off the north coast. These islands are Honduras' prime tourist attractions, offering great diving and snorkeling on their extensive coral reefs. The marine gardens are a continuation of the barrier reef that starts off the coast of Mexico and extends for 185 miles to Honduras, making it the largest reef in the Western Hemisphere and second only in the world to Australia's Great Barrier Reef.

Culturally as well as scenically, the Bay Islands are a world apart from the mainland, having been occupied by the British from the seventeenth to the nineteenth centuries. Christopher Columbus landed on Guanaja in 1502, where he found a fairly large native population. In less than 25 years, the population had been decimated by the Spaniards who followed him, enslaving the islanders and sending them to work on the plantations of Cuba and in the silver mines of Mexico.

Before long, English, French, and Dutch pirates took over the islands and from these convenient bases raided the Spanish galleons laden with gold and other treasures from the New World en route to Spain. Then, in 1782, after many attempts, the Spanish successfully

wiped out the pirates' stronghold, and once again the islands were left uninhabited. A decade later, after the Black Carib uprising in St. Vincent, the British shipped the survivors to Roatan. Although most made their way eventually to the mainland, Roatan still has one settlement of Garinigus at Punta Gorda.

The Bay Islands, along with the large Mosquitia territory in northeastern Honduras, remained British until 1859, when Great Britain ceded the territory to Honduras. Yet only in recent times, after Honduras required that Spanish be spoken in all schools, did the islanders begin to speak Spanish. English, spoken with a typical Caribbean lilt, remains their preferred language as well as their cultural orientation.

Roatan: Situated off the coast at La Ceiba, Roatan is the largest and most developed of the Bay Islands, with a population of about 10,000. The island, 30 miles long and only 1 to 3 miles wide, is surrounded by over 60 miles of reef, making it a mecca for divers. The most beautiful part of the island is at West End, a small village with an idyllic, palm-shaded, white sand beach washed by turquoise waters filled with colorful fish. Coxen Hole, the main town, is about a ten-minute drive from the airport. The island has good accommodations and dive facilities.

Guanaja: The most easterly of the three islands, Guanaja has rugged, mountainous terrain covered with forests and appears to be a mainland breakaway. Only

about 11 miles long and 4 miles wide at its widest point, the island is surrounded by miles of coral reefs and a dozen or more cays. About 90 percent of the island has been declared a national forest reserve and marine park. The island caters mostly to affluent travelers.

Guanaja Town, known as the "Venice" of Honduras and called "Bonacca" by its inhabitants, is on a small cay just off the main island's east coast. Its wooden houses with sloping roofs, all at different heights, are packed tight and rest on stilts. There are no roads and no cars on the cay; a labyrinth of walkways winding around the houses and narrow canals enable residents to bring their boats right up to their houses.

Utila: The smallest, least developed of the group has modest tourist facilities, appealing to budget travelers, and is, as yet, probably the cheapest place in the Caribbean to learn to dive.

Actually, all three islands are relatively inexpensive by Caribbean standards and have excellent diving facilities. The dive shops offer a range of options, from an introductory resort course to full certification. The islands are linked by daily air service from La Ceiba and San Pedro Sula to Roatan.

THE NORTH COAST

Honduras' entire north coast of 384 miles fronts the Caribbean Sea, with mountains of tropical jungle rising to over 7,000 feet behind it. The towns of the north coast are Puerto Cortes, the main port where cruise ships usually dock; La Ceiba, the largest coastal town and jumping-off point for travel by air or boat to the Bay Islands; and Tela and Trujillo, known for their lovely, palm-fringed beaches and good fresh seafood. Rain, heaviest on the coast from September to January, can sometimes make the roads impassable.

Puerto Cortes: Located on the sea near the Guatemala border and 34 miles from San Pedro Sula, Puerto Cortes handles over half of the country's exports. The docks are in the heart of town and are normally busy with cargo ships loading bananas, pineapples, and other produce for the two-day sail to New Orleans and Miami. There are some good beaches within a short drive, and the Spanish fortress at Omoa is a half-hour bus ride west from town.

Tela: In addition to its beaches, Tela has the Lancetilla Botanic Gardens and Research Center, begun in 1926 by United Fruit Company as an experimental station for tropical plants. The huge estate is a park with a visitors center and specimens of about every fruit tree and flower that grows in Central America. It's also a birder's

haven, as the gardens attract over 200 species.

La Ceiba: Situated on the narrow coastal plain between the towering Cordillera Nombre de Dios mountains and the Caribbean, La Ceiba is a rich fishing and farming community surrounded by banana and pineapple plantations, mostly owned by Standard Fruit. Pico Bonito National Park, a few miles behind the town and covering about 300 square miles, is Honduras' largest national park and has magnificent forests and wildlife. On the coast 12 miles west of La Ceiba is the Cuero-Salado Nature Reserve, a large estuary formed by the Cuero and Salado rivers that protects a multitude of wildlife, including manatee, howler monkeys, and many bird species.

INLAND FROM THE NORTH COAST

San Pedro Sula: Honduras' second-largest city is 34 miles south of Puerto Cortes in the Ulua River Valley, a large plain that is one of Honduras' most fertile, productive areas and the heart of banana country. Here, Standard Fruit and United Fruit, who own a large part of northern Honduras, grow bananas and pineapples for export to the U.S. Several of the vicinity's towns, ports, roads, and railways were built by the banana companies.

San Pedro Sula is a lively town with a population of about 325,900. It has an archaeological museum and a good central market where the National Association of Honduras Artisans has a wide selection of crafts from throughout the country.

Founded by the Spaniards in 1536, the town is today Honduras' major industrial and commercial center as well as the main center for the region's agricultural products. It is also the transportation hub for western Honduras and the gateway to Copan.

La Lima, 8 miles east of San Pedro, is a company town built by United Brands of Chiquita bananas fame, where you can visit the banana plantation and watch the packing operations. The Cusuco National Park, 12 miles west of San Pedro, is a mountainous cloud forest with its highest peak at 7,398 feet; there is a visitors center. The 300-foot Pulhapanzak waterfall and Lago de Yojoa, about 30 miles to the south, are popular recreation areas.

THE MAYAN ANTIQUITIES OF COPAN

Southwest of San Pedro Sula via a new road of 125 miles that climbs the hills and upland valleys through coffee, tobacco, and corn fields and terraced hill sides, are the ruins of Copan, among the most magnificent antiquites in the Americas, rivaling Tikal in Guatemala for top honors as Central America's most important archaeological site. Called the "Athens of the Mayan World," Copan was a flourishing city for hundreds of years and reached its peak between A.D. 465 and 800 in the Mayan Classic Period, when it was the artistic and scientific center. The region was inhabited by the Maya for about 2,800 years.

The main ceremonial center covers about 75 acres; the principal group of ruins includes the Great Plaza, with dozens of intricately carved stelae portraying the rulers of Copan; and the Hieroglyphic Stairway, the most dramatic monument. The stairway, 30 feet wide and 60 feet high, is covered with over 2,200 glyphs that record the history of the Copan rulers; it is the longest pre-Columbian text ever found. Indeed, the temples and monuments of Copan have more reliefs and artistic embellishment than any other in the Mayan world— one reason they are so significant. The entire site is thought to have been built over earlier temples and other buildings. New discoveries are made continuously; these findings are housed in a museum in town and a new small Mayan sculpture museum near the ruins.

The pretty little town of Copan Ruinas is less than a mile from the ancient ruins. Its cobblestoned streets are lined with typical white-washed adobe houses with red-tiled roofs; a colonial church anchors the plaza. Copan is a three-hour drive from San Pedro Sula and four hours from Puerto Cortes; there are hotels within walking distance of the Mayan site.

THE MOSQUITO COAST

Located in the northeastern part of the country, La Mosquitia or the Mosquito Coast is one of Central America's largest wilderness areas, rich in wildlife. This swampy, heavily forested region is sparsely inhabited by the Miskito and Sumo Indians. Travel is mostly by boat, as there is only one road. Adventure and nature tours reach their destinations in the region by bush plane, four-wheel-drive vehicle, cayuco (dugout canoe), on foot, and by mule pack.

The Rio Platano Reserve, established by Honduras with the United Nations in 1980, is often described as the most beautiful nature reserve in Honduras. It protects a pristine river system that flows through a tropical rain forest and has abundant wildlife. Travel is by boat on the river, with camping in the forest. Air service to Palacios, a lilliputian hamlet and the most accessible locale to visit the reserve, operates from La Ceiba. There is also air service to Puerto Lempira, a small vil-

lage and the largest coastal settlement in the Mosquito region, near the Nicaraguan border.

FAST FACTS

POPULATION: 5.5 million.

GOVERNMENT: A democratically elected government.

CLIMATE: Hot, tropical year-round in the lowlands; perpetual spring in the highlands.

CLOTHING: Comfortable, casual light clothing for the coastal areas; hiking clothes and shoes for jungle excursions.

CURRENCY: Lempira. There are 100 centavos in a lempira. U.S. $1=L 7.55.

DEPARTURE TAX: U.S. $10.

ELECTRICITY: 110 volts A.C.

Entry formalities: Valid U.S. passport; on arrival, tourists get tourist cards valid for up to 90 days.

LANGUAGE: Spanish and English on the Caribbean coast and Bay Islands.

TIME: Central Standard Time.

TELEPHONE AREA CODE: 505.

VACCINATION REQUIREMENT: None.

AIRLINES: American, Continental, Taca, Tan/Sahsa.

INFORMATION:

Honduras Tourist Board, 299 Alhambra Circle #510; Coral Gables, FL 33134; Tel. 305–461–0600, 800–410–9608.

NICARAGUA

Although it has been six years since a democratically elected government was voted into power and peace fell over the land, neither U.S. tourists nor cruise lines seem ready, as yet, to embrace Nicaragua as a major travel destination. When they do, they will find a beautiful country of tall mountains with pine-forested slopes, volcanoes, and lakes, including the largest lake in Central America, rain forests, lowlands drained by 23 rivers often traversing thick tropical jungles, and long shorelines on both its Caribbean and Pacific coasts. They will also see some of the Western Hemisphere's most historic towns, such as Granada and León, with lovely Spanish colonial architecture; and enjoy music, folklore, festivals, and markets brimming with handicrafts.

The largest country in Central America, with 57,143 square miles, Nicaragua is sandwiched between the Caribbean Sea on the east and the Pacific Ocean on the west. She is separated from Honduras, her neighbor on the north, by the 411-mile Rio Coco, Nicaragua's longest river; on the south, much of her border with Costa Rica is formed by the 120-mile Rio San Juan. Geographically, Nicaragua has three distinct regions: the north-central mountains that fall east to the Caribbean in a vast area of rivers and lowlands known as the Caribbean or Mosquito Coast; and the Pacific lowland, which has the majority of the towns, including Managua, the capital, and people. The Pacific region also has about 40 volcanoes, some reaching upwards of 6,000 feet. The Momotombo volcano on the southern shore of Lake Managua and clearly visible from the capital, is the national emblem. Just outside Managua is the Masaya National Park with the Masaya volcano. It is one of the few summits of an active volcano that can be reached by car. A road leads directly to the lip of the cone, where you can look down into the smoking crater. The town of Masaya, 15 miles from Managua, is well known for its artisans, whose wares are on display in the town's colorful market.

The rich volcanic soil has made the Pacific corridor Nicaragua's most productive farming region. The region also has many lakes, including 5,067-square-mile Lake Nicaragua, Central America's largest and the tenth largest freshwater lake in the world. Granada, 28 miles from the capital at the foot of the Mombacho volcano on the northwestern shore of Lake Managua, is Nicaragua's oldest city, founded by Hernandez de Córdoba in 1524. It is known for its Spanish colonial architecture and its conservative ways and rivals León, long a liberal stronghold and almost as old.

León Viejo, or Old León, at the foot of Momotombo, was also established by Hernandez de Córdoba in 1524 but it was destroyed by earthquake in 1610 and covered with layers of ash from subsequent eruptions of the volcano. The present city of León is 19 miles away; it served as Nicaragua's capital until 1857 when the capital was moved to Managua. Among León's many attractions, the massive Metropolitan Cathedral, begun in 1746 and completed a century later, is the largest in Central America and is famous for its huge paintings of the Stations of the Cross, considered masterpieces of Spanish colonial art.

Despite the difficulty with its image, tourism has grown with peace and already ranks second as a source of national revenue. Hotel and resort development is moving along on the Pacific coast; the Caribbean shores, however, remain undeveloped and almost inaccessible except at Puerto Cabezas in the north and Bluefields in the south.

Nicaragua is recapturing some of its past appeal to visitors through travel programs focusing on nature and light adventure. These might include visits to ranches and coffee plantations or a cruise on the Rio San Juan through the Indio Maiz National Reserve. The trip follows the course of the river from Lake Nicaragua to the Caribbean Sea along Nicaragua's border with Costa Rica. Once a major highway of commerce, the waterway was viewed by many as a more viable route than through Panama for building a channel to connect the Caribbean with the Pacific when various plans were being studied for the Panama Canal.

THE MOSQUITO COAST

Hot, humid, and scarely populated, the Caribbean or Mosquito Coast covers about half of Nicaragua and, with an average width of 60 miles, forms the widest skirt of lowlands in Central America. Much of it is covered with tropical rain forests that in some places is impenetrable jungle. The 325 miles of Caribbean shores are broken up by many river deltas and large lagoons created by the coursing of 23 rivers from the central mountains to the Caribbean Sea.

Nicaragua's Caribbean ports can be reached from Managua by air, but a preferred tourist route is via the town of El Rama and downriver by boat to Bluefields, a colorful old port on the Caribbean. The Mosquito region was never colonized by Spain and indeed, tribal leaders asked—and got—protection from the British against the Spaniards. Britain relinquished the territory to an independent Nicaragua in 1860, but English is still spoken on the coast and nearby islands and, like so many pockets along the Central American coast with their mixed populations, there's a West Indian flavor here, too.

About 40 miles or so offshore from Bluefields are the tiny, idyllic Corn Islands—Grande and Pequeña—currently the only Nicaraguan Caribbean destinations visit-

ed by cruise ships. The largest of the Corn Islands is only 4 miles square; the smallest is about 1 mile square. Both are fringed by sandy beaches, crystal-clear waters, and coral reefs and are ideal for swimming, fishing, snorkeling, and diving, including exploring the wreck of a Spanish galleon a short distance offshore. The islanders are English-speaking Creoles and Garinigus (see the Honduras section).

FAST FACTS

POPULATION: 4 million.

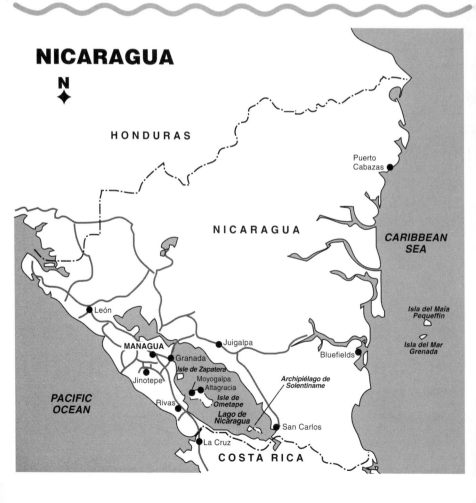

GOVERNMENT: A democratically elected government.

CLIMATE: Hot and humid on the coasts; spring-like in the highlands.

CURRENCY: Cordoba, divided into 100 centavos. US $1=6.6 cordobas.

DEPARTURE TAX: U.S. $12.

ELECTRICITY: 110 volts A.C.

Entry formalities: U.S. passport valid at least six months after entry date and a tourist card, issued for $5 on arrival.

LANGUAGE: Spanish; English on the Caribbean coast and Corn Islands.

TIME: Eastern Standard Time.

TELEPHONE AREA CODE: 505.

INFORMATION:

Nicaragua Tourist Office,
  P.O. Box 140357; Miami, FL 33114-0357;
  Tel. 800–660–7253, 305–860–0747.

COSTA RICA

Costa Rica is often called the Switzerland of Central America. A mountainous land with a long democratic tradition, no army, and one of the highest literacy rates in the Western Hemisphere, the country has managed miraculously, in recent years, to stay out of trouble.

A small, friendly country about the size of West Virginia, Costa Rica is bordered on the north by Nicaragua and on the south by Panama—countries plagued by political turmoil and armed conflicts throughout the 1980s. Yet peaceful Costa Rica succeeded in staying out of the conflicts that were tearing apart her neighbors while remaining their friends, and at the same time maintaining a good relationship with the United States and often serving as mediator for all.

Most visitors come to Costa Rica to see her natural wonders, and cruise passengers are no exception. Costa Rica has become the very definition of eco-tourism through her pioneering environmental efforts. Approximately 20 percent of the nation's land is under protection in more than 30 national parks, forestry reserves, wildlife refuges, and biological and private reserves (compared to 3 percent in the U.S.).

The designated areas protect a diverse landscape ranging from volcanic peaks and rain and cloud forests on mountain slopes, to dry and swamp forests in the lowlands, to dense mangrove and coral reefs along her coasts. The country has 12 distinct ecological systems containing 8,000 species of plants including 1,200 varieties of orchids, 750 species of birds—more than in all of North America, and 10 percent of the world's butterflies. In the national park system, which is made up of 45 areas, at least one example of each ecosystem is represented.

Three chains of volcanic mountains form the Central Highlands, where the capital of Costa Rica, San José, with its year-round spring-like weather, is located at an altitude of 3,805 feet. Depending on their ship's itinerary, cruise passengers often spend either the first or last night of their cruise in San José and visit the nineteenth-century National Cathedral and the wonderful National Museum with a wealth of pre-Columbian artifacts, and shop at the Central Market.

Sarchi, a short trip from the capital, is a handicraft center known for its workshops that create the traditional, brightly painted ox carts and interpret the colorful art onto many practical souvenirs. Shops sell other hardwood products as well as hammocks, straw, and leather.

San José is the gateway to many of the country's parks with drive-to volcanoes, rain-forested mountains, and a lush countryside fresh with rushing rivers and rich with fertile valleys.

Poas Volcano National Park, an easy 1.5-hour drive north of San José (22 miles north of Alajuela), is one of the most accessible, and hence, most popular parks, and provides the rare opportunity to drive almost to the crater rim of an active volcano at 8,000 feet, to peer down into it (when clouds don't obscure the view), and to hike in the surrounding forest. The crater is almost a mile across and 1,000 feet deep. There are small eruptions from time to time but normally not enough to close the park as in 1989, when eruption sent volcanic ash almost a mile into the air. A trail through a dwarf cloud forest heavy with mosses, lichens, and bromeli-ads, and abundant with hummingbirds and other species, leads to an extinct crater with a pretty lake.

Farther to the northwest, the Arenal National Park protects the majestic Arenal Volcano, the largest and most active volcano in Central America. From its perfect cone, the 5,389-foot-high volcano puts on a spectacular display, sending smoke, ash, and exploding rocks into the air and lava tumbling down the slopes. At night when the streams of orange-red lava glow in the night, the sight is awesome. East of San José, the Irazu Volcano National Park has Costa Rica's highest volcano at 11,325 feet altitude.

THE CARIBBEAN COAST

Like so much of Central America, Costa Rica's Caribbean coast is sparely settled and is the least accessible, less developed area of the country. Puerto Limón, the eastern gateway almost at the center of the country's Caribbean coast, is a three-hour bus ride from San

José. A hot, humid port city of about 60,000 people, Puerto Limón owes its creation in 1880 to the railway and banana industry, both of which have seen better days. In 1871, the government, eager to get the country's principal crop, coffee, more expeditiously to foreign markets, contracted Minor Keith, an American engineer, to build a railway from San José to the coast. The track took some 20 years to lay and cost thousands of lives due to malaria and yellow fever. It also changed Costa Rica forever by introducing blacks and bananas.

At first, Keith brought workers from China and Italy, but in time, he found that Jamaicans were better able to withstand the weather and disease. To help defray some of the cost of building the railway, he planted bananas alongside the track, and in Limón, he built a pier and collected a share of the fee for its usage.

The banana business was so successful that by 1884, Keith was able to help Costa Rica pay its national debt and in exchange received a 99-year lease on the railway and thousands of acres of land along the route where, of course, he planted more bananas. Five years later, Keith and a rival company joined hands to form the United Fruit Company. It extended its base of operation from Guatemala to Panama and to a great extent con-

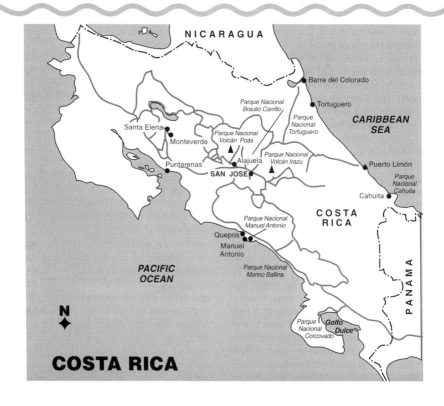

COSTA RICA

trolled the power and politics of Central America's "banana republic" for almost a century.

After the railway had been completed most of the Jamaicans stayed to work the banana plantation and railroad. Today, the descendants of these English-speaking Jamaicans make up the majority of the population, which has largely retained a Jamaican or West Indian culture. However, that they kept their separate identity is not surprising considering the fact that the rest of Costa Rica did not accept them. Not until 1952 were they allowed Costa Rican citizenship. Even a half-century later, there is little evidence of assimilation.

TORTUGUERO NATIONAL PARK

North of Puerto Limón is a huge area of jungle-thick forests, swamps, and marshland crisscrossed by rivers and canals, a large part of which is protected by the Tortuguero National Park and to the north, the Barra del Colorado National Refuge. Both are rich with birds and other wildlife.

Tortuguero takes its name from the large numbers of turtles that nest here from August to November. The national park, created in 1975 after a two-decade effort by conservationists, protects the nesting sites of four species—hawksbill, green, leatherback, and loggerhead turtles—on the beaches in the 50-mile stretch between the Matina River, which empties at Moin, and the Colorado River near the Nicaragua border.

The protected areas also include the low-lying hills, swamps, and forests that are home to monkeys, jaguars, raccoons, tapirs, and hundreds of species of birds, in addition to inland waterways that support a wide variety of fish and other wildlife, including storks, herons, crocodiles, otters, manatees, and the gar, an unusual prehistoric fish said to be little-changed for 90 million years.

Boat trips start at Moin, about 2 miles from Puerto Limón, and make their way through the swamps and marshes via a network of jungle-bordered canals with signs like a highway, used by the people of the region as transportation. The area offers good sportfishing, while divers head to the reefs south of Limón.

CAHUITA NATIONAL PARK

Cahuita, a small village about 25 miles southeast of Limón, is expanding as a tourist destination, attracting visitors for its laid-back life-style and the pretty beaches and reefs protected by the Cahuita National Park. Here, the Caribbean Sea rolls in sometimes with force and breaks against the reefs. Behind the palm-edged beaches is a coastal rain forest full of birds and other wildlife.

THE PACIFIC COAST

On Panama Canal cruises, Puerto Caldera, a modern container port about six miles from Puntarena, the traditional port, is frequently used by cruise ships for passengers beginning or ending their cruise in San José, where they arrive or fly back to the U.S. Depending on your ship's itinerary, you are likely to visit some of the national parks of the Pacific coast, some of which are remote from the capital and more readily accessible by ship.

Manuel Antonio National Park, near the Pacific coastal town of Quepos, is the smallest of the country's parks and one of the most popular. It protects beaches, rocky headlands, and a tropical forest that hosts a great variety of wildlife including ocelots, three-toed sloths, squirrel, howler, and white-face monkeys—all often seen during hikes on the park's maintained trails. The park is 3.5 hours by bus trip from San José.

Santa Rosa National Park, the first park to be established, covers 260 acres on the Pacific northwest and is the nesting ground to three turtle species: huge leather backs, the Olive Ridley, and the Pacific Green. The park protects ten different habitats ranging from beaches and mangroves to dry forests and wooded savannahs. The wildlife includes monkeys, anteaters, coatimundies, peccaries, and deer. Palo Verde National Park, a huge swampy refuge for migratory waterfowl, is also in the northwest.

Corcovado National Park in the south on the Osa Peninsula near the Panama border is remote from the capital. A popular stop for cruise ships, Corcovado's tropical rain forest and diverse habitat counts more than 500 species of trees, 285 species of birds, and 139 species of animals. Cruise ships often visit the Marenco Biological Reserve, which can not be reached by road. There, they hike a trail to the Rio Claro for swimming in freshwater pools and along beaches shaded by almond trees. This region is one of the last refuges for the rare scarlet macaw often spotted in the trees by hikers.

CRUISES

Clipper Cruise Line's light adventure cruises operate in October and from December to April, combining Costa Rica with Panama. In Costa Rica, passengers visit the Manuel Antonio National Park, the Marenco Biological Station, the Carara Biological Reserve, San José, and Poas

Volcano National Park. The cruises are accompanied by naturalist guides who give daily briefings on each of the areas visited. The ships carry their own Zodiacs to take passengers to secluded beaches for swimming, snorkeling, and hiking and to visit isolated villages.

Special Expeditions sails on a series of cruises combining Costa Rica and Panama between Colón on the Caribbean and Caldera on the Pacific. After transiting the Panama Canal, the cruises visit the Marenco Biological Reserve on Costa Rica's Osa Peninsula, the Manuel Antonio National Park, the Refugio Curu, a privately owned wildlife refuge, and other locations.

Many parks are visited on the cruises offered by Temptress Voyages. There are two different itineraries. One has almost weekly departures between November and May, and visits Manuel Antonio, Palo Verde, and Corcovado National Parks, along with other Pacific coast highlights. The second, a northern route, operates between June and October, and visits Cuajiniquil for Culebra Bay near the Nicaragua border, and the Santa Rosa and Guanacaste National Parks, among other places.

Crystal Cruises, Holland America Line, and Princess Cruises are some of the cruise lines that call at both Puerto Limón and Puerto Caldera on their transcanal cruises.

 # FAST FACTS

 POPULATION: 3.2 million.

 GOVERNMENT: A democratically elected government.

 CLIMATE: Spring-like climate in San José and the highlands; hot and tropical year-round on the coast; the dry season from October to May is the most comfortable period.

 CLOTHING: Comfortable, casual light clothing for the coastal areas; hiking clothes and shoes for jungle excursions.

 CURRENCY: Colón. U.S. $1 equals about 155 colones.

 DEPARTURE TAX: U.S. $16.

 ELECTRICITY: 110 volts A.C.

 ENTRY FORMALITIES: No visa required for U.S. or Canadian citizens, but you must have a valid U.S. passport.

 LANGUAGE: Spanish and English.

 TIME: Central Standard Time.

 TELEPHONE AREA CODE: 506.

 VACCINATION REQUIREMENT: None.

 AIRLINES: LACSA, Aero Costa Rica, America Airlines.

 INFORMATION:

Costa Rica Tourist Bureau, 1101 Brickell Avenue, #801, BIV Tower; Miami, Fl 33131; Tel. 800–327–7033 (for general information).

The Tourist Board has a toll-free line to its San José offices, where English-speaking operators answer questions: 800–343–6332.

 # PANAMA

THE SAN BLAS ISLANDS

Of all the exotic destinations cruise ships visit in the Western Caribbean, none is more ususual that the San Blas Islands off the northeast Caribbean coast of Panama. An archipelago of low-lying islands, upon approach their thatched-roof dwellings shaded by crowds of palm trees look more like the islands of the South Seas than the Caribbean.

These islands are the home of the Cuna Indians, the only tribe of island dwellers in the Caribbean who have both survived and been able to maintain their ancient folkways, more or less, intact despite 500 years of contact with Europeans and other alien cultures.

The San Blas Islands are comprised of about 400 islets plus a strip of land on the Panamanian coast, over which the Cuna claim sovereignty and maintain self-rule. There are 48 Cuna villages with a total population of about 40,000, represented in a tribal council. The people move between the islands in dugout canoes, little changed from those of their ancestors. Their main crop is coconut, which they use as currency. Despite their isolation on these islands, they are unusually worldly and have accepted certain innovations, such as communications and education, while retaining their traditional way of life.

Normally, your first glimpse of the Cuna will be from your cruise ship, where as many as ten boats, full of Cuna women, will be doing a brisk business selling their colorful, unique molas for which they are famous. Do not think these are the last of their stock. When you go ashore to visit a Cuna village, you will see the molas displayed on clotheslines strung the entire length of the village. Some are squares that can be made into pillow covers or framed; others appear on shirts and dresses. All are remarkably inexpensive, ranging from $10 to $40 depending on the intricacy of the design. There is no need to try bargaining; these women may not be able to speak your language but they understand money.

Molas represent a Cuna woman's wealth, like a dowry. They are elaborate reverse-applique in bold, bright colors, incorporating stylized flowers, animals, birds, and super-natural motifs, and are made origi-nally for the front and back panels of the blouse which the petite Cuna women wear. Occasionally you will see a mola that incorporates current events, such as the U.S. landing of troops in Panama, which crept into designs in 1990. To a newcomer, molas may all seem alike but upon closer examination, the finest of the stitches and sophistication of the motifs are the telling signs of a master craftswoman.

Cuna women also wear beaded bracelets drawn tightly on their arms and legs, gold nose rings, and layers of gold around their necks. They are a colorful bunch, irresistible to photographers. Most are happy for you to take their picture, often posing with a bright green parakeet, monkey, or iguana, but you must pay them—25 cents per click.

The villagers are friendly, although rather stonefaced unless you take the time to admire someone's beautiful child—a gesture that usually draws a broad smile from the young mother. Their straight hair is jet black and their facial features are similar to those of other Indian tribes of South America's Caribbean coast whose common ancestors were the Arawaks once populating all the islands of the Caribbean.

More and more, the San Blas Islands are being included on transcanal itineraries, particularly the westbound ones sailing from the Caribbean to the Panama Canal. See the chart at the end of the book for specific ships.

BUILDING THE PANAMA CANAL

History is replete with great endeavors but few were as bold, difficult, dangerous, and controversial—yet successful and beneficial—as the Panama Canal. An engi-

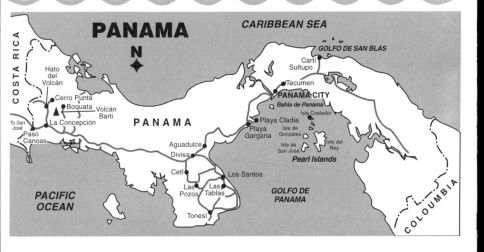

neering triumph by any measure, the Big Ditch, as it is often called, is a 50-mile-long channel traversing Panama at the narrowest point between the Atlantic and Pacific oceans. A vital link in international trade for almost 90 years, it has had a profound effect on world economic and commercial development. Annually, as many as 15,000 ships pass through it, carrying almost 200 million tons of cargo bound for destinations in the four corners of the globe.

From the time the Spanish explorer Vasco Nuñez de Balboa crossed from the Atlantic to glimpse the Pacific in 1513, the dream of a waterway through the Isthmus of Panama was born. Under Charles I of Spain, the first survey for a proposed canal was made in 1534. The California gold rush of 1849, when the lack of a safe way across the U.S. by land hampered those in the eastern U.S. from participating in the bonanza, the search for a short-cut across Panama found new motivation. With the permission of Colombia, which controled the isthmus area, a group of New York businessmen financed the building of a railroad, completed in 1855. It provided travel from the eastern U.S. to Panama by sea, crossing the Isthmus of Panama by rail and sailing up the Pacific coast to California.

Yet the idea of a waterway persisted. In 1876, Colombia gave a French financial syndicate, headed by Lt. Lucien Napoleon Bonaparte Wyse, a French army officer, permission to construct a canal. The syndicate engaged Ferdinand de Lesseps, who built the Suez Canal, for the project. De Lesseps, with little evidence to support it, said that a canal at sea level was feasible.

Despite tremendous support, enthusiasm, and feverish activity, the project was doomed from the start. For reasons of geography and topography, engineers say, digging a canal at sea level would not have worked regardless how much money, men, and machines De Lesseps had used. And if technical miscalculations had not been enough to defeat the French, tropical diseases were. Approximately 20,000 men died from yellow fever, malaria, and other illnesses in the two decades the French toiled. To these trials were added mismanagement and financial chicanery by no less than De Lesseps's son Charles and Gustave Eiffel, builder of the Paris tower. After $300 million in payout, the syndicate went bankrupt in 1889.

Meanwhile, Theodore Roosevelt, a visionary who personified the American spirit of the times, wanted the U.S. to build a canal, which he saw as strategic for an expanding America and the link between the eastern U.S. and its new Pacific possessions—Hawaii and the Philippines—gained from the Spanish-American War in 1898.

After engineers studied sites in Nicaragua and Panama and a long, public debate was held, Congress approved Panama in 1902. But the battle was not over. Colombia said no and demanded more money for granting the U.S. permission. The Panamanians, wanting the canal and eager for independence from Colombia, had their own ideas. With French aid and U.S. encouragement, they revolted; U.S. troops prevented Colombia from moving forces to stop them.

In 1903, the U.S. and Panama signed a treaty allowing the U.S. to build the canal. The following year, the U.S. bought the rights, property, and equipment of the French Canal Company for $40 million. Ironically, the equipment had deteriorated so much by then that most of it was worthless.

Faced with the difficulties of removing the rock necessary to create a sea-level canal, U.S. engineers, headed by Col. George W. Goethals, an Army Corps of Engineers career officer, concluded that a lock system would be less costly and provide better control. But the first order of business was to improve health conditions and particularly to control the mosquitoes that carried yellow fever and malaria. The job was given to Col. William C. Gorgas, who set about draining swamps and installing sewer systems. By 1906, yellow fever had been brought under control and malaria reduced dramatically.

Building the canal entailed three major projects on a grand scale: cutting a channel through the Continental Divide; digging an earthen dam—the largest ever built up to that time—across the Chagres River to create Gatum Lake, which became the largest artificial lake of its time; and designing and building three sets of enormous parallel locks and gates.

Cutting the 9-mile channel through Panama's mountain spine at the Culebra Cut—later named Gaillard Cut for Col. David DuBose Gaillard, the engineer in charge—was the most difficult part and took ten years. Enormous amounts of rock and shale were removed and hauled by rail to the Pacific to fill in marshes and build a causeway. Like the French, the U.S. team was plagued by rock and mudslides caused by the area's heavy rains.

The canal opened to traffic on August 15, 1914, six months ahead of schedule and at a cost of $387 million—$23 million below estimates. In the intervening years, the U.S. has invested more than $3 billion in the canal, 70 percent of which has been recovered, but basically, the original structure is intact. Even though ships have gotten larger, the canal can still handle 90 percent of the world's ocean-going liners. By the time the canal had marked its 75th anniversary in 1989, more than 5 billion tons of goods and 700,000 ships had transited it.

In his *The Path Between the Seas,* the leading book on the history and construction of the Panama Canal, author David McCullough says that of its many achievements, perhaps the most remarkable is that "so vast and costly an undertaking . . . [was] done without graft, kickbacks, payroll padding [or] any of the hundred and one forms of corruption endemic to such works . . . . nor has there been even a hint of scandal . . . [or] charge of corruption in all the years that it has been in operation."

The canal's value is impossible to calcuate. Just one example provides a dramatic illustration: From San Francisco, the voyage around South America is 13,000 miles and takes three weeks; via the canal, it's 4,600 miles and can be made in a week.

TRANSITING THE PANAMA CANAL

As many as two dozen cruise ships offer transcanal cruises regularly in the winter season, and another three dozen offer them seasonally in spring and fall when they make their way between the Caribbean and Alaska, or the West Coast and the East Coast, or en route to and from South America in winter and Europe for the summer. See the chart at the end of the book for specific ships.

The Isthmus of Panama, the neck of land connecting North and South America and traversed by the canal, lies northeast/southwest across mountainous, tropical jungle terrain. Due to the lay of the land, ships sail mostly on a north/south course, rather than east/west as might be assumed.

Ships approaching from the Caribbean enter the waterway at the Port of Cristobál in Limón Bay; Colón, Panama's second largest town, is to the east. Port Cristobál is also the northern terminus of the railroad that runs alongside the canal. There may be as many as 50 ships waiting to transit but cruise ships are given priority over cargo vessels. Normally, cruise ships complete the crossing in about eight hours, but it can take longer, depending on the number and speed of the ships ahead. Pilots from the Panama Canal Commission board all ships to guide them through the canal. The commission also provides every cruise ship with a commentator who gives a running account over the ship's public address system of the vessel's passage through the canal and of the history and operation of the canal.

From Cristobál, your ship follows a 6.5-mile course at sea level along a 500-foot-wide channel south to the Gatun Locks, the first of three locks where your ship is lifted 85 feet in three stages to the level of Gatun Lake. As your ship inches forward on its own steam into the first and lowest of the three chambers, a tow line is tossed to the Panamian seaman, who connects

it to a messenger line from an electric 55-ton towing locomotive known as a mule, which runs on rails at the top of the lock on each side, pulling the ship into place in the chamber. Each mule can pull 70,000 pounds; the number attached to a ship is determined by the ship's size.

Above the first chamber is the control tower where the operator controls the flow of water through huge 18-foot culverts, or tunnels, located in the center and side walls of the locks. When the pilot gives the signal, the mules begin to roll forward to position your ship into the first chamber; slowly the great doors at the stern close.

With your ship inside the huge chamber, the tower operator opens the valves and water spills out through the culverts at the rate of three million gallons a minute. It is like being on the bottom of a gigantic swimming pool, watching your ship rise as water fills the enclosure. No pumps are used to fill or empty the chambers; the system works by gravity, with water flowing from one level to another through the large culverts to smaller culverts that open to the floor of the chambers.

The huge chambers—1,000 feet long by 110 feet wide—have concrete walls from 8 to 50 feet thick and floors from 13 to 20 feet deep. Each set of locks has parallel chambers of the same size to allow passage in both directions at the same time. Each lock holds 65.8 million gallons of water; every time a ship makes a complete transit, 52 million gallons of water flow into the sea. The colossal steel doors or gates—still the originals—at the end of each chamber are 65 feet wide and 7 feet thick, and vary from 47 to 82 feet in height; the largest weighs over 700 tons. Yet they can be opened and closed with only a 40-horsepower motor.

When the water in the first chamber reaches the level of the water in the next lock, the gates between the two open, the mules pull your ship forward, and the doors behind your ship close. Again, water fills the chamber, and your ship rises to the water level of the third and final stage. When that step is completed, your ship sails onto Gatun Lake.

Covering an area of 163.38 square miles, Gatun Lake was created by carving out an enormous earthen dam across the Chagres Valley at the north end of the canal. The Chagres River flows into Gatun and Madden lakes on the north side of Continental Divide, and together with Miraflores Lake on the south side, supplies the water to operate the locks. The lakes' water levels are controled by dams, ensuring a constant supply.

Your ship sails under its own power for 24 miles across Gatun Lake to the Gaillard Cut through a pretty landscape of forested hills and islets (the tops of submerged hills), where you can observe some of the region's wildlife. The most frequent visitors around your ship are brown pelican; the treetops are often heavy with vultures; and high in the sky, magnificent frigate birds glide overhead. If you are good at spotting birds, off in the forest you might see toucan and macaw; and as the ship moves closer to the Pacific, you might begin to see bobbies.

You will also be able to watch ships transiting the canal from the other direction; most will be cargo vessels, but occasionally, a small private yacht or another cruise ship will pass, too. Expect a shower or two; depending on the time of year, the air can be balmy and pleasant or steamy. This is, after all, the middle of the jungle, even if it appears mechanized and manicured.

A few cruise ships on one-week Caribbean cruises go only as far as Gatun Lake, where they turn around and depart through the Gatun Locks back to the Atlantic side.

At about the midpoint of the canal, your ship leaves Gatun Lake and sails into the Gaillard Cut. This V-shaped channel, cut from granite and volcanic rock, is the narrowest stretch of the canal and was the most difficult to build. More than 230 million cubic yards of earth and rock were excavated from the 9-mile stretch to make it navigable. Orginially, the channel was 300 feet wide; later, it was widened to 500 feet, and there is discussion about widening it farther. It has a depth of 42 feet. While the sides have been stabilized, they are monitored constantly and dredging never stops. About halfway along the cut on the west side, a bronze plaque honors the builders of the canal and the workers who died.

The cut ends at the entrance to the first of two sets of locks: Pedro Miguel Locks with only one step of 31 feet, followed by the Miraflores Lake and the Miraflores Locks, which drop 54 feet in two steps. Here, the process is reversed. Your ship will enter a chamber full of water, and as the water is drained out, your ship is lowered to the next level, and finally to the level of the Pacific. At the exit of the final lock is the Port of Balboa and, off in the distance to the south, Panama City. Directly in front is the lofty *Bridge of the Americas,* the bridge connecting the two sides of the waterway and part of the Interamerican Highway between North and South America.

Trivia buffs may like to know that the largest cruise ship to pass through the canal is Cunard's *QE2,* which is 963 feet long with a beam of 105—just 5 feet short of the locks' 110 feet. Princess Cruises' *Crown Princess* holds the record for paying the highest fees, based on tonnage, which was $156,100 in 1996; the least is still the 36 cents paid by Richard Halliburton to swim the canal in 1928.

THE PANAMA CANAL OPERATION

Under treaties signed by the U.S. and Panama in September of 1977, full control of the canal will be turned over to Panama on January 1, 2000. Meanwhile, the canal administrator, who was a U.S. citizen with a Panamanian deputy prior to 1990, is a Panamanian nominated by Panama, appointed by the U.S. president, and approved by U.S. Congress; his deputy is a U.S. national.

The treaty also created the Panama Canal Commission with a policy-making board comprised of five U.S. citizens and four Panamanians to operate the canal. As an agency of the United States Government, the Panama Canal Commission has a legal obligation to operate on a break-even basis, recovering through tolls all costs of operating, maintaining, and improving the canal. Toll rates have been increased only four times since the opening of the canal in 1914.

The Panama Canal operation is the model of efficiency. It operates 24 hours a day and 365 days a year, with as many as 40 ships passing through daily. For most ships, the average Canal Waters Time—the total time spent at the Panama Canal, including waiting time and in-transit time—is just under 24 hours. A reservation system is available to provide a guaranteed priority transit upon request.

Its ability to work at peak efficiency is attributed to its skilled technicians and year-round maintenance, which accounts for about one-quarter of the canal's annual operating budget, or about $100 million. These include annual major overhauls of the lock gates, culverts, and valves; towing locomotives, which are reconditioned at a repair facility designed especially for them, and tow track; and continuous dredging of the 50-mile channel and anchorages. Millions are also invested in new plant and equipment, and over $5 million goes to training annually.

Some of the new equipment includes more powerful tugboats designed to canal requirements; new towing locomotives that provide faster transit through the locks; and high mast lighting with clusters of 1,000-watt metal halide lamps on 100-foot poles that light the inner walls of lock chambers, providing pilots with better visibility for nighttime transiting.

 **INFORMATION:**

Office of Public Affairs,
   Panama Canal Commission,
   APO Miami 34011;
   Tel. 507–52–3165 (Panama),
   202–634–6441.

Appendix

CHART OF CRUISE SHIPS SAILING THE WESTERN CARIBBEAN

*E*very effort has been made to ensure the accuracy of the information regarding the ships' ports of call and prices, but keep in mind that cruise lines often change itineraries for a variety of reasons. Before you make plans, you should obtain the cruise line's most current information from the cruise line or your travel agent.

Prices are for "cruise only" unless indicated otherwise and are based on per person, double-occupancy rates, ranging from the least expensive cabin in low season to the best cabin in high season. Prices do not include port charges, nor do they include holiday and special cruises or suites (unless all the ship's accommodations are suites). No price given here is guaranteed; readers need to confirm prices with cruise lines or their travel agents.

*Itinerary codes are given in parentheses: (A) alternating itineraries (not all ports are included in every cruise, nor are they necessarily visited in the order listed); (B) same itinerary except for holidays; (C) same itinerary year-round or during season indicated.

Ship (Cruise Line)	Ports of Call*	Price Range	Duration/ Season
Caribbean Prince (American Canadian Caribbean Line)	Belize City, San Pedro, Ambergris Cay, Goff Cay, Man-O-War Cay, South Water Cay, Laughingbird Cay, Placencia, Lime Cay, Pt. Livingston-Icacos, West Snake Cay, Punta Gorda, Guatemala, Fort San Felipe, Lago de Izabal, Quiriqua Mayan Ruins, Mariemonte, and West Cay; or Belize City, Goff Cay, South Water Cay, Laughingbird Cay, Placencia, Lime Cay, West Snake Cay, Punta Gorda, Livingston-Guatemala, Fort San Felipe, Lago de Izabal, Mariscos, Quiriqua Mayan Ruins, Omoa Beach-Honduras, Fortaleza de San Fernando de Omoa, Utila, and Roatan. (A)	$1,188–$2,525 with air	12 days Winter
Carnival Destiny (Carnival)	Miami to Playa del Carmen/Cozumel, Grand Cayman and Ocho Rios; or East San Juan, St. Croix, St. Thomas. (B)	$1,149–$1,569	7 days Year-round
Celebration (Carnival)	New Orleans to Tampa, Grand Cayman, Playa del Carmen, Cozumel; or Tampa to Grand Cayman, Playa del Carmen, Cozumel, New Orleans. (A)}	$1,399–$1,859 with air	7 days Year-round
Century (Celebrity Cruises)	Ft. Lauderdale to Ocho Rios, Grand Cayman, Cozumel, and Key West; or San Juan, St. Thomas, St. Maarten, Nassau. (C)	$1,675–$2,845	7 days Year-round
CostaRomantica (Costa Cruise Lines)	Ft. Lauderdale to Key West, Playa del Carmen/ Cozumel, Ocho Rios, and Grand Cayman; or San Juan, St. Thomas/St. John, Serena Cay, Nassau. (B)	$795–$2,990	7 days Winter

Ship (Cruise Line)	Ports of Call*	Price Range	Duration/Season
CostaVictoria (Costa)	Ft. Lauderdale to Key West, Playa del Carmen/ Cozumel, Ocho Rios, Grand Cayman; or San Juan, St. Thomas/St. John, Serena Cay, Nassau. (B)	$795–$2,990	7 days Winter
Crystal Harmony (Crystal Cruises)	Acapulco to Caldera, Panama Canal, San Blas Islands, Playa del Carmen, and New Orleans; or to Puerto Queztal, Panama Canal, Grand Cayman, Playa del Carmen/Cozumel, and Florida Strait; or New Orleans to Galveston, Playa del Carmen/Cozumel, Grand Cayman, Puerto Limón, Panama Canal, and Huatulco; or Ft. Lauderdale to Playa del Carmen, Grand Cayman, Panama Canal, and Caldera. (A)	$2,399–$4,668	10–13 days Winter, Spring
Crystal Symphony (Crystal)	Acapulco to Puerto Queztal, Caldera, Panama Canal, San Blas Island, Playa del Carmen/Cozumel, and New Orleans; or New Orleans to Galveston, Playa del Carmen, Grand Cayman, Puerto Limón, Panama Canal, Huatulco, and Acapulco; or Ft. Lauderdale to Playa del Carmen/Cozumel, Grand Cayman, Panama Canal, and Caldera. (A)	$2,399–$4,668 Winter	10–16 days
Cunard Dynasty (Cunard)	Ft. Lauderdale to Ocho Rios, Grand Cayman, Cancún, Cozumel, Key West; or to Cozumel, Grand Cayman, Panama Canal, Puerto Caldera, and Acapulco. (A)	$760–$6,115	7–14 days Fall, Spring
Disney Magic (Disney Cruise Line)	Port Canaveral to Nassau, Gorda Cay. Three to four days with Disney World Packages. (C)	tba	7 days Year-round
Disney Wonder (Disney Cruise Line)	tba	tba	tba
Dolphin IV (Cape Canaveral Cruise Line)	Port Canaveral to Freeport. (C)	$129–$229	2 days Year-round
Dreamward (Norwegian Cruise Line)	Ft. Lauderdale to Grand Cayman, Playa del Carmen/Cozumel, Cancún, and Great Stirrup Cay-Private Island, Bermuda. (C)	$1,649–$2,499 with air	7 days Fall to Spring
Ecstasy (Carnival)	Miami to Nassau; or to Key West, Playa del Carmen, and Cozumel. (C)	$559–$1,239	3, 4 days Year-round
Enchanted Isle (Commodore)	New Orleans to Montego Bay, Grand Cayman, Playa del Carmen, Cozumel. (C)	$498–$1,358	7 days Year-round
Fantasy (Carnival)	Port Canaveral to Nassau; or Nassau and Freeport. (C)	$559–$1,239	3, 4 days Year-round

Ship (Cruise Line)	Ports of Call*	Price Range	Duration/ Season
Fantome (Windjammer Barefoot Cruises)	Cancún or Cozumel to Isla de Mujeres, Playa del Carmen, Tulum, Xel Ha, Akumal, Xcaret. (C)	$450–$1,025	3, 4, 7 days Year-round
Galaxy (Celebrity Cruises)	Ft. Lauderdale to Key West, Cozumel, Montego Bay, and Grand Cayman. (C)	$1,675–$2,845	7 days Winter
Golden Princess (Princess Cruises)	Los Angeles to Cabo San Lucas, Acapulco, Costa Rica, Cartagena, Montego Bay, Cayman Islands, and Ft. Lauderdale. (C)	$4,062–$9,831	15 days Winter
Grande Prince (American Canadian Caribbean Line)	Central America/Panama; ports to be announced. (A)	tba	12 days Winter
Imagination (Carnival)	Miami to Playa del Carmen, Cozumel, Grand Cayman, and Ocho Rios. (C)	$1,399–$1,859 with air	7 days Year-round
IslandBreeze (Dolphin Cruise Line)	Montego Bay to Cartagena, Panama Canal, San Blas Islands, and Puerto Limón. (A)	$1,095–$2,095	7 days Fall, Winter
Leeward (Norwegian)	Miami to Nassau and Great Stirrup Cay-Private Island; or to Key West and Great Stirrup Cay-Private Island; or to Playa del Carmen, Cozumel, and Key West. (C)	$609–$1,299 with air	3, 4 days Year-round
Legend of the Seas (Royal Caribbean)	San Diego to Acapulco, Panama Canal, Cartagena, Ocho Rios, Miami. (B)	$2,999–$4,849	12 days Fall
Maasdam (Holland America Line)	New Orleans to Playa del Carmen/Cozumel, Grand Cayman, Panama Canal, Golfo Dulce, Puerto Queztal, and Acapulco; or Acapulco to Puerto Queztal, Golfo Dulce, Panama Canal, Grand Cayman, Playa del Carmen/Cozumel, and New Orleans; or to Puerto Queztal, Costa Rica, Golfo Dulce, Panama Canal, and Grand Cayman; or Ft. Lauderdale to Grand Cayman, Panama Canal, Golfo Dulce, Costa Rica, Puerto Queztal, and Acapulco. (A)	$3,000–$7,340	10 days Winter, Spring
Majesty of the Seas (Royal Caribbean)	Miami to Labadee, Ocho Rios, Grand Cayman, Playa del Carmen/Cozumel. (C)	$1,399–$2,899 with air	7 days Year-round
Mayan Prince (American Canadian Caribbean Line)	Panama City, Colón, El Provenir, San Blas Islands, Coronado de Jesus, Isla Tigre, Portobelo, Panama Canal, Taboga, Isla del Rey, Contadora, La Esmeralda, Point Alegre, Darien Jungle, and Balboa. (A)}	$1,539–$2,630	12 days Winter
Nieuw Amsterdam (Holland America)	New Orleans to Montego Bay, Grand Cayman, and Playa del Carmen/Cozumel; or to Montego Bay, Cartagena, San Blas Islands, Panama Canal, Golfo Dulce, Costa Rica. (B)	$1,212–$6,205 with air	7–21 days Fall, Winter

Ship (Cruise Line)	Ports of Call*	Price Range	Duration/ Season
Noordam (Holland America)	Tampa to Key West, Playa del Carmen/ Cozumel,Ocho Rios, and Grand Cayman; or to GrandCayman, Ocho Rios, and Playa del Carmen/Cozumel;or to Santo Tomas de Castilla, Guatemala, Playa del Carmen. (A)	$1,262–$2,128 with air	7 days Winter, Spring
Nordic Empress (Royal Caribbean)	Port Canaveral to Nassau and CocoCay. (B)	$699–$2,399 with air	3, 4 days Summer
Norway (Norwegian Cruise)	Miami to Ocho Rios, Grand Cayman, Playa del Carmen, Great Stirrup Cay. (C)	$1,299–$2,549 with air	7 days Selected dates
Norwegian Crown (Norwegian Cruise)	Ft. Lauderdale to Grand Cayman, Cozumel, Great Stirrup Cay, Key West. (A)	$1,649–$2,399 with air	7 days Spring, Winter
OceanBreeze (Dolphin Cruises)	Miami to Bahamas, Mexico, and Key West; or to Playa del Carmen, Cozumel, and Key West; or to Nassau, Blue Lagoon Island. (B)	$835–$2,095 with air	3, 4, 7 days Year-round
Polaris (Special Expeditions)	Costa Rica and Panama. (B)	$2,390–$4,090	8 days Winter
Regal Empress (Regal Cruises)	Port Manatee to Key West, Playa del Carmen, Cozumel, Grand Cayman, and Jamaica; or to San Andres, Panama Canal (Partial Transit), San Blas, Puerto Limón, Grand Cayman. (A)	$599–$1,999	6–10 days Winter, Spring
Regal Princess (Princess)	Ft. Lauderdale to Princess Cays, Montego Bay, Grand Cayman, Playa del Carmen/Cozumel. (B)	$949–$1,875 Winter	7 days
Rotterdam (Holland America)	New York to Ft. Lauderdale to Curaçao, Aruba, Cartagena, San Blas Islands, Panama Canal, Golfo Dulce, Costa Rica. (A)	$2,993–$9,995 with air	14–20 days Winter
Royal Majesty (Majesty Cruise Line)	Miami to Playa del Carmen, Cozumel; or Key West, Nassau, Royal Isle. (C)	$369–$2,099	3–7 days Winter, Spring
Royal Viking Sun (Cunard)	San Francisco to New Orleans via Panama Canal, San Andres, Playa del Carmen. (A)	$2,395–$12,075	8–16 days Spring
Ryndam (Holland America)	Ft. Lauderdale to Grand Cayman, Santo Tomas de Castilla, Playa del Carmen; or to Nassau, San Juan, Oranjestad, Panama Canal, Golfo Dulce, Puerto Queztal. (B)	$3,145–$7,975	13–16 days Spring
Seabourn Legend (Seabourn Cruise Line)	Tampa to Progreso (Mérida), Cozumel, Santo Tomas de Castilla, and Roatan Island; or Georgetown to Isla Mujeres and Tampa. (A)	$9,375–$16,410	10–16 days Winter, Spring

Ship (Cruise Line)	Ports of Call*	Price Range	Duration/ Season
Seabourn Pride (Seabourn)	Ft. Lauderdale to New Orleans, Cuba (if permitted), Puerto Rico, Panama Canal, Curaçao, Jamaica. (A)	$6,650–$22,160	15 days Winter
SeaBreeze (Dolphin)	Miami to Nassau or Blue Lagoon Island, San Juan, St. John, St. Thomas; or Playa del Carmen/Cozumel, Montego Bay, Grand Cayman. (C)	$835–$1,855 with air	3, 7 days Year-round
Seaward (Norwegian Cruise)	Miami to Great Stirrup Cay, Ocho Rios, Grand Cayman, Playa del Carmen/Cozumel. (C)	$999–$2,830	7 days Year-round
Sensation (Carnival)	Miami to Playa del Carmen, Cozumel, Grand Cayman, and Ocho Rios; or to San Juan, St. Croix, and St. Thomas. (C)	$1,399–$1,859 with air	7 days Year-round
Silver Cloud (Silversea Cruise Line)	Nassau to Grand Cayman, Aruba, Guadeloupe, Iles des Saintes, Virgin Gorda, and Ft. Lauderdale; or Barbados to Antigua, Virgin Gorda, and Ft. Lauderdale. (A)	$2,645–8,395 Fall	6–10 days
Song of Norway (Royal Caribbean)	Acapulco, Caldera, Panama Canal, Curaçao, St. Thomas, Puerto Rico. (C)	$1,849–$3,049 with air	10–14 days to Sept. 1997
Sovereign of the Seas (Royal Caribbean) }	Miami to Nassau, CocoCay. (C)	$599–$2,149 with air	3–7 days Year-round
Star/Ship Atlantic (Premier Cruise Line)	Port Canaveral to Nassau, Lucaya. (C)	$699–$1,789 with three- to four-day Disney package	3, 4 days Year-round
Star/Ship Oceanic (Premier Cruise Line)	Port Canaveral to Nassau, Lucaya. (C)	$699–$1,789 with three- to four-day Disney package	3, 4 days Year-round
Statendam (Holland America)	Ft. Lauderdale to Grand Cayman, Cartagena, San Blas Islands, Panama Canal, Golfo Dulce, Costa Rica; or Acapulco to Puerto Queztal, Golfo Dulce, Panama Canal, Cartagena, Catalina Island, Nassau. (B)	$3,145–$11,845 with air	13–21 days Winter
Stella Solaris (Sun Line Cruises)	Galveston to Cozumel, Playa del Carmen, Grand Cayman, Key West; or to Grand Cayman, Cristobal, Panama Canal, San Blas Islands, Port Limón, Cozumel, Playa del Carmen; or to Grand Cayman, Puerto Cortes (Honduras), Santo Tomas de Castilla (Guatemala), Isla de Roatan (Honduras), Belize City, Playa del Carmen, Cozumel. (A)	$990–$4,980	7–12 days Winter

Ship (Cruise Line)	Ports of Call*	Price Range	Duration/ Season
Sun Princess (Princess)	Ft. Lauderdale, Princess Cays, Montego Bay, Grand Cayman, and Playa del Carmen/Cozumel; or Los Angeles, Cabo San Lucas, Acapulco, Huatulco, Costa Rica, Cartagena, Grand Cayman, Playa del Carmen/Cozumel, and Ft. Lauderdale. (A)	$1,149–6,216	7–16 days Fall, Spring
Temptress Explorer (Temptress Voyages)	Punta Arenas to Curz Biological Reserve and Tortuga Island; Corcovado, Drake Bay, and San Josecito; Golfo Dulce and Golfito; Corcovado National Park and Caqo Island; Manuel Antonio National Park; or Golfo Dulce and Golfito; Corcovado and Caqo Island; Manuel Antonio National Park. (A)	$695–$2,095	4–7 days Year-round
Temptress Voyager (Temptress Voyages)	Belize City to Gale's Point and Rendezvous Caye, Sitee River, Hopkins, and Bird Sanctuary Caye; Coco Plum Caye, Placencia, and Seine Bight; Snake Caye and Punta Gorda; Monkey River and Laughingbird Caye; or Belize City to Gale's Point and Rendezvous Caye; Sitee River, Hopkins, and Bird Sanctuary Caye; Coco Plum Caye, Placencia; or Seine Bight; Snake Caye and Punta Gorda; Monkey River and Laughingbird Caye. (A)	$695–$2,095	4–7 days Year-round
Veendam (Holland America)	Ft. Lauderdale, Playa del Carmen/Cozumel, Ocho Rios, Grand Cayman. (B)	$1,378–$2,455	7 days Fall, Winter
Vistafjord (Cunard)	Ft. Lauderdale to Grand Cayman, Cartagena, Panama Canal, Puerto Caldera. (A)	$2,560–$4,490	7 days Winter
Westerdam (Holland America)	Ft. Lauderdale to Key West, Playa del Carmen/ Cozumel, Ocho Rios, Grand Cayman. (C)	$1,348–$3,248 with air	7 days April

Index

ABOUT THE AUTHOR

K ay Showker is a veteran writer, photographer, and lecturer on travel. Her assignments have taken her to more than a hundred countries—in the Caribbean and around the world. She is the author of *The 100 Best Resorts of the Caribbean* (Globe Pequot Press, 2nd edition, 1995); *Eastern Caribbean Ports of Call* (Globe Pequot Press, 1991), which was honored in the Benjamin Franklin Awards for 1991; *The Outdoor Traveler's Guide to the Caribbean* (Stewart, Tabori & Chang, updated 1992), which was named first runner-up as "Travel Guidebook of the Year" in 1990; and two Fodor guides—*Egypt* and *Jordan and the Holy Land*. Her latest book, *The Unofficial Guide to Cruises* (Macmillan Travel, 1996), was named "Best Travel Guide Book of the Year" by the Lowell Thomas Travel Society.

Ms. Showker writes a regular cruise column for *Travel and Leisure, Caribbean Travel and Life, Cruise and Vacation Views,* and many other magazines and newspapers across the country. She has appeared as a travel expert on network and cable television and is currently a host for "Cruise Critic" on America On Line. She served as senior editor of *Travel Weekly,* the industry's major trade publication, with which she was associated for 11 years.

A native of Kingsport, Tennessee, Ms. Showker received a master's degree in international affairs from the School of Advanced International Studies at Johns Hopkins University in Washington, D.C. She was the first recipient of the Caribbean Tourism Association Award for excellence in journalism; she was named "Travel Writer of the Year" by the Bahamas Hotel Association in 1990; and she received the 1989 *Marcia Vickery Wallace Memorial Award for Travel Journalism* given by the Jamaica Tourist Board in conjunction with the Caribbean Tourism Organization. In 1996 she became the first travel journalist to receive the *Sucrier d'Oro* award from the Martinique Government for "her outstanding coverage of the Caribbean scene." She has served as a consultant to government and private organizations on travel and tourism.